A New Moses for a New Israel

A Commentary on the Book of Matthew

By W.J. Sturm

1-1-19

Dear Hanna,

For you & Jason on
your birthday.

Pastor Bill

MT 20:28

To Kent and Mary Shepherd, friends in the faith and fellow zealots for the Lord.
To Mary specifically who over the course of 3 years invested well over 100 hours into this project, transcribing.

Preface

In May of 2009 I had, for the first time, my opportunity to teach through a book. I had been a pastor in my early 20's and did not do well. I cannot lie; I do not know how I made it the year that I did. I was awful in my quest of taking a church of 50 and building it all the way down to 25☺ Anyway, after 8 years in the United States Army I knew it was time to return to pastoral ministry in some manner and I was also not sure to what degree that would be full time church pastoring or part time while being an army chaplain eventually.

I was now not 22; I was 31. I was hired by the current pastor of the Berean Baptist Church of Fayetteville, NC and was to be a part-time pastoral intern which turned into a fulltime pastoral position within 14 months. When I first arrived, however, I was told my main task would be to build a Sunday School class of 100. To be honest I thought that would be impossible. I couldn't get 30 people to show up to hear me. Sean Harris believed in me and told me it was needed. Berean was coming out of the dogmatic approach to "small groups" and the conventional, lecture-based alternative was in view. I feverishly called all those who did not have a Sunday School class on the membership roll and I started with 44 on the first Sunday. I was ecstatic…until I went to the 30's within a month. Short story, it took me approximately 2 years to see the "100 mark" and we had Sundays in that 7 years of ministry with 130+. We basically had a class of 110+ on average.

It was my first opportunity to teach through a book of the Bible and I picked Matthew. It took nearly 3 years for myself and my assistant teachers—mainly Brother Dick Button (a father figure and big brother in Christ) who was so patient I am embarrassed about it—for us to teach through Matthew.

Then, the associate pastor took a church in a nearby town in late 2012 and I became the associate pastor which meant that I preached the midweek worship service. I finished our current series in Exodus, preached through Job (those notes are now a commentary called "Now My Eye Sees You"), and then thought about preaching (rather than merely teaching) through Matthew's

Gospel. Approximately two years had passed since finishing my Sunday School series and gave it a whirl.

I think it may have been my first experience in what it is like to see themes develop in a book; my first opportunity to see the human-ness of the author in such a vivid way (yes, I know the overall author was the Holy Spirit; save the time it would take to correct me through e-mail).

Anyway, I hope you can see how much I loved this book.

Over two years into the series I was in chapter 27 and my time had come to take my current church. The new associate pastor finished the book at Berean in my stead but I finished my preaching trip through Matthew in the Lord's Supper and Passion Week services at Sandy Ridge Baptist Church of Hickory, NC within my first year.

Table of Contents

Introduction to the Book of Matthew

There are approaches to the book of Matthew that I could take. I could cover all four Gospels at the same time, right, like a Gospel harmony? It's probable that the recipients of Matthew's Gospel didn't have Mark; they didn't have Luke, they didn't have John. So it's very important for us to understand the original understanding of the audience so I want us to hear the words in the way that the original audience would have heard the words. I have to think, "What did the writer expect the reader to already know?" He didn't know Mark. He didn't know Luke. He didn't know John. In order for us to truly appreciate what the writer is saying by aid of the Holy Spirit, we need to hear what the writer first wrote and hear it as the first hearers would have heard it.

So in your devotions you're going to be tempted to spend your time chasing Thompson's Chain References all over the place and let me just say to you that we should discipline ourselves to read what the writer wrote. This is not a topical study about why is it that Matthew and Luke have things in different order.

Regarding Authorship: It seems this Gospel could have been originally written in Hebrew. It was thought to be so as early as 100 A.D., says Eusebius.[1] This is not conclusive, but it would otherwise be that we have the Greek translation of the Hebrew text which would was the transmission of Aramaic words spoken by our Lord Jesus. It is safely assumed that Matthew's Gospel was written by Matthew for we find no argument against it early in church history.[2] Furthermore, it is rightly deemed "inconceivable" that the Gospel, whose name had Matthew attached to it by Ignatius' time,[3] would circulate around the people of God for centuries with ambiguous authorship.[4]

While we may not immediately pinpoint a date of writing, we can be relatively certain that since Ignatius is known to quote Matthew's gospel in his epistles en route to his death in Rome, the Gospel could not

---

[1] Steven Waterhouse *Papias and Matthew* (Amarillo: Westcliff Press: 2014), 3.

[2] Waterhouse, 7.
[3] Waterhouse, 29.
[4] Waterhouse, 19.

have been written afterward (around 110 A.D.).[5] It seems probable that the hints of impending doom (Matthew 23:34; 24:34) are not nearly as pungent at those in Luke 21:20-24 and 23:28-31. Since this awful thing took place in A.D. 70, it seems to place Matthew far before the occurrence. Eusebius, on the other hand, places the writing in the early 60's—while Peter and Paul were both in Rome.[6]

[5]Waterhouse, 13.
[6]Waterhouse, 10.

Chapter 1

1:1
The book of the generation

> *Genesis 5:1 This is **the book of the generations of Adam**.*
> *In the day that God created man, in the likeness of God*
> *made he him.*

We have this book of the generations of Adam in the day God created him, the book of the beginnings of Adam. Each generation ends with somebody dying. Then, this phrase is not actually found anymore in the Bible until Matthew 1. The phrase, "the genealogy of" anybody is not found until Matthew.

Matthew is saying "here's a new Adam for you." The Creator of Adam's race became the second Adam. He is the last Adam but he did so by becoming a part of the first Adam. Jesus comes and redeems Adam's race and he does so by becoming a part of Adam's race. Remember that Matthew is not writing to 2014 people in America. These are people that have an understanding of the Old Testament; these are people that have a deep love for the Old Testament. As a matter of fact, it might even go beyond deep love; they actually have their value, their confidence, their esteem, by knowing the Old Testament. In other words, there was a healthy dose of nationalistic pride and that nationalistic pride of being a Jew included knowing the Old Testament. You were an idiot if you didn't know the Old Testament. It's like saying, "You're an American?"

Yup.

"How long have you been here?"

Ah, about 20 years.

"Do you know the Pledge of Allegiance?"

No.

"What?"

Here you are, you're a reader of Matthew, and it is assumed you know about Genesis. The difference between Jesus' genealogy and Adam's genealogy is in the way that they end. You have people dying in Adam's genealogy and it ends with hopelessness. If you believe on him, you carry on his name, Matthew 28:20. The book ends in a way that you would expect it to because of the way it begins.

Mary was a lot of things but she was still a daughter of Adam: imperfect, sinful. A good woman, yes. A godly young lady. It's hard to imagine God the Father putting his Son into the womb of a young lady that did not appreciate the things of God and so the marvel still is though, as Bruce McCormack would say, "the new creation was being formed in the womb of the old creation." That is a marvelous thing. And what's even more marvelous is the fact that Adam's genealogy ends with death, death, death and Jesus' genealogy ends because of his death, with life. You are an enormous part of this new genealogy that begins in the womb of Mary, through the last Adam.

Alright, where would Jesus have read Matthew 19:3-4? Genesis. And Jesus expected that the Pharisees had read it too.

> *Matthew 26:47 And while he yet spoke, lo, Judas, one of the twelve, came, and with him a great multitude with swords and staves, from the chief priests and elders of the people. 48 Now he that betrayed him gave them a sign, saying, Whomsoever I shall kiss, that same is he: hold him fast. 49 And forthwith he came to Jesus, and said, Hail, master; and kissed him. 50 And Jesus said unto him, Friend, **wherefore art thou come?***

"Where did you come from? Where have you been?" Think about that. Did Jesus know where he'd been? Of course he did. Genesis 3: did God know where Adam had been and where he was? Yes. So, I think Matthew is trying to show us a few things here. If you believe Genesis and you believe Matthew and you believe both were written by God, I think it would be pretty easy for us to see: Matthew is trying to show us that Jesus is the last Adam and man hasn't changed and, oh by the way, Jesus is God. Who came looking for Adam in Genesis 3? God did. And he asks a question in the Garden, "Where are you?" And Jesus asks Judas a question right here, "Where have you been?" This tells us something about God and Adam's relationship in the Garden: They were friends. It says they heard him walking in the cool of the day, they heard the voice of the Lord walking in the cool of the day. Adam and Eve and God walked together in the Garden. And it says in John 18:1 that Judas knew where to take the band of soldiers because he knew where Jesus was always going to be praying. Why? Because Judas and Jesus always walked together in that garden. Now, Jesus says, "Where have you been?" That's a clear parallel.

> *Matthew 27:26 Then released he Barabbas unto them: and when he had scourged Jesus, he delivered him to be crucified. 27 Then the soldiers of the governor took Jesus into the common hall, and gathered unto him the whole band of soldiers. 28 And they stripped him, and put on him a scarlet robe. 29 And when they had platted a* **crown of thorns,**

What? Thorns? Why is he wearing a crown of thorns? Because the first Adam brought a curse which he brought thorns. The last Adam removes the curse by wearing thorns (Galatians 3:13). He took your curse. The one that our father Adam brought and resulted in thorns. Jesus begins a new race of people through faith through His work of sacrifice which included thorns.

And then, this is so difficult to imagine, what would happen if you got thorns on your brow? You would bleed. Do you remember what God told Adam in the Garden? He would "bring forth the fruit of the ground by the sweat of his brow" which resulted in thorns. And this "last Adam," in a garden, takes away the curse by wearing thorns and sweats great drops of blood (Luke 22).

And then, it gets even deeper. What did God tell Adam would happen the day that he sinned? "The day that you sin, you're going to die." Genesis 5 says that Adam was 130 years old when Seth was born. Adam died at 930 years old, that means he lived at least 800 years after he "died." That's if Seth was born that day which, of course, we know he wasn't. So, Adam lives another 800 years after he "died" so that either God was wrong or there was a part of Adam that actually died that day. We would call that death that Adam experienced "spiritual death." And how would we define that spiritual death? Separation from God.

The first Adam sins, involving a tree; it brings a curse; it brings thorns; it brings sweat from the brow and it brings separation from God.

> *Matthew 27:45 Now from the sixth hour there was darkness over all the land unto the ninth hour. 46 And about the ninth hour Jesus cried with a loud voice, saying, Eli, Eli, lama sabachthani? that is to say, "My God, my God, **why hast thou forsaken me?**"*

Jesus died Adam's death to take away our curse. Now, I suppose it's a whole separate discussion of whether or not God actually turned his back on Jesus, I just need to take you to Isaiah 53 to clear that up but it doesn't change the fact that Jesus for the first time in eternity felt separation from the Father. What if Adam "fell" when he was 100? 100 years is a long time to be walking with God in the cool of the Garden and then one day you no longer sense the presence of the Lord. Don't you enjoy sensing the presence of the Lord? Don't you enjoy the fact that he lives in you and abides in your heart? Now imagine knowing that God has departed from you and feeling that for the first time in your existence.

We could go up that far but what if it was 3-4 years? That's still an amazing amount of time because all Adam has ever known is fellowship with his Creator in the Garden. And now you take the eternal Son of God, who has walked with the Father, so to speak, Proverbs 8 says since the very beginning of the foundation of the world. He said, "I brought him up before me. He was daily my delight." They spent eternity past together and for the first time after all of eternity, the Son experiences separation from the Father? Why did he do it? To remove the curse of our father Adam.

Think about the vulnerabilities that Jesus takes on by taking on the flesh of Adam? On the other hand, we avoid vulnerabilities. That's our nature. We are survivalists. We circumvent discomfort. We disdain devaluation. We recoil at reclusivity. We ponder plans with probable productivity. We are constantly marking our survival. We are branded by instinct. We have stripes of self-preservation. But, actually we're really just telling tales of terror. We are afraid and that's why we stay away from uncomfortable situations.

The book of the generation of Jesus <u>Christ</u>

*Matthew 1:21 And she shall bring forth a son, and thou shalt call his name JESUS: for he shall save his people **from their sins***.

What is he freeing us from? What you need to know is the fact that he is Jesus "the Christ" just like Judas is Judas the Iscariot and John is John the Baptist. Those are titles. The reason he is Jesus the Christ is because he has been anointed chiefly. Is he the Son of Man? Yes. Is he the Son of God? Yes. Is he the son of David? Yes. Is he the son of Abraham? Yes, but he chiefly frees us from our sin.

Oh, what I like most about Jesus is that he never quits saving me from my sin. Ever. I was saved from the wrath of God when I believed on Christ to save me from the wrath of God, but he saves me from the sin that just checkers my heart with Adam's nature. From now until the day of redemption, he is consistently saving me from my attitudes and actions and moods and everything else that doesn't glorify him. He is saving me from my sin.

Consider Isaiah 35 and ask "when will this happen?" When is the stage perfectly set? What will be some of the things that occur when this is ready to come on the scene? You will start to see blind seeing, deaf hearing, lame walking and dumb speaking. When the highway is being laid for the King?

*Isaiah 61:1 The Spirit of the Lord GOD is upon me; because **the LORD hath anointed me** to preach   good tidings.*

*Matthew 1:18 Now the birth of Jesus **[the anointed one] Christ** was on this wise [here's how it happened]: When as his mother Mary was espoused to Joseph, before they came together, she was found with child of the Holy Ghost.*

Now, if you were to take this over to the New Testament and instead of translating it from Hebrew to English you would translate it from Greek to English you would translate "good tidings" as "Gospel." And that word "anointed" there, it's actually a verb form of the noun "Messiah." Let me say that again: the word "anointed" in verse 1 is the verb form of the noun "Messiah." "Messiah" is the Old Testament word for the New Testament term "Christ." So basically the word "anointed" in verse 1 is the verb form of the noun "Christ."

Isaiah 61:1b...he hath sent me to bind up the brokenhearted, to proclaim liberty to the captives, and the opening of the prison to them that are bound. 2 To proclaim the acceptable year of the LORD, and the day of vengeance of our God; to comfort all that mourn; To appoint unto them that mourn in Zion, to give unto them beauty for ashes, the oil of joy for mourning, the garment of praise for the spirit of heaviness; that they might be called trees of righteousness, the planting of the LORD, that he might be glorified.

Do you want to know the mission of the Christ? When the Christ is on the scene, here's what he'll do: he'll preach the Gospel to the meek, the poor. When the Christ comes on the scene, you can expect that the blind will see, the lame will walk, the deaf will hear, the dumb will speak, many will be led out of prison and the poor will have the Gospel preached to them.

What does it mean to be anointed? Elisha's anointing by Elijah shows anointing of prophets; priests from Aaron forward are ordained by anointing with oil; kings beginning with Saul and David were anointed. Central to the external ceremony was pouring of perfumed olive oil upon the person's head.

When he heard of Jesus coming and being called the anointed one, he would have thought about this particular person who was going to be anointed with oil and thought, "Is this person going to be a great prophet? A great priest? Or a great king?" Consider 1:17: there are three sets of 14 in this generation. "Abraham to David," did you know that Abraham is called a prophet? The second division is "David to the carrying away into Babylon" and did you know that David, in 1:6 is called "a king?" 1:12 finds "And after they were brought to Babylon, Jechonias begat Salathiel; and Salathiel begat Zorobabel," and Zerubbabel worked very closely as governor of Judah, he worked very closely with the high priest named Joshua, you can find that in the book of Zechariah, and Joshua was the high priest.

So you have one third of the genealogy of Jesus beginning with Abraham the prophet; you have the second third of the genealogy of Jesus begun by David the king, and you have the third part of the genealogy of Jesus begun by Zerubbabel who was the governor for the high priest Joshua. All three offices that were anointed in the Old Testament are greatly eluded to right here in the first chapter of Matthew. Remember, we're not trying to make you smart topical theologians, we're trying to get you to understand what Matthew's audience would have understood. And I cannot help you understand what Matthew's audience would have understood if you will not hear Matthew the way his audience heard him. Let me say that again: you will not be able to hear the word of the Lord like Matthew's audience did when they read this if you will not hear him the way they heard him. In order for us to hear him like they heard him, we have to know what he's saying. In order for us to know what he's saying, we have to know what is it he expected us to know before we read the book of Matthew. Guess what he expected you to know? The Old Testament. He expected you to have some bring-along information, some read ahead material and Isaiah is a great part of that. They were expecting the Christ. They were good students of the Greek translation of the Old Testament known as the Septuagint and they were expecting the one known as the Christ.

What should we know chiefly and primarily about this Messiah? First of all, it was a picture of the Spirit of God coming upon somebody. When someone was anointed to be king, when someone was anointed to be prophet, when someone was anointed to be priest, it was not that all of a sudden this oil has some sort of amazing power. No, it was because it symbolized something. It's a symbol like water baptism. It was a symbol of the Holy Spirit coming upon someone and equipping them for their calling. That was the anointed one.

What was Matthew's audience thinking about the anointed one? Well, look at verse 1 again, "The book of the generation of Jesus Christ." Well, Matthew, how exactly was Jesus anointed? Well, he was the son of David so he was anointed to be king. And he is the son of Abraham the prophet so he was anointed to be a prophet.

Now, it symbolized special empowerment from the same Holy Spirit. The question that I have for you is: when was Jesus anointed with the Holy Spirit? See Matthew 3:13-17.

Jesus was anointed with the Holy Spirit, when? His baptism. You say, "I'm not comfortable with that." Oh well, it's right there. That is when the Holy Spirit landed upon Jesus. Now, don't read into it but don't explain it away.

Look at the opening verses of Matthew 11 and see Matthew expected you to know Isaiah 35 and Isaiah 61. Why did Jesus give the response to John the Baptist's disciples the way he did? Because he expected them to know Isaiah 35 and Isaiah 61.

He was understood by John the Baptist to be the performer of six specific signs as the anointed prophet of God—the anointed prophet of God. Remember when Moses came? What things did he do? What did he do to show that he was qualified for the job? He said in Deuteronomy 18, "God is going to send a prophet just like me." Great signs were a sign of a prophet.

So Matthew 2, he was the Christ, the anointed King. Matthew 11, he's doing signs as the anointed prophet.

> *Psalm 2:5 I will declare the decree, the Lord has said unto [me, His **anointed,** verse 1], thou art my begotten, thou art my **begotten Son**. This day have I begotten thee. I will set my king upon my holy hill of Zion…*

We learned that being the Son of God was a title that went with the anointed, expected king so when Peter says, "You're the Christ," it was only natural that he should follow it up with, "the Son of God" (Matthew 16:13-16).

Now, right after Peter says, "You are the Christ, the Son of God," Jesus goes in and starts talking about the church for the first time (Matthew 16:18), which is the body of Christ. Then on top of that, in the very next verse he says,

> *I have given you the keys of the kingdom of heaven.*

So really we see once again in the same passage, "You're the Christ, the Son of God, and I have given you keys to a kingdom." Only kings have kingdoms to give keys from and so the Christ is the Son of God who is also a King. Do you see how this all works together? So he is here Christ, the anointed king. Chapter 2, anointed king. Chapter 11, anointed prophet. Chapter 16, anointed king.

*Matthew 22 While the Pharisees were gathered together, Jesus asked them, Saying, What do you think of **Christ?***

But not "what do you think of Jesus, what do you think of your personal Savior?" Rather, "What do you think of the anointed one of God?" Do you think the Pharisees knew the book of Isaiah? Absolutely. "What do you think of the Christ?

> *whose son is he? They say unto him, The Son of David. He saith unto them, How then doth David in   spirit call him Lord, saying, The LORD said unto my Lord, Sit thou on my right hand, till I make thine enemies thy footstool? If David then call him Lord, how is he his son?*

So Jesus asked the Pharisees a question about the Messiah, the Christ. Of course, the answer is that David is called the king in Matthew 1, and "prophet" in Acts 2. So you have the anointed prophet and king as the father of the Christ, right here, in Matthew 22.

Matthew 26:65 has the high priest rending his clothing. Why? Because in Daniel 7, it talks about the Son of Man which is a name for a prophet, coming before the throne of the Ancient of Days and then in chapter 9 of Daniel, two chapters later it says that there is a Messiah that will come. So when the high priest asked Jesus, "Are you the Messiah, the Christ?" And Jesus says, "Yup, and you're going to see the Son of Man." The reason the high priest was so angry was because he understood the linkage between the Son of Man (Daniel 7) and the Christ (Daniel 9). Ezekiel is the only other person called the "son of man" in the Bible and he was a prophet. So they understood that to be the Christ is to be the Son of Man so Christ all through the book of Matthew is claiming the title of anointed prophet and anointed king.

the son of David The Greek word behind "generation" is the word "genesis" in the Greek and it means "origin; beginning." So right away you know that genesis is not a Hebrew word and so it probably wasn't the title of the book Moses wrote it back there in Genesis. It means "the beginning." So you want to read it that way, we could read verse 1 as, "The book of the beginnings of Jesus Christ, the son of David, the son of Abraham."

How did he begin? The fact that he doesn't begin with God or he doesn't begin like John, or the fact that it doesn't go back to God like Luke should tell us that Matthew is talking about the human beginning of Jesus.

The word "book" there is where we would get our word "Bible" (*biblion*), and it is actually the word "scroll." So you could say that, "The scroll of the beginnings of Jesus reads like this: he's the son of David, the son of Abraham," and then for the next 16 verses or so, we find a scroll that Matthew had where it recorded the lineage of Jesus.

If Jesus gets his lineage and his namesake from Abraham and David, then the question is: who is carrying on his name? If Matthew begins with the book of the beginnings of Jesus, whatever happened to him because we don't see Jesus having a son. Now you say, "Well, of course he didn't." But the Mormons think he did. The Rosicrucians think he did. The Guardians of the Grail think he did. The Arians think he did. So there are lots of people on the planet that think that Jesus and Mary Magdalene had children but they didn't. Isaiah 53 says, "He should be cut off from the land of the living and who will declare his generation?" He was killed, Psalm 110, "with the dew of the youth upon him." He was killed as a young man and Isaiah 53 says before he could have kids; before he could be married and have children.

Jesus leaves and then what? Who carries on the name of Jesus? Well, the end of the chapter, the end of the book, chapter 28:20 says you and I do.

Then there are certain assumptions that Matthew comes with. Matthew comes with the assumption that you know your Old Testament, the book of the beginnings of Jesus Christ **the son of David**, The son of David? Why should I care? Seven brothers, and he was the least desirable, the least attractive of all of them. He's out watching sheep. He stinks horribly and Samuel comes to anoint a king and Samuel is so sure it's not him that he's actually kind of shocked and says, "Lord, are you sure?" And God says, "You look like a man looks, Samuel." But God doesn't look that way. You make an adjustment based on the cover of the book but God looks at the heart.

Think about this: David has been king for seven years now. He has been ruling in Hebron. He has been ruling primarily over one of the tribes of Israel: Judah. He is 30 years old when he becomes king. David is now 37 years old and it is time for him to capture Jerusalem and the Jebusites have control of Jerusalem.

2 Samuel 5: The king of the Jebusites in Jerusalem said, "We're going to put the blind and the lame by the gates and David won't be able to get in." Well, the result was that they actually did take the city and Joab became David's general in that episode. Meanwhile, David ends up hating the lame and the blind, the handicapped and the blind. You say, "Well, that's not nice." Yeah, I know. I didn't say it was nice, it's just part of the story and it happened this way.

Here's something that David loathed: he hated lame people and he hated blind people and the writer of 2 Samuel tells us the reason is because of this episode. He was taunted with them. David killed bears and lions with his bare hands, and crushed a pompous old windbag of a giant and then cut his head off and hung it on a wall somewhere and put his sword up on a wall. David was a man's man, so for David to be told, "You can't take the city. If you could send everybody, you've got to get through the lame and the blind to get to me," and David said, "I'll not only take the lame and the blind, I'll take your head too."

So David ended up hating lame people and blind people, but that's not the end of the story. Then David decides two chapters later that he wants to build a house for the Lord. A very admirable thing for him to do, but God shows up to him and says, "David, you've killed more people than anyone else I've had on the planet. You're a bloody man. You've crushed everyone I've put in your way. And David, you are so bloody I can't even let you build my house." But he makes a promise to David, "I will set up thy seed after thee which shall proceed out of thy bowels and I will establish his kingdom. He will build a house for my name," talking about who? Solomon.

> He will build a house for my name and I will establish the throne
> of his kingdom forever. I will be his father and he will be my
> son. If he commit iniquity I will chasten him with a rod of men
> and with the stripes of the children of men.

So we know it's not primarily Jesus because Jesus has never had to be whipped for his own sin. So there is a local fulfillment here in Solomon.

> *But my mercy shall not depart away from him as I took it from Saul whom I put away before thee and thy house and thy kingdom shall be established forever before thee. Thy throne shall be established forever.*

So the Hebrew people are expecting—not because of their good conduct…the Hebrew people were expecting God to fulfill the promise to David, not because of David's good conduct, but because of God's good character.

Promises are fulfilled not because you're a good girl or I'm a good boy, promises are fulfilled because God is a great God. Not a single one of us deserves to enter heaven's gates other than in Christ, and since we're in Christ, we actually don't deserve hell (Romans 8:32-35).

So you have a nation expecting a son of David to become a king. Why? Because God said so. In 1 Samuel: David and his best friend make a promise to each other. David and his friend Jonathan make a promise. Jonathan said, "David, when I'm gone, please don't kill all my children. Be kind to my children." And why should he be kind to his children? Because they were friends. And David said, "Because I love you, Jonathan, I will promise that I will take care of your offspring." It had nothing to do with the conduct of Jonathan's offspring. Zero.

But then, we're told of a man by the name of Mephibosheth. In 2 Samuel 9, we're finding out that David is going to be good to one of Jonathan's sons. Why? Because Jonathan was a good guy? No, because David made a covenant and David was a great friend. There is a Christ lesson there. There is a Christ lesson. David is a picture of Jesus there. Jesus doesn't die for us because we're super. He loves us and redeems us with his own blood because he loves his Father and made a promise and a covenant with his Father. The Son made the covenant with the Father and you and I are recipients of a covenant made between the Son and the Father. We've got no chips in this game, good neighbor. We had nothing to offer God. Jesus offered everything needed to God for us to get to God.

Mephibosheth, who even knows if he was even thought of. We're finding out that when Saul's whole household was killed, that the nurse taking care of Mephibosheth fled and dropped him and he was lame from then on. Now, wait a minute. There's something that David hates in his very soul in chapter 5: lame people. It's opposed to his character. He hates lame people. But because of a covenant, he takes a lame man into his house, that which is against his nature, because of a covenant that he made.

So, Mephibosheth "bowed himself," so you get the idea. Over in that town in Lodibar, David sends a messenger to go and get Mephibosheth. Mephibosheth shows up and says, "What is thy servant, that thou shouldest look upon such a dead dog as I am? Then the king," that's David, "called to Ziba, Saul's servant," remember, Jonathan is Saul's son, that would have made Mephibosheth Saul's grandson. So he says to Ziba, Saul's servant, "I have given unto thy master's son," Saul's son, "all that pertained to Saul and to all his house. As for Mephibosheth, said the king," David, "he," the lame one, "shall eat at my table, as if he were one of the king's sons." Why? He hates lame people. This act of kindness has nothing to do with the condition of the sinner. It has nothing to do with the conduct of the sinner. It has everything to do with the covenant that David made. Oh, my, in your worst of days, it has nothing to do with how good you wish you were and your best of days, it has nothing to do with how good you think you are. It goes right on back to what did Christ do for me at Calvary.

> *Matthew 9:27 And when Jesus departed thence, two blind men followed him, crying, and saying, Thou Son of* **David,** *have mercy on us. And when he was come* **into the house,**

King David said, "I won't even sit in the same house with those men."

> *9:28 And when he was come into the house, the blind men came to him: and Jesus saith unto them, Believe ye that I am able to do this? They said unto him, Yea, Lord.*

Why? Because he's the son of David.

> *...Then touched he their eyes, saying, According to your faith be it unto you. And their eyes were opened; and Jesus straitly*

charged them, saying, See that no man know it. But they, when they were departed, spread abroad his fame in all that country.

When there is something that is disgusting to the nature of God, God changes it in the man that has faith. You see Jesus, the son of David, he was better than David because he not only met in the same house with blind men, he left them seeing. So all that talk about God putting up with us who are opposed to his nature, guess what he does to sinful people? He sanctifies them and makes them less sinful than they were last week. He doesn't leave us in the mess we're sitting in. His name is Jesus and he saves his people from their sin.

> *Matthew 12:22 Then was brought unto him one possessed with a devil, **blind,** and dumb: and he healed him, insomuch that the blind and dumb both spake and saw. And all the people were amazed, and said, Is not this **the son of David?***

There is something about the son of David. He actually doesn't mind being around blind people.

> *12:23 But when the Pharisees heard it, they said, This fellow doth not cast out devils, but by Beelzebub the prince of the devils.*

You need to understand that the people in these accounts understand that Jesus is the descendent of King David, the one who restores lame people to his table.

Find a woman calling Jesus the **son of David**, he called her a dog (Matthew 15:21-26). Now, where do you think this story is going to go?

Now look at 15:27 and ask "How do you know that, lady?" Because I heard about your father David treating a lame man right and letting him who thought he was a dog eat from the master's table.

> *Matthew 20:29 And as they departed from Jericho, a great multitude followed him. And, behold, two blind men, sitting by the way side, when they heard that Jesus passed by, cried out, saying, Have mercy on us, O Lord, thou **Son of David.***

Now, why would these blind people think that the son of David cared about them? Because whoever the son of David is will live forever as the son of David and he has compassion on lame and blind people because he makes covenants and keeps his word.

They don't meet David in the temple but they meet his son there in the house of God (Matthew 20:32-21:12). The lame and the blind that are disgusting to the soul of David, his son meets them in the house of God?

> *Matthew 28:18 Jesus came and spake unto [his disciples] saying, All [authority, all kingship, all reigning] is given unto me in heaven and in earth. Go ye therefore, and [make disciples of all nations; make subjects of] all nations.*

For 28 chapters, Matthew has been trying to get you to see that this is the son of David that rules everywhere and when he gets up from the dead, he says, "All ruling power is given to me in heaven and in earth so go and make disciples, make subjects, of the nations." Jesus has a right to rule and he's taking over the world. He's taking over the world.

the son of Abraham. By the time you get to Matthew 1, Matthew writing to other Hebrews expects that audience to know Abraham.

The Gospel that Abraham had preached to him (Gatlatians 3:8-9) very simple: "Abraham, in you I will bless all nations. All nations, Abraham. I will bless all nations through you."

The son of David, the son of Abraham. Matthew expects you, the reader, as a Jew, to know who David and Abraham are. God promised Abraham that he would bless all nations. He would bless all nations. God blessed Abraham and told Abraham that he would bless all nations through him. As a matter of fact, Paul said it was the Gospel that Abraham had preached to him.

Genesis 12, and you know we're in the story of Abraham. When I say story, I mean the true account of Abraham. When you get to Genesis 12, you are at least 33% through human history. Think about that. Abraham is dated at about 1900 BC. That is more than 1/3 through human history. Now think about that. We know that this last third of human history since the time of Christ basically wasn't recorded in the Bible. That means that the first third of human history is covered in the first 11 chapters of the Bible and the middle third of human history has the other 1,178 chapters.

> *Genesis 12:1 Now the LORD had said unto Abram, Get thee out of thy country, and from thy kindred, and from thy father's house, unto a land that I will shew thee: And I will make of thee a great nation, and I will bless thee, and make thy name great; and thou shalt be a blessing.* ***I will bless them that bless thee,*** *and curse him that curseth thee, and* ***in thee shall all families of the earth be blessed****.*

It was so much about Jesus that two chapters earlier than this "Gospel to Abraham" in the book of Galatians, Paul says, "If anyone comes unto you with a Gospel other than the one I preached, let them go to hell." (1:8-9) Now think that through with me for a minute. The Gospel that Abraham heard was the same Gospel that Paul preached. Abraham got saved by the same Gospel you and I do. It was put in different words. "Abraham, I'm going to bless all nations through you."

Abraham is 75 years old and he has no son. Abraham is 86 years old and he has no son and so he is tempted and he takes, I suppose, human ingenuity to help God out with his will. Many of us are guilty of doing that from time to time. We find out God wants something and we substitute it for maybe a good way to help him out. Maybe his timing is not what we think it ought to be and so we jump the gun and we get impatient. We expect God to do something immediately because he says he'll do it eventually, you see. We're not happy with eventually, we want immediately. You see, we think in five minute increments of time and sometimes 30 if you're really lucky.

So we think in little increments of time but we're dealing with a God here who is not limited by the sitcom. He knows exactly how much time he's going to take doing something and Abraham is a little bit challenged here. You see, when we read through the book of Genesis, we see a man and a woman walking with God in the garden and they lose paradise for the many. So Adam and Eve are estranged from God and their obedience or rather disobedience leads to the ostracization of all people from the presence of God. Your sin affects more than just you. It affects more than just you. You may not know how it affects other people, it does affect other people in some way or another. You say, "Well, no. I don't know." It affects other people.

So the few become the many. They are instructed to expand. "You will go and you will repopulate the earth," and at Noah's flood, God says, "We're going to start over. Man's heart is just sinful and wicked and I can't put up with it anymore. My Spirit will not always strive with men." So eight people get on the boat. It wasn't because there wasn't enough room. God knows there was room for anyone that wanted to get on the boat but only eight did. Let that be another life lesson: no one will ever, ever go to hell saying, "I trusted Christ but there was no room on the boat." Nobody. Nobody. Nobody will ever say, "I wanted to get on the boat but I trusted and I wasn't led in." Nobody. The amazing thing about the ark is the door was huge. It was big enough for the rabbit, it was big enough for the elephant. It was big enough for anybody and Jesus Christ can handle your sin whether you're a drunk, a derelict, or a Baptist. You take your pick. He can handle your sin. The door is big enough for whosoever will.

When it's time to get off the ark, they are told, "You will go and repopulate the whole earth," and they dwelt in the Plain of Shinar. So we have people that are disobedient, once again, and they are expected to actually seek him. So you have people with bad hearts. Now remember, even though most of the population of the planet was destroyed, the sin nature got on the ark and the sin nature got off the ark. And what you have with people whose imaginations are only evil continually because you know sinners came from somewhere, and it didn't take long for Noah to show that he was a sinner. I mean, he got drunk and he got naked and things happened and so he showed that he was still a son of Adam. That's Genesis 9. So you see Noah and his kids are then ordered to love God and to seek him but, their hearts are wicked and they have no desire to love this God.

So Abraham gets a promise and what good is a blessing to people who are not always sure they need to be blessed? I mean, think about how audacious it is for God to pick one. That's what he did. He looked over the entire planet, and there were plenty of people to choose but he chose Abraham. Abraham. Now, if there could have been potentially billions alive at the flood, that was about 1,800 years after creation, then it makes good sense that you could at least have a couple million by the time Abraham is called out of Ur of the Chaldees. God picked one.

You say, "Why did he pick one?" I don't have any idea why he picked one. Deuteronomy 7 says so he could show himself to be a loving God. It wasn't because they were lovely; it was because he was loving. So those who have a problem with God's, how should we say it, discrimination, get over it. God is not asking permission from anyone if he can do anything. He does whatever he wants to. No man stays his hand or says, "What doest thou?" (Job 9:13)

So we are not going to sit back and say, "God, what are you thinking picking Abraham?" But here is Abraham who is told, "You're going to be a blessing to all nations." Abraham looks left, looks back, looks right, looks forward and says, "Well, I don't see anyone that wants to be blessed by me." So God sees a paradise restored off in the distance and mankind finding his joy in the garden, walking in God's glory. He sees Revelation 22 all the way back here in Genesis 12, but how is this supposed to happen? "I don't even have a son. I'm 75 years old. I should be playing shuffleboard, right? A descendant? A son? A mass conquering? I have over 300 armed servants. I guess we could conquer a people and bless them." That's not really blessing them, I don't know. "Trips to Egypt? I mean, we've done that twice. We could subdue Pharaoh and we could trick Abimelech. I'm not sure. Hey, maybe I could just impregnate all kinds of women like that Egyptian girl, Hagar." Did you think the Bible was squeaky clean full of Ivory soap? I mean, it is full of that stuff.

No, that's not the way to go because in Matthew 3, know what they thought about mass discipleship. He says in verse 7, John the Baptist,

> when he saw the Pharisees and Sadducees come to the baptism, he said, O generation of vipers, who has warned you to flee from the wrath to come? ....9 And think not to say within yourselves "We have Abraham to our father:" for I say unto you, that God is able of these stones to raise up children unto Abraham.

God, I don't understand. If being a son of Abraham is such a big deal and if I'm supposed to be a blessing to all nations, why can't we just have some kind of massive indoctrination and just march people through a river and call them Christians? Why can't we do that?" Well, because their hearts are still bad.

Then in one place we have Jesus, in Matthew 8, there will be people "coming from the east and the west to sit down with Abraham, Isaac and Jacob [but you Pharisees, you're going to be put in outer darkness]". So being a son of Abraham is not a popular thing in the book of Matthew.

Now, think of all the things Matthew could have begun with. I mean, Luke begins with the birth of someone else: John the Baptist. Mark begins with his baptism. That's kind of impressive, I might have started that way. John starts with his preexistence. It's tough to top that. Matthew starts with the exciting genealogy and of all the exciting things he could have started out with, he says, "He's the son of David, the son of Abraham." So it looks to me, though, like he's shooting himself in the foot because twice in eight chapters he's basically said, "Being a son of Abraham doesn't help." Well, then how in the world is a man who's been dead for 1,800 years by now…how is he supposed to "bless all nations?"

How are we going to bless all nations, Abraham? Well, we're not going to do with manipulation, maneuvering, misappropriated masculinity, masterful mobility or mass reeducation, so how exactly are we going to bless all nations who aren't even sure they want to be blessed by you? There is no substitute for the heart change. This is a worldwide blessing. Christ died for sinful men and women, mankind (Matthew 20:28).

How are you going to bless all nations? See Matthew 5:1-9.

"Wait a minute, Jesus, this is far from the domination that I was hoping for. You're blessing all nations by sitting up there in your little Rabbi's outfit and you're telling us that those who mourn are blessed? Those who are meek are blessed? Is that the very best you can do is just bless, bless, bless, bless and talk to us about blessings? Is that all we can do?"

Then if that's not good enough of God, he takes Jesus in the first years of his life and sends him to the very place he yanked his people out of 2,000 years before, 1,500 years before. He pulls people from the east and brings them to the Christ and he brings the Christ and sends him to Egypt. That is the missional heart of God right there. You thought we had to go all the way to Acts to find a God that cared about the nations. Oh no, no, no, we find God caring about Gentiles a long time before Gentiles ever wanted to be cared for because God is a God that cares about people who are lost and people who are dying without him. It's so popular to talk about theology these days. It's so popular to talk about how we have liberty in Christ and we have so much liberty and we're so right on theology that the world goes to hell tonight with over 3,000 people groups without a single verse of Scripture in their language, and we sing about the "God who saves."

Away with our pious nonsense about how, "It's not us that does the saving," for in 1 Corinthians 2:9, Paul said, "By all means, I might save some. I become all things to all people," 1 Corinthians 9:26. "I become all things to all people that I might by all means save some." Romans 11, "If by any means I might save some."

Every time you see the word "Gentile" in your King James Bible, the Greek word behind it is *ethnos* and it's the same word behind "nations" in Galatians 3:8 and it's the same word behind "nations" in Matthew 28:18 where he says, "Go ye therefore and teach all nations."

> *Matthew 4:12 When Jesus had heard that John was cast into prison, he departed into Galilee; And leaving Nazareth, he came and dwelt in Capernaum, which is upon the sea coast, in the borders of Zabulon and Nephthalim: That it might be fulfilled which was spoken by Esaias the prophet, saying, The land of Zabulon, and the land of Nephthalim, by the way of the sea, beyond Jordan, Galilee of the **Gentiles.***

There we are, chapter 4, God cares about the nations. Galilee was supplanted by 722 BC. The Assyrian Empire came and captured the northern half of Palestine known then as "Israel," took a lot of the men and put them in other nations. Made eunuchs out of most of them and took a lot of the Assyrian men and put them down there in the land of Israel. They intermingled and intermarried and really until about 104 BC, Galilee was almost completely Gentile. You couldn't really find very many Jews until a Jewish conqueror in 104 BC started putting Jews back in Galilee. It was still so much Gentile that 100+ years later, they're still calling it "Galilee of the Gentiles."

Interesting thing, all the major trade routes go through Galilee of the Gentiles. People would come from the east and cross through Galilee and they would go over to the way of the sea and go down by the Mediterranean Sea into Egypt and there was no place really to pass through the mountainous region of Judea. Very few traffickers going through Judea. Very little happening in Judea except at times of festivals when you could make lots of money off the half-Jews that came from all over the world to offer sacrifices three times a year. Other than that, business went through Galilee.

If I was a Savior, I would have put my home base in the first place closest to my people and I would have been right next to the temple. That's how Bill Sturm would have done it. We find Jesus saying, "Don't fear like the nations. Don't fear like the Gentiles." All through the book of Matthew, Jesus is saying, "The Gentiles get it wrong. The nations get it wrong." And at the same time, we have Jesus reaching out to the nations.

> *Matthew 16:13 When Jesus came into the coasts of Caesarea Philippi,*

that is so far north that it's not even considered Palestine. Here's Jesus traveling with his disciples in a land that is almost entirely Gentile and Jesus comes into the coasts of Caesarea Philippi,

> *he asked his disciples, saying, Whom do men say that I the Son of man am? And they said, Some say that thou art John the Baptist: some, Elias; and others, Jeremias, or one of the prophets. He said, But whom do you say that I am?*

So Jesus says, "Okay, out there they say who I am: Jeremiah, Elijah, Moses, but what do you say? What do you say?" Now look what Peter says in verse 16, "You are the Christ, the Son of the living God. And Jesus answered and said unto him, Blessed art thou." What? That word "blessing" is not used very many times in Matthew. He put the standard so high. There is not a single person that ever walked the planet who can live out the Sermon on the Mount other than the one who preached it. But I can live Matthew 16.

Not a single person can take credit for their knowing Jesus. Not a single person among God's redeemed can say that you were brilliant enough, smart enough, wise enough, holy enough, good enough, or that you had enough foresight. "Boy, you had your stuff together. You had enough brains." No, John 17:3, Jesus said to the Father, "This is life eternal that they might know thee, the only true God and Jesus Christ whom thou hast sent." One way to the Father is knowing Christ. One way to being blessed is knowing Christ.

Meanwhile, in the middle of this grand scheme of redemption for the nation lies broken hearts, exhausted parents, absent minded disciples, mundaneness, each day peppered with excruciating reality that things are not very messianic, not very kingdomly, not very Davidic, not very Abrahamic, not very "blessed." And probably some of you would make good audience members in that crowd reading this book and you're thinking, "How in the world can you say that all nations are blessed today?" I suppose the reason that miracles are in the Gospel is so that you can know what happens when your prayers are answered, "Thy kingdom come, thy will be done on earth as it is in heaven." For at the time when all know who Christ is, "from the least to the greatest" (Jeremiah 31, John 6, Hebrews 10) when all nations know him, they are truly blessed and we all of a sudden realize that Matthew was a foretaste of what kingdom life is like. There are no lame people in the kingdom. There are no blind people in the kingdom. There are no tax collectors in the kingdom. There are no tornadoes in the kingdom. There are no lost children in the kingdom. There are none of those unsavory things in the kingdom. But let me turn the table on you, my dear, cleaned up, religious friend: there are no falsities or pretense in the kingdom either. There are no greed for the American dream. There is no materialism. There are no lusts for cars that we cannot afford and houses we cannot maintain. There are none of those either.

So all of a sudden, the evils outside don't look as evil as the evils inside because we realize that in that kingdom when all nations are blessed, our hopes no longer melt into dismal, hapless, formless, laughable nonsense. We will see a kingdom without ventilators. A kingdom without funeral homes. A kingdom without misunderstandings and air headed comments from fellow believers who are just not sure what to say at times. We will have a kingdom where everyone will know exactly what to say when they need to say it. We won't begrudge the Lord of his praise. And we'll be in a kingdom where we won't wonder, "What's wrong with my wife tonight?" and she won't be thinking, "What a selfish arrogant pig." And we won't be having these things in the kingdom anymore. Why? Because the son of Abraham has blessed all nations and so every time you take the Gospel to the world and the Father blesses someone by opening their eyes and seeing who Jesus is, the Christ, the Son of the living God, guess what you're doing? You're saying, "Let me give you a sneak peek of kingdom life when all the families of the earth will be blessed." Blessed be the name of the Lord.

1:2-11

Abraham begat Isaac If you'd like to, you can look at Genesis 20. **Isaac begat Jacob** that's Genesis 28 **Jacob begat Judas and his brethren** that's Genesis 29 **And Judas begat Phares and Zara of Thamar** that's Genesis **34 Phares begat Esrom; and Esrom begat Aram; And Aram begat Aminadab; and Aminadab begat Naasson; and Naasson begat Salmon; And Salmon begat Booz of Rachab; and Booz begat Obed of Ruth** What book would we find that in? Ruth **Obed begat Jesse; And Jesse begat David the king; and David the king begat Solomon of her that had been the wife of Urias** That's 2 Samuel 12. **Solomon begat Roboam; and Roboam begat Abia; and Abia begat Asa.**

And Josias begat Jechonias and his brethren, about the time they were carried away to Babylon. Jechonias is kind of a key fellow. In Jeremiah 22, he was cursed with a promise that he would never have a descendant sit on the throne of David. How are you supposed to have a son of David sitting on the throne if someone down there in the downline was cursed with not being able to have that?

1:12-16

And after they were brought to Babylon, Jechonias begat Salathiel; and Salathiel begat Zorobabel, but none of them were kings.

And Jacob begat Joseph the husband of Mary, of whom was born Jesus, who is called Christ. Interesting, it doesn't say, "Joseph begat Jesus." So all of a sudden we realize that Jesus is not a natural born descendant of Jechonias and so we circumvent the curse by having a legal adoption of sorts whereby you have a descendant. Have you ever viewed anybody's adoption papers? I have seen a set with my own eyes from a particular state that says, "From now on, Such-and-such child will be counted as the biological child of So-and-so." Now think about that: "will be counted as the biological child of said adult." So for all legal purposes, the child is counted as biological but is, in fact, not. But legally is.

1:17
So all the generations from Abraham to David *are* fourteen generations; and from David until the carrying away into Babylon *are* fourteen generations; and from the carrying away into Babylon unto Christ *are* fourteen generations. That didn't just happen. That was what Matthew did with the genealogy. He left a few generations out, and it's not an error in that custom to say that Josiah begot Jechoniah, even though there is a generation between them.

All right, so here's what happened: Josiah was a great king in Judah. You can check out 2 Kings 20-24 and you're going to find out a lot of great history of how Judah, the southern half of the Israel kingdom, in the Old Testament, ended. Josiah was a great king. Great, great revivals. Smashed false gods, idols. Smashed pagan temples. Brought great reform to Israel. He didn't wait until he was an adult to become a good leader. In his 18th year, somehow, while they were cleaning out the temple, a priest found the Bible. It says that Hilkiah the High Priest came to the king and said, "We have found the law of the Lord!" It says that Josiah was on the front porch of the temple, and they began to read, and he tore his clothes, and began confessing sins. Everything from shrine prostitutes to homosexuals were put out of the land. And false religion priests were actually killed. That was a non-prophet organization.

Josiah died and his son Jehoahaz reigned for three months. He was taken by a Pharaoh, in 2 Kings 23, to Egypt. Jehoiakim , his brother, was put in place by that Pharaoh after he took Jehoahaz to Egypt, and it says he died there. Jehoiakim reigned eleven years. Jechoniah, or Jehoiachin, was the great, great, great, great, great grandfather of Joseph, the foster father of Jesus. He was the grandson of Josiah, the son of Jehoiakim. He also reigned three months. So, three months, eleven years, three months, eleven years. You can find that in 2 Kings 24. So, it was Josiah's son, Josiah's second son, Josiah's grandson, and then Josiah's third son.

This is the man that Nebuchadnezzar put in place. When he took away Shadrach, Meshach, and Abednego, he took with him Jechoniah (Josiah's grandson), and put Zedekiah (Josiah's 3rd son) in his place. Zedekiah is Jechoniah's uncle. Zedekiah did what he wanted to do and basically rebelled against Nebuchadnezzar. He was supposed to be kind of a tributary king, collect taxes to fund Nebuchadnezzar, and as long as there was peace kept, and everyone understood who the real boss was, he allowed Zedekiah to stay in charge.

After eleven years, Zedekiah wasn't behaving. And so Nebuchadnezzar put the Amorites, the Egyptians, the Moabites— everyone—against Jerusalem…Zedekiah the king in particular. And Zedekiah dealt with a siege against the city of Jerusalem for some time. And then he thought, "You know, I'm going to take some of the people in my cabinet, and we're going to sneak out into the countryside, and I think we can get away, and we'll just disappear. And maybe, one day, we'll set up another kingdom of God's people." Well, two of the people that were with Zedekiah were his sons. Nebuchadnezzar, in front of Zedekiah, killed his sons. Little boys. Killed them right in front of him, and then put out Zedekiah's eyes, and drug him off to Babylon blind. The last thing Zedekiah saw was the killing of his two young boys. And then his eyes were put out.

> Lamentations 4:19 *Our persecutors are swifter than the eagles of the heaven: they pursued us upon the mountains, they laid wait for us in the wilderness. 20. The breath of our nostrils, **the anointed of the LORD**, was taken in their **pits**, of whom we said, "Under His shadow we shall live among the heathen."*

Yĕhovah is the Hebrew behind the "all caps" "LORD," but look what that word is behind "anointed:" *Mashiyach*/Messiah.

> John 1:40 *One of the two which heard John speak, and followed him, was Andrew, Simon Peter's brother. 41. He first findeth his own brother Simon, and saith unto him, "We have found the **Messias," which is, being interpreted, the Christ.**

Now you've already seen it a couple times in Matthew. "Judas" is the Old Testament "Judah." "Josias" is the Old Testament "Josiah." So also here "Messias" is the same as the Old Testament "Messiah."

"Pits" is only used one other time in the Old Testament. So this word behind the word "pits" in Lamentations 4 is used two times in the entire 39 books of the Old Testament. The other time it's used, it's translated "destruction" in the King James. It is actually a hunting term. It's like a snare. Let's read that back into Lamentations 4:20:

> *The breath of our nostrils,* **the Jehovah's messiah, was trapped** *or destroyed of whom we said, "Under His shadow we shall live among the heathen."*

We find that this was the song of those that thought that they could duck under Nebuchadnezzar outside the city gates. They said, "Hey, prophet, priest, and king are all anointed of the Lord." Jesus is the ultimate Anointed One, that's why He is "Jesus the Messiah." The New Testament term is "Jesus the Christ." All the previews of Jesus, prophet, priest, and king, were known as anointed ones. Even Cyrus, king of Persia, in Isaiah 45, God calls him, "Cyrus, Mine anointed."

So here, we have vain imaginations. People hiding out in the city of Jerusalem are saying with king Zedekiah, "We are going to escape with this man because he is God's messiah, he's God's anointed, and we will disappear with him among the heathens, among the non-Jews, among the Gentiles, among the nations. We'll disappear, blend in, and one day perhaps we will arise with his sons, or his sons' sons, and we will have a nation once again." They were wrong.

We recognize a reality that wasn't true for Zedekiah and his followers but is true for the ultimate Messiah, the ultimate Anointed (Christ). We remember Luke 24:44, Jesus is in the Upper Room with the ten. Jesus took them through Moses, and the prophets, and the Psalms, and talked to them about Himself. This prophecy, like all prophecies for the most part, find their ultimate fulfillment in Jesus.

We believers have much in common with these people. We have all but one thing in common. Our Anointed of Jehovah did not die and stay dead. So, eleven years, Zedekiah. Eleven years those who followed him were sure that they would disappear because he's the Lord's anointed. They were wrong. We are right when we say, "Jesus is our Anointed, our Messiah, and because He was captured and killed, made a trip to hell, rose again the third day—we can say in 2016, "We will live under His shadow among the heathen."

When we're talking about the Anointed One, we're talking about Jesus the prophet, the priest, and the king. Lamentations 2:9 and 4:13 show that these three offices were on the writer's mind.

And by the way, we would probably say we're more likely to live under His shadow when we understand the first phrase of this verse. We are living under the shadow of the One who is the breath of our nostrils. Think through that for just a minute. God speaks, Genesis 2:7, into the clay and man becomes a living soul and he has God's breath in him. You and I are breathing tonight because God said so. So it seems right then that we should say "Christ is our breath, the breath of our nostrils." The Anointed of the Lord, Jesus Christ. How can we live under His shadow among people that do not appreciate our Jesus? It's very simple. He is the very breath of our nostrils. He is our life. We are obsessed with Him. This should be second nature to us. We've heard verses most of our life (Psalm 91:1-3).

He will deliver you from the pits because you are under His shadow. But you know to be in someone's shadow you have to be relatively close to them. I know if the sun is low the closer to the horizon it is, the further you can be from someone and still be in their shadow. If you've ever been out for a festival and set up a tent, you know by early morning or late evening usually you have to sit about thirty feet away from the tent to be in its shadow, but most of the time, I think it's a rule to say, if you want to be in someone else's shadow you need to stay close to them.

Now there's this mystery about the Lord. He says, "I will hold you close to Me," and yet at the same time He requires us to be close to Him. And I don't know how to make those two jive. I don't know how to gel those. I don't know how to make them match but I believe them both and so I think James is right when he says, "You draw nigh to God and He'll draw nigh to you." So all day, every year, every day this year,

I want to remember that I need God more than He needs me. He was God a long time before I made a choice for Him.

Because He loves me, He is far more concerned about my sanctification than I am. I just want to tell you that at the end of the day He is far more concerned about you staying under His shadow than you are concerned about staying under His shadow. I'm not talking about salvation. You're saved by faith alone in the blood of Jesus. And if you're saved it's because God did the work and God will complete the work until the Day of Christ, but I am telling us that there is a difference between knowing you're saved and feeling like it. And I want you to know that in the day of battle you're going to want to feel like it.

Now being in the shadow means that you're pretty close to the Lord. You're feeling close to the Lord. You're dwelling close to the Lord. But I want us to remember that sometimes it's just downright cold in the shadow. It is still cold in the shadow. Sometimes we can't explain it, sometimes it doesn't feel right, it doesn't seem right, but this coldness can actually be a bit of loneliness, and yet we would say that we're close enough to Him to be in that shadow! So, if you feel cold and alone, it's not because you're not under His shadow.

1:18
Now the birth of Jesus Christ[7] was on this wise, here's how it happened, **When as his mother Mary was espoused to Joseph, before they came together, she was found with child of the Holy Ghost.** Now, in the Jewish culture, there is this thing known as betrothal. It could be as long as a year. It could be as short as several months, rarely was it shorter than that. It was an engagement but much more important than an engagement. It was so important as an engagement that if the engagement was broken off, it was actually called a divorce. Obviously the marriage wasn't complete until there was a consummation of the union, until there was intercourse.[8] When a father of the groom, the

---

[7]Jesus must have been born before 4 B.C. since it is "almost certain" that Herod Great died in the spring of that year. If the edict of Herod in Matthew's second chapter called for the death of all those two years old and under, it seems reasonable that Christ was born no less than 2 years before this time and was therefore born in 6 B.C.

[8]Jim Bishop *The Day Christ Was Born* (New York: Harper & Brothers, 1960), 21.

father of the bride, would come together and make an arrangement for their children, often the children did not know each other very well and at any given time during the next year when the father of the groom deemed it appropriate because provisions had been made for him to care for his new wife, he would then go with a great entourage and gather his bride to himself. There would then be a great ceremony with lots of fanfare.[9]

With this explanation, you and I are amazed that we have a virgin who is pregnant when in today's world we should be amazed that we have an unmarried person who is a virgin! I'll just go ahead and say it: "This doesn't happen on accident."

Perhaps you're saying, "well, that was the culture then, and we have so much more to deal with." Really? You think what we deal with is harder than an occupation force that takes whatever women they want, does unspeakable things to them, and then returns them—maybe—to their families?

Perhaps you think God has changed His mind on marital chastity? Perhaps you think God was against fornication then, but now…"He's progressive and expressive?"

We are forced with wondering, "Joseph, what did you think when that young lady was **found with child**?"

Mary says, "Oh Joseph, it's from God."

When a young lady[10] today is pregnant and it's understood that she and her husband are expecting, she says "it's from the Lord" and we all understand what that means: it's a gift from God. But when Mary said, "The Father is God"…well, that was different.

1:19-20
Then Joseph her husband, being a just man, and not willing to make her a publick example. There were two ways to handle this: you could either stone the violator or you could privately send her away in shame. Joseph made a decision to not punish his dear espoused wife. Like I said,

---

[9]Matthew 25:1-13 gives a sort of peek into this.
[10]Bishop, 3; most young ladies were betrothed between 13 and 14.

it's a cultural uniqueness. He did not want her stoned because he loved her.[11] He was **a just man**. There are but two people mentioned as being **just** in the entire Old Testament and one of them is Noah.[12] Now think that through. Abraham, Isaac, Jacob, Joseph, Moses, Aaron, Joshua, Samuel, Eli, Solomon, Hezekiah, Manassah, Isaiah, Jeremiah, Ezekiel, Daniel. None of them are called **just**. What kind of man was a man who the only other person described up to that point as **just** is a man who was one of eight to survive a flood.

He was **just** enough to not act on his suspicion.[13] Furthermore, we have no dogmatism that Mary told him the reason of her pregnancy, but this Scripture gives the additional light that Joseph probably needed a **dream** for him to believe the story even if Mary did tell him what had happened. One wonders how much a man loved a woman to keep her suspected infidelity at a distance through divorce while being unsure enough to allow his own name to be tarnished as the 1. Suspected participant in fornication resulting in pregnancy; 2. Assumed "dead-beat dad" who left a woman after getting her pregnant.[14]

Jesus never got away from this. As you read through John, do you know what you're going to find Jesus called? A child of fornication (John 8). Jesus went through his entire adult life with everyone supposing that his mother had probably been messing around with Joseph before they were married (Matthew 13:53-55).[15]

Does anybody else think it's strange that the character of Mary is not explained? As a matter of fact, Matthew makes very little of Mary in comparison.[16] More than that, where are the shepherds? The angels? The

---

[11]Deuteronomy 22:23-24 not only identifies a betrothed as a spouse but also assigns stoning as the penalty for fornication during this betrothal period.

[12]The only other one I can find is David (in the words of Saul; 1 Samuel 24:17)

[13]John Peter Lange and Philip Schaff, *A Commentary on the Holy Scriptures: Matthew* (Bellingham, WA: Logos Bible Software, 2008), 52.

[14]One wonders how he might have avoided stoning for her in the case of public divorce or stoning for the both of them in the case of private divorce. I don't know at this point.

[15]or was messing around within a local garrison of Roman soldiers and Christ was begotten

[16]She is later known as Jesus' mother in Matthew 12 and Matthew 13:55 where it is also evident where she had other children—to include two guys known as

manger? We're all the way up to His birth and there is no talk of a taxing or anything that is famed in the Gospel of Luke. Why? Matthew wants you to notice the quality of this man Joseph.[17]

"James and Joses." They were probably "born" to her and Joseph after the birth of Jesus. <u>So much for the perpetual virginity of Mary.</u>

Now, I want you to notice the next time we see Mary is in Matthew 27:54 where she is known as "the mother of James and Joses." This shows us that she needed a Savior. At the cross, she is not known by Matthew as "the mother of God" or "the Queen of Heaven" or even… "the mother of Jesus." Furthermore, Matthew 12 describes her as Jesus' mother, yes. However, Jesus describes anybody as "his mother, brothers and sisters" if "they do the will of my Father." <u>So much for an exalted position in Heaven</u> for one who wasn't even exalted on earth.

[17]Matthew's genealogy traces Christ through Joseph, the son of Solomon (Mat 1:6) the Son of David whereas Luke's genealogy traces Christ through Mary (through the assumption that Joseph is counted as a son—being a son-in-law to Heli; Luke 3:23) the son of Nathan (Luke 3:31) the Son of David. See more in my commentary on Luke (chapters 1-2 particularly).

Mary and Joseph were engaged for marriage (Mat 1:18) and she was found with child of the Holy Ghost (Mat 1:18). This pregnancy was announced by the angel Gabriel in the 6th month of Mary's cousin, Elizabeth's pregnancy (Luke 1:26). She received the vision with great faith (Luke 1:38). Around this time, Mary journeyed away from her espoused husband to see her cousin Elizabeth in a different part of Palestine (Luke 1:39). She lived there for a short time with her and her husband Zecharias (Luke 1:40) whereupon entering, Elizabeth's baby leaped within her (Luke 1:41) and Elizabeth announced Mary pregnant (Luke 1:45). At this time, Mary sang a song of praise to the Lord much like that of Hannah's (1 Samuel 2; Luke 1:46-55).

After about three months, Mary returned to Nazareth (Luke 1:56). Joseph was willing to divorce her privately instead of having her stoned (Mat 1:19) but the angel of the Lord came to him in a dream (Mat 1:20) and named the son in Mary "Jesus" telling of His mission that "Jehovah saves" (Mat 1:21). One must assume that Mary knew before Joseph since the aforementioned vision of Gabriel which informed Mary of the same name intended for Jesus (Luke 1:31) occurred before her pregnancy (Luke 1:35). Joseph arose and formally married his wife thereafter (although he did not lay with her until Jesus was born; Mat 1:25). At some point there was a decree from the emperor of Rome that each citizen in the government should be counted in his home town (Luke 2:3). Since Mary and Joseph were both "sons of David" (Mat 1; Luke 3), they simply returned to Bethlehem (Luke 2:4).

Upon arrival in Bethlehem, Mary began going into labor (Luke 2:6) and they had difficult times finding a room because of the influx of travelers returning there so they stayed in a stable of sorts, and it was there where Jesus was born (Luke 2:7). Just outside of town shepherds were watching sheep when the angel of the Lord appeared to them (Luke 2:9) and announced the birth of their Messiah in Bethlehem (Luke 2:11)— giving them guidance for what to seek (Luke 2:12). At this time a multitude of angels chanted praise to God (Luke 2:14) and left—leaving the shepherds to seek this Messiah

(Luke 2:15-16). There were apparently many townspeople present to whom the shepherds relayed the angels' news (Luke 2:18). Mary took all of this and pondered it (Luke 2:19).

When Jesus was eight days old, he was circumcised (presumably in town). When he was just over forty days old, He was taken to the temple in Jerusalem where his parents offered a sacrifice as commanded by the Law of Moses (Luke 2:22). It was at this time that the Holy Spirit led Simeon into the temple and He held Jesus (Luke 2:27-28), pronounced a blessing upon his own life (Luke 2:29), a blessing upon the baby (Luke 2:30-33) and a prophecy concerning Mary (Luke 2:34-35). At this time also, a widow of about 100 years old named Anna prophesied of the blessed Messiah (Luke 2:36-38).

Following the birth of Christ, there is a sound of immediacy in Matthew's account where it records the arrival of the wise men (2:1) who first inquire in Jerusalem with King Herod as they search for the "King of the Jews" (2:2). The Jewish leaders narrowed down the birthplace of the Messiah to Bethlehem of Judaea (2:5) and Herod sent the wise men after the child to supposedly locate him for Herod's worship as well (2:8). The wise men then followed a star to the house where Jesus was located (2:11) where they presented Him with gold, frankincense, and myrrh (2:11). Then God warned them in a dream to return some other way (2:12) as His angel appeared to Joseph and warned him to flee to Egypt with Mary and Jesus (2:13) to avoid Herod's angry holocaust of boys two years of age and younger (2:16).

After Herod's death, a fourth dream (the 3rd from the angel of the Lord—all three of which were to Joseph) occurred where Joseph was informed of Herod's death (2:20) and at this time he passed through Israel (2:21) and landed in Nazareth (2:23).

The dilemma:
1. *Matthew 2:1 places the arrival of the wisemen in close proximity to the birth of Christ. This would still allow for the 45 or so days for Luke 2's temple episode with Simeon and Anna.*
2. *We are told in Matthew 2 that Joseph and Mary and Jesus fled to Egypt after the wise men's visit (which was in close proximity to the birth of Christ; Mat 2:1).*
3. *We are told that they went to Nazareth following their return from Egypt (Mat 2:23).*
4. *We are told Joseph and Mary and Jesus returned to Nazareth after the temple episode (Luke 2:39) and where Jesus continued to develop as a young boy (Luke 2:40).*
5. *Therefore, one must account for a return to Nazareth following the trip to Egypt and a trip to Nazareth following the temple episode when Jesus was less than two months old.*

Possible Solution:
1. Luke 2:40 says that Jesus and Joseph and Mary returned to Jerusalem (or greater Jerusalem area, perhaps) each year. It could be, then, that a full year

But it's more phenomenal than that. Matthew doesn't use that term **just** again. After looking at Matthew 27:19, The only other person in the entire book of Matthew is the one that Joseph raised. Has it ever dawned on you that Jesus was greatly influenced by Joseph? Do you have nephews or nieces that need influence? Jesus was greatly influenced by the adults in his life.[18]

Matthew, Pilate's wife (Matthew 27:19) and Pilate (Matthew 27:24) all use a term and they're the only ones that use the term; and they only used it about two different people in the book of Matthew: Joseph and Jesus. I don't believe God is doing anything but showing us that Joseph had an amazing impact on Jesus.

Was mindful to put her away privately But here's a man that was so in love with his bride-to-be that although he was suspicious of her conduct and fervent about justice…he couldn't just watch her die.[19] Banishment is harsh, but it is better than death and, who knows, maybe it's better than her damnation. "She's pregnant and she's blaming it on God. She's obviously not repentant so he doesn't even know if she's one of Jehovah's kids anymore. If she's dead, what happens to her?" With a love and concern for a woman that he wasn't sure he could even trust

---

had elapsed before their next trip to Jerusalem (to include Bethlehem to stay with family during their trips to the temple each year).

2. While Matthew 2:1 indicates the wise men arrived in Jerusalem around the birth of Christ, it does not give a definite interval to the time the wise men stayed in Jerusalem, awaiting the star to reappear (Matt 2:9). It was furthermore required of Joseph to be in town for all three major festivals (Deuteronomy 16:16).
3. It is possible that the "young child" Jesus was in the "house" (Mat 2:11) upon their following trip to Jerusalem. In other words, the Egypt episode could have taken place while Jesus was around one year old after a return from Nazareth for sacrifice (Luke 2:39-40).

[18]This is doubtless hard to swallow until we consider passages like Isaiah 53:2 where Christ grows as a "tender plant" or Luke 2 where we're told twice that he "grew in favor and grace." These seem proof positive that Jesus learned under Joseph. Please don't think for a moment that because Jesus was God in the flesh that meant he didn't fall and scrape his knee. How can you be a partaker of Adamic flesh and not trip and skin your knee? Not hit your thumb with a hammer in the carpenter's shop? Do you know that Jesus had to be shown how to put a table together by Joseph?

[19]Joseph in this episode—in this way—appears to take on Adam's perspective. Adam couldn't watch Eve die alone; so he ate.

anymore, Joseph shows himself a **just** man. So much for Christianity being chauvinistic.[20]

Clearly the **angel of the Lord** is not a Christophany as is usually supposed in O.T. contexts since Jesus is already in the belly of his mother. The "man, Christ Jesus" never expressed omnipresence and could therefore not be in two places at the same time. What a mystery that for this time…I hesitate to write this…Jesus knew nothing in the womb of His mother.[21]

1:21
Mary shall bring forth a son, and thou shalt call his name JESUS: Now, the name "Joshua" (from the book of Joshua) means "Jehovah saves," and so here's a man whose name means "Jehovah saves," and his courage comes as he is assured that God values his life more than anyone else's, otherwise why would the statement be so pronounced in the word of God, "If anyone disobeys Joshua, he gets to die?" So really, Joshua, a man whose name means "Jehovah saves," is placed sort of more important than everyone else in the nation to the point where God says through the people, "We'll not only obey you but if someone doesn't, they get to die."

He has two men to which he entrusts the campaign of Jericho:

Joshua 2:1 Joshua the son of Nun sent out of Shittim two men to spy secretly, saying, Go view the land, even Jericho. And they went, and came into an harlot's house, named Rahab, and lodged there. And it was told the king of Jericho, saying, Behold, there came men in hither to night of the children of Israel to search out the country.

---

[20]The treatment of women in Greek culture seemed to affect the 1st century Jewish world of our Lord. Many see Judeo-Christianity as this chauvinistic ideal as if it is a step down from the classical world, yet it was in the Greek world where women "had only limited access to education and social life, possessed few legal rights, and occupied themselves primarily with domestic duties and home industries" (Ibid 114). Perhaps one should remind the critic of today's believer that 1st century Judaism is a byproduct of Hellenism whereas Christianity is trademarked by truths like Paul's admonition to the Galatians that "in Christ there are no males and females" (3:29).

[21] For more on this, listen to http://www.sermonaudio.com/sermoninfo.asp?SID=1212121937452 [accessed December 8, 2016].

Here's a man whose name means "Jehovah saves." If anyone disobeys him, they die. He entrusts the conquest of the new kingdom west of the Jordan River to two trusted man called spies. Some people think that one of them ended up marrying Rahab and shows up in Matthew 1's genealogy as the father of Boaz.

We find out in verse 2, they go to a woman's house whose name is Rahab and she is known as a businesswoman in town. She did have a business and she was apparently very well known because when they needed a place to hide, they just needed to act like customers at this business. And through an act of war, Joshua crushes a stalwart city through an act of bloody war, Joshua subdues a city where a city is demolished and the city's name is Jericho.

I want you to look at verse 12 of this chapter. "Now therefore, I pray you," says Rahab, "swear unto me by the LORD, since I have shewed you kindness, that ye will also shew kindness unto my father's house, and give me a true token: And that ye will save alive my father, and my mother, and my brethren, and my sisters, and all that they have, and deliver our lives from death. And the men answered her, Our life for yours, if ye utter not this our business." All right, let's say it again: two trusted men of the man whose name means "Jehovah saves" are sent in to conquest a country, at first peaceably, it ends up and bloodshed and they go to a harlot's house and they promise a life swap. If she will not speak of their business, they will guarantee her life through their life.

So these two trusted men of the one whose name means "Jehovah saves," are sent in and they have relationship with a person and guaranteed their life for hers if she would be true to her word. Now then, they march around the city once a day for six days and then seven times on the seventh day.

> *Joshua 6:24 And they burnt the city with fire, and all that was therein: only the silver, and the gold, and the vessels of brass and of iron, they put into the treasury of the house of the LORD. And Joshua saved Rahab the harlot alive, and her father's household, and all that she had; and she dwelleth in Israel even unto this day; because she hid the messengers, which Joshua sent to spy out Jericho.*

Now, I want you to remember there was a scarlet cord hanging in the window. There are so many pictures of Jesus in this chapter and I'm simply not going to do a thorough job of showing you them all because this is not the main point.

> *6:26 Joshua adjured them at that time, saying, Cursed be the man before the LORD, that riseth up and buildeth this city Jericho: he shall lay the foundation thereof in his firstborn, and in his youngest son shall he set up the gates of it.*

In other words, it's going to cost him his family if he tries to rebuild the city. He will be cursed and his offspring will be cursed.

> *...So the LORD was with Joshua.*

So, he calls His Son, in Matthew 1:21 "Joshua" or "Jehovah Saves" or "Jesus." They are the same between the testaments. God could have named him Joel which means "Jehovah is God," and everyone would have thought, "Wow, this Jesus, this son of David, the son of Abraham, the mediator of the new covenant, the new Adam, the new Moses, he's going to be just like Joel." Or he could have named him Zephaniah which means "Jehovah has a treasured people." Well, certainly that's true of Jesus, it's true of God but it's not what he was trying to get across to his people. He could've named him Zechariah which means "Jehovah remembers," and then everyone would have thought this new Adam, this new Moses, this new Abraham, this new Aaron, this new Moses, he is supposed to be like Zechariah and they'd go back to Zechariah and do some searching to find out the character of the Son of God. All right, or he could have called him Jeremiah which means "appointed by Jehovah," and everyone would have thought, "Well, he's appointed by Jehovah," and certainly Jesus the Christ was and is appointed by Jehovah. Sure. He could have named him Obadiah which means "the servant of Jehovah," and everyone would have thought, "Well, let's find more out about Obadiah, the servant of Jehovah," and certainly Jesus could have been named Obadiah because as Isaiah 42 says, he "was and is the servant of Jehovah." He could've also named him Elijah which means "Jehovah is my God," and certainly Jesus could say that Jehovah was his God for he said on the cross, "My God, my God, why hast thou forsaken me?" He said to Mary Magdalene on resurrection morning, "I go to my God and your God." Certainly Jesus could say Jehovah was his God.

Okay, but that wasn't the name that the Father picked out to send through the angel to Joseph to have Mary name her son. He could've named him Isaiah which means "Jehovah has saved," but no. God wanted you and I and the Jewish reader to think about something particularly when we heard the name Jesus. The name Jesus comes from the Greek name which comes from the Hebrew name *Yeshua* which is where we also get our English name Joshua and it means "Jehovah saves." So both "Joshua" and "Jesus" come from different languages and they both mean "Jehovah saves." Therefore when you think about Jesus, God wanted you to know not that Jehovah has saved, not that he had a servant, not that he had an appointed people, not that he is remembering things as if he could forget, but rather that he has servants, that he can be your God. No, God wanted us chiefly to know, first and foremost, that Jehovah's character, his fiber is that He is now saving. Now saving. It's not something that he has done, it's not something we hope he did, it's not something we read about in biographies it's something, he does: He saves.

for he shall save his people from their sins. Now, think about the character of God that is continually finding Christians and saving them from their sins. The Messiah, the one better than Adam, better than Abraham, better than David, better than Joshua, better than Moses, is actually saving his people from their sins. I understand the moment of salvation that when we put our faith in Christ he saves us from the wrath of God, but even today as we trust the Lord in victory over sin in our life (whatever it is).

So I wanted you to see this. Then I wanted to show you some irony about this. The one whose name means "Jehovah saves," is in the very next chapter being saved by Jehovah. Who does God use to get Jesus to Egypt out of the clutches of Herod but his earthly adoptive father, Joseph. And all of a sudden I realized that God is saving his Son from the human hand of Herod, we find from Revelation 12 it's from the hand of Satan. Remember, the dragon stood before the woman waiting for her to bear the man child who was caught up. So really Herod was an agent of Satan, we get that. So God saves his Son, Jesus, from the hands of Herod who is being used by Satan and he uses Joseph, a carpenter. We don't have to be superstars to be used of God.

Okay, so they're not in the kingdom yet but we have two men that want to be trusted with the kingdom already (Matthew 20:17-23), and you have 10 people upset with the two guys (Matthew 20:24). 10 and two. It kind of reminds me of the 12 spies, "ten were bad and two were good." I want you to notice particularly was that we have a comparison happening here.

> *20:25 But Jesus called them unto him, and said, Ye know that the princes of the Gentiles exercise **dominion** over them, and they that are great exercise authority upon them.*

That word "dominion" there, it's very simple. If you were to turn that into a verb, "you know that the Gentiles dominate one another."

> *20:26 But it shall not be so among you: but whosoever will be* **great among you***, let him be your minister.*

They wanted to be key in conquesting a kingdom, yes? Isn't that what they were expecting with the Romans? If they learned anything from the Old Testament, what did they learn? Probably bloodshed. Jesus is saying, "It's not happening in that way. That's how the Gentiles do it."

> *20:27 And whosoever will be chief among you, let him be your servant: Even as the Son of man came not to be ministered unto, but to minister, and to* **give his life a ransom** *for many.*

What did the two spies say to Rahab in Jericho? "Our life for yours." Then it says in chapter 6 that they came and saved her. How? Because they promised a ransom of their life for hers.

Why do you think they are having that conversation in Jericho (20:29)? Because of the record of Joshua. Two men sent into a kingdom that is eventually conquested through dominion. Who wouldn't want to be part of that? No wonder James and John said, "Yeah, we can be baptized like that. Sign us up. Give me a gun. I can go over and take care of that business." No wonder they were ready to "drink [that] cup". Who wouldn't want to be a warrior and a decorated general? James and John certainly wanted to be. And who wouldn't want to be a part of a snatch and grab operation where we go in and get Rahab and her household and yank them out? But here is Jesus saying, "Well, here is how this is going to be done. I'm going to give my life a ransom for many." And where are they? Coming out of Jericho.

> *20:30 And, behold two blind men sitting by the way side, when they heard that Jesus passed by, cried out, saying, Have mercy on us, O Lord, thou Son of David. And the multitude rebuked them.*

Now why would you rebuke some blind people that need to be healed? Here's why: because they were considered cursed. Do you remember John 9 when the disciples came up with Jesus, John 9 and they said, "Lord, who sinned, him or his parents?" And at the end of the passage the Pharisees are saying, "We know that you were born in sin and you ask us about the Messiah?" They wouldn't even give respect to the man because he was blind and thought about as a horrible sinner because he was blind. Now think about it: not only was it the perception of people that he could have been a sinner but it was a perception that even according to John 9:3 with the disciples, his parents could have been sinners. Therefore it was in the perception of the reader that both the parents and the children were cursed if there were offspring that were born blind. From Joshua, Who was considered cursed if they would rebuild the walls of Jericho? The man and his family.

So here now we come out of Jericho and we come across two men that are considered cursed.

> *20:31 And the multitude rebuked them, because they should hold their peace: but they cried the more, saying, Have mercy on us, O Lord, thou Son of David.*

And look what Jesus did when those cursed human beings spoke out to him. He wasn't flippant like Joshua. Oh no! He's not just better than Moses. Not just better than Aaron. Not just better than Adam. Not just better than Abraham. Not just better than David. He's even better than Joshua.

1. You see, there are four limitations that come out to us in this passage that Joshua had. Here they are. In verses 20 through 24, Joshua equipped

those whom he deemed suitable. In other words, he called them because they were suitable. Jesus takes those two men in these verses and says, "You're not ready for this. You're not equipped, but you will indeed drink of the baptism. You will drink of the cup." Look at what he says in verse 23, "You will indeed drink of the cup and have the baptism that I have had." Do you see that? So here you have two spies in Joshua. He sends them because they're good to go. They're ready for the job, they're equipped and so he sends them. Jesus says, "You're not ready to go. You're not equipped. You're not as ready as you think you are but you are going to be sent and you're going to die." **Joshua only called those who were, humanly speaking, Grade A people.** Do I need to tell you in this culture of war we've been in for almost 13 years now in the United States, can I tell you that you can find plenty of evidence of what a real warrior looks like. These men were Grade A men and the two in this passage needed mom to talk to Jesus.

2. You might notice verses 25 to 27. **Joshua could only conquest a kingdom with means of the sword** and Jesus said, "You conquest kingdoms by becoming servants to those kingdoms." Better than Joshua.

3. Notice in verse 28, the **best Joshua could do was promise the temporal life** of Rahab and her family. Not eternal life, the temporary life of Rahab and her family at the promise of death of two men according to their word. Were they really able to keep her alive if the wrong person got to the house first? If the king of Jericho found out that she was a traitor, could they really promise what they were saying? No, and the very best they could do was give up two lives and save a household, but Jesus says, "I'm going to give up my life and be a ransom for many." Jesus is better. He provides eternal life for many, not temporary life for a few.

4. Verses 29 through 34: and we see **that Jesus doesn't ignore the cursed**. He promises a different quality of life for those who are cursed. Jesus' own character reflects the Father. The Father's character is that he saves people from their sin and not just people, his people. Contextually, I know that you can see that he is talking about the Jewish people, saving the Jewish people from their sin. 19 chapters later Jesus says, "No, I came to save many and I came to dominate Gentiles by giving my life for many." I'm a Gentile and I've been dominated by the Lord. How so? Because he threatened my life? No, because he gave his life as a

ransom, a trade. He took on my curse and that's why we see that he is able to bless those that are cursed. After all, Galatians 3:13, he was nailed to a tree and became a curse for us.

1:22

And knew her not. That's an old euphemism for he "did not have sex with her." There was no consummation of the union **until she had brought forth her firstborn son: and he called him Jesus.** Now before we go to some cerebral material about the virgin birth, I feel like a quote from Pastor Baxter is in order:

> Many ministers study only to compose their sermons, and very little more, when there are so many books to be read, and so many matters that we should not be unacquainted with. Nay, in the study of our sermons we are too negligent, gathering only a few naked heads, and not considering of the most forcible expressions by which we should set them home to men's hearts.[22]

This is not to say that the "virgin birth" is not a something with which we should be "acquainted," but rather that I wish to make an impression more upon your heart. Yet, we cannot adequately love our God without first knowing Him and knowing of Him.

We can also love God more when we love His Word more. Of course, we must embrace Scripture's veracity in order to love our God through His Word.

A God who called the entirety of the universe into existence can handle a virgin birth, a virgin conception. Do you see how that works? Look at six statements that tells us that Jesus was born of a virgin and maybe there are more but here's where I see it (Matthew 1:16, 18, 20).

1:23, to look at this baby and say God is now with us, that must mean that he's the offspring of God then. Divinity can beget only divinity.

---

[22] Richard Baxter and William Orme, *The Practical Works of the Rev. Richard Baxter*, vol. 14 (London: James Duncan, 1830), 182.

Also in this verse, we find a quotation from Isaiah 7 where Matthew clearly believed that Isaiah's prophecy required a virgin to conceive.

> *1:25 and **knew her not till she had brought** forth her firstborn son: and he called his name Jesus.*

So they had not even come together for another nine months after he found out she was pregnant. I'm assuming nine months.

Why do we need a virgin birth anyway? Well, I can think of four reasons and there are probably more.

1. You have to get around the curse of Jechonias. He couldn't have a natural born descendant sit on the throne so he needed a virgin birth. We need Jesus to become the legal child of someone in that line because he's the son of David that is also the king of Israel (Jeremiah 22).

2. To fulfill prophecy. Matthew 1:22-23 plainly cite a prophecy from Isaiah 7:14 and this commentator does a good job of giving an explanation of "virgin" in the original context of Isaiah 7:14…

> In the passage before us the reference is probably to a typical prophecy. The virgin (עַלְמָה) presented to Ahaz as a sign, was a type of the holy Virgin for the following reasons: 1) her future pregnancy and her giving birth to a son were announced even before her marriage had actually taken place;[23]

The neat thing is that while it was prophecy for the prophecy of Isaiah, destined for two fulfillments, it was historical when it was cited by Matthew as a fulfillment. Or, maybe a little easier, Mary was still a virgin when she gave birth whereas she was a virgin, as was the one in the near-term fulfillment, when the prophecy was spoken.

---

[23] John Peter Lange and Philip Schaff, *A Commentary on the Holy Scriptures: Matthew* (Bellingham, WA: Logos Bible Software, 2008), 53.

3. For God to be a man. You read all through the Old Testament and you're going to find out that God took on the form of a man but did not actually become a man.[24] Clearly God took on forms of men, but did not actually become man. Temporary versus permanent. And for us to have someone die for the sins of the whole world, we need someone who's able to do that which is infinite. If he's going to shed blood for all the sins that have ever been committed which, by the way, brings with it an infinite or endless or boundless or incomprehensible penalty of an eternal damnation from the presence of God—to satisfy an infinite God with an infinite payment for an infinite obstruction, an infinite transgression—takes infinitely righteous blood produced only by an infinite God.[25] So if Jesus were a perfect man (and there hasn't been once since the pre-fall Adam), then he could die for one other man but not every man. But because he's God and he's infinite, he can pay for the sins of the whole world: men, women, everybody. He tasted death for every man (Hebrews 9), and he cannot do that if he's not infinite and he cannot be infinite without being God.

4. To avoid the sin nature of Adam. Surely we understand that the responsibility of sin and the sin nature itself is passed down through the father. Exodus 34:7, it says that, "I will visit the iniquities of the fathers upon the children and the children's children unto the third and fourth generation." And since every father in my upline has been a sinner, that "third and fourth generation" carries well on to me and even beyond me. A Christ who was born of a man and a woman is just as sinful as you are and as sinful as I am and he can't even die for his own sins, let alone mine, because he has Adam's sin nature in him.[26]

---

[24]If you would like a couple of examples, you have the story of Abraham in Genesis 18 where three men come to his tent door. One of them is clearly the LORD and two are his angels.

[25]Acts 20:28 gives the idea of "God's blood."

[26]Romans 5:12 seems to bear this out as sin passing as almost a biological component through the father. We'll wait for science to catch up to theology as it normally does.

Chapter 2

Some introductory issues from the text of Matthew 2:

1. The lust mankind has for exaltation (2:8)
   a. Outside of Christ
   b. We also see the reality that Christ is no "mere man" (4:10) as He could have had the power if He desired it.

2. The significance of small things in the plan of God (2:5)

3. God speaks in dreams 2 through 4 to Joseph, the wise men, and Joseph.

4. Old Testament references 2 through 4
   a. Micah 5:2 in Matthew 2:6
   b. Hosea 11:1 in Matthew 2:15
   c. Jeremiah 31 in Matthew 2:17-18
   d. Isaiah 11:1 in Matthew 2:23

5. Killing babies occurred before the arrival of the babies 2 times in history. This makes us consider the future.

6. Two Josephs in Egypt by the will of God (comparing Matthew 2:13 with Psalm 105:19)

7. Christ is better than Moses…and everything else ("coming out of Egypt" is the beginning to Matthew's theme).

Consider, again, 1:21 "for he shall save his people from their sins." Now, think about the character of God that is continually finding Christians and saving them from their sins. The Messiah is actually saving his people from their sins. I understand the moment of salvation that when we put our faith in Christ he saves us from the wrath of God, but even today we trust the Lord in victory over sin in our life (whatever it is).

Now I want to show you some irony about this. The one whose name means "Jehovah saves," is in the very next chapter being saved by

Jehovah.[27] Who does God use to get Jesus to Egypt out of the clutches of Herod but his earthly adoptive father, Joseph. And all of a sudden I realized that God is saving his Son from the human hand of Herod, we find from Revelation 12 it's from the hand of Satan. Remember, the dragon stood before the woman waiting for her to bear the man child who was caught up. So really Herod was an agent of Satan, we get that. So God saves his Son, Jesus, from the hands of Herod who is being used by Satan and he uses Joseph, a carpenter. We don't have to be superstars to be used of God.

We furthermore realize that this Satan is the very one who shows up in the 4th chapter to drive our Lord Jesus to blunder in His devotion to the will of God and to, probably, disqualify Him from returning to the right hand of His Father. Satan's involvement is no marvel to us as it has been promised since the "enmity" promise of Genesis 3:15.

1. Joseph saved Jesus from Herod. Isn't it a miracle to think about the Creator being vulnerable? Think about these wonderful truths of Jesus being vulnerable:

"Jesus, joy of the highest heaven,
Born as a little baby
Under a wondrous star.
Like us, crying he takes His first breath
Held by His mother, helpless
Close to her beating heart.
Jesus, laid in a lowly manger,
Facing a world of dangers,
Come to turn me a stranger
Into a child of God.

Jesus, King of the highest heaven
Learning to take His first steps,
That He might bring us life…[28]

---

[27]It may even be said "'Jehovah Saves' is Jehovah Who needs saving!" See Appendix in Commentary on Ephesians.

[28]http://www.metrolyrics.com/jesus-joy-of-the-highest-heaven-a-childrens-lyrics-keith-kristyn-getty.html [accessed December 13, 2016]

2. Joseph saved Jehovah from Herod.
   a. Out of Bethlehem
   b. To Egypt
   c. In Egypt
   d. Out of Egypt
   e. To Nazareth through Galilee

3. Joseph saved Jehovah from Satan.

4. The Father saved Jehovah from Satan (Revelation 12:4-5).

5. The Father saved His Son from Satan.

6. The Father hid His Son from Satan.

7. The Father skillfully hid His Son from trouble.

8. The Son trusted His Father to protect Him from Satan.

9. The Son trusted His Father to protect Him evil (Psalm 22:9-10).[29]

10. The Son trusted His Father to keep Him secure in a strange land (John 1:14 and the marvel of His living in our camp).

11. The Son trusted His Father to keep Him secure in a strange land within a strange land (the marvel of taking Him to a land where His fathers were prisoners and slaves).

Marvels of any of this:

1. God uses people to accomplish things of eternal significance (the absolute understatement of the year given the context).

2. You can do what you ought to do.

3. You must only do what you must do.

4. God is mysteriously allowing things we cannot explain. While we rejoice about our salvation be secure in Egypt, hundreds of

---

[29]Listen here for more:
http://www.sermonaudio.com/sermoninfo.asp?SID=1212121937452 [accessed December 12, 2016].

mothers are weeping in Bethlehem....and we have no worthwhile explanation.

5. It is within the realm of possibility that Satan desires to harm you and that angels are active, as here, in your protection.

6. All of this trouble came from worship (2:2). How little would there be from this story if some people worthy of adoration did not wish to give proper adoration to Jesus?

2:1-2

Now when Jesus was born in Bethlehem of Judaea in the days of Herod the king,[30] behold, there came wise men from the east to

---

[30]Herod the Great ruled from 37-4 B.C. and was a generally wicked king who did things such as this infanticide, and also heavily taxed the people to build monstrous fortresses such as Masada (Ibid), Bethelehem, and Machaerus (Scott, 96). He was obviously very manipulative as seen in his dealings with the Magi here.

However, He did have glimmers of benevolence in ways which he assisted the people during famine and destitution—even restoring their center of worship, yet this too seems pragmatic as the temple was almost five decades in building this temple to bring himself notoriety (Lea, 25). Nonetheless, the white marble (Ibid) edifice had a platform that was instrumental in virtually flattening the top of Mount Zion and making it the very center of so much of early church history (and that of Christianity).

Religiously, he was hardly a Jew. He was half-Jew at best (Scott, 95) and was more Hellenistic in his philosophy (Ibid).

He was not much of a family man. He had more than seven wives and was afraid of many of them and their offspring to the point of deposing many of them (Lea, 25). When he died his kingdom was willed to three sons: Archealus, Antipas, and Philip who reigned over Judea, Samaria, Galilee, Perea, and Northeast of Lake Tiberias respectively (Scott, 97). These boys of Herod the Great were some incestuous hellions themselves—conniving to get one another's wives and kingdoms (Ibid). For that matter, it was Antipas who was lusting after his step daughter (who, by the way, was also his great niece) when he offered up to half his kingdom to her on his birthday and ended up giving away the life of a man of God (Mark 6:22-28).

Later, the Great's grandson, Agrippa I did his best to get his uncle Antipas in trouble with Rome and this ended with exile to present day France (Ibid, 99). This same Agrippa was apparently quite religious towards Judaism and as such was quite popular with the Jewish populace of Palestine. Agrippa's young son Agrippa II and his daughter Bernice along with his other daughter Drusilla and son-in-law Felix the Roman governor round out the significant history of the Herods and their mention in the canon (Ibid, 101).

Jerusalem. There shouldn't be any question in our minds why they went to Jerusalem and why they went to King Herod to find this new king. Why wouldn't they assume it was King Herod's son? A new king born, right? And here they are coming to the king of the Jews who was Herod. He's the king of the Jews. He's in Judea. He's king; he would be the king of the Jews.

2 Saying, Where is he that is born King of the Jews? Imagine the wise men coming and saying, "Where's the new King?" That would've been popular. <u>Probably Herod had no problem believing that he had a son somewhere.</u>[31] He was not a chaste man. He was not good. He was constantly killing off his sons that were competition for him. He had many female interests and he had many sons by them perhaps and he was constantly suspicious of them taking over his kingdom.

Here come the wise men. Why did they come to Jerusalem? Because that's where the king reigns and so they go to the place where the king reigns and ask the king, "Where is your new son?" basically. "Where is the one that is being born King of the Jews?" Naturally, that caused kind of an uproar in Jerusalem. The city wasn't happy because it meant another Herod was going to reign.

we have seen his star in the east, It seems like what is described in Matthew 2 can happen to a star or a combination of planets forming a star and it can appear to move and disappear and appear to move again if it's somewhere around the horizon of the earth. For example, if you're in Jerusalem and you're looking towards the southern sky towards Bethlehem, it looks like the star is above the city if the star is somewhere close to the horizon, right? And how does it disappear? It disappears below the horizon and so why does it disappear when they go to Jerusalem? Probably because on the travel path of that heavenly body, it disappeared below the horizon. Incidentally, the star's disappearance and reappearance (2:9) seems to rule out explanations of planets merging or reappearances of new stars.[32]

---

[31]His mom was an ethnic Arab and his dad was a person of Idumea which is Old Testament Edom and so he's really not even Jewish, but in any case, he's the "king of the Jews."

[32]John Peter Lange and Philip Schaff, *A Commentary on the Holy Scriptures: Matthew* (Bellingham, WA: Logos Bible Software, 2008), 57.

Just at the right time. God's timing is always perfect in every way. I want you to think about the kind of trouble, if we could say it for lack of a better term, that our Lord went through to prepare the world for the coming of Jesus, he prepared the Roman world. The Roman world. Now, I'll make you a deal, folks, I will not be distracted by the squawking if you won't be. I'm not bothered by children. Something tells me that Jesus likes them a lot so we can work with no issues with children, can't we? It will be all right.

*Galatians 4:4 But when **the fulness of the time** was come God sent forth his Son, made of a woman, born under the law.*

1. The Roman world was prepared for the coming of Jesus. A universal citizenship was called a kingdom, an empire, made up of little things throughout the kingdom known as *ekklesias* where little city councils would meet and declare judgments within every little city. The Roman world was ready for a Jewish Savior.

Efficient movement The Roman's roads, one of them named in the book of Acts is the Appian Way. There was no way in the world that anybody could get through the world at any time in the world as quick as in the time of Christ. It was the ancient world's Autobahn. And it was ready for some first century apostles that three decades after the Lord's birth would go here and yon from the west to the east as far as these spice trails of India with Thomas and as far west. We hear of Joseph of Arimathea in Britain and what were they doing but they were taking the Gospel to the world and how could they do it so quickly? Because *at the right time, God sent forth his Son.*

The Roman world had plenty of temples. Pagan gods everywhere. There was no shortage of so-called god-men. All the way back to Babylon, people were saying that gods had intercourse. The problem is that every one of those offspring, everyone from Nimrod at Babylon forward, died and stayed dead. The Roman world was ready for a God-man that would live and then live again and then never die.

2. Then there are the Greeks. The Greek language was the first universal language was found in the entire world, to the best of my knowledge it's found in the first century in that thing called Koine or common Greek

where you would not need a translator to preach the Gospel in most any part of the known world and you would not need a translator for the Scriptures in any part of the known world. If there was ever a time when it was perfect in the Greco-Roman world for a Savior of the world, it was at this time.

Then there are the philosophers: Aristotle and Plato and the rest. They set the stage for us to know the true wisdom of God, Jesus Christ. Paul says we were prepared.

3. I find that the Lord is preparing for the coming of his Son in the Jewish world. I mean, think about everything that was already set in place. They had a capital city: Jerusalem. We know that church history spawned from Jerusalem. The history of theophanies where would show up in the flesh, not just in the burning bush (Exodus 3) but as far back as God at the tent of Abraham (Genesis 18). God was setting the table. God was setting the time. God was preparing the world for the coming of Jesus, the Christ, the Son of God. A Messianic hope. They had been hoping for Jesus; they had been hoping for a Messiah for years. An ethical system known as the Ten Commandments. A Scripture; they already had an Old Testament. They were certainly ready for another word from God. They were prepared for such a thing. Then there is this thing known as a meta-narrative, the big story, Genesis 3:15 where God starts preparing the world for someone that would come and crush the serpent's head. If ever there was a time that was perfect for the coming of the Son of God, it was at the right time. Galatians 4:4, "When God sent forth his Son," born of a woman, "made of a woman, born under the law," the only one known as the seed of the woman, Jesus Christ.

Then there is this authority structure where you would go into every city where there was a Jewish population, if there were ten or more males, there was a synagogue. In every city there was a synagogue. In every city there was a representation of the monotheism that the Jews practiced. So we were ready for the coming of Christ who would set up his church and want all churches to be in all cities of the world from the rising of the sun to the setting down of the same. The sun would never set on Jesus Christ.

What a perfect time for the Son of God to come to our world—the Roman world, the Greek world, the Jewish world. How about great feasts and great signs? Surely, the world was ready for the Lord's Supper because it already knew the Jewish world had of a Passover. It was already ready for baptism because it already knew what circumcision was about. If there was ever a time when the world was prepared for the coming of our Lord Jesus Christ, it was the right time and the right time was when he came.

Conquering. They had heard in their Old Testament, the Jews did, of a conquering man by the name of Joshua and that Joshua of the Old Testament is the same Hebrew word as the Hebrew word for Jesus, Yeshua, and so they already had a great hero named Jesus and they were prepared for another one and so here came another one. So in the last half of Matthew 1, we have Jesus preparing others. Now, if you think about Joseph, we have him being talked about in verse 19 as a just man and I love this just man because Matthew only uses that term "just" for one other person in the entire Gospel by aid of the Holy Spirit, it is Jesus. Jesus and Joseph, the only two described as "just" in the entire Gospel. Who is this Joseph? What a great pedigree he has. Let's see here: adulterers and adulteresses, swindlers and liars, deceivers and deceitful, Moabites, Canaanites, Hittites, all in his pedigree.

I mean, I read as far back as Genesis 23 and I find Abraham buying a field to bury his loved one, his wife, from the Hittites and right here in chapter 1, verse 6 of Matthew, you have, "Jesse begat David the king; and David the king begat Solomon of her that had been the wife of Urias." How did a Hittite make it into Jesus' genealogy, but there he is, Uriah the Hittite. I'm not saying he was one of Jesus' great grandfathers. No, it's much dirtier than that. No, no, no, no, David stole his wife and she was in Jesus' genealogy.

From the highest of palaces to the lowest of curses, it seems, this Jesus comes and I would say "what is God thinking?" I mean, after all, it's been 400 years. Surely there was a right time before that and in Galatians 4 Paul assures us, "No, it's not true. There was no better time than this."

What about **an honorable upbringing for Joseph**? You say, "Well, how do you know he's honorable." Because he had every lawful right to have his espoused wife stoned and yet angels are coming to him three times in dreams and we heard about that and so I won't tarry there.

4. But how **about Jerusalem**? Look at chapter 2, verse 1, "When Jesus was born in Bethlehem of Judaea in the days of Herod the king, there came wise men from the east to Jerusalem." They came from the east and they came to Jerusalem and you know what happens in the next several verses, King Herod is there and King Herod is the king of the Jews and King Herod has had many, many, many, many adulterous relationships and so probably there were many sons of Herod and many of them expecting to be the king of the Jews and that wasn't good enough. No, now we need some strangers coming to town and saying, "We're looking for the new king."

Jerusalem is being prepared. It has been prepared. It was prepared back when God was cursing Israel because of the sin of David and God says to David, "What would you like? Pick one of the three things that I could do to you. You can run from your enemies for three months or you can..." and he gives him three choices, "or I could plague you for three days." And David said, "I'd rather fall into the hands of God than into the hands of men." After 70,000 Jews are killed, he sees a flaming sword over by the threshing floor of Araunah in the last chapter of 2 Samuel and guess where that is? It is Mount Moriah and we find if we go all the way back to Genesis 22, we have Abraham offering Isaac on Mount Moriah. So Abraham offers Issac or almost offers Isaac (James 2:21-24) at Mount Moriah. They built a temple there. Jerusalem is being prepared.

5. For hundreds of years Jerusalem is being prepared and **the Herods** are being prepared. Who is Herod? Herod is the offspring of one man we might know as Esau for Herod and the Herodians were Idumeans and that is the New Testament equivalent of the Old Testament word "Edom." All of a sudden, we have Genesis 26 happening where Esau is wanting to kill Jacob. You have Herod trying to kill Jesus.

Oh, who is doing all this preparation?

It is God.

6. He sends forth his Son at the right time and he has been preparing **Egypt** for 1,500 years, 1,500 years before this very account. God says to Moses, "Israel is my firstborn. You go tell Pharaoh that I will kill his firstborn if he does not allow my firstborn to leave Egypt." And you

know the story. Pharaoh's firstborn did die and that was a wonderful picture, a picture of our Lord Jesus Christ, the firstborn who had to die for God's people to go free from bondage. God wrote the whole book, the whole story. It was all prepared by the Lord God and Egypt was ready. What sweet irony it is for God to chase his Son and his Son's mother and his Son's earthly father back to Egypt. When I say "earthly father," I don't mean that Joseph begot him for you can see at the end of the genealogy in 1:16, "Jacob begat Joseph the husband of Mary, of whom was born Jesus, who is called Christ." Jesus was virgin conceived.

So all of a sudden, my dear friends, we have evidence that God has been preparing the whole world for the arrival of his Son and we learn, once again, that God is never late. What an encouragement. We learn that God visits his people in the darkest of times. I find it so odd that the angels didn't, I don't know, make the daytime visit but no, we had to have Jesus born in the evening. God still appears to his people in the darkness. He is continually poking into our worlds uninvited.

I always enjoy people who say God is the perfect gentleman who will never come into your life unless invited. Really? Ask the Apostle Paul if that's true. I found that the Lord does not always wait for invitations. He is not the perfect gentleman. When he decides you're his, he's kicking your front door open and sitting on your couch and drinking the milk out of your fridge. He is doing it with or without your permission and he proved it right here when he showed up on a dark night somewhere in God's blessed Promised Land that he has been preparing for years and years and years. So why did he create Egypt? So he could send his Son to Egypt and bear truth to the fact that, "My Son is coming out of Egypt again."

And after Herod is dead in Matthew 2, we find the firstborn coming back out of Egypt and so God has prepared Esau for Jesus. God prepared Egypt for Jesus. God prepared Jerusalem for Jesus. God prepared the Roman world for Jesus. God prepared the Greeks for Jesus. God prepared the Jews for Jesus.

7. God prepared **angels** for such a time as this. I do not find the angels bearing any kind of witness in anyone's life before Joseph's dream for the last 400 years at least. What have they been doing? God has been preparing them.

8. God prepared **the stars** (Matthew 2:2-3). Apparently the star disappeared from the view of the wise men. And then you might see, please, in verse 9, "When they had heard the king, they departed; and, the star, which they saw in the east, went before them, till it came and stood over where the young child was." Well, I have good reason to believe it was a star. When the star disappeared, it probably disappeared below the horizon and when it says that it stood over where the child was, it was probably appearing on the horizon, from their perspective, above the place where Jesus was. Right down there. Do none of them live on the horizon? Of course they do, but wait a minute, that's not crazy enough. No, no, no, God has been preparing that star and for 4,000 years by that time. That star has been traveling in its constellation and that constellation has been moving in its galaxy and that galaxy has been moving around the universe. For thousands of years God has been preparing a star and he kicked the stars on the fourth day and got them moving like a big clock and they didn't stop until this time and right at the right time, the star stood over where the Christ child was. At the right time.

8. **Mary** was prepared. She did not stay a virgin on accident. God gave her a set of parents and a culture and protected her. She was a woman of virtue and you hear me well, that did not happen on accident. Measured steps were taken. People seemed unreasonable and unreal but along with God preparing something as vast as a world empire, he prepared something as minute as a little teenage girl in Nazareth because God is in the details.

9. The **wise men** were prepared. Nothing is in here on accident. I want you to look at chapter 1 and verse 11. "And Josias begat Jechonias and his brethren, about the time they were carried away to Babylon." Why did he put that in there? If you were a Jew reading this, you would know that Jechonias was the last king or Zedekiah in the Old Testament. You would not need Matthew to tell you, "and they were taken away at this time to Babylon." Matthew is helping us connect some dots here between chapter 1:11 "they were carried away to Babylon," and 2:1, "here comes some wise men from the east."

Now listen, here's what I believe had to happen for some wise men to be prepared. Where did Zedekiah go as a defeated king of Judah? Babylon. Isn't that strange? They took him back east. A conquering king of the Babylonians came back and took him east. Now, I cannot be assured of much in this text in regards to this but hear me when I tell you that I do not believe that Matthew left it up to guesswork for us to know from where these wise men came. What is not clear from the text is how many there were, but what I think is a smidgen clearer is where they came from. I believe they came from Babylon.

Summary: You see, God is preparing everything for the way of his Son. His Son was Plan A, not Plan B. "Oh, the Jews didn't work out, those silly people. The sacrifices weren't working. I guess I'll send my Son." No, at 605 BC when the Babylonians came west and captured Zedekiah the king, I want you to know that the Babylonians were there because God put them there. Everything in our life, the untied shoes, the skinned knees and the job promotions are all from the Lord. "I don't like that." Well, when you're on the top of the mountain, you'll give credit to the Lord because that's what Christian people do. We do spiritual things. When we get raises at the job, we say, "God did it." When we get skinned knees, we say, "Why did God allow such a thing to happen?" And I want you to know, every bit of it was put in place to make big news of the Son of God.

Don't you know that the Lord could have made the Jews hold off a little bit longer until the Persians were in charge? No, he wanted them coming from Babylon. Don't you know he could have made the Jews be taken away during the Assyrian Empire? Nope, he doesn't want them coming from the northeast, he wants them coming from the east and God is preparing some wise men. Now, what is the result? The result is that because of the wise men coming to our great King Jesus Christ, really the end of the story is in Revelation 5 when you and I who have been redeemed of very kindred, tribe, people and nation come bowing before our King in the great throne room and what are we doing but casting our crowns before the Lord? We are wise because we believe on Christ. Not because we made an intelligent decision to believe on Jesus. Not because we're smarter. Not because we're Americans but because God made the Gospel the center of history. Those before it looked forward, those after it looked behind and we're all benefiters of such a thing known as the Gospel. Starting with Christ, the wisdom of God, "the *Logos* was made flesh and dwelt among us and we beheld his glory, the glories of the only begotten of the Father full of grace and truth and of this grace we have all received and grace for grace" (John 1:14-16). And why are we before his throne at the end of time saying, "Worthy is the Lamb that was slain?" Probably because we have believed on the blood of that Son who died for us and so our response is like that of Mary's when she receives news that she is pregnant with the Son of God. She said, in Luke 1

> *My soul magnifies the Lord and my spirit rejoices in God my Savior for he has regarded the lowest state   of his handmaiden. From henceforth all generations shall call me blessed for he that is mighty has done   great things for me and holy is his name and his mercy is on all of them that fear him from generation to generation. And he has shown his strength with his arm and with his might he has cast down the mighty. He has exalted the lowly and cast down the mighty from their thrones. He has satisfied the hungry with good things and the full he has sent away empty.*

That is the response of people that know what beggarly people they are and they are saved because God gave them perfect faith to believe (as much as people can with imperfection) on a Christ who came from a virgin, lived a sinless life, died on a cross in their place for every sin, and took away our sins. The Lamb of God who took away the sin of the world, slain and slaughtered, raised again the third day for our justification, interceding for us at the right hand of the Most High God, soon to return so that we, the wise, can offer our gifts before him.

His star modern star worship comes from misguided star-gazing today (astrology)[33]

2:6

And thou Bethlehem, in the land of Juda, art not the least among the princes of Juda: for out of thee shall come a Governor, that shall rule my people Israel. Here is the 2nd Old Testament quotation found in Matthew. Micah 5:2 is being quoted here.

2:8

---

[33] https://www.sermonaudio.com/sermoninfo.asp?SID=92915115051 [accessed December 13, 2017].

And he sent them to Bethlehem, By the way, there shouldn't be any question in our minds why they went to Jerusalem and why they went to King Herod to find this new king. Why wouldn't they assume it was King Herod's son? A new king born, right? And here they are coming to the king of the Jews who was Herod. He's the king of the Jews. He's in Judea. He's king; he would be the king of the Jews.

He pretended to worship and he said, **You go and search diligently for the young child and when you have found him, bring me word again that I might come and worship him also.** "I'm going to pretend to worship so that you don't see how much of an unworshiper I am."

2:11

11 And when they were come into the house, they saw the young child with Mary his mother, and fell down, and worshipped him. That's the third time the word is used. It's used in verses 2, 8 and here. Here we have a very fundamental definition of **worship.** Precious little more needs mentioning here about what **worship** really "is." It is, at least, a posture of reverence and submission. It seems reasonable as well to assume that the next action was a part of this **worship.**

And when they had opened their treasures, Now that's important. Energy in praise—did you spend that? Did you leave it as his feet? Did you spend energy in thinking and loving him with your mind? What gift have you brought for the King?

1. **This worship was, according to their status, proportional (gold brought by kings).** Maybe this is why "those who are forgiven much, love much" (Luke 7). Maybe this should make some of us wonder what it would take for us to feel like we have freedom in our spirits to worship much. "Lord, guide me to hear-felt richness so I may offer to you heartfelt and proportional worship. Such an act as this seems so simple.

   "Why travel so far to do something so little?"

   The only "little thing" in this story is the effort of the wise men. How can we, after seeing a little child that is a king and a little town that is a palace....how can we be surprised that in the middle of this account is a little gesture from some little men?

So I ask you again, "What did you bring for your King?" What thing? What vice? What weakness? What sin do you leave here at his feet in humble repentance? If he really is with us in a very clear and sensational way where you can sense his presence, then that means that you are before the presence of a King and I ask you, "What have you left him? You know the only thing we contribute to our salvation is our sin. That's all we contribute to him. But what will you leave him as a gift?

If I lay my shame from my past, would I miss it? Do I think that feeling shameful over my sin is, deep inside of me, a sort of...virtue? Or do I just need permission to lay my shame before my King?

> Might I recommend a man
> With an olive skinned hand
> Who scratches in the Sand
> and says to that woman "you're not guilty?"

> May there be such a One
> Who was born God's Own Son
> And before His sermon was done
> He says to the lame "your sins are forgiven thee?"

> Is there really relief
> Found beside that one thief
> Through Him Who in grief
> Said "in paradise, you'll be with me?"

> Then bring Him your sin
> No matter how grim.
> Find deliverance in Him
> And bow down rejoicingly.

they presented unto him gifts, gold, and frankincense, and myrrh.
What are we going to give God? God sort of said this in Isaiah 40 when he said " What will you give me? Are you going to give me the islands? I own them. Are you going to give me sacrifices when I am the one that

blows on the crust of the earth and up pop mountains? Are you really going to please me?"

Psalm 50 Don't I own the cattle on a thousand hills?

Worship is never deemed complete without gifts, gifts that are fit for a king. Gifts that forecast his fate. **Gold**, the gift of a king. **Frankincense**, found a lot in Leviticus, for the Great High Priest. When you're thinking of **myrrh** you should probably be thinking about bitterness, a prophet. It is interesting to note that after Christ is called the "Christ" (1:18) and before He is anointed as such (3:16), He is endowed with gifts fitting for all three offices of anointing. So strange…the only entourage of which we're told approaching the child-King…and yet…so few details:

> Around the Person of the God-Man, when the homage of the heathen world was first offered Him, we need not, and want not, the drapery of outward circumstances. That scene is best realized, not by description, but by silently joining in the silent homage and offerings of 'the wise men from the East.'[34]

This gifting to the Christ child was probably instrumental in financing their flight to Egypt—requiring meals and lodging for as long as Herod the Great lived. We see not only God's protection of His Son into Egypt, but we see God's provision for His Son. He'll not disappoint those who follow His Son. On the one hand, if God had not propped a star for the wise men to follow, there would have been no trial. On the other hand, if they had not followed the star, there would have been, arguably, no way to get Jesus out of danger. God provides the trial and the way of escape (1 Corinthians 10:13).

If there were no worship, there would have been no trial. But if God had not shown off His handiwork in the stars—wherein this very Gospel is found, there would have been no worship.

2. **This worship was, to our surprise, reasonable.** On the other hand, when you know One Who descended from Heaven's portals to earthly sod, it seems negligible to spend months on a

---

[34]Alfred Edersheim, *The Life and Times of Jesus the Messiah*, vol. 1 (New York: Longmans, Green, and Co., 1896), 208.

beast of burden to bring gifts to the King. They traveled a pre-determined distance—a long distance—to perform a particular act. This seems rather "unreasonable." Who would have thought they needed to go this far to do something as simple as this? This seems…avoidable…rather than "reasonable." They could have avoided the difficulty, the hassle…unless they really believe what they saw in the stars. If he really is the coming Messiah, then it seems reasonable that they should come this far.

Referencing Matthew 2:2b, It could be as close as present day Jordan, it could be as far as present-day India. We really don't know. They came a long ways and it took some effort. Imagine telling them they should consider worshiping at home in the east! They could have done that, you know. There could have been some sort of display of homage, so to speak, from a distance. Couldn't they have sent emissaries? Couldn't they have sent messenger boys? Couldn't they have sent royal diplomats? Couldn't they have sent an enclave of people to take the gold, the frankincense, the myrrh? Couldn't they have sent some kind of lackey to kneel before the new king and say, "I am here on behalf of the king of, and his name is_____, and I bring you his greetings and his worship?"

But that would've been unsuitable, improper. I'm not going to act like they knew him as the Son of God. However, they had a certain reverence for the person they deemed as king of the Jews and if they were willing to travel miles and miles and to make a certain display of worship based on their opinion of the king of the Jews, it would've been an absolute absurdity to say, "You stay home and worship there."

Real worship is never deemed "reasonable" by others who wish to have more glory. King Herod was not happy that they were there to worship the king of the Jews. Here's why, first and foremost: he was unconverted. First and foremost, King Herod needed to be saved. Do you know why Judas had a problem with the woman breaking an alabaster box of ointment and putting it over the feet of Jesus? Because he needed to be saved. Do you know the reason why many people are uncomfortable when the King of the Jews, Jesus Christ, is getting worship? It's simply because they are going to hell.

There are many among the sons of men that would give you a reason of why it is not fitting that others should receive honor. They would rather see resources given to some grander, more notable cause than to simply bolster the renown of another sovereign. "Couldn't that be given to the poor?" Judas said. Today Judas would say something like, "Can't we take that money we spent on that carpet and feed people?" or "couldn't we take the time we're spending singing to the Lord and spend it for fellowship?" But we who are saved say with the Psalmist that it is to His Name that glory belongs (Psalm 115:1-2) and that it should be for no other thing that we lift our worship (Psalm 137:5).

And so this worship thing, it bothers Herod because now people are not paying attention to him and now we're seeing Herod just as he is. If you have a new "king of the Jews" on the scene, what does that mean about King Herod? His days are numbered and when you worship someone else, it really means that everything else is just, well, temporary. Temporary. When you take out your Bible in the morning and you make the effort to journey from the east, that bedroom, and you come to that place where you enjoy meeting with the Lord in the morning, it takes a lot of effort. But a show of worship says, "No, he's worth the journey. I'm going to go to that place with my Lord and I'm going to give him worship because everything else is very, very temporary."

3. **This worship was, to those of Jerusalem and Bethlehem, visible.** You may be able to blame a lack of worship on personality and temperament and "moderation" here, but eventually you must realize that real worship must be unveiled. Real worship will show itself.

Perhaps you're thinking, "I worship inwardly and I have my hands raised in my heart." I'll be kind here, but that works for nothing else. We visibly pay taxes. We visibly show up for work. We visibly communicate with our spouses. Anything else is considered dysfunctional.

2:16

Then Herod, when he saw that he was mocked of the wise men, was exceeding wroth, and sent forth, and slew all the children that were in Bethlehem, and in all the coasts thereof, from two years old and under, according to the time which he had diligently enquired of the wise men. That word "according" means "in conjunction with" the time that the wise men had said they saw the star. Presumably, they saw the star signifying the birth of the new king about two years previously.

4. **This worship was, for this horrible calamity, responsible.** As mysterious as this is, we see that wishing to bring proper worth brought the wrath of Herod. To say it even more exactly with Revelation 12:4-5, worship the Christ brings Hellish anger on earth. If you wish to upset the halls of Hell, just give thanksgiving to the King of Glory. Satan still desires to be "like God" (Isaiah 14:12-14), and how can we but help that it is worship he desired.

5. **This worship was, as the plan of God, unstoppable.** One need only to see the difference between Matthew 1:11's sending of the people from the seat of the Messiah (a la Acts 8:1-4) to the Babylonians to see the contrasting reality that God often brings people to us. Now, I want you to consider this plan of God in two ways:
   a. God was fulfilling Scripture (Hosea 11:1).
   b. God wants His Son worshipped (Psalm 72)[35] to His Own glory as the Father (Philippians 2:11).

Apparently, there was a preacher in Adoniram Judson's life who saw the connection between this star and missions as well. It had such an amazing impact on this pioneer's life:

> "While engaged in his theological studies, Dr. Buchanan's sermon, entitled "The Star in the East," fell

---

[35]http://www.sermonaudio.com/sermoninfo.asp?SID=121912195152 [accessed 12/20/16].

into his hands, and its perusal kindled all the fire of his soul into a living and quenchless flame, and gave his thoughts a new direction. The scope of his christian sympathies became enlarged; the tone of his prayers was changed, and their subjects multiplied; and he hinted to some of his intimate friends, that it was, perhaps, his duty to engage in missionary labor..."[36]

---

[36] J. Clement, *Memoir of Adoniram Judson: Being a Sketch of His Life and Missionary Labors* (Roger Williams Heritage Archives, 1853), 19.

Chapter 3

3:13-17

We are not being told in this passage that John the Baptist's baptism and the baptism receive are one and the same. They are not the same baptism. All you need to do is look at Acts 19 and realize that unsaved people had John's baptism.

Also, we should not assume that John the Baptist knew about Jesus' divinity at this point. John 1 seems to indicate he knew nothing about this aspect of his cousin.

We are not told that Jesus' baptism requires our baptism. It makes bad teaching to say the reason we're baptized is because Jesus was. Now, that is, I suppose, a good inference but it is not Bible. It's not true. The reason we're baptized is because the Son told us to be baptized.

<u>Why did Matthew include this here?</u> Matthew wrote what he wrote and if we truly believe that Matthew wrote his Gospel first of the four, then we can't assume that Matthew said, "Well, I'm not going to mention that because they have that in Luke." No, I can't assume that. I have to believe that there was an agenda with Matthew particularly. Think of all the things Matthew doesn't mention. He doesn't mention the "shepherds in the field keeping their watch over the flock by night" (Luke 2). He doesn't mention the episode of Jesus at 12 years old. There are a lot of things Matthew doesn't mention and why doesn't he mention it? Because it doesn't fit into his agenda, his program for why he's writing the book of Matthew. So we've got to be careful about that. We want the overall scriptural view of something but we ought to trust the Scripture enough to stay put, okay?

> 1. It shows us **how Jesus became the Christ**. Matthew 1:18 reminds us that Jesus was always known as the "Christ."

Now the birth of Jesus Christ was on this wise.

That's just kind of simple to understand if you compare this to the idea of president elect, he's known as the president even before he's inaugurated. So Jesus is the Son of God and he is declared to be the Son of God with power at the resurrection (Romans 1:4). Christ is not his last name. It means "the anointed one." Well, when was He anointed? The Holy Spirit came upon him and anointed him at his baptism so though he has always been Jesus the Christ, he was actually in real time "Christed," so to speak, at his baptism.

2. We can **know where Jesus has been**. Look at the last verse of chapter 2, "And he came and dwelt in a city called Nazareth that it might be fulfilled which was spoken by the prophet saying he shall be called a Nazarene." Well then, Nazareth is a part of what third of called "Galilee." So Jesus goes to Nazareth and he becomes a part of Galilee. As a matter of fact, it says that at the end of the previous verse

*And when [Joseph] heard that Archeleas did reign in Judea in the room of his father Herod, he was afraid to go thither: notwithstanding, being warned of God in a dream, he turned aside into the parts of **Galilee.***

And where did they settle? Nazareth of Galilee.

Now we look at chapter 3:13 and what do we find Jesus is coming from Galilee. Now, why is Matthew taking the time to use those words other than the simple fact that he was inspired by the Holy Spirit to do so? Because it is to draw in contrast to the other folks.

*3:5 Then went out to him **Jerusalem and all Judea** and all the region round about Jordan.*

So surely if John the Baptist is looking out at a bunch of really religious good Jews who are from Jerusalem. They're basically coming from the hot seat of God right there at the temple. The Pharisees and the Sadducees came to John the Baptist from Jerusalem, but The Messiah had an accent. An accent? Yeah, you remember, Peter was from Galilee. Do you remember on the night of Christ's betrayal they said, "You're with him."

"No, I'm not with him."

"Oh, you're from Galilee."

"No."

"Yes, you are. You got you an accent. I can tell by the way you're speaking that you're from Galilee.

Jesus had a Galilean accent. How do you think that came over with the Pharisees? Jesus comes from Galilee of the Gentiles. Matthew says, "Hey, that's where we left him, that's where we're going to pick it up again in chapter 3, verse 13."

So for 12 verses, we don't know what Jesus has been up to, presumably he's been an honorable Son because look what it says in verse 17, "a voice from heaven, said, This is my beloved Son, in whom I am well pleased." You rest assured, I don't know how old he was at the end of chapter 2, it could have been 2, it could have been 4, I don't really know how old Jesus was. It really depends on how long they stayed in Egypt, right? If they came back right after the death of Herod, he was probably 2 but there's no need to think they came back right after the death of Herod. The book of Luke that Jesus is 30 at his baptism so it's been about 26 years, perhaps, maybe 28, and Matthew says, "All you need to know is that for these 28 years he has been pleasing his Father."

Wow, what a great epitaph that would be, huh? Wouldn't that be great to walk up to a tombstone and know that the person wasn't lying when they put a Scripture verse on the tombstone? "Precious in the sight of the Lord are the death of his saints," and that old guy ain't been in church in 77 years and the poor preacher in the funeral had to preach him into heaven because, you know, on his deathbed he said something about how he loves God and, "Oh, he must be saved because that's what saved people do." I mean, I've never been to a funeral where someone went to hell. Maybe you have and thank God you've met an honest preacher.

Alright, so Jesus had a testimony that he delighted the Father. I would love for someone to be able to walk up on my graveside service and say, "I don't know much about Bill Sturm, but I'm sure he pleased the Father because all I've seen of him..." I would love for that. I would love for one of you if I beat you into heaven to be to walk up to my tombstone and say, "I believe the Father was well-pleased with that guy. Now, I've seen him act the fool sometimes and he wasn't perfect and there were some things that he did that I probably wouldn't have done and there are some things that he did, the way he did them, I probably wouldn't have done. And I knew him pre-Christian and I knew him pre-pastor and there were some things that I might not have...but I know this, he delighted the Father." Certainly this is an ultimate way in which Jesus delighted the Father the way no other one can.

Delighting the Father is something that we can pray to do generally but, wow, what a testimony the Son had. He delighted the Father. Every time he made a table in the carpenter's shop in Nazareth, he was delighting the Father. Every time that he went to prayer in Bethlehem because they went up every year, they delighted the Father. Wouldn't that be a great testimony? That is a great prayer to pray in the morning when you turn on the coffee machine and scratch the dogs and sit on your couch with your Bible, our prayer should be something like, "Lord, help me today to bring delight to your soul." What a simple prayer.

3. **To show us the impeccable character of Jesus**. Look at verse 14, "John forbad him, saying, I have need to be baptized of thee, and comest thou to me?" This is interesting. What kind of baptism was this? A repentance. Did everyone get that? Jesus is taking part in a baptism unto repentance and he said it was a righteous thing to do, and we'll get to that in a minute as to how Jesus is taking part in a baptism unto repentance. Repentance in and of itself does not mean "turn from sin," you have to look in the context to see what you're repenting of, but clearly here in the context, we're talking about people who were repenting of sin. How do we know that? Verse 6: They were baptized of him in Jordan confessing their sins. So here you have people who are confessing their sins and repenting of their sins and are showing their repentance even more by being washed in water. I'm not saying their sins were washed away in water, I'm saying that they showed their sincerity to God by being washed in water, this thing known as baptism.

What does it tell us when John looks at Jesus and says, "I have need to be baptized of thee and comest thou to me?" Now, before you answer, let's remind ourselves that John does not yet know for sure that Jesus is the Christ. We find up in, the Gospel of John that he knew that when the Holy Spirit came down upon him. Why? Christ means anointed one and he saw the Holy Spirit anointing him and that's how he knew he was the Christ. How do you know he was anointed? "I saw him get anointed."

So we don't know that John the Baptist knew that Jesus was the soon-to-be anointed, but we do have reason to believe that John knew Jesus pretty well. Their mothers were related in some way. Salome, which is Mary's sister, was married to Zebedee and Zebedee and Zacharias were brothers and that would have made them related.

Alright, so probably we do know that in Luke 1 that Elizabeth and her family and John the Baptist lived in the hills of Judea and Mary and Joseph presumably since Matthew 2 lived in Galilee and it looks like based on Matthew 1, that Mary started out in Nazareth of Galilee. Alright, I'm saying that John and Jesus probably saw each other at least periodically: family gatherings, picnics, whatever. I don't know.

So here's the fact: you have John and Jesus know each other very well and so when Jesus shows up at a baptism unto repentance where people are confessing their sins and John says, "You don't belong here." What is John saying? "I know you and I don't know you to be a sinner." Twice in this passage we have the witness of both John the Baptist and the Father that Jesus was impeccable. You couldn't find anything wrong with Jesus and I still can't.

4. **To show us Jesus' identification with sinful people**. Okay, here is Jesus taking part in a baptism that symbolizes repentance from sin. Jesus did not have any sin to confess, verse 6, but he was still taking part in a baptism of repentance from sin. How do we justify this? Well, we have talked about how Jesus is the ultimate prophet, have we not? Alright, let's look at what an ultimate prophet in the Old Testament did (Isaiah 6:1-5).

And we find out from Matthew 1:21 that they will call his name Jesus and why? Why? Because he's going to save his people from their sin and Jesus starts the ministry of saving his people from their sin by first identifying with his sinful people.

Now, think of the miracle here. He could've waited until the day when all the peasant folks came out to get baptized, but the context at least leads us to believe that it's in the same proximity with the Pharisees. And where does he spend most of his time throwing down and landing punches in the book of Matthew? With the Pharisees. You see, the Pharisees are a picture of the worst sinner you can think of and Jesus shows up with the worst sinner you can think of, I'm talking about the one that makes you clench your fist. I'm talking about irritation so bad, you cry. Those people, God says, "I'm thinking about the worst people I know of and my Son is going to identify with them."

That means I get in because I'm the worst sinner I know and if the worst sinner of his day can be saved by the Christ from their sins, I can believe on Jesus and be saved from mine. Saved from the wrath of God upon my sin at salvation and saved from the power continually of my sin through everyday life. He chose to identify with sinful people to save them from their sin. We have a Savior who shows up and takes part in a baptism that the Pharisees weren't even allowed to take part in. Think about that. So John the Baptist says, "You Pharisees, you're not repentant. You don't belong here." And he looks at the Son and says, "You have nothing to repent of. You don't belong here."

5. If I were writing a heroes epic, here's what I would say: God sent his Holy Spirit down on Jesus and then Jesus stood up and declared us free from our sins and marched to Rome and crushed them all and buried them in the sand and we all live happily ever after. But no, that Holy Spirit anointed Jesus and it wasn't first to do great works, to open blinded eyes, to make lame people walk or even to raise him from the dead. Not at first, no. This to me is madness. **The Holy Spirit came upon Jesus to, first, drive him into the wilderness**.

I see Jesus going to the wilderness and why is he going? For one reason: to be tempted. Not to be blessed, to be tempted. But that Holy Spirit that came down upon Jesus, he came so that Jesus could be tempted of the devil. We can say the devil showed up personally in Jesus' life and the Holy Spirit is responsible for leading. And I wonder about you. I wonder, is there ever a time when you look up towards heaven and say, "What am I doing here in this wilderness? I don't see a way out. That is why the Holy Spirit is in me, to first drive me into a

wilderness where I can be thirsty and hungry and alone? That's why?"
Yes. Sometimes, humanly speaking, to go into the wilderness and
receive nothing but temptation and to come out empty handed. Did Jesus
come out with bread? Did Jesus come out feeling good about his ability
to be caught by angels? He was tempted to feel both of those. Did Jesus
come out a literal real time king over the nations? He got nothing out of
the temptation but the approval of the Father.

Chapter 4

4:1-3

Then was Jesus led up of the Spirit into the wilderness to be tempted of the devil. And when he had fasted forty days and forty nights, he was afterward hungry. And when the tempter came to him, he said, If thou be the Son of God, command that these stones be made bread. This is not a difficult idea. Moses is in the wilderness gets water from a rock. Water comes rushing out. John the Baptist told the Israelites, "God doesn't need you to be a son of Abraham. He can turn these stones into sons of Abraham." This is not difficult. God can do anything he wants with stones.

What is the temptation here? Is it just feed yourself? Is that all this is or is there more here to this? Jesus is being tempted to abuse his powers; to go beyond God's plans. So take matters in your own hands. "I'm the Son of Man, of course I should be able to do this." The way Christ responds helps us to understand the temptation. His response is, **Man shall not live by bread alone but every word that proceeds out of the mouth of God.** So God's mouth communicates God's plan.

Deuteronomy 1:1 These be the words which Moses spake.

So let's stop for just a moment and remind ourselves what is Jesus doing when he quotes from Deuteronomy? Jesus is saying, "That's the word of God." He is, in fact, validating the authenticity of the text. The historicity of Moses is validated by quoting that.

Moses goes on, in chapter 8, to say to them that God

allowed thee to hunger

God let the children of Israel go hungry. God moved them to a place where there were no Walmarts, no Food Lions, and they were going to get hungry. He takes them to a point where they're hungry and in their state of hunger. They need God.

and fed thee with manna, which thou knewest not, neither did thy fathers know; that he might make thee know that man does not *live by bread only, **but by every word that proceeds out of the mouth of the LORD.***

Jesus quotes one verse but let's remind ourselves, he's quoting that verse to an audience that knows their Old Testament well so he doesn't need to read the entire chapter to them. They immediately make the connection. Matthew's reminding them that God's firstborn, Israel, was taken to the wilderness and was allowed to be without food and water and to be at a point where the only hope for life is if God does something.

> *Deuteronomy 8:4 Thy raiment waxed not old upon thee, neither did thy foot swell, **these forty years**. Thou shalt also consider in thine heart, that, as a man chasteneth his son, so the LORD thy God chasteneth me. Therefore you and I must keep God's commandments. We must walk in his ways. We must remain in a reverential fear for who he is. For the LORD thy God brings thee into a good land, a land of brooks of water, of fountains, depths and springs out of valleys and hills.11 Beware that thou forget not the LORD thy God, in not keeping his commandments, and his judgments, and his statutes, which I command thee this day: Lest when you have eaten and you're full, thine heart is going to be lifted up and surely you're going to forget the LORD thy God which brought thee forth out of the land of Egypt, out of the house of bondage.*

"Remember, remember who led thee through that great and terrible wilderness. What was in that great and terrible wilderness? There were fiery serpents. There were scorpions. There was drought. There was no water. Who was it that brought thee forth water out of that rock? Who was it that fed thee in the wilderness with manna?"

Let's consider the nature of the three temptations: When Jesus is being told, "Maybe you should make water or you should make bread for yourself," the big question among the Jews was, "Jesus, are you as good as Moses? Are you like Moses?" Look at their expectation below:

> *Deuteronomy 18:15 The LORD thy God will raise up unto thee a Prophet from the midst of thee, of thy brethren, **like unto me**. 16 According to all that thou desiredst of the LORD thy God in Horeb in the day of the assembly, saying, Let me not hear again*

the voice of the LORD my God, neither let me see this great fire any more, that I die not. 18. I will raise them up a Prophet from among their brethren, like unto thee, and will put my words in his mouth. 20 But the prophet, which shall presume to speak a word in my name, which I have not commanded him to speak, or that shall speak in the name of other gods, even that prophet shall die.

So the children of Israel are expecting another prophet like Moses, right? Moses brought them bread.

*Deuteronomy 9:9 When I was gone up into the mount to receive the tables of stone, even the tables of the covenant which the LORD made with you, then I abode in the mount forty days and forty nights, I **did not eat bread or drink water.***

So here's Jesus in the middle of 40 days and 40 nights of fasting and the devil is tempting him. Why is the devil tempting him? Because he wants the children of Israel to know and he wants Jesus to know first and foremost, "You're not like Moses. You are not the fulfillment of Deuteronomy 18 because if I can make you make bread for yourself here in the wilderness, then that means you're not as good as Moses who didn't eat bread for 40 days and 40 nights."

4:4

But he answered and said, It is written, Man shall not live by bread alone, but by every word that proceedeth out of the mouth of God. The temptation for Jesus would be to take matters into His own hands and abuse His power to make things happen in His time—to abuse His power.

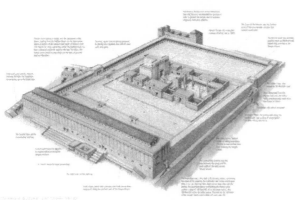

4:5

Then the devil taketh him up into the holy city, and setteth him on a pinnacle of the temple A lot of people when they hear word "pinnacle" they assume it's like, "Ah, a temple has a steeple," and so they picture Jesus and the devil standing on a steeple but really the pinnacle was on the southeast corner of what was Herod's temple. Often at the sundown on the Sabbath eve, you would see the trumpeters standing across the pinnacle of the temple and they would blow their trumpets says Alfred Edersheim in his book "Life and Times of Jesus the Messiah."

Also, right here 33 years exactly after the death of our Lord Jesus, his half brother James was martyred from that place where he was thrown from the pinnacle of the temple, says the book "Martyrs Mirror." He survived the fall and then was then beaten with clubs until his death. James, the half brother of Jesus. Passover day 33 years exactly to the anniversary of the death of Jesus.

Now, I want you to just consider for a moment that Satan has been around for the entire 30 years of Jesus' life up until this point because, if you think about Matthew 2, he was behind Herod's actions of trying to kill all the baby boys. Revelation 12 tells us that the dragon stood before the woman waiting for her to birth the man child but he was caught up to heaven before Satan could kill him. Well, that includes the lifetime of Jesus.

4:6

And saith unto him, If thou be the Son of God, cast thyself down. Satan probably wanted Jesus to become king that day so that he couldn't die, and offers Jesus a shortcut to the throne. If you're in the middle of Jerusalem, and everyone sees angels catch you…they're going to make you king. I want to remind you of John 6, after Jesus fed them in the wilderness it said they desired to make him king.

What evidence do we have that he could've beckoned the angels later in the book of Matthew? In the Garden of Gethsemane, He could've called 12 legions of angels. It wasn't that the angels were outside of the realm of Christ's authority. He was being tempted to use his authority. Jesus was being tempted to act like an American, to use his rights to benefit himself. It's very important that we do not equate Christianity with Americanism because here Jesus had the right to throw himself down. He had the right to make himself bread and he didn't do it.

All three temptations were answered out of Deuteronomy and I want you to notice that all three temptations came out of Deuteronomy. "Moses made bread. Can you make bread?"

> *Deuteronomy 33:1 This is the blessing, wherewith Moses the man of God blessed the children of Israel before his death. 2 And he said, The LORD came from Sinai, and rose up from Seir unto them; he shined forth from mount Paran he came **with ten thousands of saints**: from his right hand went a fiery law for them. Yea, he loved the people; all his saints are in thy hand.*

Now, I know when we think of saints, we think of saved people, but even Jude 16 says, "Behold **the Lord comes with ten thousands of his saints** to judge those who are ungodly of their ungodly deeds which they have ungodly committed."

So there are many times in Scripture where the word "saints" just refers to angels. Deuteronomy 33:2 is one of them. In Acts 7, Stephen preaches from here and in Galatians 3, Paul preaches from this passage. He says the law was given through angels. So here is Moses for 40 days and 40 nights on Mount Sinai in the wilderness of Sinai meeting with God and he receives the law of Moses. He receives the law from God at the hand of thousands of angels. So when we think of the second temptation and we think of Jesus who is being tempted 40 days and 40 nights and he's already been tempted to do that which Moses would not do and that is eat during the fast. Now he's being tempted to see if he stacks up to Moses. "Are you as good as Moses? Can you show angels as a part of your 40 days and 40 nights?" So he's being tempted here again. "Can you show me? Can you show these people that you are the prophet like Moses?"

4:7

Jesus said unto him, It is written again Thou shalt not tempt the Lord thy God. Here, he quotes a 2nd time out of Deuteronomy, a book that Moses wrote. Moses also wrote the Psalm which Satan quoted.

> *Psalm 91:1 He that **dwelleth in the secret place of the most High** shall abide under the shadow of the Almighty. I will say of the LORD, He is my refuge and my fortress: my God; in him will*

*I trust. 3 Surely he shall deliver thee from the snare of the fowler, and from the noisome pestilence. He shall cover thee with his feathers, and under his wings shalt thou trust: his truth shall be thy shield and buckler. Thou shalt not be afraid for the terror by night; nor for the arrow that flieth by day; Nor for the pestilence that walketh in darkness; nor for the destruction that wasteth at noonday. A thousand shall fall at thy side, and ten thousand at thy right hand; but it shall not come nigh thee. Only with thine eyes shalt thou behold and see the reward of the wicked. Because thou hast made the LORD, which is my refuge [Moses wrote] even the most High, thy habitation; There shall no evil befall thee, **neither shall any plague come nigh thy dwelling.***

Do you think Moses was qualified to say that? Two million Jews lived in Egypt and they had light in their dwelling when the Egyptians were walking around bumping into tables for three days. It was light in Goshen. There were no frogs in Goshen. There was no problem in Goshen. The plagues did not touch the children of Israel even though they were smack dab in the middle of Egypt. I think Moses was qualified to say, "Neither shall any plague come nigh thy dwelling."

Now, here is what Satan quoted, verses 11 and 12

He shall give his angels charge over thee, to keep thee in all thy ways. They shall bear thee up in their hands, lest thou dash thy foot against a stone. *Thou shalt tread upon the lion and adder: the young lion and the dragon shalt thou trample under feet. Because he hath set his love upon me, therefore will I deliver him: I will set him on high. because he hath known my name. He shall call upon me, and I will answer him: I will be with him in trouble.*

Now, let's get this: the Psalmist is speaking from the perspective of someone who is in deep trouble. That is when you can count on verses 11 and 12. Question: was Jesus in deep trouble on the pinnacle of the temple? No. Did he have any authority to claim that Psalm right there? Was it a righteous thing for him to claim that Psalm? No.

Now, let me tell you how correct Satan is. Satan was willing to take a Psalm and apply it to Jesus. Satan knew that the Psalms talked about Jesus. Luke 24:44 says the Psalms speak of Christ. So every time you see something admirable that you like in the Psalms, you need to see Jesus right in the middle of it. Moses knew what it was like to live Psalm 91, but Satan knew that the Psalm was talking about Christ and Satan was a great student of Scripture. Have you ever met anyone you just admired their Bible knowledge?

Satan knew his Bible. Satan knew the words of Moses so let us not be fooled into thinking spirituality is somehow revealed in the fact that you can win Bible trivia. "Wow, that guy is anointed." Ezekiel 28 calls Satan "the anointed cherub." He looks so much like Christ, God's Anointed One.

The words of God are the best words. Now, notice Jesus didn't say, "Well, you used the Bible wrong." Satan quotes Moses, Jesus quotes Moses.

> *Deuteronomy 6:1 these are the commandments, the statutes, and the judgments, which the LORD your God commanded to teach you, that ye might do them. 2 That thou mightest fear the LORD thy God, to keep all his statutes...4 Hear, O Israel: The LORD our God is one LORD: You will love the LORD thy God with all thine heart, and with all thy soul, and with all thy might. 6 And* **these words***, which I command thee this day, shall be in thine heart. 7 thou shalt teach* **them** *diligently unto thy children, and shalt talk of* **them** *when thou sittest in thine house. 8 And thou shalt bind* **them** *for a sign upon thine hand. 9 And thou shalt write* **them** *upon the posts of thy house. 14 You will not go up after other gods, of the gods of the people which are round about you; (For the LORD thy God is a jealous God among you) lest the anger of the LORD thy God be kindled against thee, and destroy thee from off the face of the earth.* **Ye shall not tempt the LORD your God***, as ye tempted him in Massah.*

Jesus quoted verse 16, the first part. The words of God are the best words when understood within the author's intent. That is really important. The devil didn't care about the author's intent in Psalm 91. God protecting people who are being pursued by their enemies can count on the angels of God keeping your foot from dashing against a stone. Jesus cared about the author's intent and so he came back with a

Scripture. Please notice, he didn't try to fix Satan: "Now here, Satan, let's turn over there to Psalm 91 and see where you're wrong." Nope. Jesus didn't take the time answering every little silly nitwitted notion of the devil. He came back quickly with Scripture.

Exodus 17: Here in **Massah,** We're getting to the place where the children of Israel need water for a second time. The first time was in a place known as Marah, the bitter waters. Remember, they cried about those bitter waters and I probably would do some crying over some bitter waters.

> *Exodus 17:1 And all the congregation of the children of Israel journeyed from the wilderness of Sin, after their journeys, according to the commandment of the LORD, and pitched in Rephidim: and there   was no water for the people to drink. Wherefore the people did chide with Moses, and said, Give us water that we may drink. And Moses said unto them, Why chide ye with me? Why do ye **tempt the LORD?***

Now, why is it temptation? Think about it now: why are they testing the Lord? It's like Moses is saying, "Why are you trying to see if God will do something? Why are you saying things?" Think about it now, "Why are you manipulating God with your words?"

Think about how we get people to do stuff for us. We haven't asked them directly. We haven't said anything directly, but we have gotten them to do things through this evil thing known as manipulation and here the children of Israel are manipulating God, just like Jesus would have been manipulating God if he would have jumped off the pinnacle of the temple. "Father, prove to me that you're still with me." Now, why did the Father not need to prove that to Jesus? Because Jesus had just heard God say from heaven, "You're my Son and I'm happy with you." Jesus didn't need any other proof. Jesus didn't need any other spectacle from God. So to require God to catch him from falling to the dirt underneath the pinnacle of the temple would have been tempting or testing God and would have been a heinous crime against God, His Father.

What did they do here at Massah? Well, remember everything the children of Israel have seen so far. They've seen a lot of Egypt's population die in a series of ten plagues. They saw most of the army die in the Red Sea. They saw waters stand up like walls on the left and right walking through the Red Sea. I have pointed out before that the opening had to be almost miles wide in order for 3.4 million people to get through the Red Sea in one night walking at a decent pace with all of their stuff. They had to be walking 3,000 abreast. And then to see manna drop from the sky and quail and a misting cloud sheltering them from the hot sun and a burning fire keeping them lighted in the evening and warm in that wilderness air and then to look at God and say, "Well, what are we going to do about water now?" That is tempting God.

> *Exodus 17:3 And the people thirsted there for water; and the people murmured against Moses, and said, Wherefore is this that thou hast brought us up out of Egypt, to kill us and our children and our cattle with thirst?*

I have required the Lord to jump through my hoops to prove that he's still on my team. That is tempting God.

Certainly a baby Christian can say, "Lord, if you're really up there, pay for my kid's camp." Certainly a baby Christian can say, "Lord, if you're up there, please fix my car without me taking it to the mechanic." Certainly a person who has been saved a week can get away with saying, "Lord, if you're really with me, make my wife repent and get along with me. Make my husband repent and get along with me. Pay our water bill, Lord, if you're really with me." If you're really with me? Weren't you there the night I saved you? Weren't you there the night that I troubled you over your sin and gave you faith in the Gospel? And you say "if you're really with you?"

So the name game of Satan is to get Jesus to doubt what just happened back there at the Jordan River.

> *Exodus 17:4 And Moses cried unto the LORD, saying, What shall I do unto this people? they be almost ready to stone me. 5 And the LORD said unto Moses, Go on before the people, and take with thee of the elders of Israel; and thy rod, wherewith thou smotest the river, take in thine hand, and go. Behold, I will stand before thee there upon the rock in Horeb; and thou shalt smite the rock, and there shall come water out of it, that the people*

may drink. And Moses did so in the sight of the elders of Israel. And he called the name of the place Massah, and Meribah, because of the chiding of the children of Israel, and because **they tempted the LORD, saying, "Is the LORD among us, or not?"** *That is convicting. Is the Lord really with us?*

And for me to believe that the Lord is really with me, I require him to show me a sign. If we're not careful in the next day or two, we will take this up with the Lord and we will give him an ultimatum, a manipulative ultimatum that says, "Because I'm one of God's favorites, he will never allow _____ to happen or he will do this for me."

4:8

Again, the devil taketh him up into an exceeding high mountain, and my question is, "How in the world did he get there? Just like that?" Well, you know, I suppose there's a lot going on in the spirit world and we find Philip in Acts 8 being whisked away to another part of the place of God's creation just like that. He's in another place. I don't have a hard time believing that they traveled that quickly to a high mountain.

What mountain would it make sense that they were on if we're Moses all through this passage of Scripture? We have a couple of guesses. One might be Sinai and one might be Nebo where Moses died; where Moses looked out into all of Canaan and saw what he could not have because of one act of disobedience. One act of disobedience. But because of his position, he was held to a higher standard.

The reason I would go with Mt Nebo is because it seems like they could be saying that they saw "all the tracts of the earth" or "all the segments of the land." It says he shows him **all the kingdoms of the world and the glory of them.** And I don't know, you'll forgive me if I'm not willing to get on the literalist bandwagon here and say that they saw everything from Wisconsin all the way around to Illinois, you know, because here's the fact: there's something in the way if we're talking about physical eyes and it's called the curvature of the earth. Eventually you're not going to see any further. Is it possible they supernaturally saw every kingdom of the world? Sure and it doesn't even have to be the whole globe, it could be the known world, the Roman government. Be that as it may, I think it could be figurative for they looked out as far as they could see and I understand on a clear day from a high point on the earth's topography you could see upwards to 35 miles if it's clear enough. Look, you can see 35 miles in every direction. I can see why Matthew might say, "He looked at all the kingdoms of the world," that is the known world.

Did you notice that Jesus doesn't argue with Satan here? Did you notice that he doesn't say, "What do you mean?" Certainly, if they weren't Satan's to give, this would have been a fine time to inform him, but the fact is they were his in some regard. He is called "the god of this world" (2 Corinthians 4).

4:9

All these things will I give thee, if thou wilt fall down and worship me. Well, that seems pretty audacious, doesn't it? That is what you do for a king, you fall down. The word there is to lick the hand of a master like a dog does. I don't think that Satan was hoping that Jesus would lick his hand, but I think he was looking for a respectful, customary kiss on a ring, if you would, like for a sovereign. This word is used often through the Gospels as a way for a subject to kiss his master's hand and so Satan was saying, "If you will bow to me as your king, I will share my kingdom with you." Think about it. Satan said, "If you will treat me like your king, I will share my kingdom with you."

Jesus for the third consecutive time quotes out of the book of Deuteronomy. So what's next? The shortcut to Canaan.

> *Deuteronomy 34:1 Moses went up from the plains of Moab unto* ***the mountain of Nebo****, to the top of Pisgah, that is over against Jericho. And the LORD shewed him all the land of Gilead, unto Dan, And all Naphtali, and the land of Ephraim, and Manasseh, and all the land of Judah,* ***unto the utmost sea****.*

So they looked from Nebo all the way to the Mediterranean Sea.

> *And the south, and the plain of the valley of Jericho, the city of palm trees, unto Zoar. 4 And the LORD said unto him, This is the land which I sware unto Abraham, unto Isaac, and unto Jacob, saying, I will give it unto thy seed: I have caused thee to see it with thine eyes, but thou shalt not go over thither.*

So God brings Moses up into Mount Nebo, shows him the land and then says, "You can't go in here." Think about it. Moses just spent 40 years protecting the children of Israel from God. I know God is gracious and merciful and I don't want to paint like he didn't love the children of Israel. He certainly did, but you need to read your Old Testament to remember that Moses kept the children of Israel from being burnt off the globe a couple of times. If there was anyone that was patient, it was Moses. He was even called "the meekest of the whole earth" (Numbers 12:3).

What is Satan suggesting? He is tempted three times in a manner that would remind him that he is supposed to be the fulfillment of the Moses prophet and Jesus three times responds from the writings of Moses. You should be able to see Moses is in view here. They're on Mount Nebo; he looks up to the north and it says he saw all that particular land, names it, looks to the south and he can see all that particular land, names it, and then God says, "You can't go in there."

Satan appears to be asking Jesus something like "Is this a chance you want to take? Moses couldn't even go into the land. He was not even worthy of the land. He followed the Lord for 40 years of wandering, couldn't even enter the land. He served his people for 40 years and could not even enter the land. They provoked God and provoked him and when he could not even enter the land. Their offspring went into the land. They never would have reached the land if it wasn't for him. If anybody should have been leading those people, taxing those people, having those people kissing his hand, it should have been Moses."

Jesus and Satan are looking at all the kingdoms of the world from a high mountain and it's as if Satan is saying, "Is this the chance you wish to take to serve your Father for years and years and years and get nothing that's coming to you?" How about this, "How about the kingdom is mine to share and I will share it with you if you will just acknowledge that I am the regent and then you don't have to worry about God doing to you what he did to Moses."

I dare say from Mount Nebo he could see the garden tomb. I dare say from Mount Nebo he could see the Mount of Olives from where he would ascend. I dare say from Nebo (if it was Nebo, it was some high mountain) he could see Galilee where he would fish with his disciples for a few weeks after his resurrection. I promise you that Jesus thought through the ramifications of Moses and the fact that he served the people of God for years and years and years and got nothing and now he has the opportunity to take a shortcut and be the ruler of those wicked stiff-necked people that should be crushed with a rod of iron.

Well, Jesus is better than Moses. The last time the children of Israel desired salvation 400 long years ticked off the clock. Long days of brick making, back breaking, spirit crushing work where the Israelites cried out to God like some thrashed desperate monotheists who were tempted to be agnostic or at least antagonistic and Jehovah sent a sign showing, miracle working man by the name of Moses, and this fear of Hebrew uprising brought the quaking hearts of the ancient Egyptians to the point where they were willing to commit mass infanticide, really genocide. God intervened and there came a boy who was saved from the wrath of Pharaoh. Moses was first rejected by the elders of the very people he sought to redeem. Moses spent 40 years being prepared by both temptation and triumph. The Father and the angels, the thirst and the dirth; he knew every part of the saga, Jesus knew. Jesus remembered that there would be death for the killing king before there could be an exodus from Egypt. Who was the Pharaoh of Jesus' day? Herod.

So it's been 400 years since Malachi and it's just like the children of Israel in Egypt. There are kings coming from the east now and they're coming to serve notice that a star has been born. Once again, not so great King Herod is intimidated and frightened. This new Moses is about to be born and this new Pharaoh is about to try to kill him. He arrives—not in ark of bulrushes, but in a manger in Bethlehem. And he's carried to Egypt until the death of the new Pharaoh, unlike the old Moses who left Egypt to be saved from the old Pharaoh. Until the death of the new Pharaoh named Herod, allows for the ultimate exodus. This time it is not Israel, the firstborn of God (Exodus 3-4; Hosea 11:1), who is saved, now it is Jesus, the firstborn of creation, who is saved out of this new Pharaoh, Herod.

Now we talk about Matthew 3. What do we see here but King Jesus, the hope of years, the consolation of Israel, the dayspring of heaven, the hero of our hearts. "He is here to save us from the Romans. We don't have to pay anymore taxes to the Romans. They will no longer loot us, bed our daughters, steal our wives, humble our fathers, steal our last mules. This is that Jesus that is a miracle worker like Moses that will save us like Joshua and reign over us like David. It's a new day for the Jew."

But wait. Whereas Moses spends 40 years in a desert, Jesus spends 40 days in the desert expressing himself as the Ultimate One. Moses spends 40 days and 40 nights hearing from God. Jesus spends 40 days and 40 nights apparently not hearing from God with temptation on every side. For Moses at the end of his wilderness wandering—at his mountain viewing, it was already clear that he was a sinner. But the 40 days and 40 nights that Jesus endured was to assure everyone including Satan that Jesus was better than Moses and he was not a sinner.

Moses was preceded by his older brother, Aaron, who was a prophet for the God figure Moses, but the prophet, John the Baptist, was a forerunner for the God-man Jesus. Moses is baptizing the children of Israel to himself in the Red Sea, but this new Moses is calling people to be baptized in his name unto repentance.

The old Moses spends 40 days and 40 nights before bringing commandments down from Sinai. This new Moses preaches a new law, a law of Christ, from a small mountain way off in Galilee. In this Sermon on the Mount, he takes the letter of the law which kills the soul and he makes it a spiritual matter, a heart matter, and says, "You heard Moses say this, but I tell you. You heard Moses say this, but I tell you." Six times in the Sermon on the Mount after he spends 40 days and 40 nights in a desert. He brings back a new law for a new people.

Moses is striking a rock so that water can come out of it. Jesus, the new Moses, is the smitten rock where all can find water. Moses signifies the first covenant by the sprinkling of the blood of animals to never actually wash away sin but Jesus on the night of his betrayal said, "This is the blood, my blood, of the new covenant which is shed for many" (Matthew 26:28).

The old Moses meets a fearful God on Sinai and the people stay away, but the new Moses goes up to God and brings us with him. The old Moses dies, never to lead God's people to the land of promise by virtue of disobedience, but this Jesus dies and lives again and because he was totally obedient, he is the author and the finisher of our faith (Hebrews 12:2) and he still lives today.

It's all his because he was obedient to the Father. At that moment when our names are called at death, we pass it all on the way to the throne of God. The old Moses is spending another 40 days and 40 nights in Mount Sinai but Jesus spends 40 days with his people, the disciples, before ascending again to the Father. The old Moses offers a covenant relationship with those who will become Jews, but the new Moses offers a covenant relationship valid for both Jews and Gentiles.

4:10

Then saith Jesus unto him, get away from me, Satan: for it is written, Thou shalt worship the Lord thy God, and him only shalt thou serve. Or better yet, "You should only kiss the hand of the master who made it all." Yeah. I love it when the Lord takes the words of the wicked one and uses them against him. Jesus actually wrote Deuteronomy so we're not surprised that he knows it.

Jesus could have quoted Scripture from any book of the Old Testament, is that right? But he chose a book of Moses. So Genesis, Exodus, Leviticus, Numbers, Deuteronomy, some of the Psalms, and I would even say part of Job were written by Moses. So probably 20% of the Old Testament was written by Moses. There was plenty of other Old Testament passages Jesus could have quoted from to combat the temptation of the devil and he quoted something Moses wrote all three times. That's significant. With three quotations of Moses from one section of Scripture, one might think Jesus was seeking to prove a point. Can Jesus do what Moses didn't do?

4:11

The devil leaves Jesus and, behold, angels came and ministered unto him. Now, why is that significant? Because just a few verses earlier, it was a part of the temptation to use these very same angels to do the bidding of the wicked one. You see, the angels were Christ's all along and the temptation was to do that which benefited me before it was the proper time. And here we are, the temptations are gone and now we have the very same angels that to utilize them just a few verses earlier would have been a fall of the very impeccable Son of God, but now it is holy and righteous and unspeakably appropriate for the angels of God to minister to Jesus.

Now, it's not just the word "angels," it's the word "minister" that is key here because the temptation was to have the angels carry Jesus when he threw himself from the temple. And here we have the angels ministering to Jesus and the idea in this related word is that they carried him like a man under his shoulders. Here is Jesus, he hasn't eaten in 40 days and 40 nights and he has endured a great fight of afflictions. He has endured temptations and he is very weak to the point where bread would have been good; staying in Jerusalem would have been good; bowing and maybe kissing the hand of a king might have been okay…Think about the ramifications of that. All of that would have been sin. Yes, using the angels would have been sin, but doing the same thing at the right time made it right. Matthew 4 is all about God getting glory by saving sinners and he does so through an impeccable Christ who won't jump the gun to get His kingdom.

*Hebrews 1:14 Are the angels not all **ministering** spirits? Sent forth to **minister** for them who shall be heirs of salvation.*

What did the angels do for Jesus at the end of the temptation? They ministered to him. What are angels sent forth to do for those who shall be heirs of salvation? Minister to them. Angels are sent forth to minister to you as much as they are to Christ.

4:12

Now when Jesus had heard that John was cast into prison, he departed into Galilee; It is not always time to die. John the Baptist was in Judea. Jesus is apparently close enough to Judea while he's being tempted that he has the option to go back to Judea. But he doesn't, and we're told why he doesn't. We're told that the reason that he doesn't is because he heard something. He heard that John was put in prison. It would have been easy enough for Jesus to say, "Well, it's my joint. I own the world. I just basically told Satan that. I proved it. I own this place. I'll go wherever I want to. I'll do whatever I want." He could have even thought to himself, "Maybe they will crucify me and that would fulfill the Father's plan, after all." Why exactly is Jesus avoiding a place where he knows there is trouble? This is why: because it's not always time to die for the cause of Christ. Apparently Jesus knew there was a time when you were not supposed to die for God. Everything has an appropriate time, it seems. If you're going to go down in smoke for the kingdom of God, make sure it's God's idea.

And leaving Nazareth, he came and dwelt in Capernaum, There's almost no details. When did he get there? "Matthew, when did he get to Nazareth? Aren't you leaving something out? He goes to Galilee and where is Nazareth? It's in Galilee. Can you give us a little more detail there? He went to Galilee and left Nazareth. Can you tell anything about that?" Well, that's where Jesus was raised. We find out the last part of chapter 2, right? And we find that this word is used in a similar way in the book of Acts where it talks about on their journeys, Paul and his companions saw a place and kept going. So this doesn't have the idea that he stayed at Nazareth any amount of time and if you compare it with Luke 4, there's good reason to think that he spent probably an afternoon there, maybe.

> *Matthew 13:53 And it came to pass, that when Jesus had finished these parables, he departed from **there.***

The context says he was coming to his own country. What was his own country according to chapter 2? The prophet said he will be a what? A Nazarene.

> *Whence hath this man this wisdom and these mighty works?*

He's supposed to be dumb. Look at the next verse,

> *Is not this the carpenter's son?*

"We know carpenters can't read. How in the world is he talking like an authority here? Isn't this Joseph's son? Is not his mother called Mary and his brethren, James and Joses, and Simon, and Judas? And his sisters, are they not all with us?" Then, the people of Nazareth were offended at Jesus because he came back talking like an authority.

But Jesus said unto them, A prophet is not without honour, save in his own country, and in his own house. And he did not many mighty works there because of their unbelief.

When you read Matthew 12:46…

*While he yet talked to the people, behold, his mother and his brethren stood without, desiring to speak with him. Then one said unto him, Behold, thy mother and thy brethren stand without, desiring to speak with thee. But he answered and said unto him that told him, **Who is my mother?** and who are my brethren? And he stretched forth his hand toward his disciples, and said, Behold my mother and my brethren! For whosoever shall do the will of my Father which is in heaven, the same is my brother, and sister, and mother.*

He was very clear, "Nazareth doesn't want me, the people I grew up around don't understand me and my own family thinks that somehow they have the right to call me out from doing the Father's business." Listen, if you're like Jesus, you're going to do some things to please the Father and your family is not going to understand.

15 "The land of Zabulon and the land of Nephthalim, by the way of the sea, beyond Jordan, Here are some main trade routes which goes right by the Sea of Galilee into Galilee of the Gentiles. The Jordan River goes from the Sea of Galilee down to the Dead Sea.

4:16a

The people which sat in darkness saw great light; God has a heart for all nations. Why is he east of Jordan? Why is he up in Syria? Why is he reaching people in Damascus? That wasn't exactly why he came, is it? Why is Jesus concerned about the nations? Because his Father is concerned about the nations. If we know what God thinks about the nations, it should rearrange how we're thinking today. Right here where we sit, we can reach the world if we will have the attitude that Christ had. Why was Christ reaching those other nations? Well, I suppose that it had something to do with his miraculous powers, but I think we can also say that what he was doing was showing us that the Father really is concerned about the nations.

and to them which sat in the region and shadow of death light is sprung up." 17. From that time Jesus began to preach, and to say, Repent: for the kingdom of heaven is at hand. Now look, that word "repentance" is actually related to the rest of the directions Jesus gives. "Repent." Why? "For the kingdom of heaven is at hand." When someone says, "Ah, repentance is just kind of a John the Baptist thing." No, it's actually kind of a "Jesus thing" too which means that it was "a God thing." We're supposed to be repenting. Why? Because the kingdom is coming.

So what does it mean to repent? It means to "have a change of mind." About what? Contextually, what are we to change our mind concerning? We're supposed to change our mind concerning those things that are keeping us unready or unfit for the soon-coming kingdom. So whatever it is in my life that is not welcome in the kingdom of God, I'm supposed to repent of it. That's the context. And if we build it upon what John the Baptist was preaching in Matthew 3, he was saying, "Repent, and by the way, don't even come until you bring forth fruits meet for repentance."

So in the context, repentance does mean to turn from that wicked sin that is keeping you from being ready for a coming king. And not just a coming king, but a coming king that is already reigning in your hearts because one chapter later, two chapters later in Matthew 6, Jesus is teaching us how to pray. "Thy kingdom come. Thy will be done on earth as it is in heaven." So we're waiting for the kingdom of God to both come in the future and come now. He's taught both of those realities. If you are born again, you're born again into the kingdom and since he is here to save his people from their sins, that means he is consistently making us ready for the kingdom. Consistently making us ready for the kingdom.

And Jesus, walking by the sea of Galilee, saw two brethren, Simon called Peter, and Andrew his brother, You might remember John 1 says that around the time of Jesus' baptism, one of the disciples was Andrew, Peter's brother. And John wasn't baptizing in Galilee so Jesus and Andrew and Peter have met before if you were to compare with John 1, but Jesus is finding them back in their hometown.

People say, "Well, where did they live exactly? Why are they fishing in the Sea of Galilee if he could find them somewhere around Bethabara where John was baptizing on the north end of this Dead Sea?" Well, the disciples were not poor folks. They were fishermen. They were proprietors. They had fishing businesses. John, for example, we find out was so well known by the high priest's family that he was the only disciple who was allowed in the courtyard on the night of Jesus' betrayal. A "good for nothing fishermen from Galilee" who doesn't have a house or anything in Jerusalem wouldn't be known by the high priest. Furthermore, when Jesus was hanging on the cross, do you remember one of his parting words was for the care of his mother? In that same Gospel (John's Gospel) is careful to tell us that the Apostle John took Mary, Jesus' mother, back to his home. Well, surely that was a home in Jerusalem.

So these disciples had multiple residences. One of them was in Galilee, one of them probably was in Jerusalem, and Jesus comes up and he preaches the same message John preaches in verse 17, but when he passes by Peter and Andrew and says, "Follow me," the last time anyone did that was in 1 Kings 19 when a prophet by the name of Elijah the Tishbite walked by his

	Elisha	Jesus
Elijah Forerunner	2 Kings 1:8	Matt 3:4
Damascus	2 Kings 5:12	Matt 4:15
"Follow Me"	1 Kgs 19:19-21; 2 Kgs 2:15; 3:11	Matt 4:19
Diseases Being Healed	1 Kgs 17:17; 2 Kgs 3:32	Matt 4:23-24
Syria	2 Kings 5:1	Matt 4:24
Leprosy	2 Kings 5:1	Matt 8:1-4
Military Leader with a servant	2 Kings 5:2	Matthew 8:5

understudy & successor by the name Elisha. Elijah and Elisha. Elijah was the first one, and he put his mantle on Elisha. He took the mantle of a prophet off and put it on Elisha, and Elisha said, "Let me go first and tell my mom and dad goodbye." And Elijah said, "Well, okay." Here, however, Jesus comes by and says, "Follow me and I will make you fishers of men," and I want you to notice what it says in verse 20, "And they straightway left their nets, and followed him." Elisha burned the plows and offered a sacrifice of oxen and there hasn't been another prophet who has come by since that time and said, "Hey, come with me. You're going to take over for me eventually." Well, in chapter 28, the disciples "take over" in what we call the "Great Commission."

casting a net into the sea: for they were fishers. And he saith unto them, Follow me, and I will make you fishers of men. Matthew is putting you in mind of an Old Testament prophet by the name of Elijah and his understudy Elisha.

4:21-22

And going on from thence, he saw other two brethren, James the son of Zebedee, and John his brother, in a ship with Zebedee their father, mending their nets; and he called them. 22. And they immediately left the ship and their father. Remember they left their father. Why did these men feel at liberty to leave their dad and why didn't their dad follow quickly behind and say, "Wait just a minute, you get back here and play your part of this family business"? The previous two left their nets, you might notice that in verse 20, and these two left the ship and their father in verse 22.

Why did these men feel the liberty or even the compulsion to follow Christ?

> *Malachi 4:1 For, behold, the day comes, that shall burn as an oven; and all the proud, yea, and all that do wickedly, shall be stubble: and the day that comes shall burn them up, saith the LORD of hosts, that it shall leave them neither root nor branch.*

There is coming a day when the wicked world will be burned up. There won't even be a root or branch left.

> *4:2 But unto you that fear my name shall the Sun of righteousness arise with healing **in his wings**; and ye shall go forth, and grow up as calves of the stall.*

It is translated "wings" often in the Old Testament but it is also translated as "hem," as in hem of a garment. Often in Leviticus when the priests' garments are being described, they are talked about as having a hem. It's the same word translated here as "wings." Now, what would happen if we were to use that same translation?

> *4:3 And ye shall tread down the wicked; for they shall be ashes under the soles of your feet in the day that I shall do this, saith the LORD of hosts. Remember ye **the law of Moses my servant**, which I commanded unto him in Horeb for all Israel, with the statutes and judgments.*

You will soon see that Jesus is, in the Sermon on the Mount, giving a new law as the "new Moses" and here we have the context of the coming of Jesus. Now, if that doesn't shock you, please notice that around this time the Sun of righteousness will rise with healing in the hem of his garment.

> *4:5 I will send you **Elijah the prophet** before the coming of the great and dreadful **day of the LORD.***

Remember now, we have a John the Baptist and who is he known by so many as Elijah. John the Baptist is known as Elijah and Jesus said, "If you would have received me and received him, he would have been Elijah" (Matthew 11:14).

> *4:6 he shall turn the heart of the fathers to the children, and the heart of the children to their fathers, lest I come and smite the earth with a curse.*

Now then, when we look at Matthew 4 and we realize that they were expecting a great teacher to come, and they were   expecting him to come in proximity to the day of the Lord; this teacher is pronouncing a kingdom that comes with the day of the Lord, and this teacher is preceded by a man who is known as "Elijah," and this teacher looks a lot like Moses, and this teacher is healing people. All of a sudden you may understand that this same teacher who was told that he will restore father to son or else the whole place will be cursed, gains the following of boys from their fathers—as in this case when a father was willing to let his boys leave the fishing business.

Now, this is quite the theme because if you look at Matthew 9:20…

> *And, behold, a woman, which was diseased with an issue of blood twelve years, came behind him, and touched **the hem of his garment**: For she said within herself, If I may but touch his garment, I **shall be whole.***

Why did she believe that touching his hem would make her whole? Because of Malachi 4. "Here's a kingdom-pronouncing healer and he was preceded by an Elijah figure and he is giving us a new law like Moses did. I bet there's healing in his hem."

> Then we look at Matthew 14:35
>
> *And when the men of that place had knowledge of him, they sent out into all that country round about, and brought unto him all that were diseased; And besought him that they might only touch **the hem of his garment: and as many as touched were made perfectly whole.***

Rabbis had a particular dress about them. They had a particular hem about their garments. That's why in Matthew 23, Jesus said, "You rulers of the Jews, you are so slick, you have these special wide hems of your garment and you want people to praise you, calling you Rabbi, Rabbi." Well, here's Jesus, known as a Rabbi, from Nazareth. He has the garments of a Rabbi and he is walking up to fishermen who have never been to rabbinical school and he says, "Come and follow me," and that is a signal that this man is about to restore fathers and sons to each other so that Israel can burn up her enemies (or be cursed, Malachi 4:6).

4:23

healed them. The word behind "healed" there in the Greek is the word we get our word "therapy" from. He "therapied them."

4:25

And there followed him great multitudes of people from Galilee, and from Decapolis, from Jerusalem, from Judaea, from beyond Jordan. But we also see from verse 24 that he went into Syria.

Chapter 5

5:1-2

And seeing the multitudes, He went up into a mountain: and when He was set, His disciples came unto Him: and He opened His mouth, and taught them, saying, "Blessed Why is He picking these things? Now, think about what Matthew could have done. He could have recorded any of Jesus' sayings, and the Holy Spirit could have guided and recorded any of Jesus' sayings, and Matthew picks these.

Beatitude is a Latin term that speaks of grace and blessing being bestowed upon someone. As you're reading this, I don't know if it's been anything to you other than a quaint little inclusion into a funeral home bulletin. But it is actually very, very full of meaning.

5:3

"Blessed are the poor in spirit: for theirs is the kingdom of heaven." Take a good look at Isaiah 35:1-8 and Isaiah 40:1-9 and see this as a forecast of the Messiah.

And so we have the promise of comfort to those who are burdened with their own sin. Jerusalem: a place full of sin. A place so full of sin that the prophets called her "Babylon." Full of sin, and yet a promise of comfort for those who are deep in their own sin. And for lack of a better way to say it, their sin has caused mourning in their life.

When we read Jesus' words in reflection of Isaiah 57 and Isaiah 61 we know He comforts those who mourn so that He can be glorified. Let me take it one step further. He comforts those who mourn for the problems their sin brought them. There is no need for a savior; there is no need for good tidings (Isaiah 61 verse 1); there is no need to be binding up brokenhearted if people are not brokenhearted. This is not a passivity, this is not some sort of "bad rap that I got, and really I have no sin over which to mourn," No. This is Jesus promising that He has been sent by God, anointed by God.

5:3b-4

are the poor in spirit: for theirs is the kingdom of heaven. Blessed are they that mourn: for they shall be comforted." Blessed are the poor in spirit. Why? Well, I'm glad you asked. One should compare the "blessing and cursing" language of Deuteronomy 28 and the "blessing" language of Matthew 5 & 6. There's a reason why we're saying what we're saying here in Matthew 5 and 6. It's because Jesus is the new lawgiver, coming for His new people of whom He is going to save from their sin. And so, everything you see that everything mentioned in Matthew 5 and 6 is particular distinction against Deuteronomy 28 to show you Jesus is not just like Moses, He's much better.

Jesus said, "I'm going to make it real simple on you. Here's what you do: Just don't do anything you don't want done to you." (Mattew 7:12) That's the law of the New Testament. And it's restated. Apparently Paul thought that this was the law of Christ (Galatians 6:2).

That sounds a lot like Matthew 7:12, just different words.

So, all of a sudden we have the Sermon on the Mount. And we would expect then that these Jews who are not experiencing what they were promised in Deuteronomy 28. Blessing and blessing and blessing and blessing and blessing and blessing. And that's where you get the stuff like, "I'm going to bless your lands and your houses. I'm going to bless your fields. You're going to be the head and not the tail. I'm going to bless, bless, bless, bless, bless." And then He gets in to saying, "I'm going to curse you. If you forget me, I'm going to curse you, curse you, curse you, curse you." And then we get to Jesus and you have people that haven't heard from God in 400 years. What do you think they would like to have heard? Some blessing. And they're not having flourishing fields, and their cattle are not healthy. And so Jesus says things that have proper application to everyone in Judea and Galilee in this passage: "You're probably very poor in your spirit. Well good, because the kingdom is for you."

If you read Mark and Luke it's going to be very apparent to you that the Beatitudes are not placed right here in the same order that Matthew is. And that is why we do a disservice by ignoring the intricacies of the individual author such as Matthew, in this case. If we just go into what we call, "An Approach of the Harmony of the Gospels," that may be really neat brain candy for you, but it won't be honest to the intent of the author. So I want to ask you, "What is it that

Matthew is trying to communicate, by aid of the Holy Spirit, by putting the sermon right here?" I think that there is an important thing. I think I already shared with you the scheme of showing us the ultimate lawgiver, Moses. By the way, if you think I might be making that up...

> *Galatians 6:2 Bear ye one another's burdens, and so fulfil **the law of Christ.***

Somehow Christ has a law. Paul could have easily written, "Bear one another's burdens, and so fulfill the law of Moses." Or, he could have said, "Bear ye one another's burdens, and so fulfill the law of God." But he didn't. Because Christ, being the ultimate Moses, has for us a law. For example,

> *Matthew 5:17 Think not that I am come to destroy the law, or the prophets: I am not come to destroy, but to fulfil.*

He says, " I didn't come to do away with the law, I came to fulfill it." So whatever the law of Christ is, it's not meant to badger the Old Testament, or ignore it, or sub-value it. It's actually to fulfill it, which means to take it and make it its fullest form. To show you what the shadow of the Old Testament is in its substance.

When Christ comes to us and He offers us a New Covenant, wherein the Holy Spirit moves into us and regenerates us, then, then we have the ability to walk with God and see God. When we see the heart of God through Christ, we see God, and a new law. And so, it is not an accident that six times before chapter 6 you hear this, "You have heard, but I say. You have heard, but I say." Let me point them to you:

> Matthew 5:21 ***Ye have heard*** *that it was said by them of old time, "Thou shalt not kill;" 22. **But I say** unto you, that whosoever is angry with his brother without a cause shall be in danger of the judgment.*

In other words, the God that you're used to seeing through your clouded glasses, that God gave you a law and you have determined that the law is to be followed to the letter. "But I say unto you that whoever is angry with his brother." That means, "I know what you think the law is saying, but let me give you the heart of the Father." Look at the last verse of this chapter: "Be ye therefore perfect, even **as your Father** which is in heaven is perfect." The idea here is not to get you to follow rules; the idea is to get us to be like our perfect Father. So the issue is not an Old Testament idea, "Be like God or he'll stomp you in the grave." No, the issue is "Be like God because you are now part of something new." A new thing. Five more times in Matthew 5 He says, "You have heard."

> Matthew 5:27 ***Ye have heard*** *that it was said by them of old time, "Thou shalt not commit adultery:" 28.* ***But I say*** *unto you, that whosoever looketh on a woman to lust after her hath committed adultery.*

In other words, the Old Testament disciple says, "Well what does the law say? Because I want to do the minimum, and be blessed." No. No. "You heard that, but I say, if you look on someone and lust after them you're an adulterer."

> Matthew 5:31 ***It hath been said****, "Whosoever shall put away his wife, let him give her a writing of divorcement."*

But that's Deuteronomy 24. That is in the Old Testament, folks. You can divorce your wife. But there are stipulations in Deuteronomy 24. It has been said you can put away your wife with a bill of divorcement, but verse 32,

> ***But I say*** *unto you, that whosoever shall put away his wife, saving for the cause of fornication, causeth her to commit adultery.*

That scripture is not intended to give you a treatise on all the many ways you can biblically divorce your spouse. The point of the passage is to tell you what the Old Testament said from the heart of God, and not necessarily just from the pen of Moses. See, it's easy to meet the minimum. An unsaved person can meet the minimum. Unsaved people stacked from here to the moon can say, "I've never cheated on my spouse." There are unsaved people from here to Mars that can say, "I have never committed murder." There are people here, there, and everywhere that can say, "I have never, ever done these things," but when Jesus steps up He gives us some criteria that only a saved person can fulfill because only a saved person has the Holy Spirit.

> 5:33 *Again,* **ye have heard** *that it hath been said by them of old time, "Thou shalt not forswear thyself, but shalt perform unto the Lord thine oaths:"* 34. **But I say** *unto you, swear not at all; neither by heaven; for it is God's throne.*

And so, in verse 33, scribes and Pharisees of that day saying, "God said we could swear if we wanted to." No, you're taking that out of context. It's interesting we can find verses for anything we want to do today. We really can. No. God was saying, "Don't go past this line." But a lost person, a scribe and Pharisee, can "not go past that line." A person with the heart of the Father, in whom dwells the Holy Spirit, that person can actually go on, in verse 34, and swear not at all. They can control their mouth because they have God living in them.

And so it's not, "Here's a new way of being born again. You either have the 'Matthew way' of works or the 'John way' of belief." No. Clearly Jesus is saying a lost person can keep Moses' law, the Ten Commandments…"righteousness of the Pharisees" (5:20). All you got to do is not blaspheme the Lord, don't make an idol, don't have another God beside Jehovah, make sure you remember the Sabbath Day, don't covet, don't bear false witness, don't kill. I mean, how hard is it to not do that? We're finding it's pretty hard. I get that, but a lost person can do that for a day. So you actually don't belong in heaven unless you can do more than what a lost person can do. Isn't that the point of 5:20? Your righteousness needs to exceed the bare minimum.

> 5:38 **Ye have heard** *that it hath been said, "An eye for an eye, and a tooth for a tooth:"* 39. **But I say** *unto you, that ye resist not evil: but whosoever shall smite thee on thy right cheek, turn to him the other also.*

And so, once again, He says, "I know what you heard. You heard in Leviticus that it's a good idea for you to have civil authority punish people." Well, you know what was happening with that. All you have to do is look at John 8 to see what civil authority looked like. They show up in front of Jesus with a woman taken in adultery and they are ready to stone her right there. No courts. So in their minds they had the freedom anytime they wish to take "An eye for an eye, tooth for a tooth." But Jesus says, "You're taking that way out of context. I'm going to tell you what I require. When you're being picked on, allow yourself to be picked on again." An unsaved person can keep "eye for an eye, tooth for a tooth." It takes someone with God living in them to say, "You know what? You may use me again. It doesn't profit me at all to allow that. But to fulfill the law of Christ, I'm going to put myself out there one more time." Say, "I don't like that." I'm not sure I do either.

> 5:43 **Ye have heard** that it hath been said, *"Thou shalt love thy neighbour, and hate thine enemy."*

And you know what? It does say that in Leviticus. It says you can actually pour contempt out on the enemies of God. But look what Jesus is saying.

> 44. **But I say** *unto you, love your enemies, bless them that curse you.*

So is Jesus disagreeing with the God of the Old Testament? No. He's trying to show them the heart of the Father. Look at the last verse of the chapter: Be perfect like your Father. The Father wrote both Testaments, folks. The Father wrote the Old Testament law through Moses, and the Father wrote the new law that Jesus is bringing up from the wilderness.

So what is the difference? Well, one of them is by the law minimum we expect regular citizens of the USA to keep. And for the rest of you, we expect you to have the heart of your Father, which far exceeds the minimum. And that is why in 5:20…

> *For I say unto you, that except your righteousness shall exceed the righteousness of the scribes and Pharisees, ye shall in no case enter into the kingdom of heaven.*

Are you saying, Jesus, that you have to do x, y, and z to go to heaven? No. No, we're saying that if your righteousness doesn't exceed the righteousness of unsaved people, who can keep those silly laws, then you don't deserve heaven at all. Only those who reflect the heart of the Father.

"How do I know that I am one of those?"

Because you have a heart that becomes more, and more, and more like your Father. I love context. I couldn't leave the rest of the chapter alone.

5:4

Blessed *are* they that mourn: for they shall be comforted. If context matters at all to you, you're not going to run for the hills and say that means, "If I don't get a job, if I don't get a new house, I will mourn and I have promise of comfort." Context will not allow that.

I have shown you eight quotations so far in our seventeen weeks in Matthew, of Matthew quoting an Old Testament prophet. And out of those eight times, four of them are from the book of Isaiah. Four direct quotations out of the book of Isaiah. The others are out of Hosea, Micah, and a couple others. And so we know that Matthew has Isaiah on his mind. There's no need for us to think that this verse stands alone, because if it stands alone there's a lot of questions that follow. Like, "How much do I have to mourn to be comforted?" "When do I qualify for this thing, this benefit?" And, "What does it mean to be comforted?" Well, it means nothing if you don't have Isaiah. Because in Isaiah we have people that needed comfort. They needed comfort because they were in mourning, and they were in mourning because of their sin.

When Isaiah says, "Your sins are causing you to receive double, but I'm going to speak comfort to you" (chapter 40), then we have a backdrop that Matthew is writing up against, and we see all of a sudden that you could almost say verse 4 reads, "Blessed are those who mourn over what their sins have caused, for they will eventually find comfort." You say, "You're rewriting the word of God." Well no different than you are when you explain what the Bible means to your children. "What does this mean?" And then we tell them what it means and you've basically made your own translation. Don't be so critical of me.

Those who mourn over their sin will find comfort. And by the way, that is why we can look at verse three and say it fits nicely because you're "poor in spirit." Blessed are the mourners when things are not ideal. Blessed are the mourners when they are seeking for relief. If you have not mourned over your sin, you don't have any clue what the gospel is about. Because Isaiah 61 is very clear that the gospel is preached by the one who comforts the mourner. So everything that comes up in life is related to the gospel.

The gospel! Usually we hear something on the phone saying, "And then I asked her, 'Have you ever asked Jesus into your heart?'" Stop saying that!!! For the love of God, if you can go to heaven by asking Jesus into your heart, Jesus died for nothing! We don't get to heaven because we ask for it. We go to heaven because Jesus was already crushed for it, and we accept that, by faith. That is the gospel. Christ was crushed for our sins and got up from the dead. And because of that we live forever if we believe.

This "mourning" of chapter 5 verse 4 is spiritual (see verse 3). If you're poor in spirit that means in the next verse you're mourning in spirit. That means it can't always be seen that you're mourning. It means there's going to be times when you're going to feel unappreciated. There's going to be times when people will not be able to tell that you're mourning. But I want to encourage you that Romans 8 says at a particular level the Holy Spirit knows why you're mourning, and He's praying for you. We're talking about some eternally significant mourning. So, if you're not mourning about something on a spiritual level, I'd say there should come a time when you come out of that cloud you're in.

How could we blessed if we mourn? We're told we're blessed if we mourn for one reason: because we will be **comforted.** I can't think of anything more humbling than thinking of the connection that my sin has with the trouble around me. That's very humbling. Things that I will start out saying, "They should be mourning over that because they…" And then you fill in the blank. I find out I actually had something to do with it.

If God doesn't reveal to us that we're sinful in some way, then we have no grounds for being comforted in that way. And I fear that we are very good at renaming our sin. And then we blame it on the preacher for making us feel bad. That's so strange. I heard someone say it in this way, "Saying that the gun killed the person is like saying that the fork made someone overweight." So, if it's my sin, I can't blame it on the preacher for making me feel bad.

This is interesting. Look at 5:10-12 and you'll see that while you are mourning over sin, and they are mourning over your mourning over sin. It means that your relationship with them has changed. We're not the person we were. And they don't like the new you. And so they find reasons to conveniently discount you as a friend. They'll even say you think you're too spiritual for them, when the truth is you're just so fed up over your own sin.

5:5

Blessed are the meek for they shall inherit the earth. Now the meek doesn't mean weak. Meek means domesticated. Never would you call a horse that's been domesticated weak. Never would you say that Moses, that brought the tablets of stone down Sinai and broke them in front of those disobedient Israelites, you would never call Moses weak. In fact, he was so strong that he made them drink. I heard someone say, "You can lead a horse to water but you can't make them drink." Moses made two million Jews drink. He wasn't weak and he was called the meekest of all the earth.

So verse 5 is basically saying, "You get **the earth**."

*Matthew 6:9 After this manner therefore pray ye: Our Father which art in heaven, Hallowed be thy name. 10. Thy kingdom come. Thy will be done **in earth**, as it is in heaven.*

I promise you, the kingdom will come to earth. So the promise for the meek is, "When the kingdom comes to earth, the kingdom will be yours." That's good news. For people that are downtrodden and bullied by Romans, that's good news.

5:6-7

These are to be contrasted and compared with the Law brought down with Moses, from Moses, on Mount Sinai, from Mount Sinai. Remember, we've been talking about how Jesus is the ultimate Moses.

1. We recall that as Moses came out of Egypt; Jesus, in Matthew 2, came out of Egypt.

2. We recall that as Moses took part in a baptism 1 Corinthians 10:2 says; Jesus, Matthew 3, took part in a baptism.

3. Moses was with God fasting for forty days and forty nights, in Mount Sinai; we remember that it is Jesus, in Matthew 4, who is fasting for forty days and forty nights with the Lord.

And now, just as Moses came down after forty days and forty nights with the Law of God, here comes now Jesus. Now again, you could ask yourself, "Why is this placed right here?" If you're not careful, this will be a lot like reading Psalm 23. Remember, Jesus is the ultimate Moses and He brings to us the ultimate, new law.

And so, we're going to begin reading the Sermon on the Mount that goes from chapters 5 through 7, really. This Mount of Beatitudes is on the northwest corner of the Sea of Galilee.

Blessed *are* the merciful: Grace is God giving to us what we do not deserve and mercy is God withholding from us what we do deserve. Mercy is such a big deal to God that out of the seven spiritual gifts in Romans chapter 12, mercy is one of them. Mercy is very important, so important that in the book of Matthew twice, twice in the book of Matthew, Jesus says that God would rather have mercy than sacrifice. Mercy, than worship. He told the Pharisees a third time (Matthew 23), "You tithe of mint, cumin, and anise, and you have left the other things undone, the weightier matters of the law: mercy." Mercy is a big deal to God. Mercy means that you look at someone and your heart bleeds with them. Your Bible might say "compassion." It means you are actually moved, your heart melts when you see a need. And sometimes it even means because we reflect the heart of our perfect Father, the last verse of the chapter, it means that we act like our Father. And our Father is so forgiving. Hebrews 13:2 says you "entertain angels unaware."

5:10-12

10 Rejoice, and be exceeding glad: "Rejoice" is also used in Matthew 2 where it says the wise men saw the star that was going and taking them over to the place where the Christ child was in the house, and it says, "They rejoiced to see it." So as happy as the wise men were to find the trail towards the new king, that's how happy we're supposed to be if we're **persecuted for righteousness sake.** Think about that. That's quite the comparison. As happy as the wise men are about finding the king of the whole universe that will soon rule and reign on the throne of His father David; as happy as they were to find that, we're supposed to be that happy to be **persecuted for righteousness sake**? And then on top of that Jesus says, "You're blessed." I'm blessed? "Yes, you're blessed." "Blessed" because I'm poor in spirit; because I'm domesticated (verse 5; "meek"). I feel like I'm weak but I'm really just controlled, controlled strength. We might call that a "governor" (if you enjoy working on engines). It's not that you can't be out of control, it's that you won't allow yourself to be out of control. You could go twenty-three, twenty-four, six thousand (depending on how small the engine is) RPMs, but the governor is in place and you've decided to be meek and allow yourself to only go up to a safe speed. So, it's not that the power isn't there, it's that it's under someone's control.

for great *is* your reward in heaven: for so persecuted they the prophets which were before you. Now I thought through this a little bit and I thought about the prophets that have already been mentioned in the book of Matthew:

> 1. Isaiah said, in chapter 1, "He will call His name Immanuel, which is interpreted God with us."
>
> 2. Micah said, in chapter 2, "Thou Bethlehem, Judah, though thou be small…"
>
> 3. Hosea said, in chapter 2, "Out of Egypt I have called my son."
>
> 4. Jeremiah said, in chapter 2, "there was weeping…"

Jeremiah was probably stoned in Egypt. Isaiah was cut in half by the King Manasseh. Micah was thrown from a cliff by the people of Ahab. Out of those four prophets, so far, the only one that wasn't killed by his people, that I can tell, was Hosea. Apparently he was blessed enough to die of natural causes. So when you say, "You are so blessed because you're being treated like the prophets," he's saying you're as blessed as Isaiah, Jeremiah, and Micah. That's some company.

Blessed are ye, when men shall revile you, and persecute you, and shall say all manner of evil against you falsely. Now here is the qualifier: "Because you're a nag." Oh! Wait a minute, it doesn't say that. "Because you're cross? Abrasive? Rude? You cut people off when they talk?" No, it doesn't say that, does it? Jesus says. Friends, friends, if we're going to be hated let it be because Jesus is in us.

Rejoice, and be exceeding glad: for great *is* your reward in heaven: for so persecuted they the prophets which were before you. You see, God is interested in rewarding His people. Away with the idea that God is not interested in rewarding you and I. He has a heart that is perfect and wants to reward His people.

> *5:43 Ye have heard that it hath been said, "Thou shalt love thy neighbour, and hate thine enemy." 44. But I say unto you, love your enemies, bless them that curse you, do good to them that hate you, and pray for them which despitefully use you, and persecute you; 45. that ye may be the children of your Father which is in heaven: for He maketh His sun to rise on the evil and on the good, and sendeth rain on the just and on the unjust. 46. For if ye* (look here) *love them which love you, what reward have ye?* **Do not even the publicans the same?**

"Don't the extortioners do the same thing?" The people that cheat the Jews? That collect taxes from the Jews for the Romans, because Jews were better at collecting taxes from Jews than Romans were, and so Romans hired Jews to collect taxes from Jews. Those are publicans. They were not liked. And God said, "They love their own. You want their reward?"

God is very much interested in us receiving a reward and so He takes us past the minimalist idea of the Ten Commandments, and says, "Let's see the heart of the Father behind the Ten Commandments so you can have a reward." It's not just there.

> 6:1 *Take heed that ye do not your alms before men, to be seen of them: otherwise ye have no* **reward** *of your Father which is in heaven. 2 Therefore when thou doest thine alms, do not sound a trumpet before thee, as the hypocrites do in the synagogues and in the streets, that they may have glory of men. Verily I say unto you, they have their* **reward**.

"But you! I don't want you to get your reward down here. I am interested in giving you a vast reward," God says, "Please don't get it here."

> 6:5 *And when thou prayest, thou shalt not be as the hypocrites are: for they love to pray standing in the synagogues and in the corners of the streets, that they may be seen of men. Verily I say unto you, they have their* **reward**.

God is from His perfect heart, chapter 5 verse 48, telling us in chapter 6 verse 5, "I want you to be rewarded. Don't get your reward here." When people stand and think, "Wow, he's a spiritual dude! If that is what you're seeking…you have your reward. Oh my goodness, don't get your reward here.

> 6:16 *Moreover when ye fast, be not, as the hypocrites, of a sad countenance: for they disfigure their faces, that they may appear unto men to fast. Verily I say unto you, they have their* **reward.**

God says, "I am so interested in you being rewarded. Wash your face when you fast."

> 6:19 *Lay not up for yourselves treasures upon earth, where moth and rust doth corrupt, and where thieves break through and steal: 20. But* **lay up for yourselves treasures in heaven**, *where neither moth nor rust doth corrupt, and where thieves do not break through nor steal:*

I tell you the day is coming when the kingdom is coming to earth and His will is to be done on earth as it is in heaven. Look, you're not traveling very far to get your reward, if you'll just be patient. He's a rewarding God. You say, "I want it now." I do too, but God says you're blessed and you're rewarded.

5:13

Ye are the salt of the earth: We have this idea of heaven constantly being contrasted with the idea of earth so this doesn't make any sense to the average reader. I mean, in a way, we get the impression that God's people don't belong here on earth. I mean the whole Beatitude idea is that, "You just wait for a better day coming, you don't belong here."

That's the whole idea. As a matter of fact, the closest thing we get to something positive actually being said is verse 5:5.

He spends the first part of this basically saying, "You don't belong here." It's basically what He's getting to. And you know, this shows in our attitudes. It should show in our actions. Because the rest of chapter 5, from 17 and on, He says, "You have heard… But I tell you. You heard… But I tell you. People of earth, they say this, but I—the one from heaven—tell you this." So our attitudes are supposed to say that "we don't belong here on earth." And our actions, the rest of the chapter are supposed to say, "We actually don't belong here on earth. We're kind of a different stripe." We need to be reminded that our heavenly heartbeat needs to be visible through our earthly bodies. I'm afraid it's a disservice to the King if all we're doing is talking about how you can't wait to see so-and-so again.

Ye are the salt of the earth: but if the salt have lost his savour, Now what are we talking about? Flavor. You are to bring flavor to this planet.

> *Psalm 34:8 O taste and see that the LORD is good: blessed is the man that trusteth in Him.*

But if the salt have lost his savour, wherewith shall it be salted? It is thenceforth good for nothing, but to be cast out, and to be trodden under foot of men. You understand that when an army used to conquer another army, sometimes they would burn the fields and sometimes they would salt them. And what would that do? It would keep anything from growing. The idea there is that people would walk on it and pretty soon the salt would be grinded in. You know it actually would dissolve into the soil and make it pretty unfertile. In other words, don't lose your savor. No salt desires to be trampled.

5:14-15

Ye are the light of the world. A city that is set on an hill cannot be hid. Neither do men light a candle, and put it under a bushel, but on a candlestick; and it giveth light unto all that are in the house. You can never really miss a city on a hill, especially if you're in the middle of a plain. And you're not supposed to be able to miss the salt of the earth either. We are supposed to be unmistakable. There's no better way to do that than be a light. Now I think there is salt to be had in our lives by picking up trash on a road when it needs to be, and adopting a highway, or maybe even serving at a soup kitchen, you must understand that there is no greater light you can bring to a soul than to give them the Gospel.

5:16

Let your light so shine before men, that they may see your good works, and glorify your Father which is in heaven. You see, why we want people to taste our lives is because we want them to be reminded of our Father.

Faithfulness now means fruitfulness later.

> *5:5 Blessed are the meek: for they shall **inherit the earth**.*

> *5:13 Ye are the **salt of the earth**:*

"I thought we weren't supposed to care about the earth. I mean I'm supposed to be meek so that later on when the kingdom comes I can have the earth." No. Be salt now, inherit later. Isn't it amazing the same word is used within eight verses of each other? We're told in one verse seemingly, "Eh, don't give a rip about what's going on around here. To hell with it." That is how Christians are these days! "Eh, whatever. I don't really want to hear about what's going on in the political world, whatever, whatever." Don't you understand we're salt? The attitude of, "I don't care," is so forgetful! We'll never be remembered having that attitude. Our generation will be forgettable. I want to be full of savor. One day the meek inherit the earth, but until then we are the salt of that very earth. This is the same earth in verse 5:18 we're told will pass away. Look at it. It will pass away. But until then, we're salt.

> *5:33 Again, ye have heard that it hath been said by them of old time, "Thou shalt not forswear thyself, but shalt perform unto the Lord thine oaths:" 34. But I say unto you, swear not at all; neither by heaven; for it is God's throne: 35. **Nor by the earth; for it is His footstool.***

So, when something is your footstool, don't you want it for a while? Isn't it yours? Don't you care for it? Yes, it's a sign that you conquered it, I got that. It's a sign that it's yours, I get that. I know when kings conquered kings they put their feet on the neck of the defeated king and said, "I've conquered this thing," I've got it. When it says the earth is His footstool it means that it is all His, it's all His, which I think is really ironic considering that Satan tried to give it to Jesus a chapter earlier.

So it's the same earth. It's the earth that the Lord controls, that He's conquered. It's the same earth that will pass away one day.

*6:30 Wherefore, if God so clothe the grass of the field, which **to day is, and to morrow is cast into the oven,***

What is that a reference to? It's a reference to when the earth and the heaven pass away. 2 Peter 3 talks about that. Everything will melt away that day. When will all the grass of the earth be thrown into the oven? When the earth passes away. Heaven and earth pass away, 5:18.

But until then, until then, we are the only salt that exists. The main way that we bring taste to this world is by making sure they are clear on what the gospel is. The gospel is not, "Pray to receive." The gospel is not, "Repent and do better." The gospel is, "Someone was crushed for our sins." Not because He was desperate for attention, but because the Father was unhappy with the creation that was in rebellion to Him. "For God so loved the world." That word "kosmos" is not just people, it is the whole of creation that God wanted restored to Him. Colossians 1:20, "He restored, or reconciled, the world to Himself through the blood of the cross of Christ." The whole world. Romans 8 says that the whole of creation groans and is in travail until the redemption. Friends, if Hebrews chapter 1 is correct, the earth abides forever, and I guess we might as well be salt.

You would think that if I do good works, you would think that the world would go, "Ahhh! Ahhh! It's the Father!" And they'd fall to their knees and repent. Unfortunately, if you look at the end of chapter 5:43,

Ye have heard that it hath been said, "Thou shalt love thy neighbour, and hate thine enemy." 44. But I say unto you, Love

your enemies, bless them that curse you, do good to them that hate you, and pray for them which despitefully use you, and persecute you; 45. That ye may be the children of your Father which is in heaven:...

If you want to be like your Father you have to have the rejection He feels. And what is that rejection?

...He maketh His sun to rise on the evil and on the good, and sendeth rain on the just and on the unjust.

"Hang on a second. Are you telling me that I spend all the time that I can think of being salt of the earth, so that people around me can look up to heaven and then they don't even give thanks for the good works that the Father has done? Are you telling me that?" Yeah....Or Jesus' words mean really nothing. What kind of force does it bring to Jesus' argument if He says, "Love your enemies like God never had to do." But that's not what it says.

You ever heard anyone say, "You're just like your dad?" Yeah, I would love for that to be said of me. How about you? Ok, end of the verse,

He maketh His sun to rise on the evil and on the good,

He's busy showing sun to people who curse His name... They should get nothing but rain when they want sun. Nope. No. They get sun when good people get sun. The end of the verse,

and sendeth rain on the just and on the unjust.

"Wait a minute, that's not right, that's not right." That must be a misprint because if I were God the people that want rain would get blowing sand. And the good people, the ones that are like their Father, they would get rain. And when it's time for the sun to do it's work, I would give the people that are unrighteous, I'd give them a whole lot more than sun, I'd give them scorching heat, enough to melt them where they stand. And I'd give the righteous people, I'd give them sun. But no, the Father says, "Those people that curse me, I'm going to love them. I'm going to love them with sun and with rain, just like I do the good."

And so, we share in the rejection of the Father when we are good to people around us. And remember, chapter 5 verse 16, we're thinking about context…

> *Let your light so shine before men, that they may see your good works, and glorify your Father which is in heaven.*

What Father? The Father who rains on the just and the unjust. The Father who sends sun for the good and the evil. Who are we drawing people's attention to? A Father that is a whole lot better than us. So it really is important that we point people to the Father. The one who drops rain. The one who forgives sin. Look at chapter 6 verse 14 and 15. Look there please.

> *For if ye forgive men their trespasses, **your heavenly Father** will also forgive you: But if ye forgive not men their trespasses, neither will your Father forgive your trespasses.*

That Father. The one who feeds the birds, chapter 6 verse 26. We read that. And the one who gives gifts, chapter 7 verse 11,

> *If ye then, being evil, know how to give good gifts unto your children, how much more shall **your Father** which is in heaven give good things to them that ask Him?*

I think sometimes we get so reformation-minded in our idea of justification that we forget that there really is such a thing as "good and bad things Christians do." And there are some days Bill Sturm doesn't do right. And I don't want you to taste my salt and see an imperfect heavenly Father. I've got to do right because I am reflecting my heavenly Father.

5:33

Again, ye have heard that it hath been said by them of old time, "Thou shalt not forswear If you might have a newer version it might say "perjure thyself." In fact, it's the only time in the New Testament that word is used. And obviously it has legal ramifications.

5:37

But let your communication be, "Yea, yea; (or) Nay, nay:" Let your communication simply be yes and no.

for whatsoever is more than these cometh of evil. Interestingly enough when you look at the end of verse 37 and you realize anything more than a yes and no communication comes from evil. It's not like it is in the Lord's Prayer where it is "the evil one,"

5:38-39

39 But I say unto you, that ye resist not evil: but whosoever shall smite thee on thy right cheek, turn to him the other also. So if you want to know what evil is, just look two verses later and find it's the same kind of evil that will gladly smite two cheeks. It's the same kind of evil. I can't define it, but it is the same kind of evil that walks up to you and slaps you.

5:43

45. That ye may be the children of your Father which is in heaven: for He maketh His sun to rise on the evil and on the good. Would it surprise you that the good Father in heaven sends rain on the evil? Of course it would. We would be surprised. We don't expect evil people to get rain, at least not in our human nature where we repay good for good and evil for evil. We do not expect evil people who have farms to get rain when they need it. Now of course, the Father is better than that.

There's no complicated idea here. What is the evil that produces communication that is simply more than "yes" and "no?" It is the same kind of evil that would gladly punch you in the face. And it's the same kind of evil that would curse the God who gives that person rain. That same kind of evil is the kind that works in us to be more than simple communicators. Think through that. Think through that. Think about how powerful that is. If you will, the same kind of evil that would use you, abuse you, drive across your lawn if you live on a corner; that is the kind of evil that produces a communication that is more than "yes" or "no." The same kind of evil that would look up to a God that has blessed them with fruit, season after season after season, is the same kind of evil that works in these body's members to produce complicated communication.

Let's remember please that these are the words spoken to us by the Lord who bought us with His blood. This is our Lord. He died for our sins, every sin that was ever committed. I never want to get tired of saying it and I hope you never get tired of hearing it. Every sin that we count as being colossal as the highest Everest, as deep as the lowest hell, and simple as a little white lie—those all crushed the Son of God on Calvary. They were all nailed to His cross. We never want to get over the fact that it is those sins that hung Him on the cross. Yes, the Father; yes, Judas; yes, Pilate; yes, the Romans; yes, but my sin nailed Him to a cross. There would be no Christ needed, no Savior needed, no cross needed, if Bill Sturm was not a sinner. And so the greater part that we can identify in ourselves that is sinful, the greater grace is magnified in our eyes through the forgiveness of Jesus. It is this same Jesus that testifies of His own grace every time we acknowledge some uncleanness in ourselves. It's not a pleasant job.

And here, this very Son of God, less than three years before He dies and pays an unspeakable price for our salvation, says something very clearly here. It doesn't seem like it speaks to us today. Not many of us are out there saying, "I swear by Capital Hill!" God knows there's not much to swear by. "I swear by the genie in the sky." Well, we all know the genie is not real. "I swear by…" "I swear by…" That seems like something so far out there. As a matter of fact, we don't take it very seriously and why should we?

> *Leviticus 19:12 And **ye shall not swear by My name falsely**, neither shalt thou profane the name of thy God:*

> *Numbers 30:2 If a man vow a vow unto the LORD, or **swear an oath to bind his soul** with a bond; he shall not break his word, he shall do according to all that proceedeth out of his mouth.*

And so we would say, "Ok, well that makes sense, I suppose. We should probably not break that law." And certainly, who would break such a law?

In other words, if I come to Eugene, and I say, "Eugene, I need to borrow your lawnmower and I swear by the God of heaven that I will bring it back to you tomorrow," I'm bringing now three people into the agreement – Eugene, me, and God. And Jesus says, "You don't need to do that. I know you're allowed to do that. You don't need to do that."

Craig Blomberg says the situation described is one which many Jews viewed swearing by heaven or Earth or Jerusalem or one's head as less binding than swearing by God. So here's the two-edged sword. Typically Jews had a lot of respect for the name of God. As a matter of fact, Matthew exhibits that often. Where Mark, Luke, and John will talk about the "kingdom of God," often Matthew says "kingdom of heaven" because he had such great respect for the name of God among his audience, the Hebrews. And so these good Pharisees would say, "Well, we can't say name of God, so let's say something like "heaven." Let's say "Jerusalem." Let's say "earth." Let's swear by things that He's kind of responsible for."

And on the other side, they would come up to you and say, "I swear by heaven that I will return your lawnmower to you tomorrow. And then tomorrow they could decided they needed it another day but didn't call you."

You say, "Well you swore by God."

They say, "No, I didn't. I swore by heaven."

So not only do they look more religious because they won't say the name of God, but they get out of promises they make to people because they didn't say the name of God. Works both ways for a good Pharisee. They're always bending the word of God to suit them.

And then they would get in this thing where they would try to get as close to God without saying, "God." So, they would say, "I swear by Venus that I will bring your lawnmower back to you."

"I can get closer to God than that, so I'll swear by Pluto."

"I can get closer to God than that; I'll swear by Hercules, that star out there in Andromeda."

"I swear by Orion."

"I swear by his belt."

"I swear by the empty space in the north."

"Well, I swear by the throne of God."

It's kind of like that with the Pharisees. "Well, let's see whose promise is more binding. Oh, you said by God's throne and I only said by earth. Ha! I guess you have to keep your promise." A very strange system of rules. But we are after all talking about the Pharisees.

The Pharisees were expanding oaths to technicalities much like our American legal system that often twists and turns the normal meanings of words—Evolving to the point of destroying the justice they were supposed to serve. All of a sudden, you have codes and laws so thick the legislatures don't even read it. I mean, how in the world can you read a healthcare bill as thick as a phonebook?

Apparently this was a pretty long lasting issue.

Matthew 23:16 Woe unto you, ye blind guides, which say, Whosoever shall swear by the temple, it is nothing; but whosoever shall swear by the gold of the temple, he is a debtor!" 17. Ye fools and blind: for whether is greater, the gold, or the temple that sanctifieth the gold? 18. And, "Whosoever shall swear by the altar, it is nothing; (that's what you say) *but whosoever sweareth by the gift that is upon it, he is guilty." 19.Ye fools and blind: for whether is greater, the gift, or the altar that sanctifieth the gift? 20.Whoso therefore shall swear by the altar, sweareth by it, and by all things thereon. 21. And whoso shall swear by the temple, sweareth by it, and by Him that dwelleth therein. 22. And he that shall swear by heaven, sweareth by the throne of God, and by Him that sitteth thereon. 23. Woe unto you.*

What is a promise? It's when you say you're going to do something, or have something, or something is so. It's not when you say, "I promise." Our kids shouldn't have to look at us and say, "Do you promise?" They should be able to think, "Ok, dad is a Christian. Mom is a Christian. They said that something will happen and it will happen." This stuck with the half brother of Jesus, James.

*James 5:12 Above all things my brethren, **swear not**. Neither by heaven or by earth, or by any other oath. But let your yay be yay and your nay, nay, lest you fall into condemnation.*

*Exodus 20:7 **Thou shalt not take the name of the LORD thy God in vain**; for the LORD will not hold him guiltless that taketh His name in vain.*

It seems that if a Christian makes a promise, he's including Christ and there is no greater invocation. So you got all these Pharisees saying, "I swear by Earth." "I swear by the clouds." "I swear by the angel on the clouds." "I swear by the harp in that angel's hands." "I swear…" And you know what? There's no higher name to swear by, so to speak, than Jesus. We are Christ's name bearers. And every time we disciple someone of the nations and make them a part of the community of Christ, we are making another Christ-name-bearer. You can get no higher witness than a person to say, "I'll do something." It's like Christ saying, "I'll do something." That's the way it's supposed to be when a Christian says they are going to do something.

> 1. Saying what you're allowed to say is not always supposed to be said. That's the point of Jesus. "Ok, since 1446BC, when you got the law from Mount Sinai with Moses, up until today. You've been allowed to swear by God. And you've abused it so much that I think you should just quit exercising your rights, and talk like a Christian." You want to talk about a higher standard? Because you might notice chapter 5 verse 1, who's He talking to primarily? Disciples. So disciples have a word that is supposed to be as dependable as the word of Christ.

> 2. Speaking too much doesn't become less sinful just because we use spiritual language. That's what's happening here in this passage. We've got a bunch of people acting carnal, using spiritual language like, "I swear by heaven," as if that makes them righter. "Well, this is a matter that needs to be known. It's kind of a prayer request. It's just something that everyone needs to know about."

3. Speaking emphatically about what you cannot control is simply illogical. Now, you might notice this particularly in verse number 5:36,

Neither shalt thou swear by thy head, because thou canst not make one hair white or black.

So we are so busy, worried, or concerned about things we simply cannot control and so I'm consistently, easily aggravated by things I really don't have control over, and God needs to help us   to have simple yes and no communication. When you look at someone, when we make business   dealings, when we talk with brothers and sisters, we ought to be people that follow Ecclesiastes 5:1-3.

He's in heaven and we are on earth, so let our words be few.

Are we willing to exaggerate because we really feel like we're going to accomplish a lot? "If he does that again I'm walking out!" You know full well you're not walking out. You need the job.

But we say things in an oath manner, a swearing type of manner, and we are saying things that we really don't mean. And it is as reckless as saying, "I swear by my white hair that will be black tomorrow." That's ridiculous, you can't do that! We're busy saying things like, "You do that again I'm walking out on you." And we really don't mean it. Before you know it our much speaking has created scars in the lives of other people. This demands control over the old man and it demands control that God can command in our life.

Chapter 7

7:1-6

Now, if you have a Bible like I have, you have one of those symbols that means "new paragraph" at the beginning of verse 6. That's pretty good of them to tell us what Jesus didn't. Jesus didn't say, "All right, new paragraph here." So all of a sudden, we start realizing that verse 6 really does belong with verse 5, and eventually there's a time when you quit helping people with that stuff in their eye. Why? Because, "they turn again and rend you," the end of verse 6. They hurt you with how you're trying to help them.

7:7-12

11. If ye then, being evil, He starts out calling them hypocrites in verse 5 and then He calls them evil in verse 11. Jesus has a way of speaking with people.

know how to give good gifts unto your children, how much more shall your Father which is in heaven give good things to them that ask Him? It is interesting that on the heels of "judging righteously" (7:1-5) we are to also exercise discernment (7:6), and then pray. It is fitting, is it not, that since we are about to then have the ability to make discernments in the verses that follow (7:15-20), that our prayers should be for discernment.

We have to have discernment. Discernment is the ability to look at two things, and not necessarily good versus evil, but sometimes good versus better. In this context I think you're going to find we need discernment as sound judgment, judging the right course, good from evil, holy from common, seeing outward appearances versus discerning the inward reality, and understanding the significance of events. As a matter of fact, 1 Chronicles 12, it talks about the men of Issachar who had understanding of the times. And that's what we need. We need the ability to understand what's going on around us and a desire for God to help us with prayer.

But Matthew 7 is not about say nothing, do nothing, be nothing, because you don't want to be accused of judging. No, Matthew 7 verses 1 through 5 says, "If you're going to judge, understand you will be judged with that same measure. So be careful when you judge." Because when you're extra critical people will probably notice when you do things wrong. After all, we did talk about it, chapter 5 verses 10 through 12, that the peacemakers are blessed, and then those who are persecuted for righteousness sake are blessed.

Newly born believers that have the Holy Spirit in them can decide between good and evil. I mean, hopefully you can tell when you're walking around with shorts bumping up against your rear-end, that that's probably not good. That's a new believer's issue. That's small stuff. The hard stuff is, "I have a choice between two very good choices. What do I do?"

Now, you're supposed to being some sort of fruit discerner. "Don't judge, don't ever judge, don't ever judge, stop judging." Well then how do you deal with the fact that Jesus said you're supposed to spot people that are wrong and inspect their fruit? That means there's some judgments taking place. I am making a judgment. It is simply not honest, or pragmatic in the slightest, to say we don't judge. To say, "You shouldn't judge," is actually a self-defeating statement because you're making a judgment saying that "judging is wrong."

All of a sudden, contextually, we are required to believe that it is a particular prayer for a particular need. Also, look at the very first word of verse 12.

If ye then, being evil, know how to give good gifts unto your children, how much more shall your Father which is in heaven give good things. The truth is, the reason I don't have much faith in God is because I feel like most of the time I'm a lousy dad. There are times when I know my shortcomings as a dad and it keeps me from praying because I superimpose my character as a father on God. And I assume that He is the father that I am. I don't do what I can for my kids and so God must be a rotten dad like I am. No, Jesus reassures us and says, "You know how to give, but the Father, He gives." What a thrill. What a thrill that on a bad dad my Father's perfect character to put my silliness in a shadow. Now that is not an excuse. I told you, it reflects my selfishness. I take what I know is wrong about me, and I suppose it's true about God. God's actions are weighed against my ability.

Therefore What is the point of this if it's a brand new thought starting in verse 12? What's the point of it? "Ask and you shall receive, seek and you shall find, knock and the door will be opened to you. Oh by the way, treat others as you want to be treated." Whoa, no way! "Therefore" doesn't make any sense, in that Bible of yours if verse 12 is a brand new thought. It's pointing back to how you judge people. Flow of thought requires that the "therefore" of verse 12 goes back to pulling the mote out of your eye, the beam out of your eyes. Now, do you want others to do that for you when they judge you? I do. Ok, if you want that, then pray for discernment on how to clean out your own eye. Flow of context.

Therefore all things whatsoever ye would that men should do to you, do ye even so to them: If we're always quick about making judgments for people, what we're doing is breaking what is known as The Golden Rule, in verse 12. In other words, I'm making a judgment without asking for discernment. The discernment goes two ways, "Lord, please show me what I need to pull out of my own eye. Lord, please show me how I can help this person with their miniscule speck." Jesus says the right perspective is, "I probably have the beam and they probably have the speck." You all with me? Proper perspective says that I assume I'm the worst one. I suspect myself first and so I'm looking in the mirror and I'm saying, "There's got to be something about me I'm missing, so before I get super critical here I better pull the beam out of my eye." And the only way to do that, apparently, is by praying. Verses 7 through 11.

Why do I need wisdom to judge properly a false prophet (7:14-15)? Because there's going to be times when I'm going to feel pretty close to them and it's going to feel good what they're saying. Why do I need discernment? I can think of two reasons. Our failures cause us to be extra merciful. In a way, we get discernment and we're tempted because we're like, "Oh man, I used to do that. I don't know if I want to make them feel bad because I know that I could probably be really close to doing that myself." And here's what we kind of say sometimes, "If not for the grace of God that would be me, there go I." And sometimes that keeps us from doing the right thing. Now it is true that we should be merciful. I mean right here in the Beatitudes in Matthew 5 verse 7,

Blessed are the merciful: for they shall obtain mercy.

So there is, no doubt, again, a place between the ditches. Showing nothing but mercy: "Ah, don't worry about it. I don't want to say anything to you because God knows I used to be in that sin, and I don't want to offend you," and over here, "I used to be in that sin and I don't want you in that sin, so get out of that sin." Somewhere in the middle there's this thing of, "Man, I know how hard it can be to give that up."

But what we learn from the book of Matthew is that it is the character of Christ to "save His people from their sins." So we're agents of Christ, helping people to be saved from their sins.

7:21-22a

22. Many will say to Me in that day, 'Lord, Lord, have we not prophesied in Thy name? The claim of these who do not enter into the kingdom of heaven is that they, verse 22, **prophesy in [the Lord's] name**. This contextually makes no sense if in view of verse 15, we're not dealing with false prophets all the way through. Verses 21 through 23 are dealing, in context, with false prophets. Jesus is talking, in verses 21 through 23, about false prophets. We already saw verses 7-11 as a "prayer for discernment." This chapter is full of the need for discernment as we judge. And low and behold, the last judge of the chapter is Jesus Christ Himself. The chapter starts out with, "Judge not, that ye be not judged," and then it tells us how to judge righteously, and then it tells us how we should judge ourselves, verse 13, "Enter ye in at the straight gate." Then it tells us, verse 15, how to judge false prophets, and then it tells in verse 21—there will be a Judge, who does indeed finally judge the false prophet.

I suppose the very sobering thing about these people who do not enter the kingdom of heaven is that we find out, in chapter 25, they actually enter the fire prepared for the devil and his angels. There are only two options on the table. There's everlasting fire or it is the kingdom of heaven. The book of Matthew gives us no third option, no sort of waiting room, no sort of post mortem opportunity for salvation.

It is the kingdom of heaven or it is eternal fire. It's sobering. And sometimes I wish that there were other choices. But there are not.

And what a fitting person to have as the Judge. He is known as the "altogether lovely One," holy, righteous, good, faithful, true, just, guiltless, sinless, spotless, innocent, harmless, resisting to temptation, obedient to the Father, zealous, meek, lowly in heart, merciful, patient, longsuffering, compassionate, benevolent, loving, self-denying, humble, forgiving, subject to His parents, and conforming His saints to Himself. Everything tells you that He is qualified, above all others, to judge. He's never been found guilty of any sin. None.

Look at these false prophets. Verse 22, **Have we not prophesied in Thy name?** They're either deceivers or they're deceived. These are the only two options. I mean, they're standing before Jesus saying, **"We have prophesied in Your name."** That doesn't necessarily mean that they were prophesying using the name of Jesus, although it can certainly mean that in the application, but to do something in someone's name means that you're coming in their stead. So these prophets are standing before the Judge, who is allowing or disallowing people into the kingdom of heaven, and they are saying, "We spoke in the name of the One who allows people into the kingdom." That's sobering. "We represent heaven." And so, either they are horribly deceived or they are deceivers, and we find out that these actually are twins. Paul had much to say about this time (2 Timothy 3:1-13).

The second thing I'd like you to notice about these folks in this judgment is that the fruit they are being judged of in verses 16 through 18 is easily defined. I mean, let's look at this. He says what kind of fruit they will bear and then I want you to notice 7:19:

> *Every tree that bringeth not forth good fruit is hewn down, and cast into the fire.*

Now friends, if you're like me, you have heard probably 40 or 50 devotions, sermonettes, lessons, messages on this passage, and many will say this fruit is good works, or fruit of the Spirit, or other Christians. I don't know what you've heard. But I say let we let Matthew tell us what Matthew meant (Matthew 3:8-10).

Almost verbatim with Jesus. Jesus is not developing a new doctrine from John the Baptist. And in the context, John the Baptist looks at Pharisees and Sadducees and says, "You've come to me to get a baptism for repentance. Before you do that, you bring forth fruit suitable for repentance. Show me a lifestyle that shows that you have repented." He said that you do good works to show that you have repented.

In chapter 7 the problem with the false prophets is not that they haven't done good works enough to go into heaven. The problem with the false prophets is that they haven't done good works enough to show that they have repented. No repentance! And by the way, in the context of John the Baptist, what was there to repent of? There was that to repent of which John said they must confess, which is their sins. So how do we expect people that are never willing to say that, "my sins don't belong in the kingdom of God," to somehow end up there?

The third thing to notice is that the kingdom of heaven is coming to Earth. Look at chapter 6. Notice what the Lord has asked His disciples to pray in verse 7.

> *But when ye pray, use not vain repetitions, as the heathen do: for they think that they shall be heard for their much speaking. 8. Be not ye therefore like unto them…9. After this manner therefore pray ye: Our Father which art in heaven, Hallowed be Thy name. 10. Thy kingdom come. Thy will be done in earth, as it is in heaven.*

The kingdom of heaven will soon come to Earth in answer to the prayers of God's people.

Now then, you have no room for believing that Matthew chapter 7, verses 21 through 23, is a pre-tribulation rapture. You cannot fit some sort of strange seven-year period between a rapture and a second coming of Christ in the context of the Sermon on the Mount. Know it and know it well. When does the kingdom come to earth? You can either believe Tim Lahaye or you can believe Jesus & Paul:

> *2 Timothy 4:1 I charge thee therefore before God, and the Lord Jesus Christ, who shall judge the quick and the dead at **His appearing and His kingdom**.*

Please notice, Jesus will not appear again until He brings His kingdom. There are not two different tracks of eschatology, one in which Jesus didn't know the church was coming and Paul shows up, and oh my goodness! We have this thing known as the tribulation period that the church will never see.

Fourthly, these have not grieved over their sin. Remember the context. Look at 5:3:

> *Blessed are the poor in spirit: for theirs is the kingdom of heaven.*

We're talking about the same kingdom of heaven that we just read about in 7:21-23, right? Who gets to go? Those who are poor in spirit. The next verse:

> *Blessed are they that mourn: for they shall be comforted.*

No one gets to enter the kingdom who has not first mourned over their sinfulness.

Fifth, these that are denied entrance into the kingdom are not persecuted for Christ. See 5:10:

> *Blessed are they which are persecuted for righteousness' sake: for theirs is the kingdom of heaven.*

In Matthew 7:21-23, we're told about people that don't belong in the kingdom. Earlier in the Sermon on the Mount, Here we're being told who <u>does</u> belong in the kingdom: those who mourn over their sin and those who are persecuted for Christ. 5:11…

> *Blessed are ye, when men shall revile you, and persecute you, and shall say all manner of evil against you falsely, for My sake. 12. Rejoice, and be exceeding glad: for great is your reward in heaven: for so persecuted they the **prophets which were before you**.*

Don't you think it's strange that we're told about prophets who are righteous and suffered for Christ, and the absolute flipping of the coin in chapter 7 is that you have false prophets who are not allowed into the kingdom? In 5:10, we have it that those who are persecuted for righteousness' sake, the kingdom is theirs. And yet those in 7:21-23, the kingdom is not theirs. You see that? So, if you're talking about people that have never suffered for Christ consider a verse in 2nd Timothy:

> *3:12 Yea, and all that will live godly in Christ Jesus shall suffer persecution.*

The kingdom of heaven is made up of people that have suffered for Christ.

Sixth, those who specialize in helping people disobey God are those that are spoken of in 7:21-23. Let me show you in 5:19…

> *Whosoever therefore shall break one of these least commandments, **and shall teach men so**, he shall be called the least in the kingdom of heaven: but whosoever shall do and teach them, the same shall be called great in the kingdom of heaven.*

Do you see that? People who are always trying to find a way out of obeying God don't belong in the kingdom.

Seventh, those in this verse are nothing like their Father. Look at 5:20.

> *For I say unto you, that except your righteousness shall exceed the righteousness of the scribes and Pharisees, ye shall in no case enter into the kingdom of heaven.*

The Sermon on the Mount is really about the kingdom of heaven and who belongs there. It's about what people do that belong there. And it's what people do that don't belong there.

And then Jesus gives six illustrations of people that belong there. And you see them beginning in:

Verse 21, "You have heard." Verse 22, "But I tell you."

Verse 27, "You have heard." Verse 28, "But I tell you."

Verse 31, "It has been said." Verse 32, "But I say unto you."

Verse 33, "Again, you have heard." Verse 34, "But I say unto you."

Verse 38, "You have heard." Verse 39, "But I say unto you."

Verse 43, "You have heard." Verse 44, "But I say unto you."

Six times Jesus gives an illustration of how the scribes and Pharisees give you ways around the word of God. And six times Jesus says, "No. The heart of the Father is this." And if you're not convinced, look at the last verse of the chapter.

> *Be ye therefore perfect, even **as your Father** which is in heaven is perfect.*

They are not always looking for a way out of obeying God. And they have a heart like their Father. I did not have to act like Arnold Sturm to become a part of his family. That doesn't make any sense, does it? The reason I act like my father is because I'm already a part of his family. You don't have to try to be like God to go to heaven. People who have believed on Christ act like their Father.

7:22b-29

23. And then will I profess unto them, 'I never knew you: depart from Me, ye that work iniquity.' So, you're not going in. You, my friend, are not going in to the kingdom of heaven if Christ doesn't know you. Since we're Americans and we all have a TV, I feel like it's proper to address clichés as they come up. I'm about sick and tired of everyone talking about their "personal Savior." If you can find that in the Bible, I'll lay off. Furthermore, Jesus is not desperate for you to "open the door of your heart." He was the sovereign God of the universe before I was ever conceived. He does not need me. Without God I am nothing. Without me, He is still God. So, this idea of, "Have you got a saving knowledge of Jesus Christ?"

The important thing according to this passage is that He knows you. The issue with people going into the kingdom of heaven in this Scripture is not, "Do you know Jesus?" Because they appear to at least have some idea who He is. But at the end of verse 7:23 He says, **I never knew you.** That is a concern. Now certainly an omnipresent, omniscient God knows everybody on the earth in a sense. But in another sense, He knows them that are His.

> *2 Timothy 2:19 Nevertheless the foundation of God standeth sure, having this seal, the Lord knoweth them that are His.* **The Lord knoweth them that are His.** *And, let every one that nameth the name of Christ depart from iniquity.*

If God wanted to let everyone off the hook in here by saying, "Just know God. Know God! Know God!" Then I would go there, but in this passage, this Bible preacher is not being true to the context of this passage if I don't let someone hang over hell, and tell you it doesn't matter if you think you know God. He needs to know you.

Secondly, You're not going in if you don't like the rules. I've already showed you chapter 5 and verse 20, but for your blood pressure, let's read it again.

> *I say unto you, that except your righteousness shall exceed the righteousness of the scribes and Pharisees, ye shall in no case enter into the kingdom of heaven.*

If you have a heart that is consistently bucking the heavenly Father, you are proving that you are not His son. Because, Jesus was addressing the person who hated the rules of the Father. "You have heard, but I tell you." They went around the rules, but let me clarify for you.

In 1 John chapter 5 it says that, "You that believe Jesus is the Christ, you're born of God. And by the way, those of you who are born of God, His commands are not grievous." That's 1 John 5:3. A person who belongs to God, because of faith in Jesus, is not consistently looking for a way to find a way around rules.

Thirdly, You're not going into the kingdom if you can't face judgment. Now, notice 7:1-6. The point of chapter 7, verse 1 through 7, is not to give you something to put on your bumper sticker to tell people to leave you alone. No! The point of chapter 7, verses 1 through 7, is to expect people to try to help you with the speck in your eye, after they have removed the beam from theirs.

So then, what should we assume if you never want to be helped with a speck in your eye? We should assume that you are absolutely dreading any kind of judgment. And I ask you to remember that even though people may not judge us politely every time, they may not even judge us spiritually every time, I do want to tell you that judgment, righteously or unrighteously, in the Spirit of Christ or not in the Spirit of Christ, should make us think soberly of the last day when we will be judged by Christ. And if you don't like people finding fault with you, if you don't want anyone telling you that something is wrong with you, if I have a particular problem with someone being critical of my life, I may not be ready for this day.

Fourthly, you're not going in if your words are all you have. In this passage, you have a fantastic example of a Sinner's Prayer. Now, the term "Sinner's Prayer" is not in your Bible. Please notice what happens when person prays a Sinner's Prayer and depends only on their ability to voice certain words at the right time: Nothing.

Nothing changes about their destination because they say certain words. They even accurately address Jesus. But here in this passage, we have people who go to hell after they call Jesus "Lord." Here is a great demonstration of how you can go to hell saying the right things. "We have done…" "I have done..." "I have done…" "What have I done for you? I've done it all in Your name. I've done it for you. I've represented heaven." And Jesus says, **But I will profess unto them, 'I never knew you: depart from Me, you that work iniquity.**

By the way, I realize that they were relying only on their words because Jesus called them **workers of iniquity**. These are they who had no fruit in the preceding verses. These are people that had a finely crafted prayer. They have that experience that they can take you back to. They can open the flyleaf of their Bible and they can tell you about a date when they prayed a prayer. But alas, people who trust only their words find themselves outside the kingdom.

So, I throw myself at the mercy of the Christ, who in Matthew 20:28 said,

The Son of Man came…to give His life a ransom for many.

Here's the question. I ask it everywhere, "Do you believe that Christ was the ransom for you?" Because if He wasn't, there's nothing for you to believe and hell is your home.

Chapter 8

8:1a

When He (Jesus) **was come down from the mountain,** And what was He doing on the mountain? The Sermon on the Mount. Ministry often comes in the form of full days. I have found that the Lord seems to be finding busy people and using them. I am finding that people who have a hard time finding things to do continue to have a hard time finding things to do. It's been a full day already. The Sermon on the Mount has been preached. And He comes down and He heals a leper. He gives instructions to a leper. The leper goes off and now He is ready to go to a centurion's house. And the day keeps going.

We're going to find in weeks to come that He continually does things that are inconvenient. And He doesn't do it because He feels like it. For in one of these episodes we're going to find Him sleeping on a boat. He's not sleeping because it just feels like the right thing to do, and it's that time in the afternoon, and isn't it time for tea and crumpets and a nap? You know, He really is tired and He finds Himself doing ministry. And can I just say, it's ministry that matters.

8:1b-4

3 And Jesus put forth His hand, and touched him, saying, "I will; be thou clean." And immediately his leprosy was cleansed. 4. And Jesus saith unto him, "See thou tell no man; but go thy way, shew thyself to the priest, and offer the gift that Moses commanded, for a testimony unto them."

#1. Jesus has already healed thousands. Now this might be hard to grasp, but consider this passage of Scripture from just a little while ago, Matthew 4:23.

> *And Jesus went about all Galilee, teaching in their synagogues, and preaching the gospel of the kingdom, and **healing all manner of sickness and all manner of disease** among the people. 24. And His fame went throughout all Syria: and they brought unto Him all sick people that were taken with divers diseases and torments, and those which were possessed of devils,*

and those which were lunatic, and those that had palsy; and He healed them.

Wow! How comprehensive is that? How complete? How expansive? How exhaustive? And by the way, oh by the way, in case you missed it, throughout all Syria. That is no small thing. And we're going to come back to why I think that is in just a moment.

Look at chapter 4. This is not a TV where you can see the little picture up on the screen so that your son can watch the silly Steelers game while you watch the game that matters, ok? A screen within a screen. Well, Matthew can't do that so he writes about one thing at a time. And so I'm saying that I really believe that if you were to take Matthew 5, 6, and 7, and just for a second act like it's not there, look at the last verse of chapter 4:

> *And there followed Him great multitudes of people from Galilee, and from Decapolis, and from Jerusalem, and from Judaea, and from beyond Jordan.*

And then go to chapter 8 and you start reading about the healing of a leper. We're not surprised that the last verse of chapter 4 says something about Damascus. Now we see, in chapter number 8, the healing of a leper. Just stop for a minute and think that through. Just before we see Jesus healing all manner of sickness and diseases, in chapter 4, we see Him passing by His disciples, and what does He say to them? "Follow Me." The last time we see that in the Bible is when a certain prophet by the name of Elijah passed by a certain prophet by the name of Elisha. So the last time we see someone saying, "Follow me," is the prophet Elijah calling the prophet Elisha. And do you remember? There was a certain general; a certain army leader that had leprosy, in 2 Kings 5? His name was Naaman. And there's a maiden that they took captive from Israel, and she says, "There's a prophet in Samaria that can heal you of your leprosy, I think." And they go down to Samaria and they ask, "Where is this prophet?" And they find the prophet Elisha. And he is in the northern part of Palestine. And Elisha does something that makes complete medical sense. Well, not so much. He tells Naaman, "Go down to the Jordan River and immerse yourself seven times and you will have clean skin. No leprosy."

There is a clear parallel here being drawn between Jesus and all the prophets of the Old Testament, to include Elijah and Elisha. He's better than them too.

#2. Jesus continually heals people it seems.

8:16 He healed all that were sick.
9:35 Healing every sickness and every disease.
14:14 He healed their sick.
15:30 He healed them.
19:2 Healed them.
21:14 He healed them.

Is this the only leper that gets cleansed? Well, there is one later on in the book of Matthew. His name is Simon the leper (Matthew 26:6). I don't know that it is this "Simon healed of leprosy" here in chapter 8. I doubt it. But, in any case, if you'll look at chapter 11, verse 3 you'll notice that healing leprosy was part of Jesus' normal activity.

> *And it came to pass, when Jesus had made an end of commanding His twelve disciples, He departed thence to teach and to preach in their cities. 2. Now when John had heard in the prison the works of Christ, he sent two of his disciples, 3. And said unto Him,* (Are you the one that we're looking for?) *"Art Thou He that should come, or do we look for another?" 4. Jesus answered and said unto them, "Go and shew John again those things which ye do hear and see: 5. The blind receive their sight, and the lame walk, the **lepers are cleansed**.*

#3. Jesus should not be touching the man.

8:3

He put forth His hand and touched him.

> *Leviticus 5:3 Or **if he touch the uncleanness of man, whatsoever uncleanness it be that a man   shall   be defiled withal**, and it be hid from him; when he knoweth of it, then he shall be guilty.*

You need to know right off the bat, that Jesus was doing something that appeared to be wrong. The leprosy had a way of making people ceremonially and physically unclean.

#4. Next, Jesus uses the law to glorify God.

*Leviticus 13:38 If a man also or a woman have in the skin of their flesh bright spots, even white   bright spots; 39. then the priest shall look:…44 He is a leprous man, he is unclean: the priest shall   pronounce him utterly unclean; his plague is in his head. 45. And the leper in whom the plague is, his clothes shall be rent, and his head bare, and he shall put a covering upon his upper lip, and **shall cry, "Unclean, unclean."** 46. All the days wherein the plague shall be in him he shall be defiled; he is   unclean: he shall dwell alone; **without the camp** shall his habitation be.*

This leper was doomed to the rest of his life away from the synagogue, away from the tabernacle, away from the sacrificial system, away from his family; he is now to be alone for the rest of his life. He is not allowed to be around anyone. He is to keep himself from afflicting more infection among the people of Israel. He is supposed to stay away from the crowd and cry, "Unclean, unclean." That's what he's supposed to do, yeah.

*Leviticus 14:2 This shall be the law of the leper **in the day of his cleansing***:

Well, that's kind of funny. Actually, it's hysterical, because this is written about 1445 BC. 1,445 years before Christ. And other than Miriam, we have no record of anyone needing this chapter. Other than Miriam being cursed with leprosy, and healed by the Lord, and having to spend seven days outside the camp, we have nobody, from what we can tell, in Hebrew history, all through the Old Testament…not once do we ever have record of anyone needing this chapter.

As a matter of fact, little Jewish young men would grow up in Rabbinical school at times, and they would have to memorize the entire law of Moses. What a waste. What a waste to memorize chapter 14 of Leviticus. No one has ever needed it. No one ever had a day in which they were cleansed of leprosy. The only one we can find, since Miriam, that has been cleansed of leprosy, was the Syrian who didn't even need Leviticus! We have a king who died of leprosy named Uzziah because he decided to do a job that wasn't his. That is to say, he was the state, poking into the church, and he paid for it with his life. Smoke on that one.

> *Leviticus 22:4 What man soever of the seed of Aaron is a leper, or hath a running issue; he shall not eat of the holy things, until he be clean.*

Ok, well that's nice. But we don't have any record of anyone being clean after they were a leper. Except a Syrian who didn't need it. Naaman would never serve as a priest.

So imagine, Matthew 8, Jesus tells this man who is the first record we have of anyone needing Leviticus 14. Can you imagine the day when this known leper theoretically walks into the presence of a priest, in the day of his cleansing, and the High Priest for the first time in a millennium and a half, has to listen to what Leviticus 14 says? You talk about getting glory! And maybe that's the answer to why Jesus said, in verse 4, "You don't need to tell anybody. You go and show yourself to the priest for a testimony to them." Who was Jesus trying to reach with the truth of who He is? The priest. It wasn't that He was telling this man, "Don't be a witness." Nope. But there was a particular person to whom he was to witness.

God still is sovereign, and I can't give you all the reasons as to why Jesus said, "Don't go and tell anyone, but go straight to the priest," but I do know this: if the priests find out that a man was healed of leprosy for the first time in over 1,000 years, chances are word will get out that somebody did it.

You see, when Jesus directs the way in which we witness He gets the job done. When the Lord directs our witnessing activity, it gets done. When we decide who and when and where and how we're going to witness, all of a sudden we find ourselves frustrated because things just ain't happening, like we would like.

But what if he actually did obey and finally went to the temple?[37] Can you imagine the stir that that would have caused? I've already showed you over seven verses in the book of Matthew where it says He healed all manner of diseases. Virtually, Judea was disease free; Galilee was disease free; southern Syria was disease free; every time they found out the Messiah was in town they brought someone to Him to get healed. That's earth shattering. That is astonishing. And why was He doing it? So the priests would find out.

#5. This is an issue of sin. I am not saying that you get leprosy if you are a sinner, because I'd be as white as a goose. So I'm not saying that. I'm not saying this was an issue of sin, but what I am saying is that the theme of Matthew is, "You call His name Jesus, because He'll save His people from their sin." He's not called Jesus because He heals you of leprosy.

Every one of these lessons is a lesson as to how a disease that eats you to the core is a picture of the leaven of sin that permeates our inner being, and before you know it, we look in the mirror and we say, "Well, that's not me. I shouldn't have done that. That's not me. It's not like me. I don't do that." But after a little while of doing those things, we have to recognize that really is what we are. You say, "Well, leprosy starts in the skin." That's true. But it gets all the way into the organs and then you die. Matthew is repreaching to us the sermon that Jesus saves His people from their sin, and so this healing of leprosy is God's way, once again, of showing us that there's not any sin that is so deep in your core that God can't purge it out.

#6. Worship is very often audacious to those who believe they know who Jesus is. Now think through this for just a moment. There were more diplomatic ways for the leper to make his presence known. Would you agree? And by the way, if there was ever a time for Jesus to say, "Whoa, wait, wait. I'm not God, don't bother me," this would have been a good time. But the problem is this is the first of nine times that we have record of where Jesus allows someone to worship Him. That is what your Bible says, isn't it? In verse 2, **And, behold, there came a leper and worshipped Him.** That word means "kissed His hand." If

---

[37]Mark 1:45 gives the idea that he did not.

your Bible does not have something that expresses worship in its words, I'm afraid it is a weak translation.

So this is the first of nine times where we find Jesus being worshipped, and apparently He doesn't mind. The second time is when his son, a ruler who's son was healed worshipped Him. The disciple, after a storm, worshipped Him. The disciples worshipped Him. The Canaanite woman worshipped Him. The mother of James and John, Salome, who by the way was also Jesus' aunt, worshipped Him. The Gerasene demoniac worshipped Him. The healed blind man worshipped Him. All the disciples, at the end of Matthew, worshipped Him. "Thou will have no other gods before Me. You will not bow yourself down to them." That's in the Ten Commandments, so Jesus is in deep trouble if He's not God.

So this stupidity spewed out by almost every Muslim on the globe that says Jesus never claimed to be the Son of God. Two displays of audacity. Think this through with me. Jesus is touching a leper. And perhaps the only second place thing to that is the leper coming in the middle of a crowd! What audacity. Worship takes, in some regard, audacity. You offer thanksgiving that is not comfortable, and you render honor to someone when people would rather you shut up. Yeah, that's just sort of how that works.

So, if you step back and look at it, both Jesus and the leper are breaking the law. Which one is more audacity? Well, it depends. But I would recommend to you that the reason that the man was willing to stand as a leper in the middle of the crowd is because he thought, "I won't be a leper much longer." And the reason Jesus was willing to touch the leper was because in a minute He'd be touching a man that wasn't a leper. What audacity! For a man to have such faith in the Son of God that he steps in the middle of a crowd, risking his life, and says, "I will do something that is just... dumb." No one would do that. Not in a religious setting. Why in the world would you do that? Well, because he was convinced that Jesus had power. "If You are willing, You can make me clean. I know You're able. But if You want to, You can make me clean. The power is in You, God. This is a light thing to You! All You have to do is say so! You can do this and so I know You're able, and so I want to know if You're willing." And Jesus says, **Yeah, I am willing. Be clean**.

That is the Son of God; more audacious that am. He comes and He touches a leper. But Jesus has an awful bunch of power because after He heals this leper He goes to a gentile centurion and heals his servant, and then after that, in verses 14 and following, He goes and heals a woman. Not a Jewish man, a leper. Not a Jewish man, a priest, nope. A centurion. Not a Jewish man who's a priest. Nope! A woman! What an audacious Savior, taking what people would call an unnecessary chance on some little gentile dog named Bill Sturm.

So I guess that's why we followers of Christ are full of audacity. Praying for people we may never see again, willing to let the news of their conversion wait until we may meet them in heaven. The audacity of witnessing to a person that hates you. The audacity of believing when there isn't any reason to believe. The audacity to ask for forgiveness again and again and expecting the Lord, the Holy Spirit that prompted you to ask for forgiveness, is in the other person prompting them to forgive you. What audacity!

Where do we get that? Our Master. We do things that don't make any sense. Why are we so audacious as to set our alarm a few minutes early so we can pray and read the Scriptures, and actually convince the God of heaven that we think we need Him? Because we have the audacity to believe that just a little time with God changes the whole day.

#7. Crossing social barriers to accomplish the Father's will is quite Christian. I've already said it. It's very hard to imagine anyone who calls themself a son of God saying, "I would never build a relationship with a Muslim." It's very hard to imagine someone saying God brought someone 7,000 miles and I would never build a relationship with them. It's hard to imagine that, isn't it? So, we are quite Christian when we do cross lines.

#8. Obedience is the first mark of one whose sin has been purged. You see in verse 4, he wasn't, "You're healed. Go have a nice day. Go have a picnic with your wife." No, no. Where was **the priest**? Jerusalem. There weren't no priests in Galilee, or Syria, or Samaria. This newly cleansed leper was healed when they came off the mountain. Where was the mountain? North edge of the Sea of Galilee. How far from Jerusalem were they? Seventy miles at least. Jesus said, "You're cleansed. Now go show yourself to the priest. I've cleansed you. I've made you a new man. Now go do something hard for Me. Hard. The joy that I just gave you, you're going to need that joy, because I want you now to go and carry the gospel to a person far away." It's hard.

8:5-6

And when Jesus was entered into Capernaum, there came unto Him a centurion, beseeching Him, 6. And saying, "Lord, my servant lieth at home sick of the palsy We find out from Luke's gospel that this is not the centurion himself coming to Jesus but messengers of the centurion. We would have no issue saying that the ambassador of a particular country speaks for a president.

grievously tormented." In Luke 7 Jewish elders came and talked to Jesus for him and the Jewish elders said, "This centurion has built us a synagogue. Save his servant." This is an unusual centurion. This centurion was in charge of one hundred soldiers. He was an officer. He had much wealth and he was moved by the agony of his servant because you see in verse number 6 he says, **My servant is at home sick with the palsy. He's paralyzed and he's grievously tormented.** This is a servant that couldn't sleep, a servant that couldn't get comfortable. This is a servant that couldn't find a moment's rest. And if I were Jesus I might have said something like, "Maybe you'll become a Christian now. Maybe you'll become a God-fearer now. Maybe you'll be monotheistic now." No, Jesus didn't do any of that. I'm so glad sometimes Jesus helps us despite ourselves.

8:7-8a

And Jesus saith unto him, "I will come and heal him." 8. The centurion answered and said, Luke says The centurion hears about it and sends more servants to stop Him on His way to the house. So the centurion is in the house, he sends one set of servants to get Jesus and he sends another set to tell Him to stop and to not come all the way to his house.

8:8

The centurion answered and said, "Lord, I am not worthy that Thou shouldest come under my roof: but speak the word only, and my

servant shall be healed. Now, could you please notice the order? Jesus is amazed first. And then in verse 13 He says, "Your servant will be healed." If it was a faith that knew the servant was going to be healed, then we could all sit back and say, "Yeah, I'd be amazed too." But the centurion expressed faith before the servant was healed and without any guarantee that the servant would be healed. It's the same thing as the leper, "Lord, if You want to You can make me clean."

8:9

For I am a man under authority, having soldiers under me: and I say to this man, 'Go, and he goeth;' and to another, 'Come, and he cometh'; and to my servant, 'Do this, and he doeth it.'" Here's this centurion saying, "Lord, don't even come into my house because I know how authority works. I'm told to do stuff by my superiors and I do it. I tell the soldiers under me to do things; they do it. And I tell my servant to do things; he does it. I know the power of words. So Jesus, all you have to do is say the word and I know my servant could be healed." Now I don't know if you understand exactly what he was doing there, but think about it. Do I have the idea of the centurion? What sets us apart from the world in our view of authority? Do we always find a reason to complain about the president? About the pastor? About the police? About the boss? About the new rules? Do we find five minutes a day to pray for our representatives through social media, news viewing, etc.? Or do our children just find us consistently disrespecting authority? Can I just help us out with something here? Maybe the reason our children don't respect us the way they should is because we don't respect our authority the way we should.

When the centurion says, "You have the ability to heal people just speaking," he was actually calling Him the creator God, Who spoke all things into existence.

8:10-11

When Jesus heard it, He marvelled, he was amazed. Can you imagine the King of Glory being amazed? Amazed! We're talking about the One who spun Aurora Borealis in the air like it was a scarf around His neck, and He's amazed? We're talking about the One that chucked the stars in the sky like they were oysters! And He's amazed. We're talking about the One that scooped out the Grand Canyon with one little silly flood, and He's amazed. Eight times the book of Matthew says that somebody marveled. This is the only time that Matthew says Jesus marveled. He doesn't marvel when people weep before Him. He doesn't marvel when lepers bow before Him. No, He marvels when the silly, unqualified, Gentile soldier puts faith in Him. An unexpected and an unpredictable Creator! How in the world is anyone marveling at this man but yet Jesus is marveling! I'm amazed to think about how Jesus is amazed.

Now think of all that Matthew has described Jesus as seeing. He's healing through every sector of the Jews of every sect, every level of every conceivable economy within religion, society and culture. They're being healed. They're being changed. Families are reunited. Conversions, yes. Mass baptisms, yes. John the Baptist's disciples dropping all to follow Him. Businessmen following a novel rabbi. Yet this did not prompt Matthew to tell us that Jesus **was amazed**. No. He's amazed when the under-qualified have simple faith. I can do that. I may not be able to do great things, but I can amaze Him if that's all it takes! And so can you.

11. And I say unto you, that many Unexpected people with less spiritual advantage and little opportunity. This is not a place for few and I'm glad He uses the word **many** because in Matthew 20:28 it says, "The Son of man came… to give His life a ransom for *many*." Everyone who enters the kingdom, enters the kingdom because their life has been paid for by the life of the great ransom, Jesus Christ. I'm one of the many. And you are too.

shall come Saints of all ages will be in that kingdom. Now isn't it interesting, here we are in a New Testament book, and I understand the New Testament according to Hebrews 9 begins when Jesus dies. So how much more significant is it for Jesus to tell His disciples, eleven of which will be born again in any case, that everyone from Adam forward who has been saved will be in the kingdom. Isn't that something? So think about all the people you're going to see there. Adam, Abraham, Abel, Eve, Noah, Shem, Noah's wife, think of all the people from before Calvary onward that we're going to be with in the kingdom. We could certainly have a discussion about what that is, but know this, Abraham of the Old Testament will be in the kingdom; Isaac will be in the kingdom; Jacob will be in the kingdom. We will be with them.

from the east and west, and shall sit down with this seems promised in Zechariah 8:8, specifically.

Abraham, and Isaac, and Jacob, in the kingdom of heaven. The kingdom is still coming and it is symbolized by a meal. Now, often we hear of prophetic schemes in Scripture. And we hear things like, "Immediately upon the rapture comes the judgment seat of Christ and the marriage supper of the Lamb." I'm not opposed to believing that we're going to eat. I think we will eat in the kingdom to come. Let us not forget that this thing known as a marriage supper of the Lamb is mentioned for the very first time in Revelation's 19th chapter. We're not going to go there, but I think it's very strange at the marriage supper of the Lamb I don't actually find people eating. It is actually the the oriental way of referring to a continual time of fellowship and rejuvenation and relaxation. Again, with all of the wonderful songs out there that have taught us our prophecy for the last 150 years, that seems like it might be nigh unto heresy for me to say that the marriage supper of the Lamb is not actually a meal where you get to sit and gorge yourself without getting full. The truth is we find Jesus mentioning to us this kingdom is a meal (Matthew 22:2)!

What are **they sitting** down for? Well, that is shorthand. That is another way of saying there will be great hospitality in the kingdom to come and yes, Jesus will be providing hospitality and we will be eating. And so all the way through the New Testament, all the way until we get to the reference of the marriage supper of the Lamb, will there be eating in the kingdom to come? Yes, but that is just shorthand for everything great that happens in the kingdom. Everything great. It's like a meal. It's like reclining at a meal with Abraham, Isaac, and Jacob.

And you might remember that in chapter 6 we're given right in the middle of the Sermon on the Mount, the Lord's Prayer of which part of it is,

Thy kingdom come. Thy will be done in earth, as it is in heaven.

And we found out at the end of chapter 7 there's a day coming when,

> *Many will say to Me in that day, "Lord, Lord, have we not prophesied in Thy name? And in Thy name have cast out devils? And in Thy name done many wonderful works?*

So, the kingdom is coming and it's pictured like a meal. And really it's just one of the many ways the kingdom is pictured in the Bible. Some people think that all we're going to do is be like a big choir in Heaven and I'm not against that idea, but that's just one of the things we'll be doing.

It seems like we're all made of flesh and bones. That means that we all have those things that are deep in our heart and we wonder is it passed hope? Well, the centurion says, "No." The leper said, "No." I'm glad I serve a Christ who can be amazed at simple faith.

8:12

But children of the kingdom is an old Hebrew style figure of speech, saying, "the Sons of Israel." You've heard of the "Sons of the Revolution," you've heard of the "Children of Israel," you've heard of all these short-hand things that say "by right of your birth you belong in that group." Jesus says, "By your birth you do *not* belong in this group. As a matter of fact, if that's all you have, then you're not going into the kingdom." God doesn't have any grandchildren. No one gets to go into heaven here because mom was a great lady and dad was a preacher. No one gets to go to heaven because, "My family has always been Christian."

You must believe the gospel. It hasn't changed. It's not going to change for you. You say, "Well, I don't know how to determine whether or not my children have trusted." I know. It's a frustrating thing, isn't it? So what you do is you keep preaching the gospel. When there's a lack of forgiveness, you preach the gospel. When there's a lack of understanding, you preach the gospel. When there's doubt, you preach the gospel. When they're afraid to die, you preach the gospel. When they're afraid to live, you preach the gospel. When they come to you asking questions, you preach the gospel. In every way, every sin has been crushed on Calvary and we will not serve our sin. But if we sin, 1 John 2:1,

> *...we have an advocate with the Father, Jesus Christ the righteous: 2. And he is the propitiation for our sins: and not for ours only, but also for the sins of the whole world.*

The difference between someone who's been cast into outer darkness and the person who sits down with Abraham is one of them believed and one of them didn't.

I'm glad it's that simple. I cannot tell you how many evenings I woke up in the middle of the night wondering if I missed the rapture. I can remember as a sixteen year old, now folks, I can remember walking to my parent's door, I'm talking sixteen, I'm not talking about twelve, I'm not talking about six, I'm talking about sixteen. When I woke up in the middle of the night and I'd hear a siren off in the distance… I heard the old rapture idea, you know where when the rapture happens everyone's missing out of their cars, all the planes crash and all that, so I went and stood by dad's door and if I could hear him snoring I knew I didn't miss the rapture, because I knew dad was saved. That's what believing praying a prayer saves you will do for you. In five years you'll be doubting your salvation because you wonder, "Did I mean it? Did I turn from all my sin? Did I really mean it?" You're not going to do anything more for your sins than has already been done by Jesus. Hallelujah.

shall be cast out into outer darkness: Inside the house you have full light, full celebration, a meal, a celebration. It's wonderful. It's in the evening of the day, it's at the end of the world and there is nothing but light in the house. But those to whom the door is shut, they are left outside in darkness. And you would think that that would push them to weeping and repentance but it doesn't. It turns them to **weeping and gnashing of teeth**, which is saying that they start cursing the One who put them outside. You would think that if a person wakes up in outer darkness, or a person has the door slammed in their face, you would think that they would say, "Whoa, whoa, whoa, whoa, whoa! What do I have to do to make this right?" That is not the nature of fallen man. The nature of fallen man is to, when they miss out on a privilege, they immediately get angry at the person that rightfully put them outside. And this is a theme in scripture. Just in Matthew, five times, "Wailing and gnashing of teeth," "wailing and gnashing of teeth," "weeping and gnashing of teeth," "weeping and gnashing of teeth," "weeping and gnashing of teeth," and two of those five times you find outer darkness in concert with it. You can say all day every day how unfair you think it is that people get to go to hell, but hear me well, the unfair thing is that Jesus would die for anyone's sins and that they would go to heaven.

The marvel is not that not everyone gets to go to heaven. The marvel is that anyone gets to go to heaven. And Jesus paid the price for the sins of the whole world. So when you find that scoffer that wants to talk about "the pygmy over in wherever that just loves God," they have a wretched heart like Bill Sturm's was, and it will be proven on that day when after a lifetime of living for themselves and fornicating in their tribes, and hating the God of heaven that created them and gave them life, when they are put out into **outer darkness** they will gnash their teeth against the One who put them outside. Do not give some sort of quality virtue to the person who will never hear the gospel.

"I don't like hell." Well, you want to spend forever with people with unregenerate hearts? It doesn't matter what I think. It doesn't matter what you think. It matters what the owner of the house thinks. And He'll shut the door on those whom He wants **out**side.

8:13

And Jesus said unto the centurion, "Go thy way; and as thou hast believed, so be it done unto thee." And his servant was healed in the selfsame hour. If Jesus were against war at all times, at all costs, this would have been a good time to tell the centurion. Two centurions in the book of Matthew: one of them is standing at the foot of the cross giving us a profession of Jesus being the Son of God and this is the other one. I would think that if Jesus was this pacifist that always hated war, and always hated the armies, and always hated government, and always thought that we should just sit in a circle and wear tie-dye and smoke hemp and wear flip-flops and sing "Kumbaya," this would have been a great time to tell the centurion. "You know, now that I'm here, I think I've earned a hearing. I just healed your servant. Let me tell you about war. Can't you give peace a chance?"

8:14

And when Jesus was come into Peter's house, He saw his wife's mother laid, and sick of a fever. Now I could sit right here for a minute and talk about Catholicism and how silly it is that the first pope had a mother-in-law, but you get the idea. Apparently Peter was married.

Here we find a continuity of Jesus saving the unexpected. If I were trying to reach Jews I would probably find more Jews to heal. But Jesus finds a leper, and then He finds a Gentile, a Gentile occupier by the way, a Roman centurion, and then He finds a woman. So what's the big deal about that? Well, probably one of the greatest evidences that the gospel writers were telling the truth about the empty tomb was that they allowed women to be the first witnesses in the historical account.

Back to this story, though, if I were writing the story, I would have Him maybe at the Sanhedrins' house, healing all their moms, maybe healing their sons.

One of the values of the other gospels is that it keeps us from time to time from moving in the wrong supposition. So, Mark and Luke tell us that the news came to the group that Peter's mother was sick. In other words, Peter didn't know his mother was sick before this verse. Mark and Luke tell us that they found out that his mom was sick. And so they're not walking around all day saying, "No, we don't want to heal mom yet. We have to go deal with the centurion's servant and we have to heal the leper." No. They actually just found out that Peter's mother-in-law was sick. So Peter's probably bothered because, you know, it wasn't like you could take some sort of medicine and gone goes the fever. This is really a big deal. We don't really know what was causing the fever but it was enough to where Jesus took time to heal her.

8:15

And He touched her hand, and the fever left her: Ok, how did He heal the leper? Help me. Touched him. How did He heal the centurion's servant? Spoke. How did He heal this woman, the mother-in-law of Peter? Touched. Touched, spoke, touched. **She arose and ministered unto them.** The disciples that were with Jesus, she arose and ministered to them. This is the verb form of the noun "deacon." She got up and "deaconed." And that might make some folks nervous but the truth is it could be a foreshadowing of Matthew 27 where we find women going to the tomb. It says that they ministered unto Him, they deaconed unto Him all the way from Galilee. So these women were consistently deaconing Jesus. This is not a sermon on deacons or whether or not a woman can be a deacon because there's a difference between deaconing and being in the office of a deacon.

For example, 1 Timothy 3:10.

And let these also first be proved; then let them use the office of a deacon, being found blameless. 12. ...the husband of one wife.

It's very difficult for a woman to be "the husband of one wife."

8:16

When the even was come, Now, look at this folks, He came down from the mountain, healed the leper, healed the centurion's servant. By the way you find out from Mark and Luke He actually journeyed part of the way, right? So He's had a full day. Than He gets to Peter and Andrew's house. We find out from Mark that the brothers still lived together and their mom was there.

When the even was come, they brought unto Him many that were possessed with devils: Or, you might have "demons" in your translation. Spirits.

and He cast out the spirits [with what?] **with His word,** The leper He healed with? Touch. The centurion's servant with? Word. Peter's mother-in-law with? Touch. And these demon-possessed with? Word. All right, so touch, word, touch, word. I'm just making sure we're following that. Why?

and healed all that were sick: A lot of people today wonder why Jesus doesn't perform healing miracles like He did. The fact is Jesus is showing Himself to be the One who saves us from our sin. And so He does miracles to prove that He is the next Moses. Moses came doing miracles; the last Moses needs to come doing miracles and so here He comes doing miracles. By the way, was there a Bible before Moses? No, there wasn't. Moses wrote Genesis, Exodus, Leviticus, Numbers,

Deuteronomy, right? Basically, there was no Bible before Moses and so Moses comes and he has to validate the fact that he is bringing a message from God by doing miracles. Like the leper's hand out of the cloak, like the snake on the ground, like the water into blood. And so for 400 years there's no new Bible. Malachi is the last one we hear about and so there's no new Bible, and Jesus is coming, and what needs to happen to validate that He is a messenger from God but doing miracles? And so He, like Moses, comes doing miracles. And today the only reason we would need anyone to be doing marvelous miracles is because we're about to get another testament.

And so in verse 15 clearly the reason Matthew left out Mark's info about Jesus raising her by the hand and Luke's info about rebuking the fever: so if you put all three gospels together you have Jesus coming in, taking her by the hand, speaking the word, rebuking the fever, and raising her up. But Matthew says that it happens by Him touching her, verse 15. Now, why is this? Why? I suppose it's because he's emphasizing the pattern of touch healing, speak healing, touch healing, speak healing. Now why did he do this? I'm not sure why, but probably the touching to remind us that Jesus had no risk of being ceremonially unclean.

8:17

That it might be fulfilled which was spoken by Esaias Isaiah **the prophet, saying, "Himself took our infirmities, and bare our sicknesses."** So this is the fifth quotation from Isaiah in the book of Matthew. This is the eleventh quotation from the Old Testament all along.

Christ did what was necessary to please the Father and because of this the result was He was consistently fulfilling prophecies about Him. He was audacious enough to say "I only do those things that please the Father," that He was busy pleasing the Father, and oh by the way, Matthew found out later that He was fulfilling Isaiah 53:4.

There's probably 20 years between the time of this story and the time of the recording of the story. And I believe every word of it. I'm not afraid of the scholars. They don't make me feel silly. I'm not somehow intimidated by the fact that there were 20 years between those two events. I welcome stupid comments because I'm tired of Christians feeling like they can't speak in a scholarly setting. I'm not intimidated by knuckleheads that read the Bible once or twice and then think they have the authority on what it says and what it means. I'm not the least bit intimidated by that. You're a scholar that they dream they were, in church two or three times a week, learning about your Lord by reading the word of God. That is dynamite! It is God speaking through the page and it's why we get up and read it every day.

Now the reason that is really something is because we just heard John the Baptist in chapter 3 say, "I'm not even worthy to carry Your sandals." And here is the Matthew writer saying that Jesus, the One of whom we're not worthy to carry His sandals, is willing to carry our infirmities and our sicknesses. What a God. What condescension!

Does Isaiah 53:4 which is talking about the ministry of Jesus before Calvary, you do see that, Matthew says it does. This is not crucifixion verse. This is the pre-crucifixion life of Jesus. He bore our sicknesses and carried our reproaches and our sins. That is good news because that means that that wasn't a Calvary specific thing; that is a life specific thing. Why is He doing this?

So I don't want to minimize at all here His fulfillment of taking away our sin, but what this also means is that He actually took on the nature of what caused sicknesses and infirmities. Do you suppose He was ever sick? He had Adam's flesh, yes? Then I would say that He once or twice or three times was sick. And if He was ever sick we know it wasn't because He was sinful, it was because He took on, Romans 8:3 says, "He took on the likeness of sinful flesh." Can you imagine Jesus the Son of God maybe having a sore throat? Can you imagine Him working hard to pull the nets into the boat and maybe having body odor?

He took them on Himself. Their infirmities, the weaknesses He took them on Himself. To the point where He; would try to do something about it, to be emotionally involved, not apathetic, not sympathetic; empathetic. Sympathetic means, "I kind of feel sorry for you. You're kind of cute about that little sorrow thing, run along, it will be ok. I'll be praying." Empathetic means, "I am really grieved with you. Yeah, we're in the same boat, that's right."

8:18-19

Now when Jesus saw great multitudes about Him, He gave commandment to depart unto the other side. 19 a certain scribe came, Scribes were the teachers of the word because no one knew the word like they did. They spent their time counting letters and making sure that this copy looked like that one. They're the kind that say, "I know what the word says. I'm with it all the time. I know the standard."

And here's a scribe. He has spent all his days before the age of 12 in a rabbinical school. He has memorized all of Genesis, Exodus, Leviticus, Numbers, and Deuteronomy. If anyone knew the Law, it was this guy. Why is he coming to Jesus? What is it about a man that knows everything? What is it about this guy who has spent all his time around the Bible? Why is he coming to Jesus? We might think right off the bat, "Well, it must be because he was getting saved." But I think that it was because he as a scribe found all of a sudden the possibility that he could get a better position somewhere else. After all, Jesus was coming with John the Baptist promising a kingdom.

Well, who wouldn't want that? Every time they looked around they saw the clanging of a Roman spear or a shield. Every time they turned around they'd see their daughters being raped by the Roman soldiers. Every time they turned around their last mule was being taken. Every time they turned around the taxes were being doubled. Matthew knew this all too well because he was usually the one collecting the taxes. Who wouldn't want a kingdom? Particularly a scribe who spent all of his time copying the Old Testament and knows that a kingdom is coming?

and said unto Him, Master, I will follow Thee whithersoever, wherever,   And so, if this man is doing miracles like Moses, He must be the next king like His dad David. "So I think I'd like to get on board with Him. And since I know this is a winning circus, Master I'll go with You anywhere." He was unaware that his loss was greater than he thought. He thought he would lose some friends and gain greater fame and really, the greater connection to the greatest teacher ever because Jesus is the greatest teacher ever. He's the greatest miracle worker probably since Moses. Elijah an Elisha have nothing on Jesus. You have to go all the way back to Moses to find someone impressive like Jesus. So the scribe says, "This must be my next ticket." He's that guy that can't get away from the idea of getting the best positions for his career. He was really to lose his friends and he just didn't know it. The fame that he had he was going to lose and he said, "I'll go with You anywhere."

Thou goest. And Jesus saith unto him, The foxes have holes, and the birds of the air have nests; but the Son of man hath not where to lay His head. "You'll go with Me anywhere? You'll go with Me even to the realm of the homeless? Is that really what you had in mind, scribe? Is it really what you had in mind: that you're going to give up everything? Lose everything? You really have in mind to get in this boat with Me never to return because everyone will have seen you with Me? You will not ever be allowed in the temple again if they find out you were with Me. Are you ok with living under a bridge? Are you ok living in guest rooms if someone is gracious enough to put you up? Are you ok with that?"

Scribes were teachers, not followers of teachers. This means that the man had the utmost respect for Jesus. And by the way, Jesus had no credentials. It's not like He could pull out a seminary degree or a rabbinical school degree. No. He was supposed to have been, the King James Hebrews 12 would call Him, "a bastard child." One whose father is unknown or at least his mom and dad played around before they finally got married. You can find that in John 8. He was accused of it at least twice in the Gospel of John alone, of being a child of fornication. So Jesus must have been very impressive. Everyone suggested that He was born out of wedlock. No one was guessing, "Oh by the way, I bet He's virgin born." No one could say, "Here's the Rabbi that He followed." And so it is a marvel that he approaches Jesus and calls Him "Master" in verse 19.

What was it about the presence of Christ that brought this magnanimous, world-shattering respect from someone who did not have to give it to Him? To some degree even today, I find myself praying to Jesus, "I will give it all up for You, so long as it's for a better gig." No. Let's make it personal enough so you know how human I am. "Lord, if following You means that I can stay in America, if following You means that all of my bills are paid on time every month, then I'll go with You wherever You go."

So Jesus, in other parts of Matthew we're going to get to, says things like, "You will lose your life if you seek to gain it. And if you seek to keep it, you will lose it." And so Jesus seems to be saying, "What if you knew you would lose your life? What if you knew you would lose your job? What if you knew you would lose your home? Exactly how full of conviction would you be then?"

"I'll go with You wherever You go, Jesus, so long as I don't risk losing my pension." I would like to see payback immediately from the kingdom. And so we see the honest truth is that strong profession does not really mean commitment. It might mean you can just talk loud. Let's be honest. There were plenty of people around the ship, why in the world did Matthew record this guy? What was it about this man that butted into things there and said, "I'll go with You wherever. I'll be a part of Your crowd." This wasn't some sort of yacht. This was a limited, a vessel, a ship, a boat. You're not getting a whole beach-worth of people on there, as a matter of fact just the disciples, and not all 70, probably lucky to get all 12. What makes this man think that he is going to get on the boat? Well the fact is, "I'm a scribe. I belong on the boat with the new king." So we can get into the boat tonight if we want to. Because if the scribe can, I can. But just know that the cost is the same as it is with the scribe.

And another of His disciples We don't find them named. I don't know who this is. I don't know who he is in Mark or Luke. I don't know who he is at all. It's another disciple. And we find out in Luke 10 that Jesus had 70 disciples; 12 apostles, but 70 disciples. It could have been any of those 70.

"Lord, suffer me first to go and bury my father." But Jesus said unto him, "Follow Me; and let the dead bury their dead." And when He was entered into a ship, His disciples followed Him. And, behold, there arose a great tempest in the sea, insomuch that the ship was covered with the waves: but He was asleep. Clearly Jesus needed a break. Very tired. It's been a full day. And can you see the Son of God, who has never "not been," and He is experiencing weariness. And not just weariness, but weariness with people. And not just weariness with people, but weariness with people to whom He is ministering. Who wants to get in line and tell Jesus how unspiritual He is? Why is He sleeping in a boat in the middle of a storm?

I think we should do well to realize that if we don't recognize our own physical limits they will soon catch up with us. Before you know it we're short with people. Can you imagine the Son of God emptying Himself, making Himself of no reputation, Philippians 2, to the point where He had to sit down on a well and ask a young lady for a drink? Or, get into a boat and nap?

This is the second time we find Him getting into a boat to get away from people. He was a pretty popular man. Of course, if all the hospitals in Hickory, NC were empty and it was because of one guy, probably—he would be very popular. As a matter of fact, that's what I'd like to wage to some of our healing evangelists out there. If you're so altruistic and godly, why don't we just have you come to Hickory. We'll not let you speak; we'll take you around to all the hospitals, and the funeral homes.

But what I don't find in the verses to follow is that Jesus chases this man down the beach and says, "Hang on. I know I was a little too rough there. Can we talk about this? I was kidding. The truth is I do have a place to sleep tonight. And life is good. The benefits package is pretty good. I've got lots of people with lots of money. I think that you would like it. Uh, I do need more disciples. What do you think? Would you rethink this? Can we agree? Compromise? Meet in the middle?" No. Jesus chased him about as much as He chased the rich young ruler (in Matthew 19).

8:20

Self-indulgence was not Jesus' plan. I mean, think about what Jesus calls Himself at the end of the verse. The Son of Man is homeless. The Son of Man. Now please, let me ruin Theology 101 for you. People say "Son of God refers to His deity; Son of Man refers to His humanity." You read Psalm 80:17, you read Daniel 7, what you don't get is the idea the Son of Man is a title for a human being. It's the title for someone who belongs on the throne with the Ancient of Days.

Psalm 80:17 says that the Son of Man is "the Man of Your own right hand." Excellent. "Well if He belongs at God's right hand than He belongs in Rome in charge of the Senate, and I will gladly get into His boat." "Nope. I'm not going to Rome. I'm not going to self-indulge," Jesus says. This is the first time Son of Man is mentioned in all of Matthew. It is such a big deal that when Jesus stands before the High Priest on the eve of His death, when He says to the High Priest, "I am the Son of Man," the High Priest rips his clothes out of anger in front of Jesus. If Son of Man just meant, "Hey, I'm a dude," no, this is a power packed, fully immersed word that means, "I am divine in every way and I don't even have a place to sleep tonight. So why should you?" Wow. Certainly the One worthy of such a regal, magnificent name should have lavish digs. The creator of the birds doesn't have a place? The creator of the nest of the birds doesn't have a place. The creator of the fox doesn't; the creator of the den of the fox doesn't have a place to sleep.

8:21

And another of his disciples said unto him, Lord, suffer me first to go and bury my father. Now, this is a little strange if we read it at face value. As 2014 Americans we might think, "Well that's reasonable. All he wants to do is conduct a funeral and be on his way." But the truth is in the Oriental world, "Let me go home, care for him and wait for him to die, render proper respects," which, by the way, included weeping for weeks, "Let me settle the estate and collect my inheritance." In all probability his father was not even yet dead. "Let me go bury my dad" is a middle-eastern, Oriental old-fashioned way of saying, "He's not dead but he's old, and I need to wait around until he is dead, settle the estate, give him a proper burial, do 30 or more days of weeping, get my inheritance, then I'll follow You." It seems honorable. Whether he was asking to hang out with dad until he died or whether he was seeking one more year, he wanted more time. Presumably he wanted more time with family or he wanted more money, but Jesus comes back with something that is rather alarming.

8:22

But Jesus said unto him, Follow Me; and let the dead bury their dead.

Matthew 6:33 But seek ye first the kingdom of God, and His righteousness; and all these things shall be added unto you. Take therefore no thought for the morrow: for the morrow shall take thought for the things of itself. Sufficient unto the day is the evil thereof.

And so Jesus is giving a real life example application of 8:21-22. "I tell you what, you quit worrying about when your daddy's going to die and you follow Me." And what was Jesus saying, "Your dad's not important?" No, of course not. Several verses earlier He's healing someone's mother-in-law. This is not reflective of a callous Jesus. This is reflective of a Jesus who knows the heart of a man who's using his older father as an excuse for why he's not following Jesus. Oh, but this man sounded very spiritual. "Let me take care of dad." You remember how many brothers the rich man in hell had. He had five brothers. That was probably very typical. The parable of the prodigal son, for example. There's a son who stays home and a son who's a prodigal. So probably there was plenty of help around the house. And Jesus knew what the man wanted was more time and more money. He had out-of-order priorities. It's not Jesus picking on the fact that you want to help your elderly parents, it's because Jesus is knowing it is absolutely and positively an excuse.

I know this sounds drastic, "Let the dead bury their dead." But is this any more drastic than chapter 5?

5:27 Ye have heard that it was said by them of old time, Thou shalt not commit adultery: But I say unto you, That whosoever looketh on a woman to lust after her hath committed adultery with her already in his heart. And if thy right eye offend thee, pluck it out, and cast it from thee: for it is profitable for thee that one of thy members should perish, and not that thy whole body should be cast into hell. And if thy right hand offend thee, cut it off, and cast it from thee.

If you wanted to hear it in Matthew 8 language, "Let the dead bury their dead. You do what Christians do, and you let everyone else do what they do."

8:23[38]

And when He was entered into a ship, His disciples followed Him.
Do you remember Matthew chapter 4, when Jesus finds His disciples they are fishing? They are mending nets and they are in a boat. That's the last time Matthew tells us anything about a ship and Jesus tells them, "Follow Me." Just think that through. The question one must ask is, "Is this really a message from Matthew?" I mean, what is he trying to get us to see here? The last time he shows us anything having to do with Jesus, the disciples, and a ship, He's actually calling them to leave that ship. So the only thing as audacious as being asked to leave a ship when you'd probably rather stay is being asked to board one when you'd probably rather not. They were happy with the first one. It meant security. It meant something they were ok with. Dad. Business. Future. So let me say it again. It was already audacious. It was already with audacity that Jesus invites the disciples to leave the ship that they wanted probably to stay in. And then He tops it off by asking them to get into a ship that they'd probably rather not get into.

All they knew was, "I stuck to Jesus when the scribe didn't. I stuck to Jesus when that dude right there, who was just waiting for dad to die, didn't. I feel pretty committed." And Jesus introduces them into something called a storm. Jesus wouldn't do that, would He? Was He omniscient? Would He really send His disciples into a ship that was heading into a storm? Would Jesus really do that? I'm afraid so.

Wasn't it God the Holy Spirit sent down from the Father onto Jesus? Wasn't it that same Holy Spirit, that after He comes upon Jesus, "It is not time to go on tour. It is not time to speak to coliseums. It is time to go into a dry and lonely desert." "You mean to tell me You anointed Jesus to send Him into a desert?" Given the Godhead's desire to make you and I like Jesus, isn't it at least within the realm of possibility that God would tell us to get into a boat that is heading towards a storm? Many of our theologies don't allow for that. Many of our prayer lives don't allow for that. We cannot fathom having better motives than the scribe perhaps, and better motives than this other disciple, only to be rewarded with a storm. Maybe they were thinking,

---

[38]Additional information on this episode can be found in my commentary on Mark (4:35-41).

"Here we are, willing to be homeless." Maybe they were thinking, "Here we are, ready to let the dead bury the dead."

8:24

And, behold, there arose a great tempest this comes from the same Greek word that we get our word "seismograph" from. There is a great shaking on that lake when the cool air coming up over Mount Beatitude, Mount Hermon, and all the mountains on the north shore of the Sea of Galilee and mingles with the hot air, or the warmer air, of the Sea of Galilee and it just created a horrible, shaking tempest in the sea.

in the sea. Insomuch that the ship was covered with the waves. Oh my. The One who sent them into the storm, what is He doing? **But He was asleep**. One of Matthew's purposes is to compare Christ with the greats. One such comparison is Matthew 12:38-40.

Now I wonder, who is that sleeping in the boat? Because the last time I read about someone sleeping in a boat he was running from God. His name was Jonah. And the only way to get the storm to calm was to take the sinner and pitch him in the water. Jesus doesn't immerse Himself in the water to stop the storm. He immerses Himself in our humanity, sleeps in the boat, gets up and stops the storm. Behold, a greater than Jonah is here.

8:25

And His disciples came to Him. This was a little different than the last time the disciples came to Him.

> *Matthew 5:1 And seeing the multitudes, He went up into a mountain: and when He was set, **His disciples came unto Him**.*

And then Jesus gives them hard lessons and hard teaching for three chapters. Yes, the multitude was watching. The multitude is always watching when Jesus speaks to His people. Mark that down.

> *John 13:35 By this **all men will know** that You're My disciples, because you love one another.*

The multitude is always watching. They're watching. Please don't think that all 1,700 friends of yours on Facebook are Christians. They are watching you. All of your complainings about the president; they see it, but the focus here is on the disciples coming to Jesus, and what does He do in 5:1 and following? He does what we would like for Him to do. He gives us a Bible study.

But here, in 8:25, when they come to Jesus they're not hoping that He teaches them anything. Things were not as surreal. Now see, in today's world we think that everything can be fixed with buying a book about "fill in the blank - raising kids, having a marriage, finances, you name it. Witnessing better, better prayer life…" We think everything can be fixed in our life when it comes to discipline, by sitting through one more series. And certainly you know that this pastor thinks there is a purpose for pastoring, which means "to feed." Of course I think that. But all of a sudden we realize that discipleship is not just about hearing great teaching; it's about also learning in the storm.

8:26

And He saith unto them, Why are ye fearful, O ye of little faith? In this parallel passage in Mark or Luke it says, "Why is it that you have no faith?" So really it was so little that it might have been accounted as negligible, or none.

O ye of little faith Then, I want you to notice how skillful Matthew is by aid of the Holy Spirit. I do want to remind you these are Jewish disciples, and they are men who are well versed in the Scriptures, and He calls them, "ye of little faith," when just 16 verses earlier Jesus described, in verse 10, a Gentile centurion. And He says, "I have not found so great faith, no, not in Israel." Now think about the comparison. God is clearly showing us the faith of those who should have it with the faith of those who probably shouldn't.

Do you see how He both heals a servant and calms the storm by speaking the word? I want to point out to us please that the one who had great faith in all of Israel, his servant was healed by the speaking of the word. And those who had **little faith**, who should have had vast amounts of faith—their storm was taken care of by the same mouth that healed the centurion's servant. Jesus is not the One that changes. Do you think, men, that the One who made these waters and the chemicals that comprise them is going to be swallowed up by them? I mean, do we really think that? "Jesus, You're in danger of perishing." No, the One who made the waters is asleep on the boat. When we realize that Matthew 1:21 tells us what's going on here, we see that Jesus peels back the heart in the middle of the storm and saves us from more sin.

All the while, while Jesus is marveling at the faith of a centurion in 8:10…

8:27

But the men marvelled, saying, What manner of Man is this, that even the winds and the sea obey Him! In the story of the centurion you have great faith and Jesus marvels. But when people really have an opportunity to marvel at God is when He brings calm into a life despite the lack of faith in the believer. Because then we can't say, "The reason God brought a great calm in your life is because you are a man of amazing faith!" God gets a lot of glory if He decides to bring calm to our great storm despite our un-great faith, and people step back, to include us, and **marvel** at what the Mighty Christ we serve. So God uses even our failures in faith to bring praise to Himself.

8:28

And when He was come to the other side into the country of the Gergesenes, Mark and Luke it describes one man, not two. And here's a possible reason: only Matthew speaks of two demoniacs, but he does not thereby contradict Mark and Luke. Neither of the other evangels refers to the only one, they just refer to one. Perhaps one of the two dominated the conversation, but Matthew elsewhere includes two characters. For example, he gives both accounts where two blind men were healed, and Mark and Luke, when they cover them it's one blind man; in Matthew it's always two. Could be that he was particularly interested in two people bearing witness and establishing fact in a court of law, according to Mosaic requirement. But Mark and Luke don't say "only one man was possessed of the devils." It just says "one of them was," and so that's not a contradiction.

And then there's the question of, "Well, is it Gadara or Gergesa, or the place of the Gergesenes?" You see in chapter 8, verse 28, it says, "into the country of the Gergesenes," and some versions have "of Gadara." Regardless of version solutions, in Mark and in Luke it says it's Gadara. And so which is correct? What you need to know is that they're really close. And if you decide it's supposed to say "Gergesa" or "Gadara," I want you to notice that it says **they went to the country of the Gergesenes**. It doesn't actually say "they went to the town of Gergesa." Then you might notice in verse 34 that they are not in a city; rather that they go to a city. So they are in the country during this episode and there is a city nearby. So this is, I suppose, easily handled when you just consider the fact that they could be in the country of one and the city of the other is close by. You know, there are parts of Fayetteville that are not in Fayetteville proper, but they're called Fayetteville because they're so close, right?

I just wanted you to be aware of that because there's a chance that some numbskull is going to come up to you someplace, a workplace, place of education, and they're going to say, "Your Bible has mistakes in it." And you can say, "Well, like where?" And very rarely will someone come back to you and say, "Well, here's one." No, they usually don't. You understand, of course, that they've probably never read it. But you can say, "What's the contradiction?" And they can say, "Well, Mark and Luke say Gadara, and Matthew says Gergesene." And you can say, "Well you might notice it doesn't say they went into Gergesenes, but rather **to the country where the Gergesenes live**. That area there, verse 28."

there met Him He just returned from calming the storm and now, he's about to calm a man. The story is very simple. These men, watching the storm from their hillside cemetery little know that the reason the clouds parted and the winds surrendered is because the Master of the Seas controls, yes, even the demons of hell, and He is coming to their beach.

I guess the point of Matthew, along with showing us that Jesus is the God out of Whom life-giving words come, and that God is more than able to calm the storms in us. I don't want to act like these two demon possessed men were people that were good saints before the demons found them, they probably weren't.

"Why is Jesus here?" Why does He cross over? And I'm not really sure I get the idea exactly why He crossed over. I have a couple of ideas. It doesn't say, "And by the way, here's why Jesus crossed over." Did He really cross over for these two guys? I mean, think that through for just a moment, because we're left thinking, if we compare Matthew, Mark, and Luke, that He made the trip across the Sea of Galilee, at the end of a very busy day, when He was ill-rested and needed sleep. Do you think that He knew who He was going to see when He got off the boat? So there's a possibility that He crossed over only for these two men. Would Jesus come back? Does Jesus return to the place known as Decapolis, which is from two Greek words that mean "ten cities," "deca" and "polis." And so we find there are several questions we don't get answered if we just look at Matthew.

Now, I would be tempted to treat this in a manner of the harmony of the gospels, where I take Matthew, Mark, and Luke, like I've been keeping myself from doing all along, and give you a full picture of what's happening here. But the problem is that that wasn't the intent of Matthew. The intent of Matthew was to keep you questioning—asking questions that matter and looking for answers that are provided.

29. And, behold, they cried out, saying, "What have we to do with Thee, Jesus, Thou Son of God? We suddenly realize that the demons know Jesus. Now how do they know Him? Maybe it's because in chapter 4 Jesus is casting out devils. Is it because they spoke with others from the preceding evening? I mean, it was the evening before you know.

Do you think these demons knew one another? Do you think they spoke? Eight miles away cohorts of the demons are being chucked out of people, and word is spreading. How do they know who this Jesus is? Well, because in chapter 4, old kingpin, the devil himself, figured it out. I don't know if there was an after action review after the temptation in the wilderness, but there's a strong possibility that Satan talked with his minions and identified the problem. You see, Satan said in Matthew 4, "Since You're the Son of God, would You command these...?" There was no denial. And you might say he was suggesting, "If You're the

Son of God…" but the Greek is actually double emphatic, "Jesus, You are, You are the Son of God, so make these stones into bread."

There was no doubt in the devil's mind who Jesus was. All he had to do was listen at Jesus' baptism and God told you who Jesus was, "My beloved Son." So, these demons had better theology than most so-called Christians. They address Him, the One who Matthew has previously told us is the One who is the Son of David, the great king; the One known as the Son of Abraham, the great promise; the One known as the Son of Man, the great One at God's right hand. And He is now made known to us boldly as the "Son of God," publically for the first time. At the baptism it was just John the Baptist and Jesus that heard the Father.

Matthew told us in the first chapter that Jesus was the son of a virgin and we heard again from Hosea (quoted in Matthew 2) that Jesus was the Son of God ("Out of Egypt have I called My Son"). We heard from the record of the Father at Jesus' baptism, recorded by Matthew in chapter 3, that Jesus is the Son of God. But the first person who calls Him the Son of God is Satan himself, and the first person that heralds Jesus as the Son of God is a bunch of demons in a non-Jewish region known as Decapolis. We have no record of anyone calling Him the Son of God in Israel yet, but the demons. Mark her down, tonight they know who He is too. Oh, and they fear Him!

Art Thou come hither to torment us before the time?" "Oh, Jesus, Son of God, You've come here to torment us before the time." "No, I'll give you another five minutes." I mean that's really all that happens. I don't really know exactly why the pigs decided to run into the lake other than the devil loves murdering. John 8:44, the devil's a liar, he's a murderer, and a murderer from the beginning. So, he kills pigs too. And I don't really know what happens to the demons after the pigs drown. I guess that's one of the questions I don't need answered.

8:30-31

31. So the devils (or demons) **besought Him, saying, "If Thou cast us out, suffer us** (or allow us) **to go away into the herd of swine."** We find out from the book of Mark that there were two thousand, approximately. They said, "What is Your name?" You might remember from the other gospels. They said, "We are Legion." So, thousands of demons are in these two men. Off over there was a herd of swine, presumably enough for there to be one pig for each demon although that need not be since a 1 for 1 ratio was not the requirement when they were possessing human beings.

What are we to make of what Mark and Luke call 2,000 pigs? Aren't they important to God? Didn't He make those pigs? Sure He did. But I would say that if Psalm 50 is correct, and He owns the cattle on 1,000 hills, then He probably owns the thousand swine on one hill. And He's willing to sacrifice them, for two people. Stick that in your green-tree-hugging, fruit-loop pipe, and smoke it.

So we see in this episode not just the Lord's power over the storm, but His power over the demons, and this shows His deity because He does both with His words. His words! The same words that crafted every high hill and every deep valley. Those words that spoke life into the earth. Everything that's beautiful. Oh my goodness, the 38th chapter of Job makes me want to sing! It's just amazing. They just love Him, the Creator, and they don't even have any idea what they're doing. The trees of the field clap their hands! Everything bows before the Creator and so these pigs say, "Yeah, we'll die for two men." If that's not enough, He demonstrates ownership by sheer forbearance to worthless demons in allowing them to drown an entire herd. Why? Probably because God values swine less than people.

> Matthew 12:9 And when He was departed thence, He went into their synagogue: 10. And, behold, there was a man which had his hand withered. And they asked Him, saying, "Is it lawful to heal on the sabbath days?" that they might accuse Him. 11. And He said unto them, "What man shall there be among you, that shall have one sheep, and if it fall into a pit on the sabbath day, will he not lay hold on it, and lift it out? 12. **How much then is a man better than a sheep?** Wherefore it is lawful to do well on the sabbath days."

Well there you have it. Matthew said, "I'll comment on myself and record Jesus' words here." Even sheep, the clean animals, are not as important as man.

34. And, behold, the whole city came out to meet Jesus: and when they saw Him, they besought Him that He would depart out of their coasts. So here are the townspeople beseeching Jesus to go. Now consider what Matthew is doing here: We have an entire town of people asking Jesus to go, when in Matthew 8:5 we have one Gentile centurion beseeching Jesus to come. Clearly Matthew is showing us bookends to a great narrative. He puts things in comparison and contrast to one another, and he says, "Let me show you a man full of faith. Not like anyone in Israel. More faith than that, and he beseeches Jesus to come and heal his servant. But at the end of the chapter we have an entire town of unregenerate, faithless people that do not value people more than animals, and what do they want? They want Jesus to leave."

And that's what we're finding in our society, folks. That's why we act more like animals all the time. Because we serve the creature more than the Creator, Romans 1 says. And we debase the image of the Creator like unto a four-footed beast, Romans 1 says. Why? Because we did not like to retain God in our knowledge, so God gave us over to reprobate minds.

Oh so, well here we go, our question here is revisited, "Could Jesus have done more?" Think through this with me. If they came out and gave Him a parade; if they came out and brought more demon possessed people; if they came out and brought their sick, like other cities did What would Jesus have done for them?

Now you say, "You're just introducing a meaningless scenario." Really?

> *Matthew 13:53 And it came to pass, that when Jesus had finished these parables, He departed thence. 54. And when He was come into His own country, He taught them in their synagogue, insomuch that they were astonished, and said, "Whence hath this man this wisdom, and these mighty works? Is not this the carpenter's son? Is not His mother called Mary?"*

All right, what is His own country, His own city, in verse 54? Nazareth. The last verse of chapter 2 says so. They're identifying His family members. He came into Nazareth and He spoke parables…

*"And His sisters, are they not all with us? Whence then hath this man all these things?" 57. And they were offended in Him. But Jesus said unto them, "A prophet is not without honour, save in his own country, and in his own house." 58. And He did not many mighty works there **because** of their unbelief.*

The implication is that He would have had "many mighty works."

I will not be so bold as to say He crossed the Sea of Galilee for just two men. Ultimately He was willing to do that, because that's what He did, and He knew what would happen. But I would say, humanly speaking, God was making a legitimate offer to a city on the east side of the Sea of Galilee and they would not have Him. He could have done more, and would have done more if the townspeople would have desired Him more than their precious economy.

Now, let me see if I can put this is our language. If we cared more about Jesus and souls than we did about our precious value of the dollar, I guarantee He would do mighty works in our midst. Isn't that what your Bible says? If we would care more about that than the news, we would see that He could do, and would do, many mighty works. But He doesn't because of our unbelief.

Matthew seems to be emphasizing not the response of the man who is healed of the demoniacs, because in Mark he talks. And he's not necessarily concentrating on the helplessness of a world of therapy or treatment, because in Mark it talks about they tried to bind him with chains but he broke them. The response of a people who found the souls of men less valuable than their luxury, their convenience, and their economy.

Often we'll think of our church, and we think of people who don't know how to flush toilets and it annoys us. They don't seem to respect pews enough to keep their shoes off of them and it ought to bother us, I suppose. They don't seem to respect signs that say, "No beverages but bottled water in the sanctuary," and it rightfully annoys those who appreciate order and respect. But sometimes, I will not pick somebody up for fear that they will make my car smell like cigarettes. Other times I will not hug a man who looks like he has not bathed in some time.

Think about it. Swine carcasses floating everywhere. Two men breathing deeply, hugging their families for the first time. Jesus and His disciples talking among themselves. The sun is rising in the morning with the clouds in the sky. The disciples are still rubbing sleep out of their eyes because they just maybe caught a nap right before the boat hit the beach. The fresh air blowing in from the sea and a fishing vessel across the field, sitting on a beach. Can you see it?

Now turn around. Can you see a group of people coming out of the city? And they're not happy that two men that haven't been home in years are now able to go home. They're not happy that two men that haven't been able to hug their babies before bed are now able to do that. They're not happy that two men that have a right mind for the first time in a long while are able to think clearly. They're not happy that they're able to sit calmly. Oh they'll say, "We're happy about that." But, they cared more for hogs than human souls and that often happens today. I suppose what seems not so obvious is they wanted to be rid of the effects of demons but not at the cost of having a Savior to do it.

I wonder where would I be if Jesus did not cross the sea for me? I wonder how happy I am when Jesus makes an effect in someone's life? They don't say things exactly how I say them. They don't do things exactly how I do them. All they can say is, "I believe in Jesus. He's my Savior." I wonder how we would react if we had people that don't look churchy come right and sit on this front pew on Sunday morning? I wonder if we would be more upset about our self-respect being drowned in the sea? Or upset that we have people that could be affected by a demonic world? I often wonder when we get people that come to us from other churches what it would be like if we were churches that were passionate about finding people that didn't have a church. I often wonder what would happen if we decided to go after people that didn't already claim to be Christians. Oh listen, It would get messy.

Chapter 9

And He entered into a ship. Jesus spent a lot of His time around these vessels and you might remember that we are now on the same weekend. Now it is Sunday morning of this weekend, very full weekend, and once again we're in a boat, and once again we're on the Sea of Galilee.

Now Mark's account, which I don't go to very often, but it keeps us, when we know Mark and Luke's accounts, it keeps us from making mistakes in how we interpret Matthew. And Mark makes us very well aware that **His own city** is Capernaum, not Nazareth, but Capernaum. And we also realize that at the end of verse 1 (Mark inserts this from his version) that they were waiting for the Lord when He landed the ship. Now that is a long, long ministry outing.

Let's try to remind ourselves what we've seen in the book of Matthew so far, particularly chapter 8. You might remember Jesus comes down from the Sermon on the Mount and Matthew is very careful with continuation language to make sure we know we're still happening on the same day here. He comes into Capernaum on the north shore of Galilee and He heals a leper by touching him. And then He heals a centurion's servant by speaking the word. And then He heals Peter's mother-in-law by touching her. Then He casts out devils by speaking the word. Then He wants to get on a ship because He sees the multitudes and He's trying to get away. And we see time and again that the Lord Jesus is still moving in that direction.

And so what we find is that Jesus is still in the middle of His day. He's still handling ministry, which is proving to be at times pretty exhausting and inconvenient. Not every weekend was like this. This is a cross-section. But if there's anything that's timeless truth for us to learn from today, it is that there will be times when serving the Lord will wear you out, and you need to get a break, take a rest, and you'll need to step away.

What that looks like today is it means that you're not answering your phone right away. It means that you're letting the voice message pick it up. It means that you have a particular section of your day that you answer email and that you don't feel like you have to sit down as soon as you get it and answer it. And so Jesus gets on a boat and He sleeps in the rain He created. He leaves them on the beach. And there they are watching as the boat disappears, into the sea. And not just into the sea, but into the storm that is waiting for them on the sea.

and passed over, and came into His own city. Now folks, He was just there the night before.

9:2

And, behold, they brought to Him a man sick of the palsy lying on a bed: And this is that story that in Mark[39] and Luke they tell us that they let him down through a roof. Jesus is actually preaching in a house when they let down this sick man in the middle of the preaching.

Son, be of good cheer not because your friend's roof is still intact, because it wasn't; not because you're walking around, because he isn't; not because everyone is on your team, because most people in that day assumed that he was in wicked sin. No, "Be happy, because I am forgiving your sin." And why is He forgiving his sin? We only have one answer from the text. He has faith. Isn't that what your verse 2 says? "When Jesus saw their faith, He said to the sick of the palsy." "Their" includes his. But what we don't find in this passage is a Sinner's Prayer in this passage. We don't find a trip down the aisle. We don't find a card being filled out. We don't even find a baptism. All we find is the faith of a sinner and his friends and the salvation given from a Savior. And he isn't even walking yet! All he has is forgiven sins. And Jesus says, "Get happy." That tells me that he didn't look happy. That tells me he might have been aware that his problems were brought on because of sin. He didn't look happy. "Son, be of good cheer."

How does He heal the man? By speaking the word. And that is enough to be happy about. And how? Why? What is Matthew's idea? Matthew 4:4, "It is by every word that proceeds out of the mouth of God that man lives." All through this passage of Scripture we find Jesus being portrayed as God, out of whom life comes. Think about it. Even the Pharisees knew what He was saying.

---

[39]More notes, therefore, can be found in the "chapter 2" portion of the commentary on Mark by this author.

**And, behold, certain of the scribes said within themselves, This *man*
blasphemeth. And Jesus knowing their thoughts** "Jesus saw their
thoughts"? That is actually the meaning of the text. They're thinking it
and He is seeing it. The all-watchful eye of God conveyed in the body
of His Son Jesus. What a wonder!

"What's easier for Me to say?" Remember, they didn't tell Jesus
this. They thought it. He said, "Why do you think this evil in your
hearts?" How upsetting it would be to be wicked only internally and to
have somebody know it in that very same room. And not just know it,
but say something about it. "I know your hamper is full. Let me empty
it, right here in front of everyone."

**said, Wherefore think ye evil in your hearts? For whether is easier,
to say, *Thy* sins be forgiven thee; or to say, Arise, and walk?** When
God is in the flesh, and we find out from Matthew 4:4 (the author of this
same passage) says, "Man will not live by bread alone, but by every
word that proceeds out of the mouth of God," all of a sudden this One
named Jesus who will save His people from their sin, here for the very
first time in the book of Matthew is saving someone from his sin. "Now
we're getting down to business," Matthew says. "Your worst enemy is
not leprosy, or a sick servant, or a fevered mother-in-law, or a demon-
possessed neighbor, or a disjointed disciple, or an unruly wind, or a
tumultuous wave, or demon-possessed cemetery dwellers, or even palsy.
Your worst enemy, and My greatest victory, is sin and I'll save you from
it."

And, what else do we have here to testify to the fact that Jesus is
divine? "My sins are forgiven?" Imagine the reaction of this man. "My
sins are forgiven." This man found forgiveness of sins that made his
body ache each morning. Let me say it again. Most of the time we're
limited to the guilt we feel, or the stress of covering up the guilt we feel.
This man woke up to aches and pains that his sin caused every morning,
knowing by his own countenance that his sins caused them. How
audacious. He says He can forgive sins.

9:5-6

For whether is easier, to say, *Thy* sins be forgiven thee; or to say, Arise, and walk? Now, if Jesus was interested in not embarrassing people that was the wrong move. And then He says to the man, it tells us in the parenthesis, He now speaks to the sick of the palsy, **But that ye may know that the Son of Man hath power on earth to forgive sins,** What if we would say. "Junior describe God."

"Well, He's omnipotent, all powerful…"

Yeah. Ok, well here's Jesus forgiving sins right after He got done commanding nature and corrupting demons, sending them away to pigs. That's where they belonged. So Jesus is omnipotent, and now we're seeing He's omniscient? Well no wonder He feels like He can forgive sins. If we were to describe God we would use these very same attributes! And here Jesus in the flesh, omnipotent and omniscient, and we would even say He's omnibenevolent: He is nothing but good. He shows up and He wants a man happy, and so what does He do? He gives him the cause of his weakness that day, which is sin. Apparently Jesus knew the only way a man could be happy in this situation was to cure him of his sin.

In the previous chapter, two demon-possessed men are identifying Jesus as the Son of God.

> *8:20 And Jesus saith unto him, The foxes have holes, and the birds of the air have nests; but **the Son of Man** hath not where to lay His head.*

What does Jesus call Himself? Son of Man. Then the demons in chapter 8 and verse number 29, what do they call Him? Son of God. And then here Jesus calls Himself the **Son of Man.** So, I'm not Jesus, but if I were I would be using the phrase that packs the most punch for me. Think this through. The later part of chapter 8, He's talking to Jews; He says He's the Son of Man. In chapter 8, later on in the chapter, He's across the lake in Decapolis, a place where Gentiles live, and they called him the "Son of God." He's back across into Capernaum where Jews live and He calls Himself the **Son of Man.** Isn't that interesting? Son of Man to the Jews; Son of God amongst Gentiles; Son of Man among the Jews.

Who is the first one to call Jesus the Son of God, publicly? Well, it was these demons. Before that, who? Well, it was Satan. Satan: "Since, You're the Son of God." And before that, it was God of the Father. Now think this through with me. Satan calls Him the Son of God. Around the Jews Jesus calls Himself the **Son of Man.** Demons call Him the Son of God. Around the Jews Jesus call Himself the **Son of Man**. There must be something to this title, **Son of Man.** Now hear me well, if it only meant that He was a human being that would be really pointless. What would a Jew think about that reference? No wonder they would be calling Him blasphemous. A human being can forgive sins? That's preposterous.

So here's Jesus, looking at a man who can't move because of something having to do with his sin and He says, "Your sin has an end." And that's why Jesus uses the title **Son of Man**. You see, to the Jews, the Son of Man was as good as God (considering Psalm 80 and Daniel 7). It wasn't that Jesus was saying, "Oh, no, no, no, the devil's wrong. I'm really just a human being. Oh, no, no, no, the demons are wrong. I'm really just a human being." Nope, **Son of Man** to the Jews was like saying Son of God to the Gentiles. That's why "Son of God" is so much in the book of John. Because it's written 40 years after the other three gospels and it's primarily to Gentiles.

9:7-8

And he arose, and departed to his house. 8 But when the multitudes saw *it*, they marvelled, and glorified God, which had given such power unto men. Power to do what? To heal and forgive sins. Once again, Matthew reminds us that the very presence of Jesus is the presence of God. He starts in chapter 1 with this idea of His name is Immanuel meaning "God with us."

9:9-10[40]

9 And as Jesus passed forth from thence, from there, **He saw a man**. How powerful is that? He sees everything. What's so special about that? It was special to this man.

---

[40]More details to be found in the author's works on Mark (2:13-17) and Luke (5:27-32).

He saw a man named Matthew, Matthew waited nine chapters to tell us about how he fit into this.

And He saith unto him, come here, **Follow me.** Luke says in Luke 5:42, "He left all and followed Him." Matthew doesn't include that. It might have made him feel, "Look at everything I left for Jesus." And so sometimes what Matthew doesn't say speaks as loudly as what he does say. Matthew doesn't want to be the star of this show and so he just says, "He got up and followed Him."

10 behold, many publicans. Oh my goodness. There are empty tax offices all over the city. And entire guild of thieves is empty on a Sunday. And where are they? They're eating.

This goes well with 9:2. We have a need for friends to bring their friends to Jesus. When we see Matthew being a follower of Jesus, it's only natural for him to introduce his friends to Him.

And they came and sat down with Jesus and His disciples. Around a table you'll have people almost lying down on one side and reaching over their heads to the table—leaning backward upon the person behind them when wishing to speak to them. Now perhaps you understand what it means when the rich man saw Abraham and Lazarus "on his bosom." What were they doing? Reclining at a meal in paradise. Or,

> *John 1:18 No man hath seen God at any time; the only begotten Son,* ***which is in the bosom of the Father,*** *He hath declared Him.*

9:11-13

When the Pharisees saw it they said unto His disciples, Why eateth your Master with publicans and sinners? But when Jesus heard that, He said unto them, They that be whole need not a physician, but they that are sick. 13 But go ye and learn what that meaneth, I will have mercy, and not sacrifice. He quotes from Hosea chapter 6. It's really kind of ironic and funny that He's telling Pharisees who are friends with the scribes that they should learn anything. "Go and learn." Jesus looks at the student of the Old Testament and says, "You know what you need to do? You need to go back and read Hosea 6. Go and learn what this means." Well, they're the teachers. He's telling the teachers, "You need to be learning."

We've been in this weekend now for five chapters. Perhaps this whole weekend is being included because it's the weekend in which one of the most notable apostles was converted. I mean look at Matthew 10:2, "Now the names of the twelve apostles are these..."

So maybe, maybe Matthew is including this passage to show us how it all led up to his conversion. We find out in 20:28 that the "Son of Man did not come to be ministered unto, but to minister, and He gave His life a ransom for many." So how does Jesus "save His people from their sins?" He does so by giving His life a ransom. That means that there's a lot of people out there that are hostages. Hostages to sin. Contextually, remember, they are not sitting down and reading this with a cup of coffee after they let the dogs outside. No. This is a one-sitting book. A congregation of believers is reading this perhaps, and they found out His name in chapter 1 and why He's called "Jesus/Joshua," and why in chapter 20 He promises He's a ransom. Think about that.

And now he says, "Not only will I tell you about the day I became a follower of Jesus; I will even tell you what happened that evening." Matthew is not on the boat going to Gadara or coming back from it. Matthew's not on the boat. And before we get on the boat there is a certain disciple who is told to follow Jesus and he doesn't. That would be called a rough day. When a disciple won't even follow the Master. And I think the lesson for us is that "you never know what will happen overnight."

Is it natural to assume that this tax collector was well known enough to have known about the discussion on the beach the night before? I don't know. What prompted Matthew to get up and leave everything to follow Jesus? I don't really have an answer.

13 But go ye and learn what that meaneth, I will have mercy, and not sacrifice features a double rebuke by treating them first as learners and then secondly as beginners, as if they've never read the verse in Hosea. It's interesting how Jesus shows us that we need not have identical situations, with the narrative, to have an accurate reflection of God's character. I don't know that we could call Jesus sarcastic but I'm leaning that way because you notice He didn't take the time to explain the context of Hosea 6 to them. He knew that citing one Scripture out of one chapter of the Old Testament would teach them that God hasn't changed. He would still prefer mercy to sacrifice. He's not saying, "Don't sacrifice." He's saying, "If you're going to give Me just one, give Me mercy." So it's not a different God somewhere that changes between Malachi and Matthew. It's one God. God's character hasn't changed," in 700 years at the point of this writing. God still wants us to give people second chances. Mercy. Giving favors of forgiveness. But please remember that it only occurs through the door of repentance. No **mercy** for the unrepentant. No doctors for the well.

This is the first time since Jesus has quoted Scripture since He combatted the devil in Matthew 4. Think about it, how big of a deal is this? We find Jesus quoting Scripture twice so far in Matthew, once against Satan, the other against the scribes. How very similar. They must be of the same spirit. The devil loves to destroy lives and the Pharisees would rather the sinners stay sinners and the sick stay sick. If they only knew that there's no doctor for them and no Savior for them. How unfortunate.

And here we have a man that has been saved for a few hours finding a way to get his friends around his new Master. And I suppose one of the biggest marvels of this is you have a man from the tribe of Levi following a Man from Galilee from the tribe of Judah. Life seems so empty and so he leaves all to follow Him.

This goes well with the theme of Matthew, doesn't it? Because Jesus saves **sinners** (Matthew 1:21), and the real problem with the Pharisees is they can't be saved. No good Pharisee ever gets saved. No good scribe ever gets saved. You have to become a **sinner.**

9:14[41]

Then came to Him the disciples of John, saying, Why do we and the Pharisees fast oft, or often, **but Thy disciples fast not?** Oh, the Pharisees love questions. In verses 10 and 11 the Pharisees are asking questions. Not entirely honest. I mean, we don't know if the disciples

---

[41]More to be found in the author's commentary on Mark (2:18-22).

don't fast. So, let's talk about the Pharisees and their fasting. You've heard Luke 18

> *And He spake this parable, Jesus did, unto certain which trusted in themselves that they were righteous, and despised others: Two men went up into the temple to pray; the one a Pharisee, and the other a publican. The Pharisee stood and prayed thus [Here's what I do: I fast twice in the week.]*

9:15

And Jesus said unto them, Can the children of the bridechamber mourn Maybe in your version it says, "Can the wedding guests mourn?" We see this same language in Ephesians 2's "children of wrath." **Children of the bridechamber** are those who belong with the bridal party, those who belong with the bridal procession, those who belong with the bridal ceremony.

Now the question is, why is Jesus making a connection between the fasting that the disciples are not doing and the mourning that they're not doing? So why were the disciples of John the Baptist mourning? Well, we have a clue. If you look at Matthew 4:4 we get into the temptation of Jesus. Jesus defeats the devil, no surprise to any of us. In 4:11 the devil leaves Him, and behold, angels came and ministered to Him. In 4:12, Jesus had heard that John was cast into prison, He departed into Galilee. So why are they mourning? Probably because he's in prison.

And then Matthew 14, John the Baptist is at least in prison. In Matthew 14 that didn't happen, or I should say, didn't happen on that timeline right then and there; it's recorded previously.

> *Matthew 14:1 At that time Herod the tetrarch heard of the fame of Jesus, And said unto his servants, This is John the Baptist; he is risen from the dead.*

Well in order for him to be rising from the dead he must have already died. He's already dead by the time chapter 14 comes along. He's in prison in chapter 4. So he's at least in prison, and possibly—depending on how in order Matthew records the things from chapter 4 through chapter 14—dead. And so why are they fasting? We're told it's because they're mourning, it's at least because John's in prison; it's possible he's been dead, he's been killed.

children of the bridechamber The Bible is full of wedding terminology: Seven days in a bridal chamber with Jacob, being required of Laban, to fulfill Leah's week. Wedding coordinators like John in John chapter 3. Wedding guests, here. Wedding feasts. Wedding processions, like the ten virgins. Remember that? The pre-marriage covenant where Jesus says, "This is the covenant of My blood." All marriages are covenantal. The best man, we already talked about that. The bridal chamber, which is John 14, "I go to prepare a place for you." The bride, Ephesians 5.[42] The father of the bride, Paul said, "I have espoused you to another" (2 Corinthians 11:2). The father of the groom would be God the Father.

But the days will come when the bridegroom will be taken away from them, and then they will fast. Christ here endorses the principle of Christian fasts. We have religious reasons to feast, rather than **fast.** We call it "fellowship." We're obviously expected to fast. You say, "How obvious is it?" Well, it's obvious enough that in Matthew chapter 6 Jesus says, "When you fast, anoint yourself, and your Father who sees it in secret will reward you openly." He assumes we would fast. Maybe I can just remind us that some spiritual exercises are not designed for our entertainment.

And some fasting should perhaps be incidental, like, "I'm so distraught that I haven't thought about eating," and that is probably why there is a connection here to mourning. From the disciples' perspective, Jesus is here prophesying of a time directly when He would leave them and there would be occasion to mourn, and surely one weekend there was reason to mourn. And now, there are times when we mourn, and this is not beyond the realm of possibility for a believer, for in Matthew's Sermon on the Mount Jesus says, "Blessed are those who

---

[42] Now, I don't want you to become scared. Some of you muscle-men might be thinking, "This is really weird. I don't want to be married to a man." At least that used to be what people thought, but we have legislating judges now that said it's ok. It's just a way of God relaying to us the union between Christ and His people. It's like saying "He's the head and we're the body." It's like saying "He's the vine and we're the branches." It's like saying "He's the shepherd and we're the sheep." It is just another way of saying we're one with the Son.

mourn." You're not less of a Christian if you mourn. But at a wedding, people are happy; they're eating. So it made no sense for the disciples of Jesus to spend time mourning and fasting while the bridegroom is with them.

This is the first time we see of Jesus referring to a wedding, a groom, a bride. Why is He doing it? Well, let's see if we can get in the mind of the writer one more time here. He's quoted the Old Testament several times through this gospel, but he is now for the second time this chapter referring to the book of Hosea. The first was just a verse or two previous (verse 13). That is a direct quotation out of Hosea chapter 6. Here—two verses later—Jesus calls Himself something that was referred to in Hosea chapter 2. When He says that He is the bridegroom, think of the connection that makes in the mind of the Pharisee. For it was Jehovah God who said in Hosea chapter 2, "You will call Me your husband."

And so here is Jesus, as if it wasn't already in your face enough this chapter, He claims to be the Son of Man. He can read your thoughts. He says He can forgive your sins. He just told the wind to shut-up. He just sent the raging waves to the beach. He's done everything that you would expect the Creator God to do. He's healed with His voice. Out of His mouth men live by every word. And now, now, as if that's not enough, He claims to be Jehovah by taking a reference in Hosea and applying it to Himself. "I am the Jehovah of Hosea 2 and you are My wife."

9:17

Neither do men put new wine into old bottles: else the bottles break, and the wine runneth out, and the bottles perish: but they put new wine into new bottles, and both are preserved. Animal skins. Jesus is talking about the skins of an animal expanding. Well, if you take an old skin that is already expanded and you put new wine into it that hasn't expanded, once it expands the bottle breaks because the skin is not going to stretch anymore. Jesus is saying, "Your old system is like an old garment with a new patch. It's like an old bottle with new wine. It's just not going to fit."

9:18

While He spake these things unto them. Who is speaking to whom, because apparently from verse 17 Jesus is still talking and He says to them, "Men do not put new wine into old bottles: or else the bottle breaks, and the wine runs out, and the bottles perish: but they put new wine in new bottles, and both are preserved." Presumably since Jesus is talking when verse 18 starts, it must be assumed that we are on the same day.

And when we look back at the beginning of the last discourse, verse 14, "then came to Him the disciples of John…" "Then" is a very connective word in the context. It's not just a loose, "Oh and then the next thing I'm going to tell you…" No, this is something that happened immediately upon the heels of something else. So verse 14 is in the same chronology as verses 9 through 13.

And we realize "as Jesus passed from there," verse 9…It must be taking place in the episode that takes place in verses 1 though 8. Before you know it, you realize that everything that happens in chapter 9 happens on the same day.

And, when you see that in chapter 9 verse 1 that He's leaving the Sea of Galilee, you see that that He crossed over in verses 23 through 27. Then you realize that you're dealing with the same weekend. I'm trying to get you to see is chapters 8 and 9 happen in two days time. This is impressive. It's exhausting. If we want to be able to carry ministry out we better be willing to walk with the Father, because I don't know of anything more frustrating than trying to do God's work in my power. That's even more frustrating than doing my work in my power. At least I don't expect anything when I do my work in my power. I don't expect eternal reward. I don't expect refreshment. I don't expect spiritual benefit.

Now why does this story exist? Why did Matthew put it in here? I know the short answer is God told him to, got it. But humanly speaking, why did Matthew include the story? We don't have every weekend of Jesus' life being recorded in the gospels, do we? How could that be? I mean, three and a half years of ministry, probably. If you recorded every weekend, and if every weekend took two chapters like this one, add to it the Sermon on the Mount, which probably was taught near the Sabbath…and you can fit how many weekends into three and a half years? 175? So about 175 weekends times five chapters. So we have this one weekend. Why is this one recorded? I think it's probably because one of the twelve is converted. Not only that, but here we have Jesus giving them an exercise in understanding that their old religion, verses 16 and 17, will not house the new glory of Jesus. Will not.

behold, there came a certain ruler, and worshipped Him. That has the idea once again of kissing the hand of the Son and all of a sudden our mind goes back to Psalm 2:12: "Kiss the Son, lest He be angry, and ye perish from the way, when His wrath is kindled just a little bit." Here's a man that is kissing the Son out of reverence. Kings from the East, the wise men, were found first worshiping Jesus in Matthew 2. And then a leper, the beginning of Matthew 8 bows down and worships Jesus. Think about it. An unclean leper kisses the hand of Jesus, worships Him. Now that would be yet another outstanding opportunity for Jesus to say, "Stop treating Me like God." But He doesn't. Matthew 9 has just been billowing over with proofs that Jesus was either very sick and loony, or He was absolutely God. He either was God or thought He was.

behold, there came a certain ruler, and worshipped Him, saying, My daughter is even now dead: Matthew says, "My daughter is even now dead: but come and lay Thy hand upon her, and she shall live." Mark says, "My little daughter lies at the point of death: I pray Thee, come and lay Thy hands on her, that she may be healed." And Luke 8, he doesn't speak at all. We're just told by the writer, "She lay a dying." Well clearly you can see there is a difference between what Matthew says, "She's dead," and what Mark and Luke say, "She's dying." **Dead,** in Matthew 9:18, is a verb. This is really the issue. So, if you're to take the word "dead" and make it a verb, here's what it would sound like: "While He spake these things unto them, behold, there came a certain ruler, and worshipped Him, saying, My daughter is even now dying."

9:19

And Jesus arose, and followed him, Why does it say He arose? How do we know He was sitting? Verse 10 says He was sitting in Matthew's house. What about that? I love context. Still in Matthew's house, reclining. Jesus has just got done talking through the window to some Pharisees that hated the fact He was sitting with sinners and His disciples weren't fasting. That's very important that you get that fixed at

Matthew's house. While He yet spoke here comes Jairus (named in Mark), and Jesus gets up.

I just love the words that Matthew chooses by aid of the Holy Spirit, the last time "Jesus arises" He is waking up in a ship. The words could have been found between these two places any number of times but they're found twice in this preceding context; one here, one in a ship. Once He gets up to calm the storm on the sea; once He gets up to calm a storm in a man named Jairus' life. I need to be assured that Jesus will get up and speak to my storm.

It is so very tempting to jump to Mark and Luke. We get all kinds of details from there. We find out from those passages that the girl was also 12 years old. And we find out that this ruler was a ruler of the synagogue. But Matthew could have told us those things. I can't build a sermon on the fact, "Well, the girl is 12 and the woman has been sick for 12 years." I can't do that. That wouldn't be true to Matthew. If I want to preach this not from a survey from the life of Christ but a survey of what Matthew wanted you to know about Jesus, I can't veer over to Mark and Luke. Mark and Luke keep me from making mistakes like saying, "I don't know what kind of a leader this man was. He might have been a ruler of the troops." Nope, it says in the other gospels he was a ruler of the synagogue. Matthew could have told us those things and now, now we're supposed to learn something else. We're supposed to learn that at the beginning of the chapter we had all kinds of faith, and some of the faith came from the man who was sick of the palsy. The Lord saw their faith and He said to the man, "You're sins be forgiven you." You remember that episode. Here, we don't know anything about the little girl's faith. Nothing. We have no sign in any of the passage that this little girl had faith. It would be an absolute guess for me to say this little girl believed that Jesus could heal her. It would be reading into the text. Here, we have a daddy believing for his children. There are times when the children are so weak because they haven't lived the life you've lived.

and so did His disciples. Matthew is telling us we need to take part in whatever Jesus does. "I don't know what God is up to, but I'm going to stay close to Him so I can be a part of it. He doesn't hardly do anything I want Him to do, but He does everything right so I'm going to get next to Him so that I can be a partaker of what He does." Wherever Jesus goes, no one stays dead! No one stays hungry. No one stays sinful. It just seems like everything that's evil runs away when God does something. The disciples are simple enough. They say, "Well, if He's going we're going to go." And by the way, this happened in verse 23:8 "And when He was entered into a ship, His disciples followed Him." Matthew 9:10 "They sat down with Him and His disciples."

9:20-22[43]

And, behold, a woman, which was diseased with an issue of blood twelve years, came behind Him, and touched the hem of His garment: and touched the hem of His garment: 21 For she said within herself, If I may but touch His garment, Leviticus 15:25-32 basically says this was illegal. So I don't know if you're following this or not, but if a woman is hemorrhaging she cannot really touch anything without that becoming unclean and no one can touch her without becoming unclean.

God is very serious about keeping His place clean, and this might seem very, very unusual to have such seemingly stringent rules, but it's the Lord doing basically what He wants to do. And then he goes into men that are unclean and others who are unclean.

> *Numbers 15:37 And the LORD spake unto Moses, saying, Speak unto the children of Israel, and bid them that they make them fringes in the borders of their garments throughout their generations, and that they put upon the fringe of the borders a ribband of blue: And it shall be unto you for a fringe, that ye may look upon it, and remember all the commandments of the LORD, and do them; and that ye seek not after your own heart and your own eyes, after which ye use to go a whoring: That ye may remember, and do all my commandments, and be holy unto your God.*

You are actually expected to look like you belong to the Lord God Jehovah. Now for us that might mean something different, but I just want you to be aware it is not a new concept that Christians look like Christians. So this idea, "We dress properly; be a good testimony." No,

---

[43]More can be found in my commentary on Mark (8:25-34).

we dress properly because God said so. Here we are in Numbers 15 and God says, "Here's one of the ways you're going to dress like you belong to me: you're going to put fringes on your borders." You say, "I don't know why." Well, He said why. "Because it will remind you about My commandments." And so there's a number of tassels on the border of the garment that made people realize, "Here are commandments of the Lord," and every time you looked at them you looked at commandments of the Lord. That's pretty important.

But, what I want you to notice particularly is verse 38, where it says they put fringes on the borders of their garments. Now that word borders is interesting because

Deuteronomy 22:12 Thou shalt make thee fringes upon the four **quarters**.

"Borders" (Number 15) and "quarters" come from the same Hebrew word.

Malachi 4:2 But unto you that fear My name shall the Sun of righteousness arise with healing in His **wings**.

"Wings," "borders," "quarters": all three come from the same Hebrew word. I don't know why the translators translated them that way, but when you realize in Malachi 4:2 that the Lord is promising that in the days of John the Baptist there is going to come a rabbi with healing in his tassels. Healing in the borders of his garments. All of a sudden tonight's passage makes some sense.

I shall be whole. This is not the word *therapeuō,* which is where we get our word therapy; this is not the normal word for healing found in our Greek New Testament that's been translated to English. As a matter of fact this is only the third time in the entire book of Matthew that this has been used. Think about that. If you count the verses in each of the chapters it is a big deal to look and see that you have thousands and thousands of words being used and here you have this word "whole." And it's a word that we usually find translated as "saved." Why isn't she asking to be healed?

I do want you to know though that her point was that she wanted to be saved. Now that is very strange. If she knew Malachi 4 as well as I think she knew Malachi 4 then she was expecting the Sun of Righteousness to bring her some healing. And oh, by the way, some forgiveness. Because after all, she couldn't hide behind the temple or the tabernacle. She hadn't been there in twelve years. Maybe she knew the ultimate need she had was forgiveness and there was no being fooled into thinking she was forgiven because of sacrifices that she had offered, for she had offered none. What a dilemma. A woman who has been wanting to get to the place where she thinks she can find forgiveness like every Jew thinks they can find forgiveness, particularly if you read Malachi chapter 3, where it says that He will come suddenly to His temple. "Surely the Lord is interested in working still through that temple in Jerusalem and I can't even go there. I haven't been able to go there for twelve years.

"Certainly if the Lord can heal two who had been demon-possessed…I wonder what He can do for me? If the Lord can sit with tax collectors; if the Lord can tell the Pharisees they have no part, I wonder what the Lord can do for me. I wonder, if the Lord can make a man get up and walk, I wonder what He can do for me? I wonder, if He can heal a fever of this Apostle's mother-in-law, I wonder what He can do for me? If He can heal a leper, what can He do for me? If He can heal a centurion's servant, then maybe, maybe twelve years is not too long."

Nothing else has worked. Mark and Luke go out of their way to say she spent everything she had and nothing did better, but rather grew worse. The doctors had all discharged her.

"We can't do anything for you."

"My doctors don't even want me. My family can't have me. Every day I've had, I've had alone. But He has tassels and if He is doing everything that the book says He's doing; if He really is turning the hearts of the fathers to the children, and the children to the fathers; and if He really did have a messenger before Him that brought the way of righteousness; then this is that Sun of Righteousness and He has healing in His tassels. And since he's righteous, and I have no chance of being righteous, maybe I can even have more than that. Maybe I can be saved."

This is the third time this word saved has been used in the book of Matthew. The first time was found in Matthew 1:21, "You will call His name Jesus for He will save His people from their sin." So Matthew starts out in chapter 1 by saying, "Let me tell you about this Jesus. It's His very character to save people and not just save them, no." Matthew says, "save them from their sin."

You know you have to be mighty low to grab His tassel. That's why many of us will never touch it. We've never seen the tassel because we've never been low enough to see it. Everything's going pretty well. We've never really been brought low. There's always been room for us in the crowd. We've always been accepted. People have always liked us. We've always been "most likely to succeed," the best athlete, the best soldier, the best wife, the best mother, where everyone talks about how great we are; and every now and then we should look around and realize when it's nice and thick in the crowd and we're right in the middle of it…we can't get to the tassel. Sometimes I think that those who are least accepted are the most blessed. They seem to find their way to the tassel.

22 But Jesus turned Him about, and when He saw her, He said, Daughter, be of good comfort; thy faith hath made thee whole. And the woman was made whole from that hour. And we look after the story, "Yeah, the woman who was sick 12 years, she's healed, but, my little girl is still as good as dead. Good as dead." It could have been right there that we find this ruler of the synagogue said, "Well I guess that's that. I'm glad to see that old thing is healed. Doesn't really fix my problem." Nope, they continued to walk. Because this man is learning what those at the tomb of Lazarus learned: that even when it looks like He's way too late, He's still on time.

"All hope is lost!"

"No it's not. Don't you know that man lives by every word that comes out of the mouth of God" (Matthew 4:4)? And Matthew's been showing us that for six chapters now. That this is God in the flesh and when He speaks people live. It doesn't matter if it's a leper. It doesn't matter if it's a sinner. It doesn't matter if it's a paralytic. It doesn't matter if it's a tax collector. It doesn't matter if it's a demoniac. It doesn't matter if it's a fevered mother-in-law. People live when God speaks. Here's a man with some amazing faith.

When He saw her, He said, Daughter, be of good comfort; thy faith hath made thee whole. He uses the same word she uses. "Daughter, be of good comfort; thy faith has saved you." Notice she didn't pray a single prayer, never walked an aisle. She simply believed and that believing caused her to reach her arm out and grab a tassel, and she found healing.

9:23[44]

And when Jesus came into the ruler's house. It's almost like, "Ok, back to our story. We're back to what started this episode."

And saw the minstrels and the people making a noise. And by the way, I find Jesus going into peoples' houses a lot. Chapter 8 verse 14, He went in Peter's house and healed his mother-in-law. Chapter 9, He went into Matthew's house and ate with his unsaved friends. And then we find at the end of verse 23, we find out that those who don't know the Lord, when they comfort, they're really just making noise. And sometimes they're hired to do so, and they're hired with things like superficial friendship and ridiculous flattery. There's no end of mourning for people that have no hope. That's why in 1 Thessalonians 4 is says, "We will not sorrow like those who have no hope." We'll sorrow, but not like those who don't have hope.

These mourners, they're just old bags. He puts the mourners out because they don't fit. They won't work. Jesus is here to heal. He's not here to make you feel like you're needed. **He put the mourners out.**

Now all of a sudden we have Jesus again (like when he calls the woman out who "touched" Him) wanting to be the center of attention because there are no mourners stealing attention from Him. Verse 31 says that even more people noticed him just as God desired. Only God could be so audacious and egocentric as to demand that everyone else get out of the room, "So that I can raise this little girl from the dead." Certainly if Jesus was interested in everyone knowing about it He would have kept them in the room. "Hush a minute! I can't even hear Myself

---

[44]More to be found in my commentary on Mark (5:35-43).

think!" No, He says, "Get out." Not very hospitable. These were professional mourners and once again, like Gedara, they did not like their dollars being affected. What did they do when Jesus comes in and says, "You're really crying for nothing." What did they say? They **laughed Him to scorn**. "You're just so ignorant. You think that heaven can come down to earth and heal woes on the planet? You really think that, Jesus? You're such a nit-wit." He said, "Get out." And **He put them out.**

9:27

And when Jesus departed thence. From the house of the man whose daughter Jesus healed.

two blind men followed Him, crying, Now is there any doubt in your mind what Matthew is trying to do? He's trying to show you Christ is the fulfillment of Isaiah 35, for one thing.

He's also trying to show you the most important weekend in his life. The weekend when Christ, earlier in the chapter, called him from his daytime job to follow Him. This is a very important weekend. And here we are coming up finally, after three months of preaching, on the end of a weekend. A very important weekend.

We find another ailment that Jesus can heal. Another one. And once again we have those who have much faith like these blind men and those who express no faith like the dumb man. I mean, he was demon-possessed. And so once again we find in this chapter this wide array of dilemma, perhaps. You have people who can exercise faith and people who cannot. No one is going to say that the dead little girl could exercise faith. And Jesus raises her. And no one is going to say that a demon-possessed man (or two of them from the last chapter) that are living in the cemetery could exercise faith. But we know that a man who is living and has palsy can. We know that men who are not demon-possessed and are blind can.

So, there's this pitiful Savior. Pitiful. It means He's full of pity.

This takes place, like the rest of the weekend for the most part, in Capernaum. I have to tell you though, I don't think that this is the first blind person Jesus healed. I don't think that at all because earlier in

Matthew chapter 4 it says He went out healing all types of sicknesses, all types of diseases, healing lunatics; end of chapter 4. I've got to tell you, when I know this is not the only blind man, the only blind men that Jesus healed, all I can think is "more blind people." I don't mean to be irreverent here, but more "dumb people." As soon as Jesus is done healing them somewhere in Palestine another man is born blind, or going blind. Or another person is possessed by devils. So I guess, I look at this and I think, "What is the point?" Every time He does something it seems like there remains something to be done.

So we remember that 9:5 is pretty handy here: "Whether it is easier, to say, 'Thy sins be forgiven thee; or to say, "Arise, and walk?"' But that ye may know the Son of Man has power to forgive sins, get up and walk." So remember that every sign Jesus does is to prove to you and to me that He has power on earth to forgive sins. Because you've observed Him healing physical, visible maladies. So then be filled with faith that He can heal the invisible maladies as well. The ones that nobody sees.

That the reason we clean our houses is not that dirt and filth are completely eradicated. We remember that the reason that we do things that are seemingly undone as soon as we do them, is to remind people that "the Son of Man has power on earth to forgive sins." Think about it. All day, every day we do things that will have to be done again tomorrow. Why? To draw attention to the One who has power on earth to forgive sins. All day we do menial tasks. Why? So that people, by looking at us, will see what Jesus looks like when He does them. And so they "might know that the Son of Man has power on earth to forgive sins." So, here's Jesus healing another blind man; another blind pair of men. Why do we go to work to pay bills when they need to be paid again next month? To remind people that "the Son of Man has power on earth to forgive sins."

The reason Jesus did the same things over and over and over again, He told us, was so that we could see that He has power with God to forgive sins. He drew attention to Himself by doing things that were no problem for Him. And it didn't completely eradicate; have you ever met a blind person? There are many on the earth. Why did He heal these when there are more to be healed? So that we would read the New

Testament and say, "This Man must also have the power to forgive sins."

and saying, Thou Son of David, have mercy on us. Now I want you to see with the care with which Matthew is writing. **Son of David** is used here. Look at verse 6 of this chapter, "But that ye may know that the Son of Man hath power on earth to forgive sins." So we have Son of Man, Son of David. We look back at the 8:29, "And, behold, they cried out, saying, What have we to do with Thee, Jesus, Thou Son of God?" So Matthew is showing us in less than a chapter that Jesus is the Son of God, the Son of Man, the Son of David. Very systematic.

9:28

And when He had come into the house, the blind men came to Him Remember, on our chronology it's Sunday evening. Jesus has had a pretty eventful weekend: two trips across the lake, one of them in the rain; it's doubtful that He slept much, if at all, because when He did try His disciples came and woke Him up. He's been healing people. And by the way, you know how I'm kind of a stickler about staying in the passage, but if you take Mark and Luke, this weekend is even fuller than Matthew makes it look. It's even fuller. I could add about six or eight other events that took place in Capernaum on this weekend.[45] So humanly speaking I think I know why He kept walking, but this is very much unlike the One who demons call the Son of God, and He Himself called Himself the Son of Man, and here He is now and they know, they know, He's the Son of David.

Perhaps they were using this title as a sort of hopeful manipulation. "Maybe we can say something that will make God do something." But I am really impressed, maybe amazed, maybe annoyed. I don't know; maybe nauseated, that they are continually crying, "Son of David, have mercy," as they're following. Can you see it? We already know there was a crowd following Jesus because the woman who touched the hem of His garment was in the middle of that crowd. You might remember from one of the other synoptics the disciples said, "What do You mean who touched You Lord? You are in the middle of a

---

[45]http://www.sermonaudio.com/sermoninfo.asp?SID=1101192354 [accessed 2/23/2017]; some effort was made to synchronize these accounts here.

throng and You say, 'Who touched You?'" So there is a crowd pressing in on Him. You know, the disciples are trying to get Jesus safely from place to place. And it's not happening very smoothly.

Now didn't Jesus hear them the first time? That is mysterious to me. This is not the only time this happens in the gospels, where Jesus acts like He's not listening. I do not understand Jesus in this regard.

Jesus heals two blind men twice in Matthew. This passage does not have a parallel in Mark or Luke. This healing does not. The other one in Matthew does. The other one in Matthew happens much later in the book and they also call Him Son of David and ask for healing. There's something particular that these people expected from the Son of David, about healing blind people. But they're doing two things. They are following, or rather they are crying and saying as they're following.

Think of these two men. How blessed were they to believe that this Son of David is really, first of all, the Son of David, and second of all may actually be interested in healing them. I don't want to accuse them of having full faith, but they had enough. We don't know how much faith they had. We might be able to say they had lots of faith. When given the question, "Do you believe I am able to do this?" That's an easy question because there's many things I think God is able to do. But these, these two blind men, they have enough faith to at least say something when the man who they call the Son of David walks by.

I don't know about you. You may not have perfect faith. But do you have enough to say anything? Do you have enough to keep saying it when He keeps walking? It feels like He's not listening. But if He wasn't listening He would have turned around and rebuked you, because that's what the disciples would have done. He would have said, "Stop asking. My grace is sufficient."

But they follow Him into a house that they don't belong in. You might remember blind people were seen oftentimes as cursed. Do I have to remind you in John 9 when the disciples saw a blind man in the temple they said, "Jesus, who sinned? This dude or his parents?" And they said, He said, "Neither." Do you remember that? So it wasn't hard to understand that oftentimes people thought blind people were cursed. And Matthew, "Matthew, oh my goodness my friend, you've only been following Jesus for about eight or ten hours. Are you a big enough man to realize that cursed people can come to your house?" Hard questions.

9:29

These blind men are continually tapping and groping, and poking along with their sticks or their hands along the ground, following with their hands, carefully inspecting. If you were to stand in front of them and talk they would reach up and touch your face to identify who you are. They would grab your hands, your arms. They would try to see, "Is this this person I think it is? Who is it?" And when you'd come and talk again they'd re-identify you by touching you.

But this time, verse 29, Jesus **touched their eyes**. What a day! What a day! We're not seeing the emphasis of the blind, we're seeing the emphasis of the healing. We're not making much out of the people, we're making much out of the Savior. It doesn't say anything about them touching Him, because this is not a day they are going to leave desperate blind men. No, no. Jesus the One who could be touched with a feeling of our infirmities looks at them, in a house, after being tired for two days, and touches their eyes.

But He is touching their eyes! What a compassionate Jesus. No one else would touch them. Jesus touches people. I feel driven to ask the Father, that it almost makes me want to touch the dry hand of a beggar on the corner of Skibo and Morganton. I'm talking about a real beggar; I'm talking about someone that would actually follow you across the street to Burger King if you offered. Please notice this would have been an impossibility if Jesus wasn't filled with love for the Father. I find usually when I'm critical and making fun of people who need my help, it's because the love of the Father is not in me.

9:30

And their eyes were opened; and Jesus straitly charged them, saying, See that no man know it. Why did Jesus have this fascination with nobody knowing who He was? It could be, yes, that He didn't want flimsy, miracle-based fellowship or followship. It could also be that He needed a fickle people to hate Him enough to crucify Him. And if everyone knows that He's the Son of David then that means that He's supposed to be a king, and they probably won't hate Him enough to kill Him.

> *Matthew 16:20 then* **He charged His disciples that they should tell no man He was Jesus the Christ**. *He didn't want anyone, He didn't want the masses finding out He was the Son of David or the Christ.*

> *Matthew 17:9 And as they came down from the mountain,* **Jesus charged them, saying, "Tell the vision to no man,** *Until the Son of Man be risen again from the dead…22 And while they abode in Galilee, Jesus said unto them, "The Son of Man shall be betrayed into the hands of men: And they shall kill Him, and the third day He shall be raised again." And they were exceeding sorry.*

The bottom line is the answer to why Jesus didn't want anyone knowing who He was, not so much that He wouldn't heal them, because they always went out and told, didn't they? But He scaled it back quite a bit with His warnings and we know, at least humanly speaking, the reason that He told them so was because, well, while He was making blind people see, He needed all the seeing people to be blind. And if He doesn't do that, you and I would one day wake up in hellfire. What a merciful God to blind some seeing people, and to make some blind people see.

9:32

Verse 27: "Jesus departed thence;" verse 28: "when He came into the house;" verse 31: "they when they were departed." Verse 32: "as they went out." So, we have Jesus now departing from the house of the ruler whose daughter He just healed and in verse 28 He comes into the house. Now, there have been several houses in this passage. One of them was Matthew's (9:9-10).

And these blind men. I don't know which is more surprising: the fact that Jesus doesn't answer them or the fact that they follow Him into another man's house. I would say Jesus is trying to see if they are desperate enough. "Are you just throwing a trite prayer at Me? Or am I really your only hope?" Because they're following Him and they're calling.

As they went out, behold, they brought to him a dumb man possessed with a devil. Dumb here means blunted in hearing or speech. It can mean either deaf or dumb. And, as a matter of fact, context usually tells you which, because this man ends up what? Speaking. So we know that he wasn't deaf necessarily, although he could have been. He was dumb.

Look at chapter 11. I want you to see where it's used in regards to deafness. Verse 5. Jesus is speaking to the disciples of John the Baptist and He said,

> *The blind receive their sight, and the lame walk, the lepers are cleansed, and the deaf hear.*

The word deaf in 11:5 and dumb in 9:32 are the same Greek word. Context determines whether it's blunt in speech or blunt in hearing. So it's the same Greek word. It can be translated either way.

So back to chapter 9. This is the fourth time we find Him delivering those possessed of devils. We think of chapter 4 verse 24, look there with me. Chapter 4 verse 24, I want you to see that this is a common thing.

> *And* (Jesus) *His fame went throughout all Syria: and they brought unto Him all sick people that were taken with divers diseases and torments, and those which were **possessed with devils**, and those which were lunatick,*

So please notice that there was a difference, to the writer Matthew, in the first century, between sicknesses and devils, diseases and devils, lunacy and devils. So this idea that, "Oh, such folklore. Everything to them was devils, devils, devils." No, He was healing sicknesses he did not attribute to devils, or demons, however you want to say it.

> *Matthew 8:16 When the even was come, When the even was come, they brought unto Him many that were **possessed with devils**:*

That word by the way, that phrase "possessed with devils," was one adjective in the Greek, one word. There's no noun in it. Those who were demonized, possessed or tormented with demons, He was delivering them.

> *and He cast out the spirits with His word.*

So from the context there, you should know, that spirits and devils in parallel there, are one and the same. I've known people make entire new doctrines, "Well first you have spirits and then you have devils." No, no, you need to go to bed earlier. That is not what that's saying. They're synonymous.

> *Matthew 8:28 And when he was come to the other side into the country of the Gergesenes, there met him two* (and again, it's one word in the Greek) *two* **possessed with devils,** *(*or two who were demonized) *coming out of the tombs, exceeding fierce.*

and you know the end of that story.

We're told in Ephesians chapter 6:12 that we don't wrestle against flesh and blood, we wrestle against principalities, and powers, and the rulers of the darkness of the world, and spiritual wickedness in high places. I'm not anti-pharmaceutical, but the fact is, when we know people love money and we know 1 Timothy 6:10 is in the book…

> *For the love of money is the root of all kinds of evil.*

I have no hard time believing that the powers of darkness love making money through people. They will use the love of money to hurt people.

9:33

And when the devil was cast out, the dumb spake: and the multitudes marvelled, saying, "It was never so seen in Israel." So we have two possible relationships here between faith and miracles in these Scriptures. Sometimes faith produces a miracle and sometimes a miracle produces faith. Look at this! The multitudes marveled, "We've never seen anything like this in Israel!" Well that is high praise.

9:34

But the Pharisees said, He casteth out devils through the prince of the devils. Revisited in 12:22-32.

"We are not happy about Jesus casting out devils. Surely people will start following Him. We can't have people following Him. It will mean our jobs. Who will come and hear us speak? Who will buy our books? Who will attend our coliseum events? So, the only reason He's able to do those things is because He Himself is empowered by Satan." Imagine, imagine looking at Jesus, the Son of God, the Son of Man, the Son of David, and saying, "He is possessed by Satan."

And by the way, I wonder if I could just show you that we are dealing with one grand context here

> *Matthew 10:25 It is enough for the disciple that he be as his master, and the servant as his lord. If they have called the master of the house **Beelzebub**, how much more shall they call them of his household?*

And Beelzebub is of course the "Prince of Flies," or maybe less refined, it actually in its root means the "Prince of Dung," and that was a title for Satan. And so Jesus says, in just a few verses here, "They called Me a child of Satan. What will they call you?" Quite a continuing context.

9:35

And That is a very strong conjunction. It means "immediately" or "close on the heels of." So here's Jesus. He is healing someone who's demonized. He's not getting very much credit for it. He's actually told that the reason He's doing it is because He's an agent of Satan.

Jesus went about all the cities and villages, It looks like Jesus is finally leaving Capernaum. He's been there for a very full weekend. Just read these last two chapters again, and don't forget the three chapters of the Sermon of the Mount begin the weekend as well. It's a very strong connection. Now, this wouldn't be such a big deal if we didn't already see this in Matthew 4:22

> *And **they immediately** left the ship and their father, and followed Him. 23. And Jesus went about all Galilee, teaching in their synagogues, and preaching the gospel of the kingdom, and*

healing all manner of sickness and all manner of disease among the people.

Look at 4:23 and 9:35. He's going about cities, villages, teaching in their synagogues, preaching the gospel of the kingdom, healing every sickness, every disease among the people. Very similar.

"How could there possibly be any more to do?" Everywhere He goes people are trying to touch Him. Everywhere He goes He's healing. This is really something, **all manner of sicknesses, all manner of diseases**. There was apparently nothing to do for researchers because He was healing.

teaching in their synagogues, and preaching the gospel of the kingdom, and healing every sickness and every disease among the people. Now that is really a mouthful if you think about it. He's healing every kind? Why is He doing this? Matthew 9:6,

But that ye may know that the Son of Man hath power on earth to forgive sins.

There was a time and place for miracles and signs and wonders. I'm certainly not going to say that the Lord could not do it today. For certainly He can do anything He wants to do, other than that which is against His character. We know He cannot lie. We know He cannot fail. So there are a few things He cannot do, children's songs notwithstanding. It is possible He could do miracles today. I trust that He does. I believe He does. Jesus told us why He did these miracles. He already told us why. It was so that you would know that if He can take care of the physical maladies He can probably forgive sins too.

9:36
But when He saw the multitudes. He's going out. He's seeing the work. There's more to do.

He was moved with compassion on them, because they had fainted. They had lost heart, and it drives Him to a certain emotional response. Think that through. Despite Jesus' extensive ministry, many in Israel, no doubt even in Galilee, remained unreached. Jesus' human emotions reflect a deep, gut-level compassion because they're scattered. And in the context, they're scattered by a demon-crazy world.

were scattered abroad as sheep having no shepherd. And that really is a big deal.

And remember He's very tired. He's sleeping in boats. Who does that? They're crossing the water in the middle of a storm and Jesus is very tired. And they had to wake Him up. Yes, I understand that there is some measure to the Lord's weariness here. And yet, He walks out to the rest of the cities and He sees there's more work to do and it drives Him to a deep emotional response. Imagine that. It's kind of like moving someone from one house to the next, and you've got the truck almost loaded, you've almost got it done, and then they say, "There's a shed out back."

Even Jesus saw He needed help. Was He doing great things? Was He effective? Was He efficient? Was it enough? There were still multitudes. Multitudes. I hesitate to say this, but I need to say it, because it is the spirit of the passage. Jesus needed help reaching the multitudes.

Now, I could go off into my Systematic Theology, and some of you are already correcting me. Thank you very much. I don't need it. I already know that God is sovereign. He can do anything He wants to do. I already know angels preach the Gospel from the sky in the book of Revelation. I don't need a course on that. I am fully aware of that. But the spirit of this passage, nonetheless, shows us that Jesus was emotionally overwhelmed with the work. And the issue is not, "Well, no one wants to hear." They're preaching the gospel of the kingdom and the issue is not that there's no harvest. The issue is that there's no workers. He's driven to deep, deep emotional response.

*Luke 15:1 Then drew near unto Him all the publicans and sinners for to hear Him. And the Pharisees and scribes murmured, saying, This man receiveth sinners, and eateth with them. And He spake this parable unto them, saying, What man of you, having an hundred sheep, if he lose one of them, doth not leave the ninety and nine in the wilderness, and go after that which is lost, until he find it? And when he hath found it, he layeth it on his shoulders, rejoicing. And when he cometh home, he calleth together his friends and neighbours, saying unto them, Rejoice with me; for **I have found my sheep which was lost.** I* *say unto you, that likewise joy shall be in heaven over one sinner that repenteth, more than over ninety and nine just persons, which need no repentance.*

*Luke 19:10 For the Son of Man is come to seek and to save **that which was lost.***

So when God said, "I will come and do it," He did! You can't get any more personal than coming as a man, and doing it Yourself. I can't think of anyone that would do the job better than God. So He shows up in the form of Jesus. Colossians 1:15 says that Jesus is the image of the invisible God. You're not going to get any better than Jesus. As a matter of fact, when you look at Him, Jesus told Philip, you see the Father. In fact He was so much like the Father that Isaiah chapter 9 verse 6 says:

*For unto us a Child is born, unto us a Son is given: and the government shall be upon His shoulder: and His name shall be called Wonderful, Counsellor, The Mighty God, **The Everlasting Father**, The Prince of Peace. Of the increase of His government and peace there shall be no end.*

We have someone who looks so much like God, He must be God. I mean, from the perspective of the reader and the listener and the watcher, He looks so much like the Father we even call Him the Father. And so when God says, "I will show up and find My sheep that are scattered," I just think that that is just tremendous.

9:37

Then saith He unto His disciples, The harvest truly is plenteous, but the labourers are few. We need more shepherds. In the context, isn't that what it's saying? We need more shepherds.

9:38

I find all kinds of people looking for meaningful work. But typically what ends up happening is we become discontented in the work wherein we abide and we quit doing it with our heart, and so there is no Peter and Andrew pulling their nets in, in chapter 4. We have people standing around saying, "There's nothing to do. Boy, I wish I just had something to do." Now, I may not know what I'm supposed to do tomorrow, but I bet you I can find something meaningful to do today. And I'll bet you that if it's meaningful it has something to do with the Lord's harvest. "I don't like where I work now." Well, Jesus is probably going to leave you there until you are working. James and John fishing. I don't see them standing out there looking for work. No, they're working already.

And I find that when Jesus, or even Jehovah in the Old Testament, is looking for someone, he's finding a Gideon who is threshing wheat. He's finding David who is killing bears with his hands. He's finding people that are doing things, not people that are sitting around writing poetry about how lousy their life is.

Pray for the laborers to change locations. They're laborers, and we want them in the harvest. When we find Jesus finding people, we find them doing something. So when we look for work, we see, all of a sudden, that we are joining people who are already doing work. They need help making their work better. The question is, "does the Lord, can the Lord, give me at least short-term, a work to do within that work?" We continue in this work because we understand there are some workers doing a work who need more workers, and nothing makes me look like I can work quite like being caught in the act of working. We continue in that work because we understand there are some workers doing a work who need more workers. And so we are working, waiting for the Lord, and while we're working where we are set, we are praying that the Lord will send more workers into the harvest.

We're supposed to be praying that the Lord will send laborers into the harvest. That word "send," in verse 38, I'll grant you, is a verb, but you will see the noun form in 10:2.

Meanwhile, Ezekiel 34 speaks of God firing the shepherds. "You don't have a job anymore." Of course, He's dealing with the people who should have been able to be teachers: scribes, Pharisees, priests, Herodians, you name it; they should have been able to all be people of God, feeding the sheep of Israel. But instead, they were fired. And the signal that they were fired, the signal that they were out of a job, was that the new Moses shows up, gives a new law, calls twelve new people. Do you see it? Gets baptized, has His time in the wilderness, He shows up. He is God in the flesh. It is the fulfillment of God saying, "I'll show up and seek My lost sheep. I'll show up and pastor My people." That is what a shepherd is. He feeds sheep. He is a pastor.

Chapter 10

Now the names of the twelve apostles are these. Look what He calls
them for the very first time.
Apostles is the noun form of the verb "send." Now that blows my mind.
Here's how you could probably rephrase it if you wanted to, "Disciples,
I am moved about people who are fainting. They are being worn out."
And isn't it interesting, the context, I'll come back to it, but the context
is they are fainting and scattered abroad as sheep having no shepherd.
And, it's right on the heels of a man being delivered from being
demonized. We're talking about people that are being worn out by the
wicked one. The Lord comes out and He just got done healing someone
who's being demonized, and He says, "I'm looking out and I'm seeing
an entire multitude of demonized people."

And so, what is the first thing He tells them to do? Well, heal the
sick, verse 8, cleanse the lepers, raise the dead, cast out devils, but the
main point I want you to see is not that He's sending them out to do the
exact work He's been doing in front of them, but listen to this: He says
in verse 9:38, "Pray that God will send people into the harvest." Chapter
10 verse 2, "You are my sent ones." Apostles, I'm going to say it again,
I don't want you missing it, I don't want you leaving here saying, "What
was he saying?" I don't want you doing that. I've heard it too much in
the last two years of my life; it's driving me mad. Listen to me now,
chapter 10 verse 2, "apostles" is the noun form of the verb "send." He
says, "You pray that the Lord sends people into the harvest." I have no
idea what the reaction was, but two verses later they are the ones sent
into the harvest. So, sometimes, I think I can easily say, we are the
answer to our own prayers.

> *Matthew 10:16 Behold, **I send you** forth as sheep in the midst of
> wolves: be ye therefore wise as serpents.*

Behold, I send you forth. That is another proof text. The verb
in chapter 10 verse 16, "**I send** you," and the verb in chapter 9
verse 38, "Pray the Lord will **send** forth laborers into His

---

[46]More on verses 1-4 can be found in the author's commentary on Mark (3:13-
19)

harvest." That verb is the same in both places. He said it twice, once with a noun, once with a verb, "You better be ready because when you start praying, as a body, that the Lord sends laborers into the harvest field, I'm going to send some of y'all."

We romanticize about missionaries we support. Because some of us volunteer for missions trips, and we think, "I bet all they do is knock on doors eight hours a day. I bet their just preaching to gobs of people, multitudes. I bet they're falling down before them crying, 'What must I do to be saved?' I bet it's just full days of nothing but revival. Full days of just amazing stuff and they're just knocking on doors, and baptizing converts, and planting churches, and starting radio ministries, and Bible colleges, and orphanages, and it's just amazing! I bet they don't even take vacations it's so awesome!" I want to remind us please, that if we're not harvesting here, we're hypocrites. "But I give." Good for you. I'm glad you give. We need givers. We sure do.

Some of you...you're sergeants, you're officers, you're corporate executive officers, you're presidents of branches of banks, you are way past thinking about the mission field. Well all right, then come on back to me, and listen to me for just a second about those needs in our neighbor's lives? I'll bet some of us can meet those very needs. "God meet that need!" (9:38)

"Ok, I'm sending you to do it" (10:2).

Well, I think sometimes we're busy saying, "Lord, please touch some people," and the Lord is saying, "I'm using your hands."

Are these. What is their chief requirement? To go find lost sheep and feed them (9:36-38). That's the context, right? They're supposed to be praying for people to go out and gather sheep, and so in the context these twelve people are the fulfillment to their own prayers, the prayers that they were told to pray in verse 38.

the first, Simon, who is called Peter, There are four other Simons just in the book of Matthew. We have Simon the Canaanite in verse 10:4. One of the other apostle's name is Simon. Chapter 13:55, one of the half brothers of Jesus, his name is Simon. Jesus' feet are washed in the house of Simon the leper. And then there's one who carries Jesus' cross known as Simon of Cyrene. In Acts you have Simon the Tanner.

and Andrew his brother; This is the last of two times you're going to see Andrew in the book of Matthew. Andrew is not a rock star in the book of Matthew, so to speak, as the kids say these days. There is no more Andrew in the book of Matthew after this. Do I believe he was in all of the groups? Yes, of course, he's in all the groups where it talks about the disciples, but he's not mentioned after chapter 10.

So let's find out where Jesus found Peter and Andrew. We look at chapter 4 and we find in verse 18,

> *And Jesus, walking by the Sea of Galilee, saw two brethren, Simon called Peter,* **and Andrew his brother**, *casting a net into the sea: for they were fishers.19. And He saith unto them, "Follow me, and I will make you fishers of men." 20. And they straightway left their nets, and followed Him.*

This, of course, took place at the northwest corner of the Sea of Galilee.

Remember chapter 8, Jesus visited Peter's house in Capernaum to heal his mother-in-law. All the gospel writers, when they list the apostles, list Peter first, and Andrew, because he's the man's brother, gets to tag along. However, every time I see a group of three I see the other set of brothers, James and John, but not Andrew. There are three of them, and Peter's brother doesn't get to come. Peter, James, and John, on the Mount of Transfiguration. Peter, James, and John, in the Garden of Gethsemane. Peter, James, and John, in the house of Jairus. Here, we find that Peter is the rare guy.

> *Matthew 14:28 And Peter answered Him and said, "Lord, if it be thou, bid me come unto Thee on the water." 29. And He said, "Come." And* **when Peter was come down out of the ship, he walked on the water**, *to go to Jesus.*

> *Matthew 15:10 And He called the multitude, and said unto them, "Hear, and understand: 11. Not that which goeth into the mouth defileth a man; but that which cometh out of the mouth, this defileth a man." 12. Then came His disciples, and said unto Him, "Knowest thou that the Pharisees were offended, after they*

heard this saying?" 13 But (Jesus) *He answered and said, "Every plant, which My heavenly Father hath not planted, shall be rooted up. 14. Let them alone: they be blind leaders of the blind. And if the blind lead the blind, both shall fall into the ditch." 15.* **Then answered Peter** *and said unto Him, "Declare unto us this parable."*

And here again is a Peter episode that only Matthew mentions where Peter was the first to answer questions, most of the time; the first to ask them and first to answer them (Matthew 16:15-22).

"You will not die." Well, the real issue there is that if He doesn't die He can't get up from the dead. And if He doesn't get up from the dead there's no kingdom coming. Then Peter gets the dubious award, the distinction of being the only one known as Satan.

Matthew 16:23 But He turned, and said **unto Peter**, *"Get thee behind Me, Satan: thou art an offence unto Me."*

Matthew 17:1 *And after six days Jesus taketh* **Peter**, *James, and John his brother, and bringeth them up into an high mountain apart, 2. and was transfigured before them...4* **Then answered Peter**, *and said unto Jesus, "Lord, it is good for us to be here: if Thou wilt, let us make here three [tents]; one for Thee, and one for Moses, and one for Elijah." While he yet spake, behold, a bright cloud overshadowed them: and behold a voice out of the cloud, which said, "This is My beloved Son, in whom I am well pleased; hear ye Him."*

Immediately, from Heaven: "Let me get this straight. You want Moses and Elijah to have the same thing that my Son gets. I better speak to that issue."

17:24 And when they were come to Capernaum, they that received tribute money came to **Peter**, *and said, "Doth not your master pay tribute?" 25. He saith, "Yes." And when* **[Peter]** *was come into the house, Jesus prevented him, saying, "What thinkest thou, Simon?"*

He comes inside the house, the tax collectors met him outside in the street and said, "So, are you guys going to pay taxes or what?" Peter says, "Uh, yeah," and walks into the house. And before he can even open his mouth, Jesus says, "Let me ask you a question, Peter." I love it. It's really hard to win an argument when someone knows exactly what you're about to say.

> *18:21 Then came **Peter** to Him, and said, "Lord, how oft shall my brother sin against me, and I forgive him? till seven times?" 22. "I say not unto thee, until seven times: but, until seventy times seven."*

And unless you've got one of those little punchers, like at the fair when you come in the gate, you're going to lose count and just keep forgiving. Of course, that's the point. Keep forgiving until you loose count.

> *19:27 Then answered **Peter** and said unto Him, "Behold, we have forsaken all, and followed Thee; what shall we have therefore?" 28 And Jesus said unto them, "Verily I say unto you, that ye which have followed Me, in the regeneration* (or in the "new beginning") *when the Son of Man shall sit in the throne of His glory, ye also shall sit upon twelve thrones, judging the twelve tribes of Israel."*

That should tell you that the apostles were incredibly interested in crushing the Roman idea of the kingdom, and that is why Peter rebuked Jesus when he found out that the king would be killed. And that is why Peter is looking for the glory of being a part of the new king's cabinet in chapter 19. When Jesus said, "I will build My church," Peter was all about the new church because it meant, at that time, to have a new cabinet. Jesus was using cultural terminology to relate to His disciples.

> *26:33 **Peter** answered and said unto Him* (Jesus)*, "Though all men shall be offended because of Thee, yet will I never be offended."*

And of course, Jesus promises him, in verse 34, that he would deny Him three times and then Peter, again, argues with the Lord.

Peter goes with Him to pray in the garden.

And then the last time we find Peter, by name, in the gospel is in verse 26:58. And I think you know what happens here. Peter does deny the Lord three times. Peter follows Jesus. After fleeing in the Garden of Gethsemane, he follows Jesus.

I've got to ask a question in all this. "Matthew, is that all? Are you really going to end your gospel leaving Peter a failure?" I mean, Mark is the one that tells us Peter is one of the two apostles that sets up the upper room for the last supper, and John is the one that tells us it was Peter who cut off the ear in the garden. We don't even get those two things from Matthew? I mean, couldn't you have at least mentioned what John did? I mean, couldn't you have at least told us that Peter was one of the first two apostles to the empty tomb? Couldn't you at least have done what John did, and share with us that Peter had one of the last conversations recorded with Jesus?

And I guess this leads me to the following thought. If I were to start a religion, let me tell you four things that I would do:

#1. I would do my very best to make all four gospels match perfectly. But the fact that they match just enough where you think they might have copied each other, but not enough so that it seems like they're imperfect presents a problem. But it should tell you that you weren't being lied to when you read the gospels.

#2. I would take away the "bearing the cross" idea, and I would go straight to the crown. I would take away the whole idea that you suffer for Jesus.

#3. I would probably not let the women be the first witnesses of the empty tomb. "You chauvinist." No, I'm reflecting the culture of the day. A woman was not even allowed to testify in court. I didn't say it was good. I said that's what was going on.

#4. I would make a hero out of its cofounders. And Matthew doesn't do that. Matthew didn't write another verse of scripture. Matthew leaves us thinking that Peter failed.

Apart from that of Jesus, no name is mentioned more often in the New Testament than Peter's. No other person is spoken of as often, or speaks as often, as Peter. No disciple is reproved as often, or as severely, as Peter. And only he was presumptuous enough to reprove the Lord. No other disciple so boldly confessed Christ and yet so boldly denied Him. And no other disciple is so praised and blessed by Jesus, and yet no other disciple did Jesus call Satan. So the least you can remember is that if Matthew wrote about Peter, you can probably trust your Bible, because he did not leave him looking pretty.

James the son of Zebedee, The Greek word behind James is Iakōbos. What does that sound like to you? Jacob. Yeah, as a matter of fact you might notice here that He calls him James, but it is pronounced *Iakōbos*. And so it is a form of the name Jacob. So, this James, the son of Zebedee, was probably named after Jacob of the Old Testament.

and John his brother; Now there are other James's mentioned in this book. There is James, son of Alphaeus. We don't have last names, and so we tell them whose son are they. There's one other John in the book of Matthew: John the Baptist.

Zebedee was probably, according to early church tradition, the brother of Zacharias the father of John the Baptist. We don't get that from Scripture, and so how authoritative is it? Not much, but when it's the earliest word that you have that's extra-biblical, you kind of lean in that direction until you find something that contradicts it. But this

More Than One "Judas?"

- (Amos 2:2) From "man" from "Kerioth?"
- Shares name with
  - son of Jacob the Patriarch (Matthew 1:2)
  - a half-brother of Jesus (Matthew 13:55)
  - two other ancestors of Christ's (Luke 3:26, 30)
  - another apostle (also named "Thaddeus"; Luke 6:16)
  - a revolutionary (Acts 5:37)
  - a homeowner in Damascus (Acts 9:11)
  - a prophet from Jerusalem (also named "Barsabas" Acts 15:22)

we know: ok, here we go; we know that we're told that Mary and Elizabeth are cousins, right? In Luke chapter 1. We're just not exactly sure how, because what's clear is that Zacharias and Elizabeth are of the tribe of Levi, right? And Mary and Joseph have to be of the tribe of

Judah, and so how do you get them to be cousins in a very close way? Well, it must be that you have someone who crossed family lines. And so a lot of people think Zebedee was the Levite who married a woman of Judah. It's possible. And then what ends up happening is you have Salome, who is not named in this book of Matthew: Salome is the mother of James and John, she is the wife of Zebedee, and she is, according to the other Scripture and the other gospels, the sister of Mary the mother of Jesus. So let's see how this works here: You have Mary the mother of Jesus, she is sisters with Salome the mother of James and John. She, Salome, the sister of Mary the mother of Jesus, is married to Zebedee who early church tradition says is the brother of Zacharias the father of John the Baptist.

Other places these two disciples are found in this book:

*Matthew 4:18 And Jesus, walking by the sea of Galilee, saw two brethren, Simon called Peter, and Andrew his brother, casting a net into the sea: for they were fishers. And He saith unto them, Follow Me, and I will make you fishers of men. And they straightway left their nets, and followed Him. 21 And going on from thence, **He saw other two brethren, James the son of Zebedee, and John his brother, in a ship with Zebedee** their father, mending their nets; and He called them. And they immediately left the ship and their father, and followed Him.*

*Matthew 17:1 And after six days Jesus taketh Peter, **James, and John his brother**, and bringeth them up into an high mountain apart, And was transfigured before them: and His face did shine as the sun.*

Matthew 20:17 And Jesus going up to Jerusalem took the twelve disciples apart in the way, and said unto them, Behold, we go up to Jerusalem; and the Son of Man shall be betrayed unto the chief priests and unto the scribes, and they shall condemn Him to death, And shall deliver Him to the Gentiles to mock, and to scourge, and to crucify Him: and the third day He shall rise again. 20 Then came to Him the mother of Zebedee's children with her sons [James and John]...And He said unto her, What wilt thou? She saith unto Him, Grant that these my two sons may sit, the one on Thy right hand, and the other on the left, in Thy kingdom.

Please just remember what Jesus just got done telling them: "I'm about to be crucified." I'm not sure they got it. In Matthew 16 when He said it, Peter responds with, "No, it's not happening that way." And Jesus turns around and says, "Get away from Me, Satan." Now here He tells them He's going to die and be raised the third day and here comes the mother of two of the disciples.

...22 But Jesus answered and said, Ye know not what ye ask. Are ye able to drink of the cup that I shall drink of?...

Now hang on, who's really behind mom coming to Jesus? James and John. "Hey mom, can you um?" Jesus cuts that right away and says to them, "Oh. Are you able to drink the cup that I drink? Are you able to be baptized with the baptism I am with? Are you able to do that?" And they said, "Sure are! We got the power!" End of verse 22.

...23: And He saith unto them, Ye shall drink indeed of My cup.

*Matthew 26:37 Then cometh Jesus with them unto a place called Gethsemane, and saith unto the disciples, Sit ye here, while I go and pray yonder. And He took with Him Peter and **the two sons of Zebedee**, and began to be sorrowful and very heavy.*

So who's with Him in the garden? Peter, James and John. That group of three again that was on the Mount of Transfiguration were with Him in the garden. And we find out once again that the hardest work in the world is prayer.

*Matthew 27:56 And many women were there beholding afar off, which followed Jesus from Galilee, ministering unto Him: Among which was Mary Magdalene, and Mary the mother of James and Joses, and **the mother of Zebedee's children**.*

10:3-4

Philip, the only other Philip in this book is the brother of Herod. Philip's wife, remember Herod Antipas stole from his brother Philip.

Matthew the publican. By the way this is the only gospel that calls Matthew a publican. Interesting that Matthew is the only one who called himself a publican.

James the son of Alphaeus, and Lebbaeus, whose surname was Thaddaeus; 4 Simon the Canaanite. So, our second James and Simon in the list.

And Judas Iscariot, who also betrayed Him. Judas was called and sent like the others, and presumably did what they did…all of it.

Psalm 55:12-13 is what we might call a Messianic Psalm; a message in the Old Testament that talks of Christ, and we see that in the Old Testament the writer is complaining, rightfully so, about a friend who tricked him and brought him great trouble. Doesn't it sound like this person is disappointed? The writer of this Psalm is frustrated and sad? Surely, surely. And so we see the heart of our Lord. You know we talked about in messages past about how when the Lord came looking for Adam He said, "Where are you?" And when Judas came into the garden, a different garden, Jesus asked him, "Where did you come from?" Interesting parallel there. And He not only said, "Where did you come from?" He said, "Where did you come from, friend?" Jesus called Judas friend. What a disappointment this must have been to Him.

Judas Iscariot. *Iskariōth.* It means "Judas, man from Kerioth." I think it's like a lot of people think that Christ is Jesus' last name. It's not. His mother was not Mary Christ. Christ is a title and Iscariot is a title, "Man from Kerioth." And this is where it is in New Testament time. He shares the names with a few other folks named Judas. For example, the son of Jacob the Patriarch, the half-brother of Jesus. Remember, Judas is the New Testament equivalent to what Old Testament name? Judah. So, half-brother of Jesus named Judas, two other ancestors of Christ found in His genealogy named Judas, another apostle (so another one of the twelve) named Thaddaeus. There is a Judas in Luke's genealogy, a revolutionary in Acts 5, a homeowner in Damascus, and a prophet from Jerusalem: all named Judas in the New Testament. So a pretty common name.

Matthew 19:27 Then answered Peter and said unto Him, Behold, we have forsaken (everything) all, and followed Thee; what shall we have? And Jesus said unto them, Verily I say unto you, That ye which have followed Me, in the regeneration [in the new world] when the Son of Man shall sit in the throne of His glory, ye also shall sit upon twelve thrones.

Who is that promise to if he continues to follow? Judas Iscariot. "All right, I knew it! I'm going to have a part in ruling the twelve tribes." And so, we have Judas picturing himself sitting on a throne, but Jesus keeps saying strange things like He's going to die and be delivered into the hands of Gentiles, but He'll be raised again the third day.

Matthew 26:1-14 shows there has been a change in his disposition regarding Jesus. Why? Well, something between those two passages that I just gave you. And you find there is someone who is taking money that he loved and lavishing the Lord with it, and when he has something to say about it in verses 9 and 10, you see in verse number 11 Jesus says, "You have the poor always with you, but Me you have not always. For in that she has poured this ointment on My body, she did it for My burial," and all of a sudden it is occurring to Judas they're probably not going to get those twelve thrones. He's probably not going to crush Rome. And he becomes disheartened. We find him betraying Jesus to the Chief Priest.

Matthew 26:21 is the strongest proof text that Judas was doing all the miracles, because I'm telling you right now, if for three years if he hasn't been casting out devils, raising dead folk, healing the sick, they would not have said, "Lord, is it I?" But all would have said, "Lord, it is him." Completely undetected: part of the first church, casting out devils, healing sicknesses, being sent out, being prophesied about and prophesying, preaching the gospel of the kingdom, taking part in all of the preliminaries of setting up a new kingdom. If anyone looked churchy, if anyone looked Christian, if anyone looked like he was on board with the new program, it was Judas.

26:24 The Son of Man goeth as it is written of Him: but woe unto that man by whom the Son of Man is betrayed! It had been good for that man if he had not been born.

When one considers Matthew 7:21-23, one has to wonder if Judas for a moment ever thought that he was talked about here in particular. In that one day, that Jesus that he gave three and a half years to following and preaching His kingdom gospel, would say to him, "I never knew you. You're dead to Me. Go away." I wonder how many of you readers…you've been a part of a church, you've done churchy things, you've said the right things, you've hung out with Jesus for three years, you've slept with Him under bridges, you've followed Him by the sea, you've read "Daily Bread" and had your devotions and made commitments at summer camp, you've raised children to go to church; I wonder how many of you were sent forth even on missions trips, visitation? May I just say that if that's your criteria, you're no better than Judas Iscariot. He was close, so close to the Eternal Word of God in the flesh that Jesus could reach some bread into a dish and hand it to him. So trusted that he carried the purse with the money in it for the team. He was the treasurer of the first church. He partook in worship and loved church activities. He was counted among the closest to Jesus when the multitudes walked away, having nothing but bread and fish in their bellies. They could not go with Jesus; it was not for them. When it was time for some to accompany Him on a ship to cross over to Gadara, Judas Iscariot was on board. When it was time to watch Peter walk on water, Judas Iscariot was on board. When it was time to hand out bread and fish for the pastor, Judas was there. When it was time to go and see people healed, who was it but Judas? When it was time to see devils cast out of Gadara, who was it but Judas? Judas was there!

10:5

These twelve Jesus sent forth, and commanded them, saying, Go not into the way of the Gentiles, and into any city of the Samaritans enter ye not. That should tell you right there that we're dealing with a very temporary, time specific requirement from the Lord, because it wasn't long afterwards, if you compare gospel with gospel, Jesus is talking to Samaritans (John 4). And then of course, Acts 8; you know when Philip ministered in Samaria to a certain Simon the sorcerer. In Samaria. And we saw people saved there. So this is very temporary. Much in this passage is very temporary.

And if this "go not" commission, ("Don't go to the Samaritans, don't go to the Gentiles") and if that's temporary, don't be surprised if the sign gifts are temporary too. I mean, that makes good sense, right? You have lots of temporary things in this passage. So, if it's temporary that they're not supposed to go to anyone but Jews, because at the end of the book He says, "Go ye therefore to all nations," something between chapter 10 and chapter 28 changes. Again, if chapter 10's directions are temporary don't be surprised if the dispelling demons and healing sicknesses is somewhat temporary also. After all, there are people out there today that say since we're called and sent we should be able to cast out devils. I am saying that normatively, this passage teaches us that it was temporary. I'm not saying it cannot happen. I'm saying "as a rule it does not happen." You know, in most of these situations only God could get the credit. So I would suggest that if we want to see some of these magnificent gifts seen today, that you get on a boat, raise support, go somewhere where you have to live among people where they don't have really modern medicine, and see some of this great stuff take place. I mean, that's very simple as far as I'm concerned.

10:6

But go rather to the lost sheep of the house of Israel. Isn't that lovely—to have a bookend over here, where we're dealing with sheep, in 9:36, and a bookend over here, in 10:6 which deals with sheep? So it's not just He wants us to go after lost sheep, in the context we're going after lost Jewish sheep. And we want to make sure that we're staying in the context.

10:7

And as ye go, preach, saying, "The kingdom of heaven is at hand." And what does He tell them to do? See 9:35.

With the disciples themselves not even having a grasp, just yet, of the death, burial and resurrection for the sins of mankind, one cannot be dogmatic to say anything other than…"this is the good news that a king is coming."

Matthew 3:1 contains the first one to preach this gospel of the kingdom.

*In those days came John the Baptist, preaching in the wilderness of Judaea, 2. and saying, "Repent ye: for the **kingdom of heaven** is at hand."*

And then we already read chapter 4 verse 17. Jesus is preaching,

*Repent: for the **kingdom of heaven** is at hand.*

So, what is the good news? Well, we remember that the Lord's Prayer has a particular request. Let's work through it together here. It's out of Matthew 6:9 during the Sermon on the Mount.

*Our Father which art in heaven, Hallowed be thy name. 10. **Thy kingdom** come. Thy will be done in   earth, as it is in heaven.*

The good news is that God's kingdom is coming. And when will it come? We're told in 2 Timothy 4:1, Paul says,

*I charge thee therefore before God, and the Lord Jesus Christ, who shall judge the quick and the dead at His appearing and **His kingdom**;*

If you want to know when His kingdom comes, you just need to wait for His coming, because He's bringing His kingdom with Him. So why then are they preaching the good news of the kingdom? Because it is a legitimate offer that Jesus gave the people of that day. That is indeed good news. And part of that gospel of the kingdom is also good news, that in order for that to happen, Mathew 20:28 has to happen. The Son of Man has come to give His life a ransom for many. Today's reader has the complete story.

Think about how unusual this time period is right here, and you'll be able to see why Jesus was so urgent about getting people to help Him with something, theologically speaking, He could have done Himself. There is a time restriction in His mind. There is going to be one time period when things are as they are: Jesus on the earth. The greatest prophecy of all time was about to become the greatest historic event of all time. Let me say that again. It only happened once. There was a time period when everything was looking forward to Him, and then, all of a sudden, everything was looking back at Him. It only happened once. Why are some of these requirements of the disciples unusual? Well, because they were in an unusual time. They may have lived two decades before and two decades after? And you've had to exchange your Old Testament saving faith for New Testament saving faith? How does that work? I have no idea. That's why I kind of shrug when we talk about, "What is the blasphemy of the Holy Spirit?" I mean, when were you able to look at Jesus in the body and say, "What you are doing is done by Satan," to prompt some Pharisees to say, "You cast out devils by Beelzebub," and Jesus saying, "Well, you're not going to be forgiven of that. You just blasphemed the Holy Spirit." I think, "How is that possible? How did they do that?" Well, they were living in a very unusual time.

10:8

Heal the sick, cleanse the lepers, raise the dead, cast out devils: freely ye have received, freely give. Hear me when I tell you that you do not have to fit this context perfectly to know that there are some things you can do without and that you can give in proportion to how God has blessed you. "Freely you've received. Freely give." Especially among the body of Christ, we should be amazingly good givers and receivers. There are boundaries here. Look here in verse 9:

10:9-10

Provide neither gold, nor silver, nor brass in your purses, 10 Nor scrip for your journey, neither two coats, neither shoes, nor yet staves: for the workman is worthy of his meat. Or his food. You're worthy if you work. You're worthy what you get paid, particularly for the kingdom.

10:11-14

And into whatsoever city or town ye shall enter, enquire who in it is worthy; and there abide till ye go, away or, **thence. And when ye come into an house, salute it. And if the house be worthy, let your peace come upon it: but if it be not worthy, let your peace return to you. And whosoever shall not receive you, nor hear your words, when ye depart out of that house or city, shake off the dust of your feet.** Now, friends, I want to remind us what cities we're dealing with. These are not just every city. Verse 5 tells us what cities. Israelite cities. Cities that are in Canaan proper. Israelite cities. Israelite cities. Cities in Israel, and we need to make sure that we keep that in our minds this entire passage. If they will not **hear your words**… **shake off the dust of your feet.**

10:16

Behold, I send you forth as sheep in the midst of wolves: I don't think it's a mistake that He calls them sheep and they're going, in verse number 6, to reach what? Lost sheep. I think Jesus is saying, "Don't forget who you are. Don't forget one time you were lost. So, you're sheep going to find lost sheep but I'm sending you in the midst of wolves." You see, you have lost sheep and then you have wolves. You're not going after the wolves. You're not out there winning wolves. If you find someone and they don't think they're a lost sheep, well, that's not the one you're looking for.

I send you forth as sheep in the midst of wolves: be ye therefore wise as serpents, and harmless as doves. I don't think we ought to be repulsive people. Titus was told by Paul, "Let no man despise thee." They are going to hate your message enough; they don't need to hate us. They might hate us for our message. Let them hate us for our message and not for our attitude. I just think that a lot of Christians get that mixed up and they think that in order to stand for God you have to be a jerk, and you really don't. So we're supposed to make calculated risks.

10:17

But beware of men: for they will deliver you up to the councils, and they will scourge you in their synagogues; There's no evidence that this ever happened before the death and resurrection of Jesus. There's plenty of evidence that it happened in the book of Acts. This should tell us that the scope of this passage is not just immediately these next several weeks because Jesus does rejoin them, and they do continue ministry together, and yet He's sending them out, verse number 16, "I send you forth." So He's sending them out but He's going to join them again, so He's obviously looking not just immediately, but also telescopically. There's going to be a time when you're going to be brought before councils and governors and kings.

10:18

And ye shall be brought before governors and kings for my sake, for a testimony against them and the Gentiles. By the way, that right there should tell you, hear me well, that this passage of Scripture not only deals with the immediate, but the distant. How do I know that? Verse 5, "Don't go to the Gentiles." Verse 18, "When you are before the Gentiles." You all see that? All right, so you need to understand this is more than just the immediacy of the Apostles; this is the Apostles and as Jesus would say in John 17, "Those who believe on them for My sake." So these are Apostles and Apostles' apostles. You need to see this as standing orders.

10:19

But when they deliver you up, Not, "They may deliver you up." Nope. **When they do**,

take no thought Now that's amazing. Here's a pep talk basically telling us that, "If you're made to speak, you don't need any sermon prep time in those situations."

… it shall be given you in that same hour what ye shall speak. I heard a preacher one time say that he used that as a proof text for why he didn't have to prepare a message, and he said that he preached for five minutes on, "Boy it sure is hot in here," and then had a seat. Realized that he should have prepared some remarks.

10:22

And ye shall be hated of all men for my name's sake: We should expect to be hated. We should pray for people to repent but we should get over the fact that they're not going to. In fact, they're going to go as far as hating us. If we will set it in our hearts not only that there is a possibility that we're going to suffer, but a probability that we're going to be hated, we'll do ok in this witnessing thing. We'll do ok in this kingdom-living thing. If we'll get over the fact that we're going to be hated if we preach the right message long enough, well then that means we can get over it ahead of time. Just get you a drink of cold water and move onto the next person because someone will receive you and be worthy of the peace. Someone will be worthy of your peace to rest upon their home. I know this is directly applicable to disciples going out and bringing the gospel of the kingdom to these households in every city of Judea, which by the way they won't get to, verse 23, but I think these are timeless principles.

but he that endureth to the end, Well, we know one who didn't. But those that do are saved.

10:23

But when they persecute you in this city, flee ye into another: for verily I say unto you, Ye shall not have gone over the cities of Israel, till the Son of Man be come. There have been many atheists in the last 130 years who have written that they are not Christians today because clearly Jesus was mistaken about the timing of His coming. Let's just be honest here. He's talking to people, he's calling them "you": "You'll see this, you'll experience this, you'll have this. I'm sending you on an errand you won't even have time to finish because the Son of Man is going to come." That makes it sound like it's happening quickly.

till the Son of Man be come. Son of Man is a very peculiar title because, if you want to get just really basic, we're all sons of men.

So Matthew 10:23 is pretty basic in that we understand that He is promising that the Son of Man will come. Now I want us to understand that the Son of Man is a title that has been used of Jesus twice, and if it just means "son of Adam," well then I guess we all are "sons of man." But you might remember the first time it's used is in Matthew 8, when a man wants to follow Him and Jesus says, "The Son of Man has nowhere to lay His head."

Then in chapter 9, He is healing a man who has been brought by his friends, the paralytic is brought by his four friends, and the Pharisees say, "Who can forgive sins but God only?" because Jesus looks at the man and says, "Your sins be forgiven you." And the man says, "Who can forgive sins but God only?" and Jesus responds, "What is easier for me to say, 'Your sins are forgiven,' or 'Get up and walk.'" And then He looks at the man and says, "But that you might know that the Son of Man has power on earth to forgive sins, get up and walk." That is the second time the title Son of Man is used.

So really, here's the third time: the coming of the Son of Man. It's the first time we find Matthew referring to the coming of the Son of Man and really, here's the challenge as we go through any New Testament book: "What does the writer Matthew expect his reader to know so well that he doesn't have to mention it?"

What would the reader have thought about the coming of the Son of Man? What did Matthew expect his reader to know so well that he didn't have to say it? That's a good question, isn't it? Because he's using the title "Son of Man" and he's using the term "the coming of the Son of Man." Here's the only Old Testament occurrence of the coming Son of Man (Daniel 7:1-14).

Please notice what it does **not say**. Verse 7:13

> *I saw in the night visions, and behold, one like the Son of Man* ***came to Earth***.

And the context is the defeating of a particular people, the judgment of a particular people. How do I know that? Verse 9, thrones are done away with, do you see that? "And the Ancient of days did sit." Now, I am not about to tell you that this happened in the time of Jesus, so don't be afraid. But I want us to be honest enough in our Bible study, to say that Matthew used certain terms on purpose to convey certain meaning to the people he was writing to.

There's one place in the Old Testament where the Son of Man is coming. It is Daniel 7, and it is when He is judging nations, and it is when He is coming to the Ancient of days. There's nothing that says that during this coming He comes to Earth.

But what I am saying is that Matthew 10 is very clear. Think of all the things Matthew could have said. "You will not finish these cities before the Son of God comes." He didn't say that. "You will not finish these cities before the Lord Jesus comes." That terminology is used in the New Testament. "The coming of the Lord Jesus Christ" is not what Jesus said. He used a particular title, and let's remember, the demons said He was the Son of God, the devil said He was the Son of God, and Jesus, Himself, when He said, "the coming of the Son of Man," He could have said, "Son of God," but He didn't. Why? Because He was trying to convey to those people listening to Him, the twelve apostles…; and Matthew recording it was trying to convey it to his reader: particular connections with the Old Testament.

Now, let's just remember that when the Son of Man comes, He does not have to come to Earth, and what is my proof text? Daniel 7. Don't tell me what is not on the page. I want you to see that this theme continues all through the Scripture.

Revelation 1. Let me just share with you that that title, "Son of Man," has not been used since Acts chapter 7 when Stephen said, "I see the heavens opened and the Son of Man standing at the right hand of God." "Son of Man" has not been used by any author, since then, until here.

> *Revelation 1:9 I John, who also am your brother, and companion in tribulation… 10. I was in the Spirit on the Lord's Day… And here's what I heard, 11. A great voice, as of a trumpet, saying, "I am the Alpha and Omega, the first and the last:" and, "What thou seest, write in a book, and send it unto the seven churches which are in Asia: unto Ephesus, and unto Smyrna, and unto Pergamos, and unto Thyatira, and unto Sardis, and unto Philadelphia, and unto Laodicea.*

These are real churches, right? We've heard some teachers out there who say, "No, it's seven ages of the church." That's wonderful, but it doesn't say that.

> *1:12 And I turned to see the voice that spake with me. And being turned, I saw seven golden candlesticks; And look who John saw. 13. And in the midst of the seven candlesticks one like unto,* **the Son of Man**. *Clothed with a garment down to the foot, and girt about the paps… Or I think we can tell you that that is around the torso area… with a golden girdle. 14. His head and His hairs were white like wool, as white as snow; and His eyes were as a flame of fire; 15. and His feet like unto fine brass, as if they burned in a furnace; and His voice as the sound of many waters.*

It really looks like he's describing Him just like Daniel described the Ancient of days and the Son of Man in Daniel 7. And look, he calls Him the Son of Man. Isn't that interesting?

> *1:16 He had in His right hand seven stars: and out of His mouth went a sharp twoedged sword: and   His countenance was as the sun shineth in His strength.*

In the context, are we talking about the coming of the Son of God (Revelation 1:7), the coming of the Son of Man? Where do we get that? Revelation chapter 1.

> *2:1 Unto the the church of Ephesus 4, Nevertheless I have somewhat against thee, because thou hast left thy first love. 5. Remember therefore from whence thou art fallen, and repent, and do the first works; or else **I will come unto thee quickly**, and will remove thy candlestick out of his place, except thou repent.*

Would you agree that if you are going to make the coming of verse 5 literal you have to make the candlestick literal? It seems like the Son of Man (1:12) is telling them, "I'm going to come, in a way, in sense, I'm going to come and remove your candlestick." Is He threatening, "If you don't behave I'm going to move My second coming even closer." Does that make sense? Let me get this straight, "You're threatening me with a second coming and "catching away rapture" if I don't shape up, and if I do shape up You're going to not come back?" Clearly this is not the second coming. This is a coming of the Son of Man to remove a candlestick.

> *2:16 Repent; or else **I will come unto thee quickly**, and will fight against them, those people in your church that are not behaving, with the sword of My mouth.*

"Let me get this straight, Lord. The second coming will be delayed if we all behave?" That doesn't make sense, does it? Who's talking in the context? That's Jesus, who's known as the Son of Man, and He's saying He's going to come to the church of Pergamos. I think we could say, if it would be easier for you to understand, and easier for us to accept, and kind of put it in a box so we can package it and talk about it, "He's going to come in judgment." But is He going to come to earth? It doesn't say that. Will He come to Earth one day? Yes. Is that what He's talking about here? No. That's two times now, right here in these seven churches.

Let me show you one more. Look at chapter 3:1.

*And unto the angel of the church of Sardis write, "These things saith He that hath the seven Spirits of God, and the seven stars; I know thy works, that thou has a name that thou livest, and art dead. 2. Be watchful, and strengthen the things which remain, that are ready to die: for I have not found thy works perfect before God. 3. Remember therefore how thou hast received and heard, and hold fast, and repent. If therefore thou shalt not watch, **I will come on thee as a thief**, and thou shalt not know what hour I will come upon thee.*

Think that through. What happens if they misbehave? He'll come upon them as a thief? Did He come to Earth in the time period of this church? No. So it doesn't mean and it cannot mean that because the threat is, "I'll come on you unexpectedly." And in the context, it seems like he's saying (like to the first church) "I will come and remove your candlestick. I'll make you, I'll turn the lights out on you! You will not be a light to your generation."

I was reminded of how North Africa used to be almost entirely Christian. Augustine, Cyprian, Tertullian, Arius, all North Africa. 100s, 200s, 300s AD. Now for about a thousand years it's been completely overrun by Muslims. You know what happened? God removed some candlesticks of some liberal churches. Did Jesus come and step His feet on planet Earth? No. Did He come and remove their candlestick? Yes. Where do I get the authority to say that? Daniel 7 and Revelation 2-3.

Now, Matthew, we're going to read back into you in just a one moment, but one more opportunity to see what I'm talking about. Look at Revelation 14. We have not heard Jesus called the Son of Man since the letters to the seven churches now. It is eleven chapters later. It's chapter 14 and John has another vision (Revelation 14:14-20).

So, at least you can see the Son of Man comes, but He doesn't come to Earth, He comes on a cloud, in a vision, and what happens? There is much blood outside of a city.

So, Matthew 10:23, They are being sent out to preach to "the lost sheep of the house of Israel" (Matthew 10:5-6). What kind of cities are they supposed to flee to in verse 23? Cities of Israel. So what cities, verse 15, will suffer worse than Sodom and Gomorrah, in the context? Israelite cities.

But when they persecute you in this city, flee ye into another: for verily I say unto you, ye shall not have gone over the cities of Israel, till the Son of Man be come. And we all of a sudden realize that we have no Bible authority for believing that this verse means "when the Son of Man comes to Earth." We have zero authority to say that. Remember, we're not supposed to read back into it what we believe about the second coming. We're supposed to let the Scripture teach us. And Scripture says that the first time the coming the Son of Man is used, Matthew doesn't tell us what it means. We're expected to know it as the readers. We find it in Daniel, and look all the way to the end of the Bible and we see it used there in the very same way. He comes, in a way, comes in judgment.

So, I think it's fair to say that Jesus is telling these people, "You're going to be preaching through Israelite cities, you're going to be persecuted from city to city, and then there will come an end. The end to that," verse 22, "if you reach it, if you just hang on, I'll save you from that persecution." How will He do it? Well, it seems like, based on what we know from Daniel 7, that the coming of the Son of Man will stop that persecution. And "the coming of the Son of Man" is shorthand once again, for His "coming in judgment."

So the question is, when did He judge the Israelites and their cities? 70 A.D. I am not saying that the rapture happened in A.D. 70. I am not saying that the resurrection of the dead happened in A.D. 70. I do not want to put myself with Hymenaeus and Philetus. I do not believe that Jesus came to earth in A.D. 70. Based on what I've showed you in these last few minutes, I believe He came in judgment upon Israel, in A.D. 70.

So what happened there? Josephus said the war which the Jews made with the Romans had been the greatest war known, not only of those that have been in our time, but in a manner of those that were unheard of. He furthermore said 1,100,000 Jews died just in Jerusalem between A.D. 66 and A.D. 70. A time, oddly enough, that covers three and a half years.

The big player, in this little saga, is Titus Vespasian. He was the general that was in charge of this Roman operation and later became emperor. Two people recorded what happened in A.D. 70. One of them is a Roman historian by the name of Tacitus; the other is a man by the name of Josephus. Josephus was a Jewish priest and general who was captured by the Romans and used to write the Jewish history.

And so here's what happens. In A.D. 66, the son of the Jewish High Priest in Jerusalem outlawed the Romans from offering their sacrifices to their many gods in the temple. Why did this effort last almost four years? Because Josephus was captured and the Romans thought that there would be a better way to do what they were going to do to Jerusalem, and they got the Jewish army's plans from the Jewish general they captured, named Josephus.

Also, the main effort leader changed. It was now Titus Vespasian. Siege warfare was employed. Siege warfare means that they surround the city, particularly Jerusalem, but also surrounding the surrounding cities making sure nothing can get in and nothing can get out.

In A.D. 69, Titus approaches the city with about 20,000 soldiers and surrounds it—using battering rams. In May of 70 A.D., the first battering ram strikes the wall. With the 10th legion providing covering fire with catapults that could hurl 100-pound stones into the wall, they breach the wall with the aid of siege towers. The surrounding cities had already been dealt with. Jerusalem was the last prize.

Over the next four days, this is the 2nd of June 70 A.D., the legions wore parades and full dress uniforms as Titus ceremoniously doled out the pay of every legionary. This was done in full view of the people in an attempt to awe the defenders into surrender, the ones on the wall defending Jerusalem. People crowded the walls and windows of the city to watch the process. Josephus was sent again to negotiate a surrender, but to no avail.

The starving within the city began resorting to cannibalism. Raiders entered the city, violently taking food from women, children, and aged while killing any who resisted. Jews seeking food outside the walls were whipped and crucified. Upwards of five hundred people a day were crucified until there were no more crosses to accommodate the victims.

After breaching the walls, they made their way to the altar in the Temple area, and started offering Jews and pigs on the altar. A single Roman soldier threw a firebrand into one of the Temple's windows starting a raging fire. Titus then committed what Daniel called the "Abomination Desolation." He offered a sow on the altar in remembrance of Antiochus Epiphanes, who did it for the Greeks.

So, if Matthew 10:23 says that Jesus is not talking about the second coming where He comes to Earth, well does that mean that there are no second coming passages? No.

All of a sudden we realize Matthew 10:22 is not a proof text for, "You got to hang on to be saved and go to Heaven." No. "If you will keep running from city to city eventually you'll be saved from that persecution." Why? Because the Jews will be slaughtered in those cities.

> *Matthew 10:15 Verily I say unto you it, it shall be more tolerable for the land of Sodom and Gomorrha in the day of judgment, than for **that city**.*

> *Isaiah 1:9 We should have been **like Sodom**, and we should have been **like unto Gomorrha**.*

> *Amos 4:11 As God overthrew **Sodom and Gomorrha**…*

So, here are two more prophets, in addition to Matthew, who speak of Jerusalem being threatened with the same fate of these two cities from Genesis 19. So the day of judgment, in the context, is the day when the Son of Man comes. In the context, it would make the most sense to these people listening to Jesus that it was in their lifetime. And we have

Biblical authority for saying that it wasn't Jesus coming <u>to earth</u>. It was Jesus coming in judgment and He came in judgment of the Israelites.

Look at Matthew 22:1-10. What about that? The armies of Rome were the armies of the Lord. And that's not new. God said that Nebuchadnezzar, and Babylon, that those armies were His armies. God said in Isaiah 45 that Cyrus was His "anointed."

It is a common theme throughout Matthew that they are in the generation that will suffer worse than Sodom and Gomorrha. Never has a generation ever killed the Son of Man and said, "His blood be on us and on our children."

How long would all this take? Do you remember Exodus' account of Moses being raised in Pharaoh's palace? He went out one day and saw a taskmaster of the Egyptians beating up an Israelite. Then, after he killed the Egyptian who was beating the Israelite, he went out the next day and saw two Israelites and said, "Why do you fuss with your brother?"

Do you remember what the man said? "Who made you a judge between us?" In other words, "We don't need you calling the shots." And Moses went to Midian for forty years.

Jesus, the ultimate Moses, comes back forty years after His rejection (Luke 19:12-14) from the Israelite nation—to those same people that said, "Who made you a ruler and a judge over us?" and destroys their city. And they take four years to perish. It was much worse for them than it was for Sodom and Gomorrha.[47]

10:24-25

The disciple is not above his master, nor the servant above his lord. It is enough for the disciple that he be as his master, and the servant as his lord. If they have called the master of the house Beelzebub,

---

[47]Comment from listener: "I had already listened to this message twice, trying to digest everything that was in it. Absolutely incredible. I have never been satisfied with the fly-over, weak explanations like, "Oh the title Son of Man speaks of His deity, while the title Son of God speaks of His humanity," as if the juxtaposition was the point. THANK YOU. This will forever be one of my top favorite sermons. And now I'm fairly certain I could actually speak intelligently on it."

how much more shall they call them of his household? They did say it about Jesus (9:34). In 10:25 Jesus says, "If they have called the master of the house the Prince of Flies," that's what Beelzebub means, and actually if you go right to the etymology of the word, it's the God of Dung, but typically it's short-handed to the Prince of Flies, "If they called Me, Jesus, the One who's casting out demons, 'the Prince of the One Who Dwells on Dung, that is flies'," what do you think they're going to say to you?" They're not going to roll out the red carpet for you when they've been calling your Lord "Satan".

The disciple is not above his master. "For the next 40 years you're going to be chased from city to city and I will save you by coming on the clouds, by coming in judgment over Israel," (verse 23), "and what would you expect" (verse 24)?

10:26

Fear them not therefore. Now this is not new to us. Jesus said in John 6, "Take no thought for tomorrow. You know, don't be careful for anything." He said, "The lilies of the field, they don't clothe themselves; the Lord looks after them. And the sparrows of the air, they don't feed themselves; the Lord looks after them. Stop being afraid of tomorrow." Then you remember in Matthew 8 when they awake Him in the ship, what do they say? "Why are you so afraid?" Fear is definitely something that is not very Christian. Can I say that again? Fear is not Christian.

10:27

What I tell you in the darkness, that speak ye in the light: and what ye hear in the ear, that preach ye upon the housetops. And all of a sudden we realize that there's relatively little that is secret. And sometimes we wonder if we're fearing because of the secrets we're trying to hold. You know, fear is a crippling thing: it's fear of failure, fear of beginning, fear of ending, fear of starting, fear of stopping, fear of rejection, fear of misunderstanding, fear of being misused, fear of being underestimated, and so we see that fear can have a lot to do with what we hope to be secret.

10:28

And fear not them which kill the body, but are not able to kill the soul: but rather fear Him which is able to destroy both soul and body in hell. That is wonderful! He basically says, "I'll give you a license to fear somebody. Just fear Me. After all, I'm the only one who can touch you after death."

10:33

But whosoever shall deny me before men, him will I also deny before My Father which is in heaven. I think it's safe to say, based on what we know of salvation, you don't get saved by telling everyone you are. So that is certainly not the message of this passage. I mean, what sense would it make to say, in verse 32, if you say you're saved then you really are. So that is not what gets you or keeps you saved. But, you should not expect a saved person to be ashamed of his Lord.

> *Romans 10:9-10 That if thou shalt confess with thy mouth the Lord Jesus, and shalt believe in thine heart that God hath raised Him from the dead, thou shalt be saved. For with the heart man believeth unto righteousness; and with the mouth confession is made unto salvation.*

And people typically stop right there and say, "Yup, there you are. There's two things you've got to do to be saved. You have to confess with your mouth and believe in your heart." But the next verse has the key:

> *10:11 For the Scripture saith, "Whosoever **believeth on Him shall not be ashamed.**"*

Ashamed of what? In the context, to confess. So confession comes from real belief, from Matthew 10:32 and 33. You confess because you are a believer. So if you deny, verse 33, knowing Christ you should probably not expect to be in heaven until you confess Christ. Now don't get bogged down there. The fact is, you get saved because the Son of Man came to seek and to save that which was lost.

> *Matthew 20:28 Even as the Son of Man came not to be ministered unto, but to minister, and to give His life a ransom for many.*

So our salvation has everything to do with Jesus Christ giving His life a ransom for us.

10:34

Think not that I am come to send peace on earth: I came not to send peace, but a sword. Now that is not the meek and mild, sweet, longhaired, flip-flop wearing Jesus that I want to believe in. He just wants to talk about love and peace all the time. No! In His first coming He said, "I came to bring a sword."

10:35-37

For I am come to set a man at variance against his father, and the daughter against her mother, and the daughter in law against her mother in law. And a man's foes shall be they of his own house hold. Jesus is quoting Micah 7:6 without any regard of clarification as to whether He was the ultimate fulfillment or another fulfillment. At any rate, we're not surprised at this usage of Micah since he's already been referenced in chapter 2 (Micah 5:2 and the birthplace of Jesus). **He that loveth father or mother more than me is not worthy of me:** And we should not be surprised that Jesus says this because in two short chapters they say to Him, "Your mother and your brothers and your sisters are outside," and He says, "You," as He points to His disciples, "Are my mother and my brothers and my sisters." So we're not surprised that Jesus says those who do the will of the Father are His family and beforehand says, "You need to love Me more than your family." Jesus did it. Jesus was willing to say to His mom at a marriage feast, "What are we talking about here? It is not my time. What do I have to do with your problem?"

10:39

He that findeth his life shall lose it: and he that loseth his life for (not the Father's sake) **My sake shall find it.** So Jesus is incredibly fooled or incredibly deceitful, or incredibly correct.

He that receiveth you receiveth Me, and he that receiveth Me receiveth Him that sent Me. Well that's interesting. All of a sudden we're seeing that Jesus is the first apostle. Now I'm not the only one that uses that language. In Hebrews 3:1 Jesus is called the Great

Apostle, the Great Sent One. John 20:21 ("As My Father hath sent Me, even so send I you.")

So, the only reason that Jesus has the authority (10:2, 5, 16) to say, "Go, go, go. I send you." The only way that He has the right to say in chapter 9:38, "Pray to the Lord of the harvest, the Master of the harvest, the Master of the fields, that He will send people. And oh, by the way, you are the sent ones," the only reason He can say that with such authority is because He has lived everything that He is stating in this passage. He loved the Father more than He loved His mother. He loved the Father more than He loved His brothers. He loved His Father more than He loved the children He would have had if He lived long enough to have them. Even Isaiah 53 foresaw that because it says, "Who will declare His generation? For He was cut off out of the land of the living." Jesus was killed before He could have children, from the human perspective. So Jesus loved His Father more than He loved even having sons and daughters. Now of course ultimately He has sons and daughters. We are it. We carry on His name. Psalm 22, at the end of the Psalm, it says, "They will be accounted to Him as a generation; a seed." The people that He says, "I will stand in your midst and sing praises to God."[48]

So, this is very audacious. And now we understand why it will be more tolerable for Sodom and Gomorrah than for the Israelite cities (10:15-16). Sodom and Gomorrah never had the Son of God visit them. Sodom and Gomorrah never had a single gospel preacher. Maybe they should have, maybe Lot should have been, but He wasn't. And that's a discussion for a different time. If God knew what it would take to get somebody to repent, why didn't He go to that extent (11:20-24)? And my goodness, that's a conversation I've had with people for as long as I can remember. Hasn't everyone?

It's one of those, "Why did God create the serpent?" and all those other hard questions that I don't have the answer to. Don't email me about it. I don't have the answer to it. The point is the serpent existed and here we are. And long before the serpent crawled into the garden, Jesus was foreordained by the Father to be our propitiation (1 Peter 1:20; Revelation 13:8).

---

[48]It's quoted in Hebrews 2.

10:40

I want to just make this really clear. When they reject the preacher they reject the Son of God. If the preacher is demonstrating that he's preaching Christ, you better not reject him. Now, he might be ugly, he might be out of shape, he might have a silly profile, he might say dumb things, but you cannot reject a speaker just because he's imperfect. You say, "I don't really like the way he looks…" He's not paid to look at you a certain way. He's paid to represent Jesus. You say, "Well, I don't think Jesus would act like that." Well it's interesting that you think Jesus would whine like you do. How can we hold the pastor up to the measuring stick of Jesus but not the person being critical all the time? Before you decide, "I don't want to go to that church," or, "I don't want to stay in that church because the pastor…" just remember why the pastor is here. He's here to speak for Christ, and to reject that is to reject the Son. I did not make that up. **He that receives you receives Me**.

He that receives Me receives Him that sent Me. Away with the idea you can have a religion without Jesus. Now you might have a false religion, my dear friend, but I want to make something abundantly clear to you: God has a Son. You say, "Well, I serve the Creator." Well then, your Creator has a Son.

10:41-42

He that receiveth a prophet in the name of a prophet shall receive a prophet's reward; and he that receiveth a righteous man in the name of a righteous man shall receive a righteous man's reward. When you see 11:9, you see He is talking about John the Baptist in the context. See, He wants them to see the ultimate prophet they should have received in His name, so it goes into talking about John the Baptist.

He receives a prophet. A lot of modern translations say, "He that receives a prophet because he is a prophet." But the problem is that's not consistent. Let me please show you, if I could, in that same version, this won't make any sense to you unless you have one of those versions; I'm not trying to get you to throw it out, but I would like you to look at Matthew 18.

*Matthew 18:20 For where two or three are gathered together in **My name**, there am I in the midst of them.*

It's interesting those modern translations translate it "in My name" there but they don't translate it that way in Matthew 10:40. It's the same Greek phrase.

*Matthew 28:19 Go ye therefore, and teach all nations, baptizing them **in the name of the Father, and of the Son,** and of the Holy Ghost.*

In other words, "Baptize these people as if you're doing it on behalf of Father, Son, Holy Ghost." It's the same Greek phrase in all three places. So why some of these modern translations translate it as "receive a prophet because he is a prophet," I don't know.

He that receiveth a prophet in the name of a prophet shall receive a prophet's reward. One comes in Christ's name and therefore received, he is received because he comes in the name of Christ, the prophet and the righteous man. In other words, in verse 41 Jesus is saying basically, "He that receives a prophet in My name." One thing is certain: whatever this phrase means, I get the reward of the person who's being represented. I get the reward of the person who's being represented. I've read no less than 50 commentaries on this verse and no one agrees. And so, as my dad would say, where people disagree that you respect a lot, you probably shouldn't be very dogmatic.

Take a look at 1 Peter 5:1-4, and look at Matthew 10:41, would you say that it's a true saying that a prophet gets a crown of glory?

Consider 10:11: Would you agree that that person who receives the apostle is also receiving the message of the apostle? Is it fair to say that chapter 10 and verse 41 is a summary of that action? It seems like a person who is receiving the apostles into their home, receiving their message, those apostles sure enough will get a reward. Who else gets the reward? The one who receives them.

"Prophet" and "righteous man" in 10:41 are in parallel.

*Matthew 23:29 Woe unto you, scribes and Pharisees, hypocrites! (Look here.) Because ye build the **tombs of the prophets, and garnish the sepulchres of the righteous**.*

Do you think that Jesus was saying that there's a difference between tombs and sepulchers? No. He's saying the same thing two different ways. So if tombs and sepulchers are the same thing then, you should see this whole parallel structure thing, righteous men and prophets are the same thing.

42 And whosoever shall give to drink unto one of these little ones
And so, who, what is this? Is this, is this "little ones," is this kids? No, because in Matthew 25 He says, "When you gave unto the least of these My brethren, you did it unto Me": same word. So "little ones" doesn't mean kiddos. It's not like there was toddlers everywhere and He said, "Let Me talk to you about apostles, prophets, righteous men, and toddlers." That wouldn't make much sense would it, in the flow of context? He's talking about the ones that aren't worth much to you.

And whosoever shall give to drink unto one of these little ones a cup of cold water only in the name of a disciple, verily I say unto you, he shall in no wise lose his reward. In addition to His twelve disciples there are these ladies and gentlemen. Gentleman that make up the seventy (Luke 10) that we read about in Luke and ladies that make up the group of women who attended to the needs of the ministry (Luke 8). They are considered **little ones**. And Jesus is very clear here that if you just so much as give them **a cup of cold water** in His name, in the name of a disciple even, if someone would just give a little one a cup of cold water, and they don't even really have even the perfect theology, they do it because they follow a disciple of Jesus! That tells me that the Lord sometimes rewards people and they don't deserve it. That goes back to chapter 6 where He "rains on the just and the unjust."

Are you frustrated because you are not a prophet? Are you frustrated because you feel like that you could do so much more if the Lord would just let you? Maybe you've never sat in the dark and thought, "I've wasted so many years." Are you feeling frustrated because you feel like there's no reward for you because you have calloused your heart through less than perfect decisions? You feel like you are no longer even eligible to be a star of the show? You feel like you can't hold a high enough office in the kingdom. This passage tells me that you don't actually have to be a prophet to get a prophet's reward. That's an encouragement! So little as **a cup of cold water** can actually count as "receiving a prophet, in the name of a prophet, and receiving a prophet's reward."

Just as sure as I would tell a twelve-year-old, "Don't waste your life. You'll have regrets forever," I would say to a fifty-five-year-old who's wasted their life, "You can still have a reward." I just want to extend a hand and say if you're breathing, you can do this. You can fill a cup and refresh someone. You can find a messenger of the Lord. You can find something to do in God's kingdom. It may not be the script you wrote, it may not be the way you pictured it, it may not be the way you would have planned it, but you can have a prophet's reward, a crown of glory that fades not away.

Are you feeling inferior because you have no great name of your own? Think about the apostles. They weren't supposed to go in their own name. He says in Matthew 5:

> *Blessed are ye, when men shall revile you, and persecute you, and shall say all manner of evil against you falsely, **for My sake.***

Don't go out representing yourself. And I think sometimes we get frustrated because people don't recognize our contribution. Do you feel like maybe you've been given the short end of things because no one knows you or what you do? I want you to know that when you carry the name of Christ there is no higher calling. "You're gracious and loving and patient and kind," and then, if you're not careful, you're going to sit back one day and say, "Look what I got for being loving and patient and kind. I never got that position, and I never got that raise, and no one ever knew me." But I want you to know there's coming a day when everyone will know you. You will be rewarded publicly, the nature of the judgment seat of Christ.

Are you angry because the Lord has not given much to you to give to others? Are you shuffling around, feeling under-resourced? Do you sit sometimes and think, "I would give if I had more to give. I would do if I had more energy. I would think if I could. I would do this if I could." Look what you need, verse 42. If you're feeling low, if you're feeling broke, if you're feeling under-resourced, underestimated, underappreciated; look what you need to be a blessing: a cup of cold water. That's what you need.

10:28

This is handled in my commentary on Revelation (20:11-15).

Chapter 11

11:1

And it came to pass, when Jesus had made an end of commanding His twelve disciples, He departed thence to teach and to preach in their cities. So He sends them out and then He goes out.

11:2

Now when John had heard in the prison the works of Christ, he sent two of his disciples, Now the first question I have is how did John get there? It'd be nice if Matthew told us. And he did (See 14:1 and following which tell us how John found himself in prison while also telling us that he was dead by chapter 14).[49]

And said unto Him, Art thou He that should come, or do we look for another? Best I can tell, John is the only one who saw the dove descend upon Jesus at His baptism. Best I can tell, John is the only one that heard the voice out of heaven saying, "This is My beloved Son in whom I am well pleased." John the Baptist heard the voice out of heaven. He saw heaven open, heard the voice out of heaven, heard the voice of God saying, "This is the Son of God and I am pleased with Him." John the Baptist saw the Holy Spirit come down and anoint Jesus. Jesus, for all intents and purposes, on a timeline, becomes the Christ. I'm not saying He became perfect there, I'm not saying He became the Son of God there, I'm saying that He was anointed right there with the Holy Spirit in front of John the Baptist. So, I'm having a hard time believing that John the Baptist is asking this question. The Jews are expecting a Messiah. Well, let's remember what John saw. John saw Jesus being declared as the Messiah. And now John apparently is asking, "Are You the One that we're supposed to be expecting or should we keep looking?"

I've heard a lot of people say, "Well, this wouldn't be John doubting. He's probably wanting the disciples to ask for their benefit." I suppose the problem with that is it's not the natural reading of the passage. John the Baptist is in prison. He's in prison for doing right.

---

[49] More can be seen in my commentary on Mark (in chapter 6).

He's in prison for doing right in the name of God. And he's in prison after he himself declares he is the voice of one crying in the wilderness. John the Baptist knows he's the fulfillment of Isaiah 40, knows Jesus is the Son of God, or at least that's what he observed…and here he is sending two of his disciples saying, "Are you the One that's supposed to come or should we keep looking?" Wow. And then Jesus gives an answer.

11:4

Jesus answered and said unto them, Go and shew John again those things which ye do hear and see: And you may not get the idea from Matthew, but you certainly would if you looked at the parallel in Luke, Jesus, with them watching, does many other works. The two disciples of John the Baptist are now going to see with their own eyes and hear with their own ears and experience what Jesus says in verse 4:
The blind receive their sight, and the lame walk, the lepers are cleansed, and the deaf hear, the dead are raised up, and the poor have the gospel preached to them. Why is Jesus using this language? Because Jesus knows that John the Baptist is expecting something:

> *Isaiah 35:1 The **wilderness** and the solitary place shall be glad for them; and the **desert** shall rejoice, and blossom as the rose.*

Where was John baptizing? The wilderness. Where did Jesus go to be tempted? The wilderness,

> *35:2 shall blossom abundantly, and rejoice even with joy and singing: the glory of Lebanon shall be given unto it, the excellency of Carmel and Sharon, they shall see the glory of the LORD, and the excellency of our God. Strengthen ye the weak hands, and confirm the feeble knees. Say to them that are of a fearful heart, Be strong, fear not: behold, your God will come with vengeance, even God with a recompence; He will come and save you.*

Read the rest of Isaiah 35 to see these signs that were forecasted for the Messiah.

Jesus sends the disciples of John the Baptist back to John the Baptist with signs that He is the Christ. Why are these things being included in chapters 8, 9, and 10 of Matthew? Because Jesus needed to confirm in chapter 11 verse 5 that He did them. He did everything that Isaiah 35 talks about, so if that's true…Why is John now a little bit disenfranchised about the whole idea?

Because there are no ransomed of the Lord returning to Jerusalem (Isaiah 35:10). Surely you can see that if you were John the Baptist, and you are the forerunner, and you see Jesus and all these signs are happening, then why am I in prison? And why is Jerusalem still being ruled by a bunch of thug Romans? That would take someone who is convinced that Jesus was the Christ and maybe make them wonder.

> *Isaiah 61:1* **The Spirit of the Lord GOD is upon Me**; *because the LORD hath anointed Me to preach good tidings unto the meek….*

When did the Spirit of the Lord come upon Jesus? At His baptism.

> *He hath sent Me to bind up the brokenhearted, to proclaim liberty to the captives. 2* **to proclaim** *the acceptable year of the LORD, and* **the day of vengeance of our God**; *to comfort all that mourn; To appoint unto them that mourn in Zion, to give unto them beauty for ashes, the oil of joy for mourning, the garment of praise for the spirit of heaviness; that they might be called trees of righteousness, the planting of the LORD, that He might be glorified.*

John the Baptist is in prison, and God is not bringing vengeance. We wonder, "what is John doubting?" Hopefully you can see that John is doubting. Isaiah 35, Isaiah 61, is a lot like looking at two mountain ranges separated by an apparent valley that cannot be seen from the observer's perspective. And John the Baptist can see what's happening in the first but Jesus is not bringing vengeance. And I've read a lot of people that say, "Well the 'day of vengeance' in Isaiah 61:2 is talking about AD 70." Ok. Well, if it is talking about AD 70, let's at least admit that there's still a 40-year separation that would cause John the Baptist to doubt in his prison.

Matthew loves Isaiah

1. Isaiah 7:14 regarding His Virgin Birth (1:23)
2. Isaiah 11:1 regarding His origin (2:23)
3. Isaiah 40:3 regarding His forerunner (3:3)
4. Isaiah 9:1-2 regarding His scope (4:14-16)
5. Isaiah 53:4 regarding His empathy (8:17)
6. Isaiah 35:4-6 regarding His depth (11:4-5)
7. Isaiah 61:1-2 regarding His preaching (11:5)
8. Isaiah 8:13-14 regarding His surety (11:6)
9. Isaiah 42:3 regarding His tenderness (11:7)

> *Isaiah 8:13 Sanctify the Lord of hosts Himself; and **let Him be your fear, and let Him be your dread.** 14 And He shall be for a sanctuary; but for a stone of stumbling and for a rock of offence to both the houses of Israel, for a gin and for a snare to the inhabitants of Jerusalem. And many among them shall **stumble**, and fall, and be broken, and be snared, and be taken.*

Isaiah 8:13 sounds a lot like Matthew 10:28 while Isaiah 8:14 sounds a lot like Matthew 11:6. Clearly Matthew 10:28 through Matthew 11:6 are foretold in Isaiah 8.

Then, we see that Matthew 10:41 we have promise to those who support a prophet followed by the trial of a man (in these opening verses of chapter 11) who everybody knows is a prophet (John). And you have a very unhospitable nation in Israel. And where is their prophet? He's in prison. So we're not surprised.

The forerunner of Jesus is wondering if He is really the Messiah or should they keep looking.

11:7

As they departed (the two disciples)**, Jesus began to say unto the multitudes concerning John, What did you go out into the wilderness to see? A reed shaken with the wind?** "Were you looking for some limp-wristed sweetheart out there? You didn't find him, did you?

John the Baptist is low and feeling it and he sends two disciples to Jesus and says, "Jesus, are you the one that is supposed to be coming or should we keep looking?" Jesus gives them some things out of Isaiah 35 to take back to John the Baptist, not John the apostle. "Were you looking for a bruised reed that has broken," in other words?

11:8

What went you out for to see? A man clothed in soft raiment? That is an effeminate term. On purpose, Jesus is sort of making fun of their expectation. "Were you looking for a dude with matching purse and pumps?"

No, He says at the end of the verse, **They belong in a palace.** Now that's funny.

Behold, they that wear soft clothing are in kings' houses. But what went ye out for to see? A prophet? "Yeah, you found one. **Yea, I say unto you, and more than a prophet. For this is he, of whom it is written, Behold, I send my messenger before thy face, which shall prepare thy way before thee.** He's quoting Malachi and so then you understand why the Elijah reference happens in verse 14.

11:9

What were you looking for? A prophet? "Well, you found more than that, didn't you?"

Yea, I say unto you, and more than a prophet. For this is he, of whom it is written, Behold, I send My messenger before Thy face, which shall prepare Thy way before thee. You see, while John is wondering if Jesus is who He says He is; while his disciples are bringing back word of what they saw, Jesus is not doubting what He said about

John. <u>Bless the Lord. Let me say it again.</u> John is doubting what God says about Jesus but Jesus is not doubting what God said about John.

11:11

Truly, I say unto you, Among them that are born of women there hath not risen a greater than John the Baptist. Well that doesn't sound like a failure. John feels like a failure. Maybe John should have known better. Maybe John should have allowed for there to be distance between phrases of fulfillment in Isaiah 35 and Isaiah 61. Whether he should have or not, he's feeling mighty low in the prison. And Jesus says, "In case you are wondering, multitude, whether or not I think differently of John, let Me tell you what I think of him. There's never been a greater man born." Phenomenal.

Then I see legitimate questions being asked and I don't see Jesus getting angry. I'm afraid that I might have. "After all I've done for you, John. After all you've seen, John. After all you heard, John. You're going to doubt me?" But Jesus is not only patient, He's incredibly persistent. I mean think about what Jesus did at that moment. He invited the disciples of John with Him and did works in front of them, for them to take to John.

But I must say there's something even more striking than that. In verse 6 Jesus says, "Blessed is he that is not offended in Me. Blessed is that person that doesn't trip over Me. Blessed is the person that doesn't stumble upon the hard days of following Me. You are incredibly blessed." Now I must tell you I would have probably sent a card. "Cheer up. It'll get better. Thanks for being a good friend." And I would probably have included a Psalm. Jesus tells these two disciples, "You tell John to get up and keep walking. Blessed is he who does not trip and stay down. Happy is the one who does not allow dark times to keep him on his hind end." Apparently it's possible for you to walk in faith even in a cell because that is exactly what Jesus is requiring the discouraged John the Baptist to do. Does Jesus offer a patient hand up? Yes, and a persistent shove in the back.

notwithstanding he that is least in the kingdom of heaven is greater than he. Well, that is really saying something, isn't it? There has never been a greater man born than John the Baptist, yet the one who is the smallest in the kingdom is better than John? Now, think that through:

there is no one greater that has been born than John until the kingdom and then the smallest in the kingdom is greater than the greatest among men. That's what it says, right? Incidentally, you might notice that the word translated "least" in the King James, "he that is least in the kingdom of heaven," is the same word translated "little ones" in chapter 10, verse 42 so we have a connector there. Verse 42 of chapter 10, "And whosoever shall give to drink unto one of these little ones," unto the least of these, "a cup of cold water."

We're not given full window into this thing called the kingdom of heaven but whatever it is, it's big time because whoever is the puny, paltry, unimportant one in the kingdom is far more important in the eyes of God than the greatest among the children of men. So heaven knows your address if you're one of his. You might not rank very high among men but you can't get any higher than you. That's phenomenal. That's a comfort. There will be a time when you won't win the popularity contest. There will be a time when you aren't selected for promotion. You will be the person that will have to deal with realities that you're not the greatest among those who are born of women. Oh, but you are greater than the greatest of those born of women. That's phenomenal.

11:12

And from the days of John the Baptist until now the kingdom of heaven suffers violence, and the violent take it by force. Or "the violent are pressing into it."

For all the prophets and the law prophesied until John. "Prophets and law" or "law and prophets" is shorthand for the "Old Testament." **All the prophets and the law prophesied until John.** Now, that could be taken in a couple of different ways: it could be that it's saying that the Old Testament spoke of John up until John but I don't think it means that because the Old Testament speaks of those things happening after John as well so it is probably saying that John is the last Old Testament prophet which makes sense considering he's not in the kingdom, verse 11.

We understand from this passage that John the Baptist is apparently not in the kingdom, whatever that is. I'm not saying he won't be, I'm saying at this time he's not and apparently whatever the kingdom is, the law and the prophets prophesied of it up and until and through John. So while I understand that you're in the New Testament as far as books in the Bible are concerned, it starts in Matthew, the New Testament itself does not begin until the crucifixion. Hebrews 9:17 Says that the covenant takes force with the death of a testator. the New Testament begins at the crucifixion so that means that John is the last Old Testament prophet. It should also tell you that the thief on the cross is probably the last Old Testament convert because he died before Jesus.

11:14

If you will receive it. "It" is in italics which means that it is implied and the translators think that you should put it there, no pun intended. But apparently Jesus is saying, "If you will receive this, this is Elijah, who was to come." Why is Elijah mentioned in such close proximity to verse 10? Because Malachi 3 is quoted in Matthew 11:10 and Malachi 4 promises Elijah. And Jesus seems to be saying, "If you'll receive what the law and prophets said about the kingdom, John is your fulfillment of the Elijah promise." It's conditional.

11:15

He that hath ears to hear, let him hear. It's interesting, I think, that we're having to be told that. It's as if sometimes we think that it's enough to simply hear and Jesus says it's somehow possible to hear and not hear.

11:16

But whereunto shall I liken this generation? It is like unto children Notice, please, who is being indicted in this warning: "this generation" that is being indicted as children. Jesus is saying, "Let me tell you who is acting like a bunch of kids: this generation." Jesus has a lot to say about that generation. Now, how many generations could you say have had Jesus, God in the flesh, performing miracles? Just one. Jesus says, "Let me tell you what this generation is like: they're **like children sitting in the markets, calling to one another, their fellows, And saying, We have piped unto you, and ye have not danced.** In other words, "we were happy and you weren't and we're really upset about it that you won't mirror us. Be like us. Then they say, **we have mourned unto you, and ye have not lamented.** So this generation is really strange. "They want me to rejoice when they do and they want me to weep when they do, but they're like kids. They rejoice and weep over the wrong things. Their priorities are completely misplaced. They put things on the list of importance in the wrong order of importance." "Mourned" in verse 17 is the idea of a dirge. We have danced like there is new life and we have mourned like there has been a funeral and you won't play our game.

11:18

For John came neither eating nor drinking, "so he didn't party like you wanted him to, and you say, 'He had a devil.'"

11:19

The Son of man came eating and drinking. "He rejoiced with you and didn't mourn when you wanted him," and **you say, he's a glutton and a winebibber, a friend of publicans and sinners.** "So you are upset because John won't rejoice with you and you're upset because I won't mourn with you. Neither John nor I can win. You want Elijah the prophet and if you would have received his message, he would have been Elijah the prophet but you've rejected both the prophet and the Messiah." Incidentally, I think it's interesting to note that in the latter days when the Jews are going to be under great onslaught from the beast, he's going to have a false prophet who calls fire out of heaven. The false Christ will have a false Elijah to suit the Jewish people.

Wisdom is justified of her children. "I'll tell you what: if you want to know if I'm from God, just look at my fruit and you'll declare me 'righteous' and you'll declare my wisdom 'righteous.'"

11:20

Then began he to upbraid the cities wherein most of his mighty works were done. This probably goes back to verse 1 after he gets done giving the disciples orders.

> *11:1 And it came to pass, when Jesus had made an end of commanding his twelve disciples, he departed thence to teach and to preach **in their cities.***

So I really don't know how much time has elapsed between verse 1 and verse 20 but apparently it was long enough because Jesus begins scolding the cities. Maybe a year. Maybe months.

because they repented not. What an interesting demand that the Son of Man brings to people. He requires that they repent. Repentance is a change of mind that results in a change of action. It's interesting that you have promise of a kingdom coming. In chapter 3, John the Baptist comes preaching, "Repent for the kingdom of heaven is at hand." Why would you repent? Because a King is coming. Matthew 4: Jesus says that men should repent and he preaches the Gospel of the kingdom in every way. These are in context one of another. Then in chapter 11 we have this kingdom talk of verse 11 and then he says in verse 20, **they repented not**.

When a King is coming, we ought to make ourselves ready for the King and Jesus said that these cities did not do it. Whatever they needed to change to be ready for the King, they failed to do it. Notice the main fruit that showed that they failed to do it was the fact that they rejected the message of the King's messenger.

for if the mighty works, which were done in you, had been done in Tyre and Sidon, they would have repented long ago in sackcloth and ashes. But I say unto you, It shall be more tolerable for Tyre and Sidon at the day of judgment, than for you. I want you to notice where Tyre and Sidon are. They're over in the Gentile land. In Isaiah 42 we have a prophecy of coast lands in Gentile land waiting for light and who does Jesus talk about in Matthew 11:22? "It would be more tolerable for Tyre and Sidon at the day of judgment than for you."

Well, so far that doesn't make a whole lot of sense to me because he hasn't been to them yet. What do we do about that? We keep reading. We read four more chapters. We look at Matthew 15:21:

> *Then Jesus went thence, and departed **into the coasts of Tyre and Sidon**. And, behold, a woman of Canaan came out of the same coasts, and cried unto him, saying, Have mercy on me, O Lord, thou Son of David; my daughter is grievously vexed with a devil. But he answered her not a word. And his disciples came and besought him, saying, Send her away; for she crieth after us.*

But he answered and said, I am not sent but unto the lost sheep of the house of Israel.

Clearly Jesus is setting this thing up because he's nowhere near the cities of Israel.

*15:25 Then came she and worshipped him, saying, Lord, help me. But he answered and said, It is not meet to take the children's bread, and to cast it to dogs. And she said, Truth, Lord: yet the dogs eat of the crumbs which fall from their masters' table. Then Jesus answered and said unto her, O woman, great is thy faith: be it unto thee even as thou wilt. And her daughter was made whole from that very hour. And **Jesus departed from thence**. and came nigh unto the sea of Galilee.*

He had one stop in the Tyre and Sidon coasts. Why? Because Isaiah 42 is showing up in front of them and he offers them a yoke that is easy and a burden that is light. After noticing 11:28-29, you will agree, "Yes, yes, you and Tyre and Sidon, come on over here. Little ones, undesirable ones, dogs, come on. No one wants you, but Jesus does."

11:21-22

Woe unto thee, Chorazin! woe unto thee, Bethsaida! Woe unto you. It's like Jesus is saying, "I brought you blessing but you have desired woe." A "woe" is a distress signal. You are about to receive the thumping of your life. Why? Because you didn't repent. Who has woe? That generation. Why? Because they looked at the prophet and the King and said, "Because you didn't dance when we wanted dancers and you didn't mourn when we wanted mourners, we don't want you." I wonder with over ¾ of America claiming to be Christian, I wonder what kind of king they would like? I wonder what kind of prophets they would like? Maybe they would like a king that guarantees them heaven but requires nothing of them. Maybe they would like a king that requires no suffering and no cross, only benefits and entitlements. I wonder what heaven's King requires of us.

if the mighty works, which were done in you, Chorazin and Bethsaida, **had been done in Tyre and Sidon, they would have repented long ago in sackcloth and ashes. But I say unto you, It shall be more**

tolerable for Tyre and Sidon at the day of judgment, than for you. And if you'll read the history of Tyre and Sidon, they were wiped out. They were rebuilt in intertestamental period since their destruction, but they were destroyed in relative short amount of time (unlike Sodom), never to have been rebuilt.

Chorazin and Bethsaida are towns, Jerome from the fifth century says, that were within miles of Capernaum and Capernaum, you might remember, is all chapter 8 and 9. Most of what happens in chapter 8 and 9 happens in Capernaum. Think about this now: when we read **And thou, Capernaum, which art exalted unto heaven, shalt be brought down to hell.** So he's naming three towns that are within really close location, proximity to each other—all around the Sea of Galilee and he says, "You have great distress coming upon you." Why? Because there were millions on the earth but not everyone had Jesus and the prophet. There were thousands of towns on the earth but only but a relative few had Jesus and the prophet. There were hundreds of towns in Israel probably but only a few were named. Think about the density, the tightly packed targeting of Jesus' ministry when he can reference Tyre and Sidon which are in present day Lebanon and say, "They never got what you're getting." Think about it when he can reference Sodom—basically south Palestine and say they were there. He can talk about towns that were within 100 miles and he says, "They would have changed."

We're told that Tyre and Sidon would have repented **in sackcloth and ashes.** They would have torn their clothes and dumped dirt on their head to show their lowliness and their humility and really their self-contempt. If they would have seen what you all see and he says, "in the day of judgment, it will be more tolerable." Get that. He doesn't say it will be tolerable for any of them, it says it will be more tolerable for Tyre and Sidon. Oh, our God is to be dreaded. It is fearful to fall into his hands, Hebrews 12 says. He is a burning fire, and at the same time, mysteriously, in the day of judgment, it will be more tolerable for those who have had less to think about.

The day of judgment could be and in the context I believe it is, based on the language of verse 16, this generation, I do believe we're still talking about the destruction of Jerusalem in AD 70. I think context requires it. I don't think that you have to believe that to get the purpose of the passage, for indeed, at the great white throne judgment, Revelation 20, there are books opened and the dead are judged according to their works. Now, we know you don't go to heaven or hell based on your works; you go based on what Jesus worked on the cross. Somehow it is the same lake of fire for those who die uncoverted, yes, but somehow more tolerable for those who had less light in the night.

11:23

And thou, Capernaum which art exalted unto heaven, shalt be brought down to hell. How are they exalted to heaven? This sounds an awful lot like Isaiah 14:12

> *How art thou fallen from heaven, O Lucifer, son of the morning! thou which didst weaken the nations! You are brought down to Sheol,*

Capernaum, you sound so demonic. You sound so Satanic, Capernaum. How is it that you can sound so Satanic? How is it? How are you exalted to heaven? Well, I don't know anyone else on the globe that can say, "We had the King of kings anchor his ministry here for three years." Think about that.

Matthew loves Isaiah

1. Isaiah 7:14 regarding His Virgin Birth (1:23)
2. Isaiah 11:1 regarding His origin (2:23)
3. Isaiah 40:3 regarding His forerunner (3:3)
4. Isaiah 9:1-2 regarding His scope (4:14-16)
5. Isaiah 53:4 regarding His empathy (8:17)
6. Isaiah 35:4-8 regarding His depth (11:4-5)
7. Isaiah 61:1-2 regarding His preaching (11:5)
8. Isaiah 8:13-14 regarding His surety (11:6)
9. Isaiah 42:3 regarding His tenderness (11:7)
10. Isaiah 14:12-14 regarding Capernaum (11:23)

What a level of responsibility to say, "The Son of God based his ministry in this town for 3 1/3 years and, Capernaum, you were pretty important." How important? Important enough apparently that in Matthew 8 there were Centurions stationed there because one of their servants was healed by the Lord. Important enough apparently, that they could have tax collectors there. Matthew was converted there in Matthew 9. Apparently they were mighty prosperous and important.

They might have been considered exalted and Jesus said, "You're poor. You're dirt poor. You're brought down to hell, the land of the dead." Why? He says, **if the mighty works, which have been done in thee, had been done in Sodom, it would have remained until this day**. See that the Spirit of God is one that says, "Israel, you have a real dilemma and here's the dilemma: you are not urgent about anything."

How do I know they were not urgent? Because Jesus had to remind them they were in a battle. Verse 12, "And from the days of John the Baptist until now the kingdom of heaven suffers violence, and the violent take it by force." Why is he saying that if he didn't need to say it? The fact is he did need to say it because there are people that weren't aware of the fact that there was a mighty struggle happening for the kingdom.

I think another reason we know that they are not very urgent is because in verses 11 through 14, Jesus has to tell them that all history is watching. I mean, he says in verse 13, "all the prophets and the law prophesied until John." Please understand what Jesus is saying.

Israel is not urgent and how do I know? They had no right to rule according to Rome. Why wouldn't they have wanted a kingdom? And yet they still had a level of frivolity. They wanted people to dance with them. They had a level of pettiness and they whined when no one danced with them. The small things matter a lot.

11:24

But I say unto you, That it shall be more tolerable for the land of Sodom in the day of judgment, than for thee. Well, how will Israel pay? By the way, I wish I could limit it just to this generation but unfortunately Israel said something incredibly crazy in Matthew 26, Matthew 27. They said, "His blood be on us and our children." As pro-Israel as I am, you need to understand that much of what they've endured is because of the prayers of that generation as they handed over the only begotten Son of God to the Romans to crucify. So how will they pay?

They will pay by missing the kingdom, verse 11. How will they pay? They will pay by suffering more than previous generations.

11:25

At that time Jesus answered Answered what? No one asked him anything. I think that's kind of funny. What did Jesus answer? He answered their lack of repentance. He answered their obstinance. He answered their insolence. He answered the thoughts of their heart.

and said, I thank thee, O Father, Lord of heaven and earth. That is huge because Jesus just got done talking about these cities: Bethsaida, Chorazin, Tyre, Sidon, Sodom. Then he turns to his Father, he answers their lack of repentance and he answers them and prays to his Father and says, "I give you thanks, Father, who is the boss of all heaven and earth. The Lord. Not just of Chorazin or Bethsaida; Not just Tyre and Sidon and Sodom, but the Lord, the Master **of heaven and earth**, I thank you."

Because thou hast hid these things from the wise and prudent. I don't know if you get the full weight of this. Jesus is thanking the Father for hiding truth. It won't be the last time you see it and only a sovereign God deserves the right to be thanked for withholding truth. We will see it again in Matthew 13 where it says that Jesus spoke in parables because he did not want them to convert. "I thank you, Father, the boss of heaven and earth and basically everyone that's in it."

> *Psalm 24:1 The earth is the LORD'S, and **the fulness thereof;** the earth, and all that dwell therein.*

You show that you're the Master of everyone who lives in it because you have chosen to withhold revelation to **the wise and the prudent.** The wise. Those are the ones that the Greeks loved; the people that could think and debate and philosophize and sound really smart. They did not have these things revealed to them. **These things.** What are these things? They're the things that Jesus preached in those cities and he preached to Bethsaida and he preached to Chorazin, scolded them for not repenting and then thanked the Father for not giving them the ability to repent and Matthew does not butt in and say, "Now, let me see if I can fix this paradox. A God who is requiring you to respond and withholding the revelation possible necessary to let you respond."

"Well, then why missions? Why evangelism?" And Matthew doesn't sort that out for us. No, no, he doesn't. As a matter of fact, he adds a little bit more to the problem. At the end of the book he says, "Go and teach all nations. Make disciples of them and baptize them and teach them all things." Why should I? Because you're told to, that's why. We go because the Master said to go. That's why. We don't go because we have the promise of success or the odds or the potential or the likelihood. No, we go because we're told to go. We go where Christ has not been named and not because it makes sense, but because our Master said, 1. To go; and 2. Because the end of the book says that there would be some there before the throne of every kindred, tribe, people and nation (Revelation 5:9-10).

the prudent "Prudent" is a word that it's kind of shorthand for the one who shows foresight in planning. "Father, you have looked at the wisest among men and you have withheld your truth from them and I thank you for doing so." That doesn't seem like something we should be thanking God for unless you understand that it's his character to do right no matter what. And he says, "I thank you not only that you withheld them from the people that seemed best qualified to handle those truths and you've given them to the little ones, the least."

> *Matthew 11:11 I say unto you, Among them that are born of women there hath not risen a greater than   John the Baptist: notwithstanding he that is **least** in the kingdom of heaven is greater than he.*

And "least" in that verse is the same Greek word as "babes" or "babies" in verse 25 which is the same Greek word found in 10:42…

> *If you give drink of a cold water to **a little one**.*

I mean, the smallest in God's kingdom are greater than the greatest among men. The Father is revealing these things to little ones, insignificant ones. Why is the Son thanking the Father for that? I would expect a Master who finds the most suitable Master-worthy people and give them truth, but God doesn't get much glory out of that. Somehow God looks really good when he takes people that are not fit for much of anything and gives them truth and makes them His. I am overwhelmed with the notion that the Son of God is thanking the Father when he knows what it's going to cost him for this transaction, for we were not free. Salvation is free for us but it certainly wasn't cheap. Being given truth and regenerate hearts made possible by the shed blood of Jesus was free for us but it wasn't free for the Son of God and he looks at the Father and thanks him for this scheme. What a supernatural Son of God!

11:26

Even so, Father: for so it seemed good in thy sight. And that really is the character of the Son, isn't it? "Whatever the Father wants, I'm good with that." I sit back and I consider my own heart and I know that's not me. The things that I worry about, complain about and talk about are so petty. I can't say that I sit back very many days and think "Father, whatever seems good to you, I thank you for it."

11:27

All things are delivered unto me of my Father. So think about Jesus, he preaches to these cities; he says, "You haven't repented and if other cities that weren't so special were given what you were given, they would have repented." Turns to the Father and says, "And I thank you for making it this way for it seemed good to you." Then he turns back to the crowd and says, "All things are delivered unto me of my Father: and no man knoweth the Son, but the Father; neither knoweth any man the Father, except the Son, and he to whomsoever the Son will reveal him."

If Jesus really did have Isaiah 42 on his mind (take a look at Isaiah 42:1-5), consider what he was saying in Matthew 11:27. **All things are delivered unto me of my Father: and no man knows the Son, but the Father; neither knoweth any man the Father, save the Son.** That's pretty awesome if Jesus sees himself in Isaiah 42.

Look at Isaiah 42:6-7. It is sort of what Jesus has been doing, yes? "To bring out the prisoners from the prison," and that is why we said John the Baptist was a little confused because he's still in prison even though blinded eyes are being opened. "And them that sit in darkness out of the prison house."

In Isaiah 42:8 you have Jehovah in Isaiah 42 saying, "I don't share my glory with anybody." In Matthew 11:27, Jesus has already found himself in Isaiah 42 and he says in Matthew 11:27, "I share everything with the Father." **All things are delivered unto me of my Father, we have them in common, and no man knoweth the Son, but the Father; and no man knows the Father, but the Son, and he to whomsoever the Son will reveal him.** Here's what the Son said, "I'm the only one who shares glory with the Father."

If he wasn't claiming to be Jehovah God here, I want to ask you: what exactly was he saying? He finds himself in Isaiah 42 early in chapter 11 with that "reed" and "smoking flax" talk. He is clearly quoting Isaiah 42. Matthew is about Jesus in Matthew 12.

11:28-30

Come unto me, all ye that labour. "I'll take the Chorazins. I'll take the Bethsaidas. I'll take the Sodoms. Just come on. Everyone that **is laboring and heavy laden and I will give you rest."** This is forecasted in chapter 23 when he says to the Pharisees, "Woe unto you for you bind heavy burdens on people and you won't even lift your finger to help them carry it." And Jesus says, in contrast, "Come to me if you feel like you're weighed down. If you feel like the demands of the world are bad enough and then you step into a world where the demands of the religious are even greater. Are you feeling like you're under a heavy load? **Come to me and I will give you rest. Take my yoke upon you."** Please notice that he doesn't say, "Come unto me and remove your yoke and then be on your way."

29 Take my yoke upon you and learn of me for I am meek and lowly in heart and you will find rest unto your souls. For my yoke is easy, and my burden is light. If the Father is the Lord of heaven and earth and the Son reveals him to us, then who do you think is pulling most of the weight under that yoke? **The Lord of heaven and earth** and it's **easy** and **light.** Ezekiel says the way of the transgressor is hard, so before we start talking about "how hard it is to be a Christian," something is going wrong.

30 For My yoke is easy, and My burden is light. One might ask, "Does some of our restlessness reflect a longing in our souls to be with Christ?" I think that while contextually speaking, we're safe in saying that you can ease your restlessness by taking Christ's yoke upon you, it's because most people are generally not known as restful. But, when it comes to the believer, is there a certain amount of restlessness we get in waiting for the coming of the Lord? I suppose, but we need to be very clear what that restlessness is. I want to give you a couple of different Biblical ideas and I think we'll be able to see that Jesus, and Paul, and David, do actually agree.

I feel pretty certain that those in the original context would have understood that the way of the Pharisees and the way of the present day Judeans was not restful. It was not easy. It was not light. I am a little bit weary of Christians who talk about how hard the Christian life is. It's only hard if you're not under the Lord's yoke. He said His **yoke was easy and His burden was light**. The **yoke** is the plowing implement that is used on a farm. Christ says, "I will plow with you, and I am meek and lowly, and you'll find rest for your souls."

1. Philippians 4:11, Paul said,

...I have learned, in whatsoever state I am, therewith to be content.

I would say if there's an antithesis to rest it would be discontent. I would say that the opposite of contentment is restlessness. And we find this in a number of ways: you don't need an update on your home. You desire an update and so you go into debt to get cosmetic things done on your home. That could be considered discontentment. That could be considered restlessness.

2. Paul said in 1 Timothy 6:8,

And having food and raiment let us be therewith content. For it is certain we brought nothing into this world and we should be certain that nothing will be carried out. Don't even desire to be rich because it will trap you.

Paul is pretty clear. Contentment is supposed to be the rule of the Christian. Here's Paul, writing from prison, "I've had a ton in my wallet, or I've had to ask for food from a brother, I've learned to be content." So clearly this contentment and restlessness have a similar idea.

Again, I'm uncomfortable about taking one Scripture and running it into the face of another because I think that that is not the natural way of reading Scripture. I think Jesus was speaking to a particular context. But the question introduces a dialogue. We do need to at least entertain the good question of, "Is some of my restlessness righteous? Here I am waiting for the coming of the Lord." And I would say that that is a different kind of restlessness. Christians don't typically exercise their weary souls by turning up their intensity for the coming of the Lord.

This is tricky, because we're sinful people and we always want our sinfulness even to look righteous, and so we'll say, "Oh, I don't know why the Lord just doesn't come and take me out of this." But really what you're doing is murmuring and complaining. You don't love the coming of the Lord; you hate your burden. You don't love the presence of Jesus in a physical body in front of you as the risen Lord of Revelation 1; no, you love the idea of being yanked out of your lack of riches, relationship problems, dead-end jobs, lack of progression at your job. I hope you get what I'm saying here.

So, what would we call that holy restlessness? Because the unholy kind is certainly analogous to the discontent Paul eludes to. So is it possible to be content and still somehow righteously discontented with the current world, ready for the Lord to come? I think that David speaks to this:

> Psalm 17:13-15 *Arise, O Lord, disappoint him, cast him down: deliver my soul from the wicked,   which is thy sword: from men which are thy hand, O Lord, from men of the world, which have their portion in this life, and whose belly thou fillest with thy hid treasure: they are full of children, and leave the rest of their substance to their babes. But as for me, I will behold thy face in righteousness: I shall be **satisfied**, when I awake, with thy likeness.*

At resurrection morning, then I'll be truly satisfied. I'll feel like I'm at home. There's a big difference between saying, "I don't feel at home here," and saying, "My soul is weary and I feel like I could just quit." There's a big difference between saying, "I cannot wait to get to my eternal home in the presence of God," and saying, "I wish I had this; I wish I had that; I wish…" Now again, this is very, very, very introspective in nature. We can seriously re-label our discontent with the world with a love for Christ. And all I'm asking us to realize is that there is a difference between contentment and satisfaction. I could not possibly be satisfied in anything worldly if I'm a Spirit-filled believer. I am however, supposed to be content in whatever state I am placed in by the Lord, directly or indirectly.

David said, "The only time that I'm going to find real satisfaction is when I am back with the One with Whom I belong, totally in His presence for the first time, wonderfully satisfied, with a perfect body. I'll awake in His likeness, and then, and only then, will I find perfect satisfaction."

So the answer to the question is that the weary soul is the one who's been plagued with Phariseeism, and first century deadness, and expectation of unreasonable religionists, and an expectation of people who have served their sin. They can expect a weary soul. They're sheep scattered abroad, not having a shepherd. And Jesus said, "I have compassion on that multitude," Matthew 9:36-38.

So, let us be, first of all, very careful that we're not relabeling our sin as if it were something righteous. If that's you, and you find yourself continually embittered by this world, that is not the will of the Lord. Take His yoke upon you. But if you are continually reminded of a better place, and a better time, and a better destiny, an ultimate time with Jesus, then yes, that is a weariness in the soul that is not in Matthew 11:30, and you can take great consolation in that you share it with David.

28 Come unto Me, all ye that labour and are heavy laden, and I will give you rest. Here's the idea: "I will give you rest." That is three words in the Greek and it is, "I will cause you to rest." Sometimes Jesus says, "I am going to make you rest. You are weary because of you. You are heavy laden because of others. I've got the cure. I'm not asking for your permission. I'm going to make you rest." I don't know if you've ever been in that position in your life, but God just sometimes kicks the door open and says, "I'm here and you're going to rest." He loves us that much. What seems like an inconvenience is the Lord's way of saying, "Enough! I'm sorry you don't have the money for that. You are going to rest. I'm sorry you don't have the time to do that. You're going to rest. I'm going to cause you to rest." It sounds a lot like Psalm 23:2. He makes us to lie down in green pastures. He makes us. He doesn't ask for permission. So here's the lesson I want you to get: If you're feeling inconvenienced and doing without, it could very well be just that you're not resting very well on your own.

> *Jeremiah 6:9 Thus saith the LORD of hosts, They shall throughly glean the remnant of Israel as a vine: turn back thine hand as a grapegatherer into the baskets. To whom shall I speak, and give warning, that they may hear? Behold, their ear is uncircumcised, and they cannot hearken: behold, the word of the LORD is unto them a reproach; they have no delight in it.*

Let that sink in. They have no delight in the word of the Lord. They have no delight in being corrected by the word of the Lord.

Now look at Jeremiah 6:11-12, and you know this happened. It happened to Israel: the northern ten tribes with the Assyrian empire in 722 BC, and it happened with the Babylonians in 605 BC. God did have a rapture of sorts of His people. They were snatched away. It says the husband and wife will be taken together. Doesn't that sound a little like Matthew, "where two will be in the bed; one will be taken and the other left?" But here, both will be taken in judgment; a snatching away. There's coming some people, that will be working for the Lord, that will take everything of yours.

> *6:13 For from the least of them even unto the greatest of them every one is given to covetousness; and from the prophet even unto the priest every one dealeth falsely. They have healed also the hurt of the daughter of My people slightly, saying, Peace, peace; when there is no peace. 15 We're getting to the point. Were they ashamed when they had committed abomination? Nay, they were not at all ashamed, neither could they blush. Therefore they shall fall among them that fall: at the time that I visit them they shall be cast down, saith the LORD.*

It's one of those "fix it before I come down there" sort of things.

> *6:16 Thus saith the LORD, Stand ye in the ways, and see, and ask for the old paths, where is the good way, and walk therein,*

and ye shall find rest for your souls. But they said, We will not walk therein.

God says, "I want you to have rest in your souls." Now I am truly awestruck by this. Because He is offering them rest for their souls and there's no indication in this passage, the one before it, the one after, that anyone in that land was looking for peace in their heart or rest for their soul. That speaks to the character of God. He offers rest to people who are not sure they need it, and certainly are sure that if they do need it they're not going to get it walking in the old paths. How sad it is to find restless souls.

So, I want to know what these old paths are.

18:13 Therefore thus saith the LORD; Ask ye now among the heathen, who hath heard such things: the virgin of Israel hath done a very horrible thing. Will a man leave the snow of Lebanon which cometh from the rock of the field? Or shall the cold flowing waters that come from another place be forsaken? Because My people hath forgotten Me, they have burned incense to vanity, and they have caused them to stumble in their ways from the ancient paths, to walk in paths, in a way not cast up.

"They've caused My people to walk in ways that are not ancient. They're not old ways." We can describe it as purity, innocence, simplicity (verses 13-14). How about from verse 15? Cold and refreshing. Verse 14. Cold flowing waters that come from another place. Snow that comes from a rock. Somehow old paths are to be seen as those things that are clean, refreshing, innocent, pure, simple.

29 Take My yoke and learn of Me. The word behind "learn" there is the same word we get our word "disciple" from. It has the idea of God saying, "I am not only going to take and put My yoke on you but you are now going to be My disciple." Whatever the old paths is, it is not a lazy man's position. "You are now going to learn from Me." "You are going to learn from Me." *Apo* is the word in the original. "You're going to learn, you're going to take things from Me as you're sharing My load."

30 For My yoke is easy, and My burden is light. find is *eureka* in the Greek. It has the idea of, "You have been searching and here it is! You have found it! And it is rest!" The idea is in your souls, deep in the core of you, "rest" is going to become part of your fiber. "I'm going to make you rest to the point where they're going to have to do dynamite operations to get My rest out of you." Now that will be a day.

Now, how do we make the connection between the God of the Old Testament and Jesus in the New Testament? How is it that they're saying the same thing? It's the same one speaking in both places: Jeremiah 6 and Matthew 11. And God is still interested. I am amazed! Hundreds of years have passed, and God is still interested in His people having souls that are at rest.

Come. I wish I could say He was kind of suggesting it, but it is in the imperative. **Come to Me, all you that labor and are heavy laden.** It is, "You who are laboring yourselves, and are laden from others. You who are exhausted because of what you put on yourself and you who are exhausted because of what other people put on you." He says, "I don't care if you have caused the problems in your life. **Come. Come**. I don't care if other people have caused the problems in your life. Someone has laden you down. **Come."** And immediately I wonder, "Bill Sturm, is there anyone that you're putting a burden on?" Because I don't want Jesus calling someone for relief from me.

I know what the old paths is not: the way of the Pharisees.

> *Matthew 23:3 You go land and sea to make a convert and you won't even help them with the slightest burden. You lay things on them, more things to obey, more things to observe, more things to do, and you won't even drive by the house and pick them up to do it.*

If your idea of old paths, if your idea of purity, if your idea of innocence, if your idea of simplicity from Jeremiah 18, if your idea of old paths, Jeremiah 6, Jeremiah 18…if it's anything like the Pharisees, please know this: #1. You're wrong. #2. You do not have rest in your souls.

So here Jesus speaks as a rabbi. That whole **yoke** language is what a rabbi would say. Even today if you find a Jew, orthodox, liberal, or otherwise, they love their favorite rabbis. They quote their favorite rabbis, some from as recently as the thirteenth century, some more recent than that, especially the *kabbalah*. You've got all kinds of recent sects of Judaism, you have ancient sects of Judaism and they all have their favorite rabbis, and when you were going to follow a rabbi you would take on his **yoke**, his burden of teaching. You say, "I'm a follower of rabbi ben-so-and-so," that meant you took on his **yoke** and that even the additional traditions that he added to the law, to the Torah, that meant that you took those on as well. And Jesus says, "I'll be your rabbi. Things are not working for you so well. Come with Me. **My burden is light.**"

Chapter 12

12:1-2[50]

At that time The time that Jesus spoke Matthew 11:28-30 concerning His easier yoke. We are about to see that this thing known as the **Sabbath,** which was meant to be a blessing, became a burden.

12:5-8

5 Or have you not read in the law that on the Sabbath the priests in the temple profane the opposite of "consecrate" (or desecrate). That is, it was not "consecrated for the priests; It was not set aside." Is Jesus not as good as Aaron? Jesus, is now comparing Himself to David and Aaron...and then the temple. **the Sabbath, and are blameless? 6 Yet I say to you that in this place there is One greater than the temple.** "I'm better than the table of showbread, the priest, king David, and the Sabbath. You appreciate the architecture. Appreciate me." **7 But if you had known what *this* means,** He says to Bible scholars..."If you understood Hosea 6 and not merely read..." *'I desire mercy and not sacrifice,'* Apparently, this is the "yoke" Jesus intended for His people (Matthew 11:28-30). If God has not changed, then you can well rest assured that if your actions come from "compassion" or "tender mercy," you're probably acting in a godly way.

Incidentally, many of us who think of ourselves as servants and see our service as sacrifice should take note that it is far more impressive to God to show **mercy.** The priest and Levite in the "Good Samaritan" illustration Jesus gave in Luke 10 were busy being "sacrificial" or "ministerial" and didn't have time for **mercy.** We'll know we're under the same yoke when this takes place in our lives. This has nothing to do with "looking the other way," but rather, it is about withholding what the evidence says belongs to the person. When we don't profit from an act, we can say we are legitimately offering **mercy.**

12:11-13

---

[50]More on this episode in the author's commentary on Mark (2:23-3:12).

11 Then He said to them, "What man is there among you who has one sheep, and if it falls into a pit on the Sabbath, will not lay hold of it and lift *it* out? "Everyone of you would rescue your pet. So not only am I better than David and Aaron and the temple and the Sabbath...; and not only is 'mercy better than sacrifice'; but this man is better than your sheep." This certainly goes well with chapters 6 and 10 where He declares that we are more important than sparrows and flowers. **12 Of how much more value then is a man than a sheep? Therefore it is lawful** in answer to verse 10's question. By the way, He quotes Hosea in verse 7 and then calls it **lawful.** This means the whole of the O.T. is deemed as "the law" at times by Biblical authors.

to do good on the Sabbath." Apparently, it was well within Moses' intent—more than that, Jehovah's intent, to do well on the Sabbath. It is, therefore, lawful and orderly and godly to do well on the Sabbath.

12:15-21

But when Jesus knew it, He withdrew from there. It isn't always time to die, and I can't do everything, but I can "heal" some. **And great multitudes followed Him, and He healed them all.** On the Sabbath day...as **withdrew,** He was touching everybody as He went. There is a grand difference between giving all you're your time to something and giving none of your time to something. In Jesus' case, He can't help but heal people; it's a forecast of the kingdom promised in the Isaiah passage to be quoted (verses 17-21 out of Isaiah 42). In the grander context

Similarities between Isaiah 42 and Matthew

- Isaiah 42:1 "My Spirit upon Him" (Matt 3:11-15)
- Isaiah 42:3 A broken reed (Matt 11:11)
- Isaiah 42:5 Lord of Heaven & Earth (Matt 11:25)
- Isaiah 42:7 Opening blind eyes (Matt 11:5)
- Isaiah 42:8 The Son shares glory (Matt 11:27)
- Isaiah 42:1-4 Quoted (Matthew 12:17-21)

If Jesus really did have Isaiah 42 on His mind (and Matthew caught wind of it), consider what this means for those "on the coastlands."

(since the beginning of the passage), we will be healed entirely on the ultimate Sabbath rest, and He will not say, "Don't tell anybody." **16 Yet He warned them not to make Him known,** why? Again, why?

Because of what is quoted in the passage soon to be quoted by Matthew. Perhaps this privacy of ministry is to forgo his kingdom so that He buys more time for the people of Israel to repent? If everybody wants Him, and He's made King, He will have to "crush their bruised reed?" Today, they get another chance…and so do their families.

12:22-24

Then one was brought to Him who was demon-possessed, blind and mute; This word is typically translated as "deaf" in other parts of the New Testament. **and He healed him, so that the blind and mute man both spoke and saw. 24 Now when the Pharisees heard it they said,** This is the 2nd possible reaction.

12:25-30

But Jesus knew their thoughts, again, as in early last chapter. The Creator, the One Who spoke all things into existence, gave these created beings their mouths and their oxygen to utter such sick tings about the Lord. **and said to them: "Every kingdom divided against itself is brought to desolation, and every city or house divided against itself will not stand. 26 If Satan** Matthew 9:32 and 10:25 and 13:19 and 25 show this is a continuing theme. **casts out Satan, he is divided against himself.** This should tell us that though Judas partook in apostolic power (in some shade), he did not cast out demons. (referencing John 6:66). **27 And if I cast out demons by Beelzebub,** this proximity to verse 26 shows the connection between this title and Satan. **by whom do your sons cast *them* out? Therefore they shall be your judges.** "Does this mean that their friends were casting out devils by **Beelzebub** or by the Holy Spirit? How do you know?" an indictment against hteir own friends. If they could cast out devils by the Spirit of God, why couldn't Jesus do the same? **28 But if I cast out demons by the Spirit of God, surely the kingdom of God has come upon you.** They have two choices; only two. If Jesus is casting them out by the Spirit of God, then the Kingdom of God has come, and the Pharisees are automatically on the wrong team. Somehow, the kingdom has not yet come (Lord's Prayer, Matthew 6), yet in a sense, it has come already. **30 He who is not with Me is against Me, and he who does not gather with Me scatters abroad.** Again, a 2nd time…only two choices.

12:32

Anyone who speaks a word Matthew 12:10 and 12:38-39 show that "speaking a word **against the Son of Man** gives the idea that speaking against Christ is a "stair-step" to this "blasphemy." Those who speak against Christ have a heart against Christ (verse 33). Verse 34 speaks of a heart that feeds a mouth that speaks against Christ that blasphemes the Holy Spirit (in this passage). I say "speaks" because "blaspheme" is in the aorist tense. In other words, it is not related to a time, but leaves the door open for a state of unforgiveness so long as there is a sin of blasphemy ongoing. If the blasphemy discontinues, speaking against Christ discontinues, and forgiveness is available.[51]

it will be forgiven him; but whoever speaks against the Holy Spirit, it will not be forgiven him, The implication, of course, is that Jesus did all of His "mighty works" (term used in last part of chapter 13) by the power of the **Holy Spirit.**

12:33-37

"Either make the tree good and its fruit good, Matthew 7:15 and Matthew 13's four soils show this is a continuing theme through this passage. **or else make the tree bad and its fruit bad; for a tree is known by its fruit. 34 Brood of vipers! How can you, being evil, speak good things?** "I would expect you to say something stupid…because you're evil." **For out of the abundance of the heart the mouth speaks. 35 A good man out of the good treasure of his heart** Matthew 5:8 and Matthew 13:15-18 shows this is a continuing theme to and through this verse. **brings forth good things,** Matthew 6:19-21 and Matthew 13:52 show this is a continuing theme to and through this verse. **and an evil man out of the evil treasure brings forth evil things. 36 But I say to you that for every idle word men may speak, they will give account of it in the day of judgment.** Matthew 11:32 and 12:41 show this is a continuing theme to and through this verse. **37 For by your words you will be justified, and by**

---

[51] The time element of this sin and a summary of the sin as a whole, I think, are better handled in the author's commentary on Mark 3.

your words you will be condemned." Seeing, then, these six continuing themes throughout this episode, we can say that the blasphemy of the Holy Spirit:

12:38

Then certain of the scribes and of the Pharisees answered. That requires us to ask the question, "What are they answering?" And they're answering His words, Jesus spoke in verses 33 to 37. Well He spoke well before that but He told them in verse 36: But I say unto you, "That every idle word that men shall speak, they shall give account thereof in the day of judgment. For by thy words thou shalt be justified, and by thy words thou shalt be condemned."

Then certain of the scribes and of the Pharisees answered, saying, Master (Teacher, Rabbi)**, we would see a sign from Thee.** I guess casting a devil out of a blind, dumb man wasn't a sign.

12:39

And Jesus says, **there shall no sign be given to this wicked and evil and adulterous generation but the sign of the prophet Jonah.**[52] **but the sign of the prophet Jonah:** Please notice: as **Jonah** was a sign to

---

[52]Mark 8:12 does not contain this "sign." He is the only one that does not mention the sign of Jonah. In other words, mentioning the sign of Jonah may have been meaningless to Mark's audience. Mark wrote to somebody. What if the people he wrote to didn't know anything about Jonah? So why introduce it and get them thinking about something else?

It's like me looking at my three children one day and saying, "We will not be going anywhere this summer except for Grandma's house." One child says to her boss at work, "We're not going anywhere this summer except for a week in July." Why would her boss care? He's got to work that schedule. Child #2 tells his soccer coach "We're not going anywhere this summer except for just under a week in July." Why would the soccer coach care? He needs to build practices around the individual roles of the players. The third child tells the neighbor girl, "We'll be here all summer." It's generally true. It's mostly true. It's so true it's virtually true. It's functionally true. It's essentially true. The neighbor girl can count on Leah to be around all summer, generally. The neighbor girl could be around so much that from the beginning of the three-month summer it's good enough to say, "We're going nowhere," when vacation constitutes a mere 8% of the summer. So it could be that to Mark's audience it was generally true. There was no sign going to be given to this generation because his audience was completely uninterested and completely unaware of the sign of Jonah.

the Ninevites, so shall also the Son of Man be to this generation. Somehow Jesus, in Matthew, says that the burial of Jonah in the whale and his being spit out again was a **sign** of the Son of God. But that's not the completion of the sign. That's not the totality of the sign. There's about four to five hundred miles between the Mediterranean Sea and Mosul (or Nineveh). You know the men of Nineveh were not standing on the beach that day. Somehow a Jonah that spent three days and three nights in the belly of death was a **sign** to the Ninevites. And Jesus says, "That's the only **sign** y'all are getting." The resurrected Christ is going to appear in a magnified sort of way and you're going to know that it is He and He is quite alive.

> *Matthew 24:29 Immediately after the tribulation of those days shall the sun be darkened, and the moon shall not give her light, and the stars shall fall from heaven, and the powers of the heavens shall be shaken: And then shall appear **the sign of the Son of Man** in heaven: and then shall all the tribes of the earth mourn, and they shall see the Son of Man coming in the clouds of heaven with power and great glory.*

This **sign** of the Son of Man in heaven is also **the sign of Jonah**. How do I know that? Very simple: Jesus said that generation would get one sign. They get one **sign**.

> *24:31 And He shall send His angels with a great sound of a trumpet, and they shall gather together His elect from the four winds, from one end of heaven to the other. Now learn a parable of the fig tree; When His branch is yet tender, and putteth forth leaves, ye know that summer is nigh. 33 So likewise ye, when ye shall see all these things, know that it is near, even at the doors. **This generation** shall not pass, till all these things be fulfilled.*

You have the generation of Christ's day seeing a "sign of the Son of Man" in heaven. And we're told, twelve chapters earlier, that that generation gets one sign and it's **the sign of the prophet Jonah**. You have a resurrected prophet appearing to people to preach to them.

Both chapter 12 and chapter 24 recipients are **this generation**. Isn't that what it says? And in both verses, not only does it say **this generation**, the **generation** of Jesus, but it also says **the sign of the Son**

of Man. Isn't that what it says in both chapters? And we're told that **generation** only gets one **sign** and it will appear in heaven, in **this generation**.

12:40

For as Jonas was three days and three nights in the whale's belly; It appears to be the only time the word whale is used in the entire New Testament. That is why some versions say "great fish." The word comes from a Greek word that means a gaping fish.

so shall the Son of Man be three days and three nights in the heart of the earth. Is it three days and three nights total? Is it 72 hours? If so, how will you get 72 hours between Good Friday afternoon and Sunday before dawn?"

> *Esther 4:15 Then Esther bade them return Mordecai this answer, Go, gather together all the Jews that are present in Shushan, and fast ye for me, and neither eat nor drink **three days, night or day**: I also and my maidens will fast likewise; and so will I go in unto the king, which is not according to the law: and if I perish, I perish. So Mordecai went his way, and did according to all that Esther had commanded him. Now it came to pass **on the third day**, that Esther put on her royal apparel, and stood in the inner court of the king's house.*

She's standing before the king on the third **day,** and she says here that it would be after **three days and three nights** that she would go to the king. Now how is it possible to say it will be three days and three nights and yet it will take place on the third day?

> *Matthew 16:21 From that time forth began Jesus to shew unto His disciples, how that He must go unto Jerusalem, and suffer many things of the elders and chief priests and scribes, and be killed, and be raised again **the third day**.*

Now, how can both passages of Scripture be true? How can this be true that says that He'll be raised the third day, and the one we're examining here in chapter 12 that says He'll be in the grave **three days and three nights**? Yet we see in Esther that somehow in the Jewish mindset it was possible for three days and three nights to somehow still be true as well as her entering "on the third day."

> *By Jewish reckoning a part of a day was considered to be a whole day. And it was common Jewish idiom to refer to even a part of a day as a day and a night. So three days and three nights might refer to as much as seventy-two hours or as little as twenty-six. One full twenty-four hour day together with one hour of the preceding and one hour of the following. This explains why Jesus could be said to be in the tomb three days and three nights when He was buried late Friday and rose on early Sunday.*[53]

So if you can think like a Jewish person long enough to read this verse you realize that any part of Friday counted as a day and a night. Any part of Saturday counted as a day and a night. Any part of Sunday counted as a day and a night. So it is possible that He did die on Friday, having been raised from the dead just before dawn on Sunday.[54]

Shall the Son of Man be three days and three nights in the heart of the earth It either means exactly what it says or we have to find a pretty good reason for not thinking it means exactly what it says.

> *Psalm 139 I will praise Thee; for I am fearfully and wonderfully made: marvellous are Thy works; and that my soul knoweth right well. My substance was not hid from Thee, when I was made in secret, and curiously wrought **in the lowest parts of the earth**.*

The Psalmist seems to be calling his mother's womb the lowest parts of the earth. Many times in Jewish custom they saw the womb and the tomb both kind of the same; the womb is a sort of a tomb. And so the birth of a child was kind of like a resurrection, because there he is, hidden in a tomb so to speak, hidden in a womb, and he comes out at birth. The reality is, children often died before they were born and so it was a great thing when a child and a mother endured pregnancy and a child was delivered. There's another possibility.

---

[53] Stuart K. Weber, *Matthew*, vol. 1, Holman New Testament Commentary (Nashville, TN: Broadman & Holman Publishers, 2000), 179.

[54] Luke 24:21 does introduce another dilemma, having occurred on Sunday afternoon.

*Ephesians 4:8: Wherefore He saith, When He ascended up on high, He led captivity captive, and gave gifts unto men. (Now that He ascended, what is it but that He also descended first **into the lower parts of the earth?** He that descended is the same also that ascended up far above all heavens, that He might fill all things.)*

It really looks like the writer of Ephesians is saying that the Lord went into the center of the earth, or the lower parts of the earth. Or is he using it in the same way that the writer of Psalm 139 was using it to refer to the tomb? I believe He went to the lower parts of the earth. See my commentary on Revelation (9:1).

12:41

The men of Nineveh shall rise in judgment with this generation, and shall condemn it: because they repented at the preaching of Jonah; One might allow for a reference of a fictional character named **Jonah** here, but the problem is that the folks of Nineveh are spoken of as nonfictional people that will take part in a future judgment. And so Jesus is referencing the people of Nineveh, and they'll be at the future judgment. So it doesn't make any sense that Jonah didn't exist. Jonah is one of many Old Testament personalities that have been mentioned in Matthew so far. He's mentioned Moses and Abraham and Isaac and Jacob in chapter 8, Elijah in chapter 11, David in chapter 12.

shall rise in judgment with this generation. Somehow, either in a very literal sense in a future judgment, or in a very figurative sense in a figurative judgment, and we're not going to reargue our case here, but somehow, in verse 41 we're told that there's going to be a future judgment with witnesses. Witnesses. Now we already know there's going to be evidence there. Revelation 20 says there will be books opened. We're told that there will be a great white throne. We already know there's going to be a judge there. We already know there's going to be a judge, there's going to be books; we know there's going to be a courtroom. We know all of this and now we get word from Jesus that there will be witnesses that will condemn it. Maybe even strong, beyond the language of witnesses. You'll understand of course that the Lord did not author the constitution, so you'll have to forgive Him if it doesn't fit that whole bicameral house and the three branches of government. But there's this idea that there are witnesses who will act as a jury against you and pronounce your guilt. And they're going to condemn this generation because they, the men of Nineveh, they repented. They changed their mind, they changed the direction, they had a different attitude because of the preaching of Jonah. Now that is really something. We're going to see why that's something. But Jesus would say, now get this: Jonah lived about 800 years before Jesus did. Think about the weight, think about the gravity of such a statement as saying something like, "Preaching worked back then. It should work now." And He holds them accountable because it doesn't work with them.

rise in judgment I'd like you to also see that there's the contextual connection of judgment.

> *Matthew 10:15 Verily I say unto you, It shall be more tolerable for the land of Sodom and Gomorrha in **the day of judgment**.*

> *Matthew 11:21-24 Woe unto thee, Chorazin! woe unto thee, Bethsaida! for if the mighty works, which were done in you, had been done in Tyre and Sidon, they would have repented long ago in sackcloth and ashes. But I say unto you, It shall be more tolerable for Tyre and Sidon at the day of judgment. 23 And thou, Capernaum, which art exalted unto heaven, shalt be brought down to hell. 24 But I say unto you, That it shall be more tolerable for the land of Sodom in **the day of judgment**.*

> *Matthew 12:36 Out of every idle word that men shall speak, they shall give account thereof in **the day of judgment**.*

Jesus is far more concerned about the day of judgment than typically we are. If Jesus believes that day is so dreadful that He will continually warn us, then I say to you we need an eternal perspective once again. Oh, I'm afraid we're not thinking eternally.

Apparently, the people of that generation will stand at the judgment with great accountability, great accountability. And here's the scary thing: somehow people from this life will be at that judgment and quite possibly bear witness against you and I. You say, "Where do you get that from the text?" I don't. I get the possibility from the text. Jesus says the men of Nineveh will rise with this generation and condemn it.

They're going to be witnesses at the judgment of that first century people. Only that generation can look forward to such things Biblically, but I wonder if by application America will give a special account for the riches that it has experienced, and the wisdom of God preached from pulpits, thousands, tens of thousands of pulpits, and they would not repent. I wonder.

They repented at the preaching of Jonah; and, behold, a greater than Jonah is here. See my commentary on the Minor prophets for more on this (Chapter on Jonah).

12:42

The queen of the south shall rise up in the judgment with this generation, and shall condemn it: for she came from the uttermost parts of the earth to hear the wisdom of Solomon; and, behold, a greater than Solomon is here." What were the names of the two Old Testament characters? Queen of the south and Solomon. And what were the names of the two parties that were involved who actually repent or at least were enthralled with the presence of God in these two parties? The Ninevites and The Queen of Sheba. If you cross references this with 1 Kings 10 you would find that **the queen of the south** is the Queen of Sheba. Good, good.

Who's going to **condemn** that generation at the judgment? **The queen of the south** and **The Ninevites.** So, what does that sound like if you have a judicial setting? Who do we know that are usually at these courtroom dramas? A judge; a jury; a defendant; a plaintiff; and witnesses.

What does that mean they have to do? They have to witness. So, it seems like since we're told that both parties repented, there's a strong possibility, that since the indictment is against those in Jesus' day who did not repent, it seems like the Ninevites and the queen of the south, are in heaven, or at least with God, and that they are gathering evidence against those who lived in Jesus' day who did not repent at His preaching. How can you condemn someone when you didn't see anything? It seems reasonable, then, that those in heaven can still see what is occurring on earth. Does that prove that people can see from heaven in 2016? No. It allows for the possibility. Some people saw some things during a certain time, it allows for the possibility that all people can see everything all the time, because we don't have a scripture that says they cannot, right? We're going to be skillful with the Word and go as far as it does.

> *Revelation 7:9 After this I beheld, and, lo, a great multitude, which no man could number, of all nations, and kindreds, and people, and tongues, stood before the throne, and before the Lamb, clothed with white robes, and palms in their hands; 10. and cried with a loud voice, saying, "Salvation to our God which sitteth upon the throne, and unto the Lamb."*

All right, stop. Where are these people that no one can number? Before the throne and before the Lamb. So, multitude which no man can number, standing before God, right?

> *11. And all the angels stood round about the throne, and about the elders and the four beasts, and fell before the throne on their faces, and worshipped God, 12. Saying, "Amen: Blessing, and glory, and wisdom, and thanksgiving, and honour, and power, and might, be unto our God for ever and ever. Amen." 13. And one of the elders answered, saying unto me, "What are these which are arrayed in white robes? and whence came they?" 14. And I said unto him, "Sir, thou knowest." And he said to me, "These are they which came out of great tribulation, and have washed their robes, and made them white in the blood of the Lamb." 15. Therefore are they before the throne of God, and serve Him day and night in His temple: and He that sitteth on the throne shall dwell among them. 16. They shall hunger no more, neither thirst any more; neither shall the sun light on them, nor any heat. 17. For the Lamb which is in the midst of the throne shall feed them, and shall lead them unto living fountains of waters: and **God shall wipe away all tears from their eyes**.*

Ok. So, what we have here is God wiping tears from their eyes and they are coming out of great tribulation. Now the question you have to ask yourself: is it because they don't see anything sad? Or is it because they are taken up with a particular labor? And I think you know I'm loading the question. They are busy doing something for the One on the throne.

Yet, chapter 8 verse 1, when the Lamb opened the seventh seal there was silence in heaven for about half an hour.

As as this drama's unfolding in Revelation 7 and 8, whatever is happening on Earth is of such magnitude that it causes everyone in heaven to be quiet. That's really something. Apparently it's possible for both things to be true, in a matter of two verses. Apparently, in chapter 7 verse 17, it is possible to have your tears wiped away, and in chapter 8 verse 1, to be fully aware of what is about to be unleashed on Earth. So, the fact that there's no tears is a very general statement saying that this is not a place where you experience heart-wrenching grief, but it is a place where you are aware of the grief taking place on Earth. Now I don't know what happens to us on our way to heaven. I don't have any idea. But somehow what happens here affects us differently when we're there. I guess that's why those same people in heaven are able to rejoice when whole cities are being destroyed (like Revelation 17's Babylon). Because it's right. What God does is right.

she came from the uttermost parts of the earth to hear the wisdom of Solomon. She came from the edge of known civilization. She came from a mighty long way and she came to hear the wisdom of Solomon.

There was a man named David who was the son of Jesse, who was the son of a man who was the son of a man, who was the son of Boaz. And Boaz was in the line of Judah. And David was the youngest of eight sons, if memory serves. David was the runt of the litter. He was unimpressive in his appearance to the point where when Samuel was looking for a replacement for King Saul he comes to the house of Jesse in a town called Bethlehem, he was not brought forth.

David, for a couple decades it seems, is being run away from Jerusalem and all things regal by King Saul. He is a very loyal follower of King Saul. He has the opportunity to kill Saul and he does not do it. I must tell you, I'm not sure I would have let those chances slip away. I'm not sure I could be accused of being a man after God's own heart like David was. David reigned seven years in Hebron and thirty-three years in Jerusalem after all of Israel was united under him. He reigned a total of forty years and during that forty years Solomon was born. Solomon was the second son of David and Bathsheba. The first one died, and so, now you have Solomon. And you know it says in 1 Samuel

18:17 that David "went in and out among the people," and he was loved by the discouraged and the despondent and the broken and the people that were not popular. They loved David. He was one of them, sleeping under the same stars and enduring the same cold with them. In 1ˢᵗ Kings, David is dying and he is so cold, and like it or not I'm just relaying the story to you, they bring a younger lady in to keep him warm. And I don't believe it has any sexual inference, because honestly I don't think David was in that mood. And he was dying or almost dead and freezing.

And so David tells his son Solomon, "Show yourself a man." And one of the first things Solomon does is he offers up a prayer to God when God appears to him in the night, and he says, "Lord, I need your wisdom to lead your people." This is what Solomon says: "I don't know how to go in or out among your people." Complete opposite of his dad. Dad was a soldier who slept in the woods with Saul's men that then came to David, and even some foreigners found their way to David. And often it was basically the foreigners who made up David's group, four to six hundred men at different times, until he became king. And so Solomon is told, "Show yourself a man."

David meanwhile had aspirations of building God a house. The Ark of the Covenant was the presence of God on earth ever since it was built by Moses in the wilderness, right after the exodus. Along with about five other pieces of furniture: the brazen altar, the table of showbread, the menorah, the altar of incense, and the laver. Those things have been traveling around in a tabernacle, which is basically just a beautiful tent. God said to David, "You are not going to build My house for Me because your hands are full of blood. You've killed so many that the girls in the streets sing about it." Tens of thousands, and that was before he was even king, you know. How much had he killed after forty more years of campaigns spreading all the way to the Euphrates (which in some ways is a shadow of the fulfillment of the land promise to Abraham made in Genesis 15) to the river of Egypt.

David dies and Solomon, in the fourth year of his reign begins, we're told in 1 Kings chapter 6 verse 1, the building of the temple. Then on the day of dedication they have thousands of animals sacrificed on the day of dedication. A very bloody sight at the dedication of Solomon's temple and yet there was nothing more glorious going on in all the world than going on at that moment.

*1 Kings 10:1 And when the **queen of Sheba** heard of the fame of Solomon concerning the name of the LORD, she came to test him, prove him with hard questions.*

This lady was probably from current day Ethiopia and she came to Jerusalem. This is probably the reason why there's an Ethiopian traveling from Jerusalem back to home, in Acts chapter 8.

10:2 And she came to Jerusalem with a very great train, with camels that bare spices, and very much gold, and precious stones: and when she was come to Solomon, she communed with him of all that was in her heart. And Solomon told her all her questions. And when the queen of Sheba had seen all Solomon's wisdom, and the house that he had built, And the meat of his table, and the sitting of his servants, and the attendance of his ministers, and their apparel, and his cupbearers, and his ascent by which he went up unto the house of the LORD; there was no more spirit in her.

No more breath. There was no more breath in her lungs.

And she said to the king, It was a true report that I heard in mine own land of thy acts and of thy wisdom. Howbeit I believed not the words, until I came, and mine eyes had seen it: and, behold, the half was not told me.

"They couldn't tell me all that I'm seeing here."

Thy wisdom and prosperity exceedeth the fame which I heard. Happy are thy men, happy are these thy servants, which stand continually before thee, and that hear thy wisdom. Blessed be the LORD thy God, which delighted in you, to set you on the throne of Israel: because the LORD loved Israel for ever.

"He set a Solomon on the throne and it's not because He loves you, Solomon. It's because He loves Israel." He loves Israel forever. He loves His people so much that He gave them Solomon as king. "With all this wisdom everyone's happy, even God is blessed," verse 9.

And she rounded out her visit by giving him a hundred and twenty talents of gold.

By the way, that's in the hundreds of millions of dollars.

And of spices very great store, and precious stones: there came no more such abundance of spices as these which the queen of Sheba gave to king Solomon.

And, behold, a greater than Solomon is here. I think we are authorized, by Jesus, to say that when we read 1 Kings 10 and almost everything surrounding the life of Solomon, we are authorized to see a very perfect version of King Solomon in Jesus Christ; a very perfect version of King **Solomon. A greater than Solomon is here.** "You think that **Solomon** was rich? He has nothing on Me. You think **Solomon** was wise? He has nothing on Me. Do you think **Solomon**'s servants are happy to be ministering before him? They have nothing on My servants. Do you think that people will come from the end of the earth for **Solomon?** Wait for the day when people from the ends of the earth will come and see Me. Do you think **Solomon** was rich? Do you think he was wise? Do you think that people adored him, loved his beauty? Do you think they enjoyed coming to his Jerusalem? You wait until the world comes to My Jerusalem." And that is how the book ends, isn't it? Revelation 22.

I showed you in chapter 12 that the Lord is greater than David, and that is why Jesus allows His disciples to pick food from the field because David allowed his people to pick the bread off of the Table of Showbread in the tabernacle. Here, then, we seem to have this authorization to make the comparison between the time of Solomon and the time of David.

Two people were sent back from captivity to lead temple-rebuilding efforts (among others): Haggai and Zechariah were given twin ministries basically, and it was within the same neck of the woods as Ezra's ministry as a scribe and Nehemiah's ministry as governor. So we're over here about 500 years before Jesus. Haggai is back in town in Jerusalem and he's observing, he's trying to motivate people to rebuild the temple. What happened to the first temple, the one that took seven years to build by King Solomon? It was destroyed by King Nebuchadnezzar, and so now they're going to build their second temple.

Haggai 2:1 In the seventh month, in the one and twentieth day of the month, came the word of the LORD by the prophet Haggai, saying, Speak now to Zerubbabel the son of Shealtiel, governor of Judah, and to Joshua the son of Josedech, the high priest, and to the residue of the people, saying, Who is left among you that saw this house in her first glory?

How old did those folks he was speaking to have to be? 40? 50? "Who among you is left who is 70 years old? How do you see it now?"

Is it not in your eyes in comparison of it as nothing?

"Look at what we've built here. Isn't this garbage?" Have you read Ezra? It says that the young men were shouting for that new temple while the old men wept because they remembered the glory of the former temple seventy years earlier.

2:4 Now be strong, O Zerubbabel, saith the LORD; and be strong, O Joshua, son of Josedech,

This is not the Joshua that followed Moses, this is a different Joshua.

the high priest; and be strong, all ye people of the land, saith the LORD, and work: for I am with you, saith the LORD of hosts.

"We're going to build the second temple. We're going to make it elaborate. We're going to decorate it."

According to the word that I covenanted with you when ye came out of Egypt, so My spirit remaineth among you: don't be afraid. For thus saith the LORD of hosts. Yet once, it is a little while, and I will shake the heavens and the earth, the dry land, and all nations. 7 and the desire of all nations shall come.

He's going to shake the heavens, shake the earth, shake the sea, shake the dry land, and look what He says: the desire of all nations shall come. And here's what the Lord says:

I will fill this house, the second temple, I will fill this house with glory, saith the LORD of hosts.

Ok, you're going to have a hard time finding that in your Old Testament. You're going to have a hard time finding that in your New Testament. The second temple was destroyed in 70 AD. So when did this occur in the 2nd temple?

2:8 The silver is Mine, and the gold is Mine.

I'll decorate this joint. I own everything." This goes well with Psalm 50. "I own the gold, the silver, the mountains, and I own the cattle on it."

2:9 The glory of this latter house shall be greater than of the former.

How's that possible? Anyone that saw Solomon's temple saw that everything was overlaid with gold. Everything was made out of gold. It was oriented so that when the sun would rise up in the east that it would shine off that gold of that temple in Jerusalem and would blind the approacher coming up Mount Zion. The glory was magnificent to the point where it was bringing royalty from deep Africa. Everything about Solomon's temple was a "wow" factor. Everything was amazing. Everyone was aghast when they saw this thing. They were amazed and they thought, "Well this can't be topped. This is us." And here is what the prophet Haggai says in verse 9: "The glory of this house shall be greater than of the former." Well we know the calendar. We go 500 years forward and we find ourselves in 70 AD and the latter house falls flat, so you better do some explaining, because either God is wrong or Haggai is wrong about what God said.

and in this place will I give peace, saith the LORD of hosts.

"In this place will I give peace. In this house that will have glory that is greater than Solomon's temple. Glory and peace will fill this house." That cannot be a millennium fulfillment. The temple was crushed in 70 AD. We are not waiting for Haggai 2:9 to be fulfilled. It must have been fulfilled because the temple is now gone and the glory of that second house will be greater than the glory of the first.

Now it's true that Herod took 46 years to build the temple but I doubt for even a minute that Herod, an Idumean, the Old Testament term is an Edomite, not even a son of Isaac. He added to the second temple and he did it for 46 years. Are we to assume that because some son of Esau shows up and is in charge as the so-called King of the Jews, that now that second house has glory that is greater than the first? No way would I ever say that God said an Edomite brought glory to that house. Never, because he certainly didn't bring peace.

Luke 2:8 [Three or four miles south of Jerusalem we find] shepherds in the field, keeping watch over their flock by night.

And why were they keeping watch in the cold months by night? Because they were in sacrifice season. This was the field in Bethlehem, Micah 4 says, was the "watchtower of the flock." This is where there were sheep year round. This is not a proof text that Jesus was not born in December. This is the place, we're told by Alfred Edersheim in his work "The Life and Times of Jesus the Messiah" where sheep, sacrificial sheep, were kept year round because of its proximity to Jerusalem. And this was where they would bring them to the sheep market in Jerusalem, from this very field. And here are the shepherds watching over the sacrificial lambs.

Luke 2:9 the angel of the Lord appeared, and the glory of the Lord shone round about them: and they were sore afraid. And the angel said unto them, Fear not: for, behold, I bring you good tidings of great joy, which shall be to all people. For unto you is born this day in the city of David a Saviour, which is Christ the Lord. And this shall be a sign unto you; Ye shall find the babe wrapped in swaddling clothes, lying in a manger.

And if I were to tell you something as obvious to the reader then, as when little lambs were born they would be wrapped in swaddling clothes and laid in a manger, it would make you flip, wouldn't it? So he shows up to these guardians of these sacrificial lambs and pronounces news that they're going to find a little lamb somewhere, a Savior who is Christ the Lord, the Messiah.

Luke 2:13 And suddenly there was with the angel a multitude of the heavenly host praising God, and saying, Glory to God in the highest, and on earth peace, good will toward men.

We find glory and peace being announced on the evening of Christ's birth. And I've seen some commentators stop here in Haggai 2:9. The problem is, even if I were to say the new temple is the body of Christ it's not literal enough because Haggai 2:9 says this second temple will have glory in it that will outshine the first. So, we have to find Jesus in a temple.

Luke 2:22 And when the days of Mary's purification according to the law of Moses were accomplished, they brought Him to Jerusalem, to present Him to the Lord; (As it is written in the law of the Lord, every male that openeth the womb shall be called holy to the Lord;) And to offer a sacrifice according to that which is said in the law of the Lord, a pair of turtledoves, or two young pigeons. And, behold, there was a man in Jerusalem, whose name was Simeon; and the same man was just and devout, waiting for the consolation of Israel: and the Holy Ghost was upon him. And it was revealed unto him by the Holy Ghost, that he should not see death, before he had seen the Lord's Christ. And he came by the Spirit into the temple: and when the parents brought in the child Jesus, to do for Him after the custom of the law, Simeon took Him up in his arms, and blessed God, and said, Lord, now let your servant depart in peace, according to Your word: For mine eyes have seen Your salvation, which you have prepared before the face of all people; A light to lighten the Gentiles, and the glory of Your people Israel.

Right there, in that second temple, in the form of a boy that was about a month old, according to Levitical Law, the glory of God filled the house. The earth shook, the heavens quaked, and the sea and the land were shaking, and God was filling His house with a **greater** glory **than** that of **Solomon.**

12:43-45

When the unclean spirit is gone out of a man,

*Matthew 12:22 Then was brought unto Him **one possessed with a devil**, blind, and dumb.*

he walketh through dry places, seeking rest, and findeth none.

*Matthew 11:29-30 Come unto Me, all ye that labour and are heavy laden, and I will give you rest. 29 Take My yoke upon you, and learn of Me; for I am meek and lowly in heart: and **ye shall find rest** unto your souls.*

*12:43 When the unclean spirit is gone out of a man, he walketh through dry places, **seeking rest**, and findeth none.*

I'm trying to show you that Jesus and Matthew the writer have certain themes on their heart and mind, and this is exactly where it ought to be in the Scripture. Exactly where it ought to be.

44 Then he saith, I will return into my house from whence I came out; and when he is come, he findeth it empty, Do you know why that demon found room in that house? Because there's no one in it.

45 Then goeth he, and taketh with himself seven other spirits more wicked than himself, and they enter in and dwell there: I must say the fact that this demon was able to go back into the house because there was no strong man there from his exorcism leads me to believe that you need not worry about demon possession if the Spirit of Christ, lives in you. If you want a good reason to get saved, here's two in the passage: There's a coming judgment day in which there will be witnesses; two: you are, best I can tell, guaranteeing yourself you will never be victimized by demon possession. You have a pretty good chance of staying in your mind and having clear thoughts if you can guarantee that you'll never be demon possessed.

and the last state of that man is worse than the first. No doubt Peter was influenced by these words from the mouth of Jesus when he wrote the closing verses of 2 Peter 2. The Holy Spirit never has taken up residence and after they're done with their little fling with Jesus. You're going to see that they are twice damned, really at the end of it all. They tried Jesus and He didn't work like the therapy or the pills or the new thing. "We're going to try another spouse, another job, another car, another duty station." People are busy replacing emptiness with things and stuff and manmade fixes, and there are some people who even try Jesus. They don't put faith in Jesus, they don't trust Christ for salvation, and so they find none. They find a great mask. They find, for a little while, deliverance from their old life, deliverance from the old lust, deliverance from the old anger, deliverance from the old entanglements with heresy, but it's so short lived because they never had a faith in Christ as Lord and Savior. They simply became admirers and fans of Jesus. And they got cleaned up for a while and maybe they started coming to church because the wife got happier. Maybe they started coming to church because husband started acting more himself when the wife went to church, and the kids wanted to somehow make up for the rotten week at school so they got saved. Tried all kinds of things and then after a while we realize that there's still an empty house, even though it looks like for a while the demons had departed.

Even so shall it be also unto this wicked generation. Over and over again in the book of Matthew we find this happening and I want to tell you: in this part of the book, it's easy to accept. There's very little that will ruffle your theological feathers by accepting it in this part of the book. We will probably get to some uncomfortable portions of Scripture that deal with **this generation**. But I want you to see this phrase used over and over again.

> *Matthew 11:16 But whereunto shall I liken **this generation**? It is like unto children sitting in the markets, and calling unto their fellows.*

Jesus is constantly saying things about that generation.

> *Matthew 12:41 The men of Nineveh shall rise in judgment with **this generation**.*

That generation is the only generation that looked at the Son of God and said, "His blood be on us and on our children." I have some feeling that the Holocaust was an answer to prayer of the Jews of the first generation. "His blood be on us and on our children." I am so frustrated, so frustrated with people that mean well saying stupid things like, "God never blamed the Jews for the crucifixion of Jesus." That sounds really good, except the New Testament disagrees with it in every way.

In Acts 2 Peter said, "You men of Judea." He goes and preaches to them for 15 or 20 verses and says, "God has made this Jesus, who you crucified, both Lord and Christ."

In 1 Thessalonians chapter 2, where Paul lays the guilt of the crucifixion at the Jews' feet.

12:46-50[55]

---

[55]Discussed at length in my commentary on Mark (3:31-35).

Chapter 13

13:1-23

See the author's commentary on Mark 4:1-20

13:25

But while men slept, his enemy came and sowed tares whatever "tares" are, they apparently look like wheat, which is the point of the passage.

13:31

Another parable a third one upon which he offers no explanation.

13:33

Another parable really, a 4th one with no explanation.

13:35

That it might be fulfilled which was spoken by the prophet, Asaph out of Psalm 72 **saying, I will open my mouth in parables; I will utter things which have been kept secret from the foundation of the world.** Whatever these parables mean, they have been reality for a long, long time—even though they may not have been explained to anybody. Gravity existed before it was labeled.

13:36

Then Jesus sent the multitude away, "Well that wasn't very nice of Him." Apparently the reason for this is that He was tired. Contextually, he is on a boat teaching (verse 2). This probably got tiring. Projecting to those on the shore can get tiring. Perhaps, more than that…the disciples had questions. Sometimes you're simply not supposed to be with the masses as much as the future leaders of the masses. If he were writing books today, He would teach until the last one left the beach, right? Wouldn't that be the counsel? Well, Jesus said sometimes it's just time to send people away. Sometimes, we need to make time just for questions; and not just questions, but questions with eternal consequence. **and went into the house: and his disciples came unto**

him, saying, Declare unto us the parable of the tares of the field. It seems like we ought to find those who know more than us on certain topics and ask pointed questions.

Notice, by the way, the disciples didn't ask for explanations of all the parables.

13:37-41

This set of verses is found in my commentary on Ephesians (1:21).

41 ...they shall gather out of His kingdom all things that offend, and them which do iniquity. Lawlessness. Those who live without a law. There are no lawless people in the **kingdom**. If you're one of these people that just talks about your liberty in Christ, and to you that means you don't have to do anything you're told to do?...You don't belong in the kingdom. It's not for you. Kingdom people don't specialize in telling you what you don't have to do anymore. You don't get to be immodest in the kingdom and no one talk to you about it. If you have a problem with rules than you don't belong in the kingdom. You don't get into the kingdom by keeping rules but you don't get into the kingdom so that you don't have to keep them anymore either. We have a God of order and He has rules, and if you don't like rules the kingdom is not for you.

And this Son of Man with His angels, His angels **shall cast them**, that is those who offend and those who do iniquity and those who, in the parable, are identified as what? Tares, yeah. He said He's going to have His angels **cast them into a furnace of fire:**

13:43

Then shall the righteous shine forth as the sun in the kingdom of their Father... And I don't think I caught what was going on with Matthew until I was driving a few minutes ago, and I thought, "I better record that because I'm not going to preach another sermon on that parable."

Then shall the righteous shine... Now I have to tell you, up until this point I had been putting the emphasis on the word shine. But it's possible that Matthew, recording the words of Jesus, was saying that in that furnace of fire there will be some shining. Now it might seem sadistic to say that you will be glowing in a furnace of fire.

And then shall the righteous shine forth as the sun in the kingdom of their Father. So both are shining. Interesting that it is a fire in both cases. One is in a furnace. One is in a kingdom. Now that is really something. The entire thing is a contrast to being in a furnace of with the weeds. But what I want to point out here is they are both shining with fire.

So you say, "Well, it's a reach." Maybe it's a reach if I don't have an Old Testament Scripture to at least give me some idea that I might be right here. Isaiah is already mentioned, quoted, or alluded to, some ten times in the Book of Matthew before we get to chapter 13 so I don't find it to be a reach at all to go to Isaiah 13 with this analogy.

> *13:1 The burden of Babylon...Howl ye; for the day of the Lord is at hand; it shall come as a destruction from the Almighty. Therefore shall all hands be faint, and every man's heart shall melt: and they shall be afraid: pangs and sorrows shall take hold of them; they shall be in pain as a woman that travaileth:* ***they shall be amazed at one another;***

they will stare at each other as amazed people,

> ***their faces*** *shall be as flames.*

And I pointed out, quoting 2 Corinthians chapter 3, that the reason we are able to shine with the radiance of the Son, in the kingdom to come, is because we'll be looking on the Father, and our countenances will reflect the countenance of the Father.

Much like 2 Corinthians 3:13...

> *And not as Moses, which put a vail over his face, that the children of Israel could not stedfastly look...Upon him, because he was looking at the face of God.*

So, just like when they will be looking at one another, and we will see radiance and glory and brightness, in the kingdom to come, as forecasted by Moses with the time that He looked at the radiance of God in the Old

Testament, so I believe there will be a time in which those who are being punished by the Lord will look at each other and Isaiah 13:8,

> *their faces shall be as flames.*

So, I really do believe that this book that we hold in our hands is so amazing. Here's another way that this passage could be viewed, is that the tares will shine in the furnace, looking at each other, Isaiah 13, aghast at one another, their faces looking like flames. But the righteous shall shine with the radiance of the sun in the kingdom of their Father. Because they're looking on His face their faces have the radiance of the sun. So, I think Matthew, I think Jesus, is drawing a contrast that the wheat and the tares are both shining. One in a furnace of fire; one in the kingdom of their Father.

Then shall the righteous shine forth as the sun in the kingdom of their Father.

> *Isaiah: The nations shall see Your righteousness and all the kings, Your **glory.***

> *Daniel 12:3 Many of those who sleep in the dust of the earth shall awake. Some to everlasting life and some to shame and everlasting contempt. And those who are wise **shall shine like the brightness of the sky above and like the stars forever and ever.***

Who hath ears to hear, let him hear. Two items: beginning of the book of Matthew, you have wise men coming to Jesus; end of the book of Matthew, you have Jesus going to the nations with His disciples. Two episodes: Jonah going to the godless; and the godless coming to King Solomon. Two realities in these parables: You have birds coming to the tree; leaven into the whole of the meal.

So next I want to talk about this **kingdom.** It's a great place. It's a great thing. It shows up often in the book of Matthew. It shows up so often that you cannot afford to go years and years without being able to define **the kingdom**.

You have Matthew, Mark, Luke, and John, and Acts, "through tribulation you will enter the kingdom," and Romans, "the kingdom is not meat and dress and holidays, but love, joy, peace, and the Holy Ghost," and 1 Corinthians, "know ye not the unrighteous shall not inherit the kingdom of God," and over, and over, and over again, all the way to Revelation 12:10, "now the kingdoms of this world are become the kingdoms of our Lord and His Christ." The **kingdom** is the New Testament message. You're not allowed to not know what it means. It's insanity to not know what it means. You're not allowed to let your eyes roll back in your skull every time you hear it mentioned in the passages of Scripture or in preaching or in teaching. It's absolutely irresponsible to do so. You're not allowed to. You say, "Well I might let it slip." You're not allowed to. You are not allowed to let this theme pass you. "I'm an American." God's not. You're not allowed to not know what **the kingdom** is talking about. "Except a man be born again he cannot see the kingdom of God." You're not allowed to not know what that means. You're not allowed to be Biblically ignorant about this topic. And since in the Lord's Prayer we are told to pray, "Thy kingdom come, Thy will be done on earth, as it is in heaven," then that is a second grand reason why we better know what we're praying for, because we're praying for it to come.

In this parable both the wheat and the tares, planted by separate parties, are planted in the world and gathered out of the **kingdom**. Let's remind ourselves of the Lord's Prayer: "Thy **kingdom** come, Thy will be done on earth, as it is in heaven." So headquarters is in heaven. That's why it's called **the kingdom** of heaven.

Now let me go ahead and just head something off at the pass, before your mind is eaten up with Schofield notes. There is no difference in the Bible between the kingdom of heaven and the kingdom of God. You say, "Well I believe there is." You're wrong. All you have to do to know that is put the parables side by side between Matthew and Mark, or Matthew and Luke, and you will notice that the parables are almost identical other than Matthew uses the term "Kingdom of Heaven."

*Matthew 6 Your **kingdom** come. Your will be done on earth, as it is in heaven.*

*Matthew 7:21 Not everyone who says to Me, 'Lord, Lord,' will enter into the **kingdom** of heaven, but the one who does the will of My Father who is in heaven.*

There's nothing that will happen in the kingdom to come that does not fit perfectly within the character of the Father. Revelation 7 says, "They will serve God in His temple forever and every tear will be wiped away from his eye." I mean, we'll do work again without the curse. Adam was put in a garden to tend it before the fall, and he started sweating after the fall, and it didn't yield its increase after the fall. Can you imagine being able to work and all of your work produces fruit?

*Matthew 8:11 I tell you many will come from east and west, and recline at the table of Abraham, and Isaac, and Jacob in the **kingdom** of heaven.*

The kingdom of heaven will be a place of refreshment and reunion. I don't want to reduce heaven to playing harps and eating food. I never understood where we got that image. "Can't wait for heaven. We're going to have the marriage supper of the Lamb," as if we're going to sit around and gorge ourselves. But, the reason the kingdom is called a feast in Matthew 20 is because of how amazing it will be. And I don't know why I'll need a mansion if I won't be tired. And I don't know why I'll need to eat if I'm never going to grow weary or need nourishment. Part of what will make heaven heaven is that people who don't belong there won't be there.

In addition to 1 Corinthians 15:33-47, Romans 8:17, and Colossians 3:4, we see here why are we shining forth with the radiance of the sun? Because we are with the Son as He shines forth with the radiance of the sun. And I would say probably that this is a great place to end up, in the last book: "And the city had no need of the sun."

*Revelation 21 Neither the moon to shine in it: for the glory of God did lighten it, and the Lamb is the light thereof. And the nations of them which are saved shall walk in the light of it: and the kings of the earth do bring **their glory and honour into it**. They will see His face and His name will be on their foreheads. And night will be no more. They will need no light of lamp or* *sun; for the Lord God will be their light: and they will reign forever and ever."*

And so why do we shine forth with the radiance of the sun? And I was saying, "God, would You just give me a little taste of what that even means?" Well, apparently it is mostly because we are in the face of God. Now if you want an example of this, think of Moses meeting with God on the mountain (in Exodus 32-33). And when he came down, they made him wear a veil over his face because his face shined with the radiance of the sun. They couldn't look at him because he had a face that was just, it was too much. And why was it too much? Because he looked at God, it said, face to face.

This is the end of the story. The beginning of the story is, well, really, in the mind of God before the foundation of the world; but the beginning of human history has Genesis 3:9, where Adam and Eve are hiding from the face of God. When the sin is removed and the shame is removed and the curse is removed, then we can look at God in the face again and wear His glory. The future is bright. What a ridiculous pun. The future is bright!

Let's talk about now. The present is not so bright. The wicked one has come and sown his tares. It says in 13:25, "The enemy came and sowed tares among the wheat, and went his way." He's awful snaky. We're not ignorant of his devices (2 Corinthians 2:7). He says, "Listen in, you're going to shine with the radiance of the sun." You say, "Well, I get that. It's on the page." No, no. You don't really get it,

*Matthew 13:13 Therefore speak I to them in parables: because they seeing see not; and hearing they hear not, neither do they understand. And in them is fulfilled the prophecy of Isaiah, which says, By hearing ye shall hear, and shall not understand; and seeing ye shall see, and not perceive: For this people's heart is waxed gross, and their ears are dull of hearing, and their eyes they have closed; lest at any time they should see with their eyes, and hear with their ears, and should understand with their heart, and should be converted, and I should heal them. **And blessed are your eyes, for they see: and your ears, for they hear.***

*Matthew 13:43 He who has ears to hear, **let him hear.***

Only the wheat can hear. Only the good ground can hear and see and understand.

As a matter of fact, He wanted it so that He clouded their minds with parables. He said, "Lest they hear with their ears, see with their eyes, and their hearts are converted." So as you look around and you feel like you're the only one who really knows what's going on, it's because you are the only one who really knows what's going on. The world is mad. They're as mad as soldiers who get thrown back on their keister, staring up at the night sky, after Jesus's "I Am" in answer to their question, "Who are you looking for?" …on their backsides, staring up at a Judean sky. And then they get up, brush themselves off, and Jesus says, "Who are you looking for?" And they answered again. Insanity. You know why? They're tares. They're as insane as homosexual sodomites in Genesis 19, that are struck blind by the angels and then they grope for the doorknob to get inside to the angels that struck them blind! Insane. You know why? They're tares. They have no idea. Behind the scenes the Son of Man sewing good seed and the enemy sewing tares.

So what? What about now?

> *Psalm 34:3-5 Oh magnify the Lord with me, Let us exalt His name together. I sought the Lord, and He answered me, and delivered me from all my fears.* ***Those who look to Him are radiant.***

David said, "Not in the kingdom to come, but right now. Those who look to Him: they're radiant." They're radiant for a number of reasons, but since I'm not preaching Psalm 34, you're stuck. I'm not going to talk about it.

> *Matthew 5:14* ***You are the light of the world.*** *A city that is set on a hill cannot be hid. Neither do men light a candle, and put it under a bushel, but on a candlestick; and it gives light to all that are in the house. So, let your light shine before men, that they may see your good works, and glorify your Father which is in heaven.*

And here is what Jesus says before He gets to chapter 13. "Just go ahead and play the part here. There's going to come a time when there's a harvest, and you will shine in the kingdom of your Father. And since you're going to shine in the kingdom of your Father, just go ahead and shine for your Father now. Just go ahead and do it."

Notice how wise men come to Jesus and the disciples go to Gentiles at the end of the book. Notice how Jonah goes to the Gentiles and a Gentile coming to Solomon in chapter 12. Then in these parables you have leaven going to the meal and birds coming to the tree; as well as a man going to the treasure or the pearls, and fish coming to the net.

13:44

See my commentary on Ephesians (5:25-33) for treatment of this Scripture.

13:47-48

48 Which, when it was full, they drew to shore, and sat down, and gathered the good into vessels, but cast the bad away. The idea of fishing; the idea of fishing for fish; the idea of fishing for fish that are people is found only one other time in the book of Matthew, and of course it is 4:12-20 where Jesus called some to be "fishers of men." Now, fish are mentioned in several miracles. You know that. They are mentioned when you talk about someone's trade but fish are identified with people only this other time in the book of Matthew and so I don't think it's a mistake.

Well, what do we say about these bad fish and these good fish? 1. They all come by way of the same fishermen. Now, I know when I showed you Matthew 4, I showed you the human side. We are called to be fishermen. But here's the God side. In these parables we have showed that there is a good strong chance that Jesus is the main character. We see that the angels are the ones separating the fish but we are not told that it's the angels pulling the net to the beach. We are told that a net is pulled to the beach. We are told that it's in verse 48, "when it was full, they drew it to the shore." They drew it to the shore and sat down but the angels, it doesn't look like they're even in the act until verse 49.

I want you to notice, please, that you have good and bad fish in the net. Are you catching this? In the final analysis, the good fish and the bad fish both had the same fishermen. And what determines who is good or bad? Well, not the fishermen. We are already promised that at the end of the world we are going to find out we caught some bad fish. What a relief. I'm grateful that I'm also promised I'll catch some good fish. That's wonderful. But we've already talked about. However, I am really comforted to know that after all of my toil and labor, I am promised I will catch some bad fish. They are not all going to turn out saved.

Yes, they got in through the net and what is the net? Well, if the net is a consistent thing at all, look in 13:19 "When any one hears the word of the kingdom, and understands it not, then comes the wicked one, and catches away that which was sown in his heart…23 But he that received seed into the good ground," what is the seed? The word of the kingdom. We find out that Jesus is the doer of most the action in these parables and we find out now that it looks like the tool of getting people into the kingdom is the word of the kingdom. So we are all preaching, if you are preaching the unadulterated Gospel of Christ came to be a ransom for many (20:28), then we are all casting the same net.

"So you mean to tell me I cast the correct net and I still get bad fish?" Now, here's what a bad fish kind of sounds like. This is the person that's in the middle of a crisis and they "get saved" but when the crisis passes (joblessness; marriage issues; a storm that just came through and took out their power; a career not going where they want it to; failure). I want you to know that sometimes God uses that to save some and they come in the net and we find out, yep, they truly were saved when they said they were saved. But then there are others, they look like the real deal, they are in the same net, pulled by the same fishermen to the same beach and we don't even find out whether or not they are good or bad until the end of the world. But we are still called to be fishermen. We don't control the net. We cast it. We don't control the one dragging it. In fact, we are so out of the game, we don't even separate the fish.

13:49-50

50 And shall cast them into the furnace of fire: there shall be wailing and gnashing of teeth. Please notice it's the rejects that get cooked. In a way I feel poorly for anyone going to the furnace, and hopefully

hopefully everyone in here, saved or not, dreads the idea of hell. And honestly that is a truth that puts some people just completely out of the running for faith. In their mind how could a God of love, how could a God of love send anyone to hell. And I will flip the table on you and say, first of all, it's not your right to judge your Creator.

Secondly, he proves he is a God of love by allowing you to hear the escape route. It's called the Gospel and here you are hearing it. So if you want proof that God is a God of love, how about the fact that you are in a place, some of you multiple times, where you can hear that you don't have to go to the furnace. You can sit and find fault with the furnace if you want to but it's still going to happen.

I got saved and I was 21 when I put faith in Christ and settled that thing once and for all and quit praying the sinner's prayer over and over and over and over again. It just doesn't do the trick, friends. Put faith in Jesus, then your testimony will fit John 3:16 and you can go on with your life, "Trust Christ and you will not perish but have everlasting life." I'm going to tell you this: that is pretty awesome. The not perishing part made me very happy. I can sit around and talk about how wrong it is that God allows people to perish all day. It doesn't settle for you probably that you're not going to have all your questions answered. We're not going to be able to figure out why God allows some people to perish. The fact is we are not going to get rid of the furnace so you might as well avoid it.

A word to the fishermen: you are not in any control over who does and who does not go to the furnace. You are in control of casting the net and at the end of the world, you let God sort them out. Catch all you can and let God sort them out.

Now, you don't have to be quite as direct or rambunctious as I am. You could actually do something very crazy, you could get out of your car before you shut your garage door and see if your neighbor is outside and get their name. Please notice no one gives a rip about your personality in this parable. "But it's not my...." No one cares. You are called to be a fisherman.

So let's see how long we are supposed to do this:

*Matthew 28:18-20 Jesus came and spake unto them, saying, All authority is given unto me in heaven and in earth. Go ye therefore, and teach all nations, baptizing them in the name of the Father, and of the Son, and of the Holy Ghost: Teaching them to observe all things whatsoever I have commanded you: and, lo, I am with you alway, even **unto the end of the world.***

There it is—that same phrase that we read where the fish are sorted out at "the end of the world." I know we are concerned. We don't want to witness to someone because they're just going to get me off their back and say the right thing and do the right thing just to get me off their back. Take the risk. Take the risk. They might be a good fish.

"Oh, they are such a manipulator."

Maybe not this time. And we are required while we are waiting for the angels to come and separate the fish, we are commanded right here to keep pulling the net.

Some additional thoughts on these last few parables:

#1. These mysteries, these parables have been around a long time. Look at verse 35:

*Matthew 13:35 That it might be fulfilled which was spoken by the prophet, saying, I will open My mouth in parables; I will utter things which have been kept secret from **the foundation of the world.***

Things that are mysterious to us in this life are not a mystery to God. Paul over and over in the book of Ephesians says, "I'm going to share something with you and you've never heard it before because God just revealed it to me." Jesus is speaking about the year 28-29 AD in this passage and He has no issues saying that things that have been around for 4,000 years plus are being revealed by Him.

And I think that there is a great application here for us because in verse number 30 we're told that the field is the world. And I mentioned last week that if you have a King James this "world" is actually the word *kosmon,* which refers to the creation, and not the *aiōn,* the age, which is seen in the other words translated "world" through the rest of this parable. "What are we saying?" Well, contextually you have to understand that Matthew is using words on purpose. Words that he heard Jesus use, yes, but he's not using all the words Jesus used because there are many things Jesus said that are not recorded. The book of John says if we were to record everything that Jesus both said and did, the planet couldn't hold the books. So, if that's true, then we should not be looking passed any of these very important words in the text.

#2. God permitted Satan. We all want answers and perhaps one of the biggest mysteries is why God even allowed Satan to occur. And I can sit up here and theorize and philosophize with you as to why that is, but I want you to see in the text that the enemy came and sowed tares, in verse 25, among the wheat. I ask you, can the Lord of all the Earth stop the enemy from sowing tares? It's His field. I promise you, He could have stopped the numbskull from sowing tares.

We have this false dichotomy in Scripture, this false sort of battle going on between Satan and the Lord. Be aware, at any point that the Lord deems fit He could put a lump on Satan's head so big he'd have to climb the universe to get to the top of it. We are not going to put God in such a small box that we're going to make Satan His archenemy. Every time we find Satan battling anyone in the Bible it's an angel. Zechariah chapter 3: it's an angel. Jude verse 9: it's an angel. Revelation 12: an angel. Daniel 10: an angel. Job: he's bowing before God asking for permission to bother Job.

God permitted Satan. And you say, "Would have sure been a lot easier on the earth and on people if God would have just stopped the devil from getting in the garden, where he started sowing tares among the wheat." Yeah, you're right. But God is not interested in what's easy. God is interested in His glory. He is absolutely, positively egocentric and He should be. When you have no one with which to compare yourself, I say that you should have a good self-esteem. When He allows Satan in the garden you understand that the end game is Hebrews 2:10:

*For it became Him, for whom are all things, and by whom are all things, to make the captain of their salvation perfect through sufferings, in **bringing many sons unto glory**.*

It's debatable as to whether or not there would have been anyone brought to glory, to share in the glory of the triune God, if there were not first a fall. Because the pre-fall Adam was not in Christ. The pre-fall Adam was not in God. And those of us who are redeemed, we have a distinction.

God permits Satan to keep working even after people are aware of his work. "Would you that we gather them up?" verse number 28. And the Lord said, the Man who is sowing seed in the field, who we find out in verse 37 is the Son of Man says, "Nope. Harvest is coming." Oh, I know. It looks like the world is out of control. Oh, I know what we're thinking.

#3 There are those who saw tares (13:27). Now I've already told you that I don't know who the servants of the householder are, but I have a feeling that when I read Acts 20:28 and I find out that the Holy Ghost made overseers for the church which Christ purchased with His own blood, and later in that verse when Paul warns those Ephesian elders that there are wolves among them, I feel like that is a great parallel to this passage. It seems like, there are people who are aware of the tares and the wheat. They're aware of them and guess what they're doing? They're pointing them out to the Lord.

Where are they? According to 13:38, they're in the world, yes, they're in the world, but where else are they? They are, in verse 41, in the kingdom. The tares are raveled up in the wheat to the point where, in verse number 29, it says we can't yank them yet because they are bound up with the wheat. Apparently they are stealing the sun energy, that photosynthesis energy, from the wheat. They're stealing energy from the wheat, taking moisture from the wheat, taking that food in the soil from the wheat, and the servants of the householder know they're stealing from the wheat. And those servants of the householder just get so fired up. We're so sure someone's a tare that oftentimes when we're trying to yank them out in our own wisdom, we're hurting the wheat. You can see them. They're in your Sunday School classes, they're in the water cooler discussions at your workplace, they're claiming to be Christian and they're f-bombing, they're claiming to be Christian and they're shacking up, they're claiming to have the same Jesus you do. And there's some wheat in that crowd, and if you spend energy battling with all the tares, I'm afraid you're going to hurt your ministry to the wheat. Just wait until the end of the harvest. We're told yanking the tares out is the job of someone else.

> #4 In 13:41, the kingdom is the field. You have wheat and tares sown in the world and in verse 41. It's called "the kingdom." That should tell you that the Lord's kingdom, for now is spreading around the *kosmon* and in answer to our prayer, "Thy kingdom come, Thy will be done, on Earth as it is in heaven," God is gaining influence through the preaching of His gospel.

> *13:31 The kingdom of heaven is like to a grain of mustard seed, which a man took, and sowed in his field: Which indeed is the least of all seeds: but when it is grown, it is the greatest among herbs, and becometh a tree, so that the birds of the air come and lodge in the branches thereof. 33 Another parable spake He unto them; The kingdom of heaven is like unto leaven, which a woman took, and hid in three measures of meal, till the whole was leavened.*

When you're out there in the world, the *kosmon*, you need to know that it's God's place, it's His kingdom. He's removing tares. Are there holes? Sure! But one thing I do know: somehow the kingdom of heaven is like leaven. It is permeating the whole.

This passage seems to be saying that this kingdom influence is increasing with "the seed that is sown in the field" (same parallel). Somehow, just like the seed that has grown in the field has wheat that soon outnumbers the tares, so also the good seed becomes a tree that the birds of the earth come and nest in. And that good seed is like leaven that permeates the whole lump and I would say that it is both expectation and promise. That those who are committed to preaching the gospel will see the world soon tackled by its influence. I believe that. We're not allowed to sit back and be passive when you have the most powerful message in the universe! We have the most earth shattering message that Jesus Christ came into the world to save sinners. And that is enough to break hard hearts. And somehow we believe that enough to keep preaching it. God is not American, and if America hits the tub tomorrow, the Kingdom of God is still like leaven in the lump.

"Are you post-millennial?"

I don't particularly care what label you throw on me. I believe the Scripture says if you preach the gospel it will spread through the entire lump, the entire lump. I'm not so sure that the gospel is being preached as it ought to. It hasn't lost its power; it's losing its mouthpieces. So if you're frustrated that the gospel is not being believed and people are not being converted, be frustrated that in Sandy Ridge Baptist Church we typically have 95% of a membership that has never personally given the gospel to anybody. Yes.

> #5 The order of the tares and wheat is not significant. There are many people that have built theology out of the fact that the tares are removed first, verse 30, and then the wheat is gathered later on. "There'll be this big finale. The angels will storm down from the sky and gather up the tares and then throw them right in the lake of fire and then they'll gather the wheat." I think you need to be aware that that is not a consistent order. Look at verse 47.
>
> *Again, the kingdom of heaven is like unto a net, that was cast into the sea, and gathered of every kind: Which, when it was full, they drew to shore, and sat down, and **gathered the good into vessels, but cast the bad away.***

What's gathered first in that parable? The good. So you see the order is based on the articles He's using in the parable, not necessarily a doctrine He's establishing.

> #6. The furnace is not symbolic (verses 42 and 50). I wish it were. I was hoping there was another explanation. Are you ever that human, where you wish the Bible said something different than you've always been told it said? Verse 42 says that these tares will be cast into a furnace of fire, and in verse 50 they're going to cast something from a completely different parable into this furnace of fire. What is it? It is the "bad" pulled out of the net. The furnace I'm afraid is not a symbol. It is reality. Two separate parables with different things in them. I wish it wasn't true. And all it makes me want to do is preach the gospel more, and the gospel is that Christ died for sinful men. Matthew 20:28:

The Son of Man came not to be ministered unto, but to minister, and to give His life a ransom for many.

So we are aware that the gospel is Christ died for people that didn't deserve it, died for all their sins, all of them, rose again the third day according to Scriptures, and will save all who believe on Him. If all I had was the warning of a furnace of fire, I would preach it.

Chapter 14

14:1

At that time Herod the Tetrarch heard of the fame of Jesus, and said unto His servants, "This is John the Baptist; he is risen from the dead; and therefore mighty works do shew forth themselves in him." So in the context you can see that Jesus is in His hometown in the last part of the previous chapter. Here's Herod the Tetrarch hearing of the fame of Jesus and saying, "This is John the Baptist; he's risen from the dead." And it behooves us now to ask, "Well, how did he die?" If you're just reading Matthew all the way from chapter 1 verse 1 up to this point, you're not sure how John the Baptist died.

> *Matthew 4:12 [After the temptation of Christ] Now <u>when Jesus had heard that John was cast into prison</u>, He departed into Galilee;*

Jesus hears that John the Baptist is arrested by Herod, and He goes, instead of going back into Judea or Jerusalem, into Galilee. So, now we're in chapter 14, and now we have this John the Baptist that was arrested and he's dead. Now, we're going to have a flashback into how he died. We know he's dead because Herod says Jesus is John reincarnated.

14:6-8

When Herod's birthday was kept, the daughter of Herodias, so his stepdaughter,

14:9

And the king was sorry: nevertheless for the oath's sake, and them which sat with him at meat, or at the meal, **he commanded it to be given her.** Such a strange thing. "You're such a pretty girl dancing there, what could you possibly ask for?" Well, she asked for the head of a preacher, but didn't want to be known as someone who didn't keep his word. You remember a king in the Old Testament that struggled with this very thing? He made a law, someone was caught guilty that he loved, and he was sorry he made the law but he couldn't break the law? Darius.

14:10-11

And he sent, and beheaded John in the prison. And his head was brought in a charger, and given to the damsel: and she brought it to her mother. This ought to give you a distant understanding of what was going on in these royal families, where mom and dad aren't talking. Now what do you think? Do you suppose that this was a square dance sort of variety? Where it's kind of a Sunday school picnic setting? Nope, probably not. Probably lots of debauchery and probably some alcohol involved, and I think it would be safe to say that Herod is lusting after his stepdaughter. And his wife probably knew.

Now where did she learn how to be a little hussy? Well, you might remember what John the Baptist is preaching about, right? Remember, what he just got done preaching to Herod about was that Herod was stealing another man's wife. And not just another man's wife, his brother's wife. So Herod is stealing his sister in law from his brother. So his niece, who is now his stepdaughter, is dancing in front of him and getting basically anything she wants, and mom had already briefed her because she knew how to get men to do things.

14:12

And his disciples came, and took up the body, the disciples of John the Baptist. And we've seen them before. Back in chapter 9, the disciples of John the Baptist came to the disciples of Jesus and said, "How come your disciples are not fasting and dressed in mourning clothes like we are?" You might remember that; remember? They were in sackcloth and that kind of thing.

and buried it, and went and told Jesus. So now the disciples of John the Baptist are coming to Jesus and letting him know that His cousin, John the Baptist, is dead.

14:13-15

When Jesus heard of it, He departed. Now, do you see the pattern? In Matthew 4, He hears John is arrested and He changes where He is going from Judea to Galilee. Twice in this book Jesus hears something about John the Baptist and goes in a different direction because another man is involved named Herod. **When Jesus heard of it, He departed**

thence by ship We're safe in saying it's the Sea of Galilee or the Lake Tiberius or the Sea of Gennesaret, whichever Gospel writer is using it.

into a desert place. Before you think this is blowing sand and this is a desert in how we think of it, think of it more of a desert is a place that is deserted. We've taken that word and changed it to sandy place, a big sandbox. But that's not what it means in the context and you'll see why in a minute.

14:16

But Jesus said unto them, "They need not depart; give ye them to eat. There are some details here that are not mentioned in the other Gospels. And as is my custom I don't always mention what happens in the other Gospels unless it's pertinent to what Matthew is trying to tell us. In other words, it keeps you from making bad guesses. So, He says, "You give them something to eat." And you might remember in the book of John, Philip says, "Two hundred pennyworth is not enough to feed this crowd."[56] Which, by today's standards is about $38,000, about two-thirds of a year's income. The average income of a household in Fayetteville is $54,000, so if you say two-thirds annual income, basically, John tells us that Philip was saying, "Two hundred pennyworth is not enough to feed all these people." Was that saying they didn't have two hundred pennyworth? I think there is good reason to believe that Judas was carrying two hundred pennyworth. We find out in chapter 12 he was carrying the purse, or the bag. So if you can imagine a team so large; we find out in Luke 8 that there were women following Jesus on His ministry. So, if you can imagine a team so large, so involved, having so many needs, that they would carry around multiple thousands of dollars, and the dude who betrays Jesus is carrying it all. In any case, they said, "We don't have, to give."

14:17-18

And they say unto Him, "We have here but five loaves, and two fishes." And in the book of John we find out this came from who, or what? A boy's lunch, right. All right. So, which again has different meanings for today. You pack a lunch for second shift sometimes, but

---

[56]This figure also mentioned in Mark.

lunch is usually around noon for us. Which part of the day is this? Into the evening. So words are incredibly flexible, aren't they?

So in any case, **He said, "Bring them hither to me."** Bring what? The five loaves and the two fishes.

And He commanded the multitude to sit down on the grass. There's your first hint we are not talking about a sandy desert, because He has them sit down on the grass. All right, is everyone with me?

14:19-21

He commanded the multitudes to sit down on the grass, and took the five loaves, and the two fishes, and looking up to heaven, He blessed, and looking up to heaven He blessed, and brake, and gave the loaves to His disciples. "Well, where's my proof text for 'bow your head and pray before you eat'?" Here it is. The Son of God is blessing the food before He eats it. That's pretty simple stuff. I figure if the Son of God can do it, Bill Sturm can do it. I'm not too spiritual to praise and thank God for my food and ask Him to bless it.

Nothing mystical is going to happen if you're shoving a brownie down your throat and you're asking God to bless it to your body. Don't expect that to turn into something nutritious on the way down. No, you may as well hold your prayers.

And they did all eat, and were filled, and they took up the fragments that remained twelve baskets full. And they that had eaten were about five thousand men, beside women and children. Well I don't think it's a bad guess to say that there were probably at least 15,000 people there, right? I mean, for all the single people that were there you probably had a married person that was there with two or three kids. So I don't think 15,000 is a bad guess.

Now 2 Kings 4:38-44 is interesting, isn't it? You might not even remember that from your Bible reading. But here's Elisha the prophet, who's feeding a hundred people with twenty loaves of bread. You have the reality that everything in Matthew is for two purposes. To show us:

Matthew 1:1 That Jesus is the son of David, the son of Abraham…

Matthew 1:21 His name is Jesus: for He shall save His people from their sins.

We know we have this theme going on where Matthew is showing us all these things Jesus outclasses from the Old Testament. Matthew, written by a Hebrew, to Hebrews, has a specific purpose in this regard. Well, we also know it has something to do with Jesus being the fulfillment of the Son of David/Son of Abraham promises, and it has something to do with Him being a savior from sin. Saving His people from their sin.

Maybe this is talking about that you need to care for people's physical needs before they will listen to spiritual instruction. Often the "social Gospel" is coined by, "Make sure that you feed the hungry and shelter the homeless, because Jesus met physical needs before He taught." But, that's not true. These people were fed after Jesus was done teaching. So we're not interested in making planet Earth a better place from which people can go to hell. It's still doctrine that's the big deal. I'm glad that you will go to bed with a full stomach, if that happens for you. Sometimes, I think hunger is a great motivator, but I will do my best to keep people around me from going to bed hungry. But know this! That is not the point of this passage. Jesus is not about this philosophy that says, "Meet people's needs so you earn the right to teach them." Because that doesn't happen in the passage. He teaches them and then He feeds them.

I think the reason that this passage is here, is all about the baskets. You say, "Why?" Well, here's why, two reasons basically:

If Mark, Luke, and John are correct, the multitudes sat down in companies of fifties and hundreds. Let's say they sat down in groups of fifty within the groups of hundred, and let's say there really were just 15,000 people in attendance, how many groups of 100 is that? 150. Don't you think it was an extra bit of work to collect up all the scraps? They didn't have to do that. What's the point of doing that?

"Well, the lesson is we're not supposed to waste." Seriously? If they didn't have to collect up the baskets, but they did, that's unusual. I believe there's a big deal here with the baskets. For who? Well, if it's for the multitude, Jesus failed in every way, because in John chapter 6 they want to make Him king and He avoids them. It says they wanted to make Him king and He fled. If the message was for the multitude, Jesus failed, because He didn't stay with them. They didn't have a visitation program; He didn't go knock on their doors. Nothing. He leaves them. And what they want to do for Him, He doesn't want. He doesn't want the kingdom. So apparently, the message was not for the multitude.

I believe the message was for the disciples, and here's why: Everything in the book of Matthew it seems is done for the disciples. For example, you might think the Sermon on the Mount was for the crowd. No.

> Matthew 5:1 *And seeing the multitudes, He went up into a mountain: and when He was set,* **His disciples** *came unto Him: and He opened His mouth, and taught them.*

The multitudes followed, as usual, but the lesson of the Sermon on the Mount was for the disciples.

> Matthew 8:23 *And when He was entered into a ship,* **His disciples** *followed Him…25 And* **His disciples** *came to Him, and awoke Him, saying, "Lord, save us: we perish."*

The storm on the sea. Who would was it for? The multitudes? Nope. They experienced the sleeping Jesus, on a stormy sea, for them.

> Matthew 9:10 *It came to pass, as Jesus sat at meat in the house, behold, many publicans and sinners came and sat down with Him and* **His disciples***.*

> Matthew 9:19 *And Jesus arose, and followed him, and so did* **His disciples***.*

> Matthew 9:37, 10:1 *Then saith He unto* **His disciples***, "The harvest truly is plenteous, but the labourers are few… and when He had called unto Him* **His twelve disciples***, He gave them power…*

> Matthew 12:1-2 *At that time Jesus went on the Sabbath day through the corn; and* **His disciples** *were an hungered, and began to pluck the ears of corn, and to eat.* Verse 2: *But when*

*the Pharisees saw, it they said unto him, "Behold, **thy disciples** do that which is not lawful to do upon the Sabbath day.*

*Matthew 12:49 And He stretched forth His hand toward **His disciples**, and said, "Behold my mother   and my brethren!*

*Matthew 13:10 And **the disciples** came, and said unto Him, "Why speakest thou unto them in parables?"*

*Matthew 13:36 Then Jesus sent the multitude away, and went into the house: and **His disciples** came unto Him, saying, "Declare unto us the parable of the tares of the field.*

The multitude didn't get the interpretation of the parables, the disciples did.

Everything Jesus has done in the book of Matthew, up to this point, has been for the disciples. So it seems that this miracle has something to do with the baskets primarily, and secondarily it has something to do with the disciples.

These two things occur in the book of Matthew and do not occur Mark, or Luke, or John. Matthew's point here is that God requires impossible things out of His disciples. They give Him their meagerness and He rewards them.

*Matthew 19:27-28 Then answered Peter and said unto Him, "Behold, we have forsaken all, and followed thee; what shall we have therefore?" And Jesus said unto them, "Verily I say unto you, that ye which have followed me, **in the regeneration**, ["new beginning"] When the Son of Man shall sit in the throne of His glory, ye also shall sit upon **twelve thrones**, judging the twelve tribes of Israel.*

It doesn't say that in Mark, or Luke, or John. Not in those words. So, I don't think it's a stretch, I'm leaning in the direction, when I see that Matthew gives a basket after the miracle to all the disciples, or at least there's enough for all the disciples, and then in chapter 19 he says that in the world to come every one of them will get a throne. Now, please understand, this is not some kind of spooky doctrine where he says Judas is going to come back from hell a saved man. So He says, "You will have a place next to me, on your own throne, in the kingdom."

In Matthew 26:52-53, Jesus didn't say "eleven;" He didn't say thirteen; He didn't say ten; He didn't say one hundred. He said twelve. Here's what we know: We know there are twelve disciples. We know there are twelve baskets after the miracle of the feeding of the five thousand. We know that there are twelve thrones in the new age, and we know that apparently there are so many angels that each of the disciples, who are angry about the arrest of Jesus, could each have a legion. Interesting. Because Mark doesn't say that. Luke doesn't say that. John doesn't say that.

So what I'm trying to say, is if we're back in Matthew 14, the miracle is about disciples knowing this: You use your meagerness and God rewards you, not in this life, but in the life to come. I'm not saying He won't reward you in this life. I'm saying that this miracle does not promise you that He will reward you in this life.

I don't know what the disciples were thinking. They didn't even bring their own lunches, right? That's weird. And Jesus provides them the strength, the energy, the little boy, whatever it is in Matthew's scope, and they get a lunch. They give it to Jesus. Jesus multiplies it by speaking it into existence. For the first time since day five of creation week He creates fish. Very strange. At least it seems that way. And, oh, the bread. That must have been pretty tasty bread. In any case, they each have a basket.

> *2 Timothy 2:12 If we suffer,* **we shall also reign** *with Him: If we deny Him, He also will deny us.*

In Revelation 20:6 they sat on thrones surrounding the king, those who were beheaded for their witness of Jesus.

So I guess I'm just trying to say, "Payday is coming."

14:22-31

Discussed, in part, in my commentary on Job (9:8).

Chapter 15

When this is in the life of Jesus? We say that Jesus was about how old when He died? Thirty-three. Here's how we believe we know that: #1. The book of Luke says that He was about thirty when He was baptized. Now, how do we get the additional three years? The gospel of John mentions, we believe, four Passovers (John 2, 5, 6, 18). And so if there are only four Passovers in the ministry of Jesus, that means that just over three-and-a-half years were covered in His ministry. The feeding of the 5,000 was the only miracle found in all four gospels. It's found in John 6 and it happens around the time of the Passover. So if this happens after the third Passover and there are only four in Jesus' life, and He died on the fourth one you know, that means that this account tonight, in Matthew 15, is less than a year before His death as the feeding of the 5,000 takes place in Matthew 14. That means that Matthew 15 through 28 deal with 1/33 of His life. That's how precious little we have recorded about His life. And then to complicate matters just a little bit more, chapter 20 is the last week of His life. Basically, you have Matthew 20 through Matthew 28:1 covering one week of Jesus' life. Twenty-five percent of the first gospel deals with one week of Jesus' life. Fifty percent of the first gospel in the New Testament deals with one year of Jesus' life. Think about how little we know.

15:1

See commentary on Mark 7 for more on this passage.

15:2

And they were **saying, Why do Thy disciples transgress the tradition of the elders?** The word behind transgress there, it's pretty important because you and I read the words sin, iniquity, transgression, unrighteousness, we kind of throw them all in the same boat: "it just all means sin." And I suppose if you want to make a beeline for the definition that is true. But they are different words. For example, the word behind transgress here is the Greek word *parabainō,* which means to walk around, to go around. So the disciples of, "Thy disciples," the scribes and Pharisees are asking, "Why do Your disciples *go around* the tradition of the elders?"

15:3

But He answered. Up until this point Jesus has been asked four questions in the book of Matthew. Once He was asked the question by the disciples of John the Baptist, "Are you He that should come or should we look for another?" And He answers them. Another time He's asked a question by the disciples, "What did You mean by the parable of the wheat and the tares?" And He answered them. But this is, out of the four questions, the second question that's been asked by one of Jesus' antagonizers, and Jesus does here what He did in chapter 12 when he said to Him, "Is it lawful for Your disciples to pick grain on the Sabbath day?" And what does Jesus do when His enemies ask Him questions? He answers with a question.

Why do you go around (since they wanted to talk about "going around" things) **the commandment of God by your tradition?** So now we know, based on the fact that tradition has been used twice in this passage so far, that this is not normal wash your hands before you go to dinner, this is wash your hands the way we teach in our tradition. And then He says, "Here's the real deal, guys. Y'all are the ones that walk around things. You might be true to your tradition, but in so doing you walk around the commandments of God." Well what do You mean, Jesus?

15:5

That's quite the tradition, isn't it? Jesus says, "Who's the one that's really transgressing things here? Who's the one that's trespassing? Who's the one that's really walking around things?" Jesus doesn't even answer the question, "Why do My disciples transgress your tradition? You guys are actually worthy of death. Do you think I'm going to answer a bunch of guys that are worthy of death?"

15:7

Ye hypocrites, well did Esaias prophesy of you,[57] saying, This people draweth nigh unto me with their mouth, and honoureth me with their lips; but their heart is far from me. But in vain they do

---

[57] Once again we see Matthew is a fan of Isaiah, so for the eleventh time he either quotes or references Isaiah, and we're in chapter 15.

worship me, teaching for doctrines the commandments of men. I think it's interesting that the Lord says in verse 9 "Your worship is as empty as You have made My word." You might notice in verse 6 He says, "You have made My commandments empty because you love your traditions, and so since you have made My commandments empty," in verse number 9, "I have seen your worship as empty. It's meaningless. You're so busy saying what you don't have to do." By the way, we're not allowed to look at this passage and say that if someone has high standards they are a Pharisee. This passage is dealing with people that put their traditions on the same level of the word of God. You are not allowed to thumb your nose at people that have higher standards than you and call them "legalistic."

15:10

He called the multitude. This is the first time He does it in the entire book. All the time up until this point Jesus is sending away the multitude. They find Him; He sends them away. Why does He do it? It is to call out wicked people.

15:12-14

Then came His disciples, and said unto him, Knowest Thou that the Pharisees were offended, after they heard this saying? Here's what Jesus said: "Oh, I'm very sorry. Please put out a letter and some stationary for Me. I'll sign it before we head out of the office today. I didn't mean to offend anybody. I'll take another swing at it. I can really tone down my language. I didn't want anyone to be offended." No.

Here's what Jesus said: **Every plant, which My heavenly Father hath not planted, shall be rooted up. Let them alone:** That's why in Galatians 1:6-9, Paul says, "If one comes preaching another gospel other than that which you have received, other than that which you have received, well make sure you run them down and give them 1,000 gospel tracts and try to get them to friend you on all social media." It doesn't say that at all. "If one preaches another gospel unto you other than that which you have received from us, even if it's an angel from heaven, let him be accursed."

"I'm going to spend all my time going after religious leaders."

Then you need to know that you are going contrary to what Jesus told His disciples. You look out for the people they are leading.

they be blind leaders of the blind. And if the blind lead the blind, both shall fall into the ditch. You know, there's Jesus again, talking about that whole predestination thing. I have a problem with people who have a problem with that. Another passage of Scripture where we're told the reason someone is not going to get saved is because the **heavenly Father** didn't **plant** them.

We win who we can by God's grace and on the other shore we're going to look around and we're going to see all kinds of people that the Father planted.

15:18

And this is why James says in James 1:26: If any man among you seem to be religious, and bridleth not his tongue, but deceiveth his own heart, this man's religion is vain.

> *Matthew 12:34 O generation of vipers, how can ye, being evil, speak good things? For out of the abundance of the heart the mouth speaketh. A good man out of the good treasure of the heart bringeth forth good things: and an evil man out of the evil treasure bringeth forth evil things. 35 But I say unto you, That every idle word that men shall speak, they shall give account thereof in the day of judgment. For by thy words thou shalt be justified, and by thy words thou shalt be condemned.*

15:21-22[58]

Then Jesus went out from there and departed to the region of Tyre and Sidon. By the end of this episode, we wonder if this was yet another long trip for the sake of one family—much like the demoniacs of Decapolis (chapter 9). This region belongs to Asher, but they couldn't flush out the Canaanites. Many things have occurred there through the Kings and Amos conveys a judgment against them.

---

[58]See more in my commentary on Mark (7:24-30) and in my commentary on Revelation (3:7-8).

22 And behold, a woman of Canaan Yet another Gentile mentioned in the book of Matthew (besides Tamar, Rahab, Ruth, Bathsheeba, wisemen, centurion in chapter 8). **came from that region and cried out to Him, saying, "Have mercy on me, O Lord, Son of David!** See the notes under Matthew 1:1 where this title is studied. Jesus does have a "key of David" (Revelation 3:7-8) and He opens to whoever He wishes. He lets people in and out. Probably Solomon was the last **Son of David** to send anybody to Tyre and Sidon, and that was to have an envoy to be with that king(s) as he furnished Israel with materials for the temple (1 Kings 5:6).

Eleven times, so far, Matthew has clearly conveyed the spirit of Isaiah and I think this is the 12th instance. Isaiah 7:14 shows us that the House of David is expecting a "virgin" to conceive. Isaiah 9:6 references again the kingdom of David. He will reign forever and be born of a virgin. Isaiah 22:20 begins with the house of David having a key and one who holds the key. Jesus, then, says He's the fulfillment of this passage (Revelation 3:7-8). There is power, then, in the hands of Jesus to open the door for anybody into the House of David. If He lets you in, nobody will keep you out. Wow, but look at Isaiah 23:1 and see a pronouncement against Tyre! It will be awful! Isaiah 23:12-17 says Sidon is basically damned.

What a masterful book! Here's a woman who knows that only words of damnation pronounced from the prophet Isaiah are for her people, and yet…if anybody can give her a seat under the table…it's this Man. Then, Matthew 11:21 we have what appears to be a hint…that if "Tyre and Sidon" saw His miracles, they would repent. Is this the "if" here in chapter 15? Jesus, then, is in the business of letting Gentiles in to where they don't belong.

My daughter is severely demon-possessed." This is a participle in the Greek language and carries the idea of "my daughter is demonized."

15:23-24

But He answered her not a word. We might think this means Jesus is cold-hearted…as if He is busy pleasing Himself. Yet, His silence is an act of mercy to drive His disciples to feel things and say things they would have otherwise not said.

Do we not see God doing the same when he guards the way of the tree of life in Genesis 3 to keep us from defiled immortality? Do we not see the same thing when God scatters the crowd at the tower so that they don't degrade themselves beyond redemption (Genesis 11)?

And His disciples came and urged Him, saying, "Send her away, for she cries out after us." Maybe the response of Jesus in the next verse indicates that the disciples were implying here that they wanted Jesus to "heal her and **send her away." 24 But He answered** I used to think that this meant Jesus didn't answer her, but rather the disciples with the following phrase, but Mark's Gospel doesn't allow for this perspective.

and said, "I was not sent except to the lost sheep of the house of Israel." Matthew 10:5 shows this same conviction in Jesus' instructions to His disciples. For just a little while, then, Jesus seems ethnically discriminatory…until you see that the totality of no ethnicity will be saved. Furthermore, we see that God **sent** Jesus, and that Jesus is simply being obedient. There was nothing more important to Jesus doing the will of the Father. Do you call yourself a Christian? Do you think you have a better plan than Jesus? Doing the will of the Father?

On the other hand, we find no other errand here—other than to perhaps find rest? Was Jesus intended to reach anybody here? Did He really have to walk 50 miles to find rest? And if any sheep are to be found here…why not her? She wants to be included and is not allowed? Does this allow for the theological possibility that there are those for whom salvation is not intended that can change the Master's mind? I would quake to even entertain such ideas.

15:26-28

But He answered and said, "It is not good to take the children's bread and throw it to the little dogs." A very obvious reference to Gentiles (Matthew 7:6; Philippians 3:2), and yet not so much **(little)**.

27 And she said, "Yes, Lord, There are now two people interested in "truth." She agrees with Him more than the "bleeding hearts" of the day.

She has a better sense of right theology than the disciples do. She knows a lot about David and his dealings, and she knows she doesn't belong in the house of David…but "maybe I can still have crumbs." She had a choice: find fault with the Lord, or keep asking.

28 Then Jesus answered and said to her, "O woman, great is your faith! Only said of two people in this book, and the other is about a centurion—in a book by a Jew to Jews about a Jewish Savior bringing a Jewish salvation.

By the way—given the preceding passage—we don't have to speak filth; we can speak **faith.** This lady's heart was not one of defilement—at least not in this moment.

Then, there's the comparison with Peter in the previous chapter. Walking on the water? Teachings and discipleship for years? "Little faith." They both pray three words, yet one walks on the water while the other is willing to crawl on the floor. Think about Peter now. Wouldn't we think about the so called **faith** of those back in the boat and Peter is accused of "little faith?"

Let it be to you as you desire." Just like the centurion. They both speak for somebody else and have "great faith." They both get what they **desire.**

And her daughter was healed from that very hour. Matthew doesn't tell us anything about how we make these theological issues work. No talk about predestination or election or anything. Deal with it. Somebody who did not belong…now belongs. By the way, you may notice that she still had to have **faith.**

15:29-31[59]

30 Then great multitudes came to Him, having with them the lame, blind, mute, maimed, and many others; and they laid them down at Jesus' feet, and He healed them. This is the 5th time in Matthew He

[59]These notes are primarily from a midweek service on July 1, 2015: http://www.sermonaudio.com/sermoninfo.asp?SID=71151936129 [accessed 9/4/17].

does this indiscriminately (4:23; 9:35; 12:15; 14:34) **31 So the multitude marveled when they saw the mute speaking, the maimed made whole, the lame walking, and the blind seeing; and they glorified** Is this some "glory cloud" around the heads of saints? Is this some sort of intangible…thing? It rather means they put the stage lights on Him…"all the lights are on Him." He is in His right place…being noticed. **the God of Israel.** In Matthew 9 we find people glorifying the Lord, but this is unique because they are seen as those who are worshiping somebody else's **God**—the **God of Israel.** These are Gentiles doing this. It makes sense that the Israelites (chapter 9) would do it. Matthew 5:16 told us this was the point of the potentially Messianic Israel (those who believed Jesus was Who He said He was): to make the whole world (all Gentiles) glorify the Lord **God of Israel.** This has always been the goal of Jesus: to get people to notice His Father. Jehovah is not a tribal deity. He is the **God** of the nations. Now we know who the recipient of this coming miracles really is. Now, instead of 5000 Jews getting fed, we are finding 4000 Gentiles eating.[60]

15:32[61]

Now Jesus called His disciples to Himself and said, "I have compassion Three times Matthew tells us Jesus has this kind of feelings towards people.

15:33

Then His disciples said to Him, "Where could we get enough bread in the wilderness to fill such a great multitude?" I would almost think Matthew was making this up to teach us a lesson, but in 16:7-11 Jesus references both these miracles (the 4000 and the 5000).

15:39

---

[60]My old boss, Pastor Sean Harris, did a great job in his series on Mark in giving some similarities and differences between the two feedings at about 11 minutes into this recording: http://www.sermonaudio.com/sermoninfo.asp?SID=129121227410 [accessed 9/4/17].

[61]This passage is dealt with in more detail in my commentary on Mark (8:1-10).

38 Now those who ate were four thousand men, besides women and children. Some have said Matthew is trying to get the reader to identify with both Moses (quail and manna) or Elisha (2 Kings 4). This could have been Matthew's way of saying "You've never met a prophet like Jesus."

Chapter 16

16:1-4

Then the Pharisees and Sadducees they are annoying and ask leading and loaded questions while the disciples **came, and testing Him asked that He would show them a sign from heaven.** Didn't we already do this in chapter 12? Both times it comes after He heals many people. Oddly enough, I am not sure why these clowns are asking for a sign a second time any more than I know why these disciples are asking about where they are going to get bread.

4 A wicked and adulterous generation seeks after a sign, and no sign shall be given to it except the sign of the prophet Jonah." It seems that 16:21 gives us another connection with **Jonah.** Jesus has compassion on Gentiles and that drives Him to preach to them whereas **Jonah** wanted them all to fry.

16:7-12

8 But Jesus, being aware of it, He's reading minds again (as in 9:4, 12:15, 12:25, 16:8). How disgusting to those wishing to conceal their thoughts.

Event/Fact	Moses	Jesus
Mass Death of Children preceding arrival	Exodus 1	Matthew 2
A trip to Egypt	Exodus 3	Matthew 2
An Exodus from Egypt	Exodus 12-14	Matthew 2
Preceded by a prophet	Exodus 3	Matthew 3
Major Opposing Figure	Exodus 4	Matthew 2
A baptism	1 Corinthians 10:1-2	Matthew 3
Miracle Worker	Exodus 3	Matthew 4
A mountain for law	Exodus 19	Matthew 5-7
12 "heads of tribes"	Numbers 13:3-14	Matt 10:2-4
Two Feedings of God's people	Exodus (manna); Numbers (quail)	Matthew 14; Matthew 15
They each had a church.	Acts 7:38	Matt 16:18

12 Then they understood that He did not tell them to beware of the leaven of bread, but of the doctrine of the Pharisees and Sadducees. It really seems like Psalm 78 gives us the reason for this reaction of Jesus. Jesus is the new Moses, we have seen while the disciples are the New Israel. They are, then, in the wilderness around their Moses. Psalm 78:16 begins the rundown of a faithless Israel asking whether "God can" make a table in the wilderness. These disciples are finding themselves in Psalm 78:36 where they flatter and lie—leading others to believe they are the ones with faith while they are really questioning the ability of this God Who has visited them (Psalm 78:41-56).

Matthew 13:9, Matthew 13:34-39, Matthew 15:3-6, Matthew 15:7, Matthew 15:32 also reference Psalm 78. It becomes quite obvious with 15:33 and the reference of "bread in the wilderness" and 16:1 that the disciples are nothing but "doubting children of Israel, 2.0". All the signs God has done in their midst and ask ridiculous questions like "what are we going to eat now?!"…just like the children of Israel.

Now we know why Jesus responds with "How dumb can you be?" (16:11) Our questions…are somewhat the same…after all God has done in our midst:

1. Can God give calm after a troubling divorce?
2. Can God give grace to the believer in a crumbling America?
3. Can God finish repayment to those who have been wicked to me?
4. Can God furnish me with purpose in the workplace
5. Forgiveness through me to those who don't love me, misuse me
6. Grace with racists towards me (white, black, and Hispanic)
7. Strength in responsibilities in my family

Don't mistake those so-called pious musings for what they really are…mocking, doubt-filled, anxious questions to a God Who has lived up to His Word and His character time and time and time again.

So the question is wrong: "Can God?" is absurd. He can furnish a table with fiscal responsibility and common sense and mercy for tomorrow…

The 3rd day is coming and He is waiting for our food to be gone. Then God will be glorified.

16:13

…He asked His disciples, saying, "Who do men say that I, the Son of Man, That continued usage of this title all equated with God's special agent. **am?"** Jesus is still asking questions. He's doing it for their benefit. He's reading thoughts this entire book. He's not seeking information.

16:14

So they said, "Some say John the Baptist, some Elijah, and others Jeremiah or one of the prophets." Deuteronomy 18:18 is probably in view here.

16:17

Jesus answered and said to him, "Blessed are you, Simon Bar-Jonah, Now, maybe his dad's name really is **Jonah,** but I don't think so. It seems that Jesus is making a difference between Himself ("Son of Man" or "Son of God") and Peter, the "Son of **Jonah."** This is the man who was mentioned in the early part of this chapter. This is no accident. It seems as though Peter's temperament is similar to **Jonah's.** If you do this in real time, it's quite the response to Peter's confession. By the way, both were/will be confronted in Joppa about the fate of Gentiles (Jonah 1; Acts 10). Peter did not like Jesus' redemption ideas either. He is not interested in death on a cross (16:22), but rather a sword (Matthew 26:51).

16:18-19

And I also say to you that you are Peter, Mark 3:14 tells us Jesus gave "Simon" this name. By the way, **Peter** is the Greek form of the Aramaic "Cephas" (John 1:42). **Peter** and **rock** are contrasted with **this. and on this rock** is the confession Peter voices (16:16) with the help of the Father (16:17). Peter furthermore knew Christ was the ultimate **Rock** when he spoke of Him in 1 Peter 2:5-7.

I will build My church, Since this is the first time this word is used in the New Testament. It must therefore be rich in meaning and the original reader must have really had some things come into their mind when they heard this word. Notice how the chart (earlier in this chapter) shows us the member of Matthew's Hebrew audience would not have understood this in the common Greek understanding of *ekklesia* but rather the

Hebrew's understanding of this Greek translation of their Hebrew word. With all of these parallel with Moses that have been mentioned in this book, we should find out that Acts 7:38 will provide this Hebrew backdrop. Therefore, Matthew's audience would have pictured a gathering in the wilderness around Moses (Matthew 15:33 uses this very word)—the New Moses. Both Moses and Jesus have a **church** in the wilderness.

Jesus, then, is promising to have a people that He will lead like Moses. Apparently, an exaggerated class on ecclesiology is not needed.[62]

and the gates of Hades The Greek word behind what is usually "Hell" in some older translations, and it simply means "the realm of the dead." It is probably being brought up because of the 16:15 reference to "Living God." What good is a "Living God" who has a Son Who has a church that is conquered by death anyway?

Maybe an even better question: What Good is an assembly that is always dead once dead? We should all, then, as followers of the Son of the Living God, expect a full-on resurrection. Well, what good is a belief in the resurrection that doesn't disarm the fear of death itself? This is

---

[62] The "body of Christ" idea should be used sparingly regarding the O.T. as the "body of Christ" had no "head" until the ascension (Ephesians 1:22-23). Since we know that "church" usually has *ekklesia* as its underlying word and "called out assembly" as the understood meaning, then when did it begin?

If we are talking merely denotation, then I would say when God "called Abraham out" of the Ur of the Chaldees and "assembled with Him and Melchizedek" (Genesis 13).

If we are talking actually, then before the foundation of the world (Revelation 13:8; Eph 3:1-6).

If we are talking denotation in a New Testament sense, then it would be when he "called out his disciples and assembled with them" (Mat 16:18; Ephesians 2:20).

If we are talking effectively being made the house of God through administration of the Holy Spirit, it seems like it is the process of approximately 10 days to include the ascension and Pentecost (Eph 1:22-23; Acts 2).

If we are talking redemptively (calling out sinners to meet with Him), then Genesis 3:8 with Adam and Eve.

If we are talking about actually assembling as a universal body of redeemed, the church starts when we are all assembled around the Lord (1 Thessalonians 4:18, Hebrews 12:22).

precisely why Jesus' words are not well received by His disciples 16:24-26.

will not prevail as absurd as it is to conceive of the church, in this context, going into **Hades,** there are many who preach it thus. It seems more natural, rather, to place the church with Christ Who went into and came out of **Hades.**[63]

19 And I will give you the keys of the kingdom of heaven, and whatever you bind on earth [8]**will be bound in heaven, and whatever you loose on earth will be loosed in heaven."** He certainly exercised this at Pentecost. The sense of this passage is that those here conducting the business of **Heaven** are only doing what has already been done in **Heaven.**

> But the matter is not quite so simple; the actions described in heaven are future perfect passives—which could be translated "will have already been bound in heaven … will have already been loosed in heaven." In other words, the heavenly decree confirming the earthly one is based on a prior verdict.[64]

See this same guidance behind the passage in the "church discipline" passage of Matthew 18:15-20.

16:22

Then Peter took Him aside Along with the Hebrew understanding of *ekklesia* there is a Greek understanding that drives **Peter** to take exception to this idea.[65]

16:23

---

[63]Here is a short recording on the topic:
https://www.sermonaudio.com/sermoninfo.asp?SID=1016119207 [accessed November 8, 2017].
   [8]Or *will have been bound* … will have been loosed
   [64] William D. Mounce, *Basics of Biblical Greek: Grammar*, ed. Verlyn D. Verbrugge, Third Edition. (Grand Rapids, MI: Zondervan, 2009), 122.
   [65]See this lesson for that Greek understanding:
http://www.sermonaudio.com/sermoninfo.asp?SID=35171934456

But He turned and said to Peter, "Get behind Me, Satan! He was just called "Rock" in 16:18 and now things have quickly changed.

You are an offense This is the word where we get our word "scandal," and it is often used of Jesus being the "Rock of offense" over which people may stumble. Here, the term is used of Peter and the implication is that he is getting in the way of God. Matthew 13 uses this same "stumbling" language when Jesus would have done more, but there was too much "stumbling" going on. Here, though, Jesus is not going to allow somebody to get in the way of His following the Father. "Rock of stumbling! Move behind me!"

to Me, for you are not mindful of the things of God, but the things of men." How is it possible to have the keys of the kingdom (16:19) and not be **mindful of God?**

16:24-26

26 For what profit is it to a man if he gains the whole world, and loses his own soul? Not sure why this unfortunate translation since **soul** is the same Greek word as "life" in both cases in verse 25. In any case, "your life is so valuable, don't waste it!"

16:27-28

According to verse 13, we are still in Ceasarea Philippi. Remember all the similarities between the Moses and Jesus parallels. We're going to see in the next chapter another one: Just as God spoke to Moses out of the heavens (Exodus 19-20) and the people pled for Moses to do the talking with God whereas Peter, James, and John show the same fright. We can sort of call this next episode the "New Sinai" for this same reason: Jesus is the ultimate Moses.

28 Assuredly, I say to you, there are some standing here who shall not taste death till they see the Son of Man coming Both here and in verse 27 we do not have the word *parousia,* but rather *erchomai* and can be simply the action of "coming" or "going." **in His kingdom."** "…Until they are rewarded (by implication, verse 27)."

This is very awkward, it seems, since we have what appears to be a very clear reference to the "second coming" and a very clear understanding that these men are all now dead. 3-4 of them, however, did live another 40 years or so.

1. Is this a reference to the very next chapter? If it really is only six days later, then we can see how awkward this is to look at a group of men and say "some of you are going to live another six days!" Well…the implication is that some of them would die…and there is no indication that any died in that next week.

2. Is this Pentecost? Well, that's only another six months or so. Is this really any less awkward when we know all but one (Judas) was alive than the previous possibility? Isn't it a little anti-climactic to say so?

3. Is this the destruction of 70A.D.? It's hard to fathom that the **Son of Man** and He came with His angels and He **reward**ed folks, and all were able to see it who were alive. Of course, we're faced with asking, "If it happened? How?" 2 Timothy 1:15 shows people believed it did happen literally during this time.

4. Was Jesus mistaken? Perhaps He was hopeful like Paul was in 1 Corinthians 15:51 and 1 Thessalonians 4:13 and his "we statements." This seems hard: "The Son of God was wrong."

5. Is this just a progressive reality? During revivalism in different eras—moving westward? Not good. That would mean the apostles—some of them—are still alive.

6. Is this speaking of John only? Since he saw the book of the Revelation, does he qualify? Was that the fulfillment? It cannot be John only since this passage here speaks of 2nd person, plural (not singular) that would not "die." Therefore, it must be more than John among the 11, if it's John at all.

7. Is this Daniel simply going to the Ancient of Days in Daniel 7? If so, how will he **reward** every man from Heaven's throne **according to their works?**

8. Is this simply a postponed promise? Was it a legitimate promise that was postponed since the Jews rejected Jesus? It would be Jesus, once again, uncertain of their rejecting them.

Let's talk about "dual fulfillment." This is the idea that Scriptures can be fulfilled in more than one way. I don't particularly care about this because it sounds like a "cop out." However, there are examples (3 to be shared here) of Scripture having dual fulfillment:

1. Daniel 11 speaks of Alexander the Great's coming and all of his exploits—to include the splitting of his kingdom into four sections. One of these four kingdom-ettes was led by Antiochus IV, and Daniel 11:35 very clearly speaks of his influence in the temple of Jerusalem. It's prophecy. By the time Jesus speaks of it, it is history. However, Jesus takes this history of Daniel 11:35 and says it is <u>also</u> prophecy in Matthew 24:15. Is Jesus wrong?
2. Hosea 11:1 speaks of the history of the Exodus of the Israelite nation, and Matthew calls it a history of—not Israel, but of Jesus, and his trip out of Egypt (Matthew 2:15). Is Matthew wrong?
3. Zechariah 12:9 speaks of a prophecy that John says occurred at Jesus' death on Calvary (John 19:34) while he said it will also occur at Jesus' second coming (Revelation 1:7). Is John wrong?

We don't think any of these were wrong. So we will here enunciate two choices. First, the mount of transfiguration was the primary fulfillment:

1. All three Synoptic Gospels place the Mount of Transfiguration after this promise. No variation of the order or proximity of these two episodes.
2. We do think Peter makes no equivocation that the Mount of Transfiguration was the Coming of Christ (2 Peter 1:16-18).
3. The continued Mosaic comparison which places the Sinai "coming of Christ" [angels, for example taking place at Sinai (Exodus 19:9) according to Deuteronomy 33:2 and Psalm 68:17 with Stephen in Acts 7, Paul in Galatians 3, and Luke (?) in Hebrews 2] with this Mount and its "coming of Christ" (Matthew 16:27).

Secondly, I will say that I believe this was ultimately fulfilled in A.D. 70 (in view of Matthew 10:23 and it's notes in this commentary). In other words, for Jesus to say "some of you will still be alive" when really…all of them were alive "6 days later" (17:1) is nonsense for the person (especially in light of the fact there were only three involved) on the Mount of Transfiguration. If Peter, therefore, didn't tell me this was "a fulfillment" of Matthew 16:27-28, I wouldn't even write it.

Matthew 22:1-7 leaves no question that the destruction of Jerusalem was a **reward,** and called it a **coming.** Matthew 23:34-38 reinforces that it was Jesus who sent prophets to this generation and their fathers and that that generation would catch the full weight of the sins upon their city. If the **coming** can be pictured in a parable, it can be re-used in this promise of His **coming.** Matthew 24:34 and 26:63 also make it clear that this awful judgment was coming to those then living.

27 For the Son of Man will come in the glory of His Father with His angels, Psalm 78:48 and following speak of **angels** providing trouble for the Israelites in the wilderness. We are otherwise told only of one. It seems reasonable that **angels** could be nothing but figurative language of might and power surrounding the **coming of the Son of Man.**

and then He will reward each according to his works. Reflecting on 16:1-4, it seems like this could be **each** in that "generation." It could be, therefore, a generic statement to those then living in that nation of Christ rejectors. **Each** in Christ's sphere of influence and those in their generation will be **reward**ed **according to his works** particularly the **work** of rejecting Jesus. **28 Assuredly, I say to you, there are some standing here who shall not taste death till they see the Son of Man coming** in the same way in which the "LORD came" in Isaiah 19:1? The Babylonians actually did this, but "the LORD" is pictured as "riding on a swift cloud." What if, this time, it is not the Egyptians being judged, but rather Jerusalem; what if it was the Romans rather than the Babylonians? It is entirely acceptable to say the **the Son of Man** is **coming** when in fact, it is the Romans. **in His kingdom."** We now have another parallel between Moses and Jesus: there was 40 years between their separate appearances to the people to whom they were sent to deliver (Jesus having died around 30 A.D.).

is, by the way, **Jesus** promoting the children of God (already mentioned) above the "son of God" (known as "Israel" in Exodus 4 and Hosea 11).

27 Nevertheless, lest we offend them, or make them stumble. **go to the sea, cast in a hook, and take the fish that comes up first. And when you have opened its mouth, you will find a** [1]**piece of money;** Jesus is either omniscient and knows of a fish that swallowed a coin somewhere or He is omnipotent and made this happen. He made a coin which would not have had the proper impression on it? Maybe it was a mix? He drove a fish to swim to a dropped coin that He knew about: a good mix of both "omni"'s. He knows everything: in Matthew 9 and Matthew 12 (and so forth), and He can furthermore avoid everything at His will. So why not here? Simple: Jesus lives way below His rights to remove stumblingblocks from those who might think less of Himself. Phenomenal! He pays the stupid half-shekel, not because He owes it, but because people were watching. In other words (a la Matthew 5:16), some times we do things we don't have to do because somebody is observing the Father…and His "sons."

We pay the "half shekel" so that we don't even offend the "little ones" (next chapter). "I don't care what anybody thinks!" is not in keeping with the Spirit of Christ here demonstrated. Some of us have hard choices to make and we should be asking "what would Jesus think of this and what would the world see?"

take that and give it to them for Me and you." Jesus always shares His lavishness with us (Romans 8:15; Titus 3:7). This is a glorious forecast for us (especially with Matthew 6:19-21 as a backdrop). He gave Peter, however, "daily bread" (Matthew 6); not tomorrow's tax.

18:1[66]

At that time the disciples came to Jesus, saying, "Who then is greatest maybe everybody thought **Jesus** was going to say "Peter"— specifically since whoever it is would be greater than John the Baptist

---

[1]Gr. *stater,* the exact temple tax for two

[66]Much of what follows as additional treatment in Mark 9-10's version (found in my commentary on Mark).

(11:11). Who among the disciples would fit this description besides him? **in the kingdom of heaven?"** This is a great continuation from the last chapter. This question is probably prompted by those who are amazing! The disciples just called the "sons of God!"

18:3

A man must be "converted" to enter the Kingdom and "become like a little child". This is no different than John 3:3. They both speak of being "born again to enter the kingdom." By the way, considering 18:9, there is no alternative to "conversion" and entrance into the "kingdom" other than "Hell fire."

18:6

"Whoever causes one of these little ones who believe "receiving" (18:5) and **believ**ing in Christ are what is necessary to be saved. This is "becoming like a little child" (18:3). What must they **believe?** 17:22-23 and 20:28 tell us! In these fantastic contexts we see this chapter break is so unfortunate.

to sin, This is that same word "offend" in verse 27. We have transitioned from "offending" tax collectors to "offending" children.

18:7-14

Woe to the world because of offenses! A clue that Jesus is on the same vein of thought: scandalize or make to stumbling or **offend. For offenses must come, but woe to that man by whom the offense comes!** Basically restating verse 6: We know that children will be kept from being saved, but if you're one of them...**woe to** you.

10 "Take heed that you do not despise one of these little ones, This is a clue that we are in the same context going all the way back to 18:1 (this is after we see the connection between 17:22 and 18:5 because of the Gospel and 17:27 with 18:9 concerning "offenses"). **for I say to you that in heaven their angels** This is very interesting indeed. Take a look at Hebrews 1:14 and see this discussed. Does this imply there is a time when a child does not have an **angel,** right? Then, what happens if they die? There is no answer provided in this passage. **always see the face of My Father who is in heaven. 11 For the Son of Man has come to save that which was lost.** The "little ones" in the context. Children are not perfect and still need to be found by **the Son of Man,** or they won't be in the kingdom.

12 "What do you think? If a man has a hundred sheep, and one of them goes astray, does he not leave the ninety-nine and go to the mountains to seek the one that is straying? Can we do too much to reach children when we know this contextual teaching of Jesus going through such extents to reach them? **13 And if he should find it, assuredly, I say to you, he rejoices more over that sheep than over the ninety-nine that did not go astray.** "And if you get in the way of the seeking shepherd from His little one," there's "Hell fire" to pay. **14 Even so it is not the will of your Father who is in heaven that one of these little ones should perish.** This with the "angel talk" of verse 10 should at least give the Calvinist pause to think through their system.

18:15-17

Moreover another clue that we are in the very same context! Instead of me "offending a little one" (preceding context), now it is a "little one" offending me! **if thy brother shall trespass against thee,** "if He breaks God's law in how he deals with you." **go and tell him** this is not about cornering or strong-arming; it is about reconciliation—or else why do we want the offender to "hear."

16 But if he will not hear thee, then take with thee one or two more, that in the mouth of two or three witnesses every word may be established. Deuteronomy 19 gives this precedence, and it demonstrates that this action is to give fear to those observing.

17 And if he shall neglect to hear them, tell it unto the church: but if he neglect to hear the church, This is probably not a 3-step method, but rather drives home the point of escalating accountability ultimately ending at dismissal.[67] The intent of Jesus is to ultimately restore, as

---

[67] Jesus' intent is not formulaic, but rather progress-driven. Otherwise, do women get to take part (after all, 1 Corinthians 7 speaks of either a father or a husband

discreetly as possible, one who fears for their salvation. **let him be unto thee as an heathen man and a publican.** There are two clues here that the church is not intended for the unbeliever. First, it supposes that if there is a problem within the church, it is with a "brother." This would certainly be a believer. Secondly, if one is to be treated as a "heathen and a publican," heathens and publicans are not typically a part of this church/assembly. An unbeliever, then, should not feel "welcomed" in the church. This is not about simply voting rights, this is about feeling welcomed or not. This is not just about membership. This is about anybody who "identifies" as a part of a particular "church."

Furthermore, if you are treated, by the whole church, as **a heathen and a publican,** you should assume that you are, in fact, **a heathen,** and that you are not saved. No **heathen** should therefore feel welcome at any "church," but rather the "church" corporate (all assemblies) should respect the authority of the local assembly/church which dismissed the **heathen.** By the way, this process here would preclude the need for law suits and would empower pastors to work with their respective members if they catch wind of law suits taking place between their members.

Churches, then, should not feel "welcomed" in that they should not feel like it is designed for them. Think with me for a minute. If you have a person to your home and you decide to cook them a meal. Let's say they have children. Are the children "unwelcomed" in your home? No, but it is understood that the children by themselves would not have been invited. The meal was intended for the parents.

It is the same way church is to be designed. For whom is the worship of God designed? His people. For whom is the meal of the Word of God prepared? God's people. Over whom do the shepherds of the flock watch? The sheep of His pasture. Who do we, the pastors, care for? The flock; the church; the people who comprise our membership.

There is evidence that unbelievers will naturally join the church (1 Corinthians 14:18-25). Let it be observed, then, that it is believers acting like believers as if it is only believers which convinces the

---

having a part in the accountability of a lady, so also does Moses' law)? Is 4 witnesses too much? How much time is required between steps?

unbeliever He must be a worshipper of their God. The gifts and the assembly are designed for the believer. The unbeliever should not feel like they are "a part" of things at "First Church of Corinth." Let your unbelieving friend hear the Gospel in other places, but do not feel like your pastor is the only evangelist. Remember, that unbeliever will feel out of place. The church is simply not designed for them....and that's the point of church membership. They are treated as **heathen and publicans** because that's what they probably are.

and a publican Imagine the **publican** who wrote this smiling as he realized that since this passage had a main concern of repentance, Jesus wanted His church to have those who were as far gone as him!

let him be unto thee as an heathen man and a publican. Jesus just said that in the church you don't have people that cause dissension without accountability, and if you have them, well then, they have got to go. If they won't repent, you have to assume they're lost and send them on their way to determine if it's so! The following passage proves this actually works when Peter learns how to deal with those who may actually return and repent.[68]

18:18

"Assuredly, I say to you, whatever you bind on earth will be bound in heaven, and whatever you loose on earth will be loosed in heaven. Twice in three chapters (16:19 also)—both of which are in the context of

---

[68] Well, this does seem somewhat of a contradiction. It is a paradox in any case. It appears to be a contradiction of Matthew 13 where He deals with the removal of the tares (Matthew 13:28). There it is described as something on which to wait. I would say that right there you have the basic difference between these two passages. We're supposed to leave the tare alone until the harvest. Ok, that means that we're not supposed to be having this sort of theocratic thing where, like Calvin says, the civil law is supposed to bear the sword and get rid of all those who will not be a part of the kingdom. So the kingdom is like this: its jurisdiction is worldwide. But it is to be done specifically, according to God's will, in the church. There's supposed to be a moderate level of toleration in the world, of which the church is not a part, strictly speaking.

So the difference? In one passage the disciples are not allowed to get rid of the tares and in the other passage the disciples are commanded to get rid of those people that are obviously unconverted. They are supposed to be treated **as heathen and publicans**. We are not supposed to go out into the world and try to purge it of all unbelievers, but we are supposed to do so in the church.

the "church." We don't have to be totally clear on what this means to know that the same stuff is happening in both places in answer to the Lord's prayer (Matthew 6).

The Scripture does not speak of business meetings, but it does speak of conducting business at meetings. We can't say there was a vote taken, but some level of corporate action was taken and that had to be measured in some way. These "business meetings" conducted, says this verse, "Heaven's business." There are no other entities that conduct Heaven's business.

18:19-20

"Again I say to you that if two of you agree on earth concerning anything that they ask, it will be done for them by My Father in heaven. 20 For where two or three as witnesses as seen in verse 16.[69] These are meeting to conduct business with Jesus. We are talking about "getting rid" of "heathen" and "publicans." And if **ask**ing is for anything, it is to ask the "Father" (verse 19) to restore the "heathen" (verse 17).

are gathered together for discipline, in the context. **in My name, I am there in the midst of them."** Jesus is saying that "whatever you do down here, I am doing in Heaven." So, since we see that the church is made up of believers seeking to expel the unbeliever, we know that our churches should not seek to be "seeker sensitive."

Furthermore, if there is any place where we believers should be counted on to have Heaven's will done, it should be in the church...a home for believers, and not for "heathen or publicans."

18:21-22

Then Peter came to Him and said, "Lord, how often shall my brother sin against me, and I forgive him? Up to seven times?" Here

---

[69]The O.T. was much easier. You merely died whereas in the New Testament the action by "two or three witnesses" indicates that you belong in Hell.

we have the scenario of the church discipline actually driving somebody to repent. **Peter is asking,** "what if this works?"

Well we're still talking about a brother who sins (18:15), and look what Peter introduces as a possibility: **Then came Peter to Him, and said, Lord, how oft shall my brother sin against me, and I forgive him?** Now, it's not like he's forgiving him without any kind of repentance. We're not told to just haphazardly forgive people that are just flippant and careless in our lives. If you look at the cross-reference sometime, Luke 17, it, actually the entire thought is implied here but it's explicit there. And the only reason I'm referring to it is because I don't want to make you think something that's not true. You're not required to just willy-nilly forgive everybody, because that's really not love. Remember, one of the principles that we find in the gospel is justice. And it's very hard to show people gospel love if you're not requiring justice. Let me say that again. I don't think you hear that enough. We're not showing gospel-centered Christianity if we don't require justice. You can't enjoy God's grace and His mercy if you are not under some sort of sense of obligation to Him. So, in Luke 17 it says, "If your brother sins against thee and says, 'I repent,' you forgive him." Here it's implied.

So here is what happens when a brother wants to get it right. Peter says, "What happens if a brother wants to get it right?" And he says, **Lord, how oft shall my brother sin against me, and I forgive him? till seven times? 22 Jesus saith unto him, I say not unto thee, until seven times: but, until seventy times seven.**[70] In Genesis 4, you have this guy named Lamech. And he kills a man and he says, "I killed a man for wounding me. If Cain would be avenged sevenfold, truly Lamech seventy and sevenfold." Or, seventy times seven. It's kind of like in a math problem. If you leave the "x" in there it's the same as just putting the number in parenthesis. So, I just wanted you to see they're using the same numeric formulas here and I don't know the point, but it's the only times in the Bible where you can find this sort of idea. And maybe one day I'll get really smart and I'll find the connection.[71]

---

[70]There are four hundred and ninety years in Daniel's seventy weeks.

[71]How do I know there's a connection? Look what Jesus is referencing in Matthew 19:3-5 (just a few short verses away). He's referencing Genesis, so I have no issue saying He's referencing Genesis just verses earlier. If Genesis is on Jesus' mind

18:23-25

I think when we read the Proverbs 6, "These six things does the Lord hate, yay, seven are an abomination,"[72] Jesus is saying "Look at that perfect number and go one beyond it." If you want to find it in about six times in about three chapters, look at Amos. I have a feeling this is another Hebraic formula of saying "countless," because if you're keeping a tally and you're up around seventy three, and you're like me, you lose count and you have to start over. "Just keep forgiving."

Therefore is the kingdom of heaven likened unto a certain king, which would take account of his servants. And when he had begun to reckon, one was brought unto him, which owed him ten thousand talents. Again, you could weary yourself for the next three hours trying to figure out what that means, but a talent is a year's wage. There's no way this guy is going to repay ten thousand years worth of labor. So you're getting the story of a fixed fight. Jesus is setting the stage to make a point. He wants you to consider something that is just as bombastic, or even more, than four hundred and ninety forgivenesses. And so He says, "Here's a man that owed ten thousand years of labor to his master."

But forasmuch as he had not to pay, his lord commanded him to be sold, and his wife, and children, and all that he had, and payment to be made. Seems kind of harsh, until someone gets indebted to you ten thousand years worth of salary. Then it doesn't seem so harsh to be owned and sold. Who in the world lets themselves get so far into debt? And I guess that's the point of the Lord, isn't it? How in the world can we let ourselves get so far into debt to God?

18:26-27

The servant therefore fell down, and worshipped him. That word worship, you probably see something different if you don't have a King James. It means that he lies prostrate. The servant therefore fell down flat. In the Greek, the idea is to lick the hand of the master like a dog

---

or on Matthew's mind in 19:4 and 19:5, then I have no problem believing it was on His mind in 18:23. I don't know the connection but it does appear to be on His mind.

[72]Proverbs 30 showcases the "three, yes four" formula as well.

does his master. And if you don't have a dog you don't have any idea the frustration that that can produce.

Saying, Lord, have patience with me, and I will pay thee all. Well that's pretty arrogant. How patient would you like the master to be, for you to pay back ten thousand years of labor? We'll say just about anything in a foolish vow though to get out of trouble. And here we are having our character displayed to us.

Then the lord of that servant was moved with compassion, and loosed him, and forgave him the debt. Loosed is the same idea as **forgave him**. Right there in the verse we have forgiveness defined for us. It actually means "to let go or to disregard." When you forgive someone you're disregarding what they've done for you. It's like you're deciding to not care about it anymore. That's very hard. And the reason it seems so very hard to us is because, well, the answer is found here in this parable.

18:28

But the same servant. We'll call him Servant A.

The same servant went out, and found one of his fellowservants, which owed him an hundred pence. a denarii, which is a day's wage. So this guy owes him what amounts to be three months worth of wages, which is quite a bit different I think than ten thousand years.

He laid hands on him. That is a judicial term. It's not like he's shaking him; it's that he's grabbing him and pulling him to the magistrate to settle, which was certainly in the right of the person who was owed.

Took him by the throat, saying, Pay me what you owe. Drags him in front of the judgment seat and says, "Pay me those three and a half months worth of wages."

18:29

Now, it is striking how similar verse 26 is to verse 29. In fact, it's almost a carbon copy. Servant B fell down at Servant A's feet and besought him saying; and he says the same thing, **Have patience with me, and I will pay thee all.** Servant B is a little bit more realistic.

Servant A really doesn't understand what he owes but he does totally understand what Servant B owes him.

18:30

Servant A **would not** He would not have patience with Servant B. **But went and cast him into prison, till he should pay the debt.** Now here's my question, how are you going to do that? Now that you're in prison; how do you work it off in prison? It's not like you could earn a Master's Degree back then in jail. Make license plates. This is not Angola State Pen. That seems so contradictory. "You owe me this money. I'm putting you in jail." Well the idea is that if you put someone in prison your family would feel sorry for you and pay off your debt. Might be kind of considered like posting bail except it was actually the payment for your crime; It was actually the settling of your debt. Maybe that's a better way to say it. But any case, putting him in prison would perhaps get others to feel sorry for him and pay the debt. Three and a half months.

Now, I'm sure that's a lot of money. You know what you make every month. Multiply that by three and that's what this man owes you in this story. It's a lot of money, there's no question. But now, take your annual salary and multiply it by ten thousand and you'll know what you and I owe the king. It's astronomical. And that's the point. This is not a real deep passage.

18:31

These **fellowservants** are C through Z: **So when his fellowservants saw what was done, they were very sorry, and came and told unto their lord all that was done. Then his lord, after that he had called him, said unto him, O thou wicked servant, I forgave thee all that debt, because you simply desired it: Shouldest not thou also have had compassion on thy fellowservant, even as I had pity on thee? And his lord was wroth, and delivered him to the tormentors, till he should pay all that was due unto him.** Once again, this would be absurd if we didn't understand that people would feel badly that this man is being tortured in jail until someone pays his debt. You've already decided it certainly doesn't mean purgatory "because we don't believe in that," and already the Scripture has been stymied before it can even do any work in our hearts. It sounds like all of a sudden not only are you going to be tortured until someone pays your debt, but it also sounds like you can actually lose your salvation.

18:35

So likewise shall My heavenly Father do also unto you if ye from your hearts forgive not every one his brother their trespasses. First of all, I feel like I need to talk about this idea of Paul. Is this in agreement with Paul? Does the, first of all, church discipline square with Paul? Now folks, I'm asking you these reasons on purpose. Well, I want you to see they actually do very much agree. Especially when you look in verse 15 through 20. Please notice how much this has in common with 1 Corinthians 5:1-10. Paul sounds a lot like Jesus.

So I guess what I'm trying to say is we're not surprised. Remember the last verse of chapter 17. Jesus tells us that He did not want to give offense to people so He paid His taxes that He really honestly didn't owe (sounds like Paul, 1 Corinthians 10:32). **So also My heavenly Father will do to you if everyone of you do not forgive your brother from your heart.** This, again, sounds like Paul (Ephesians 4:32). Then, we find that Genesis 2 is quoted by Jesus (Matthew 19:1-6) and Paul (1 Corinthians 6). Paul and Jesus sound a lot alike. So with four straight episodes that are like Paul, we should expect whatever salvation is being spoken of in this passage to be much the same.

Now let's talk about three things that are not in this passage that <u>are</u> in salvation as Paul would preach it:
1. In this passage there is no evidence of salvation by faith, only a presumptive arrogance that one could repay a debt. That is not Paul's salvation. We don't see anything in here about a servant having faith in a God who will forgive him. That's not what we believe about New Testament salvation. You are not going to find salvation this way.
2. We don't find propitiation in this passage. Now propitiation is the satisfaction of an angry ruler by paying a debt and satisfying his wrath. But no debt is being paid here. Here's the reality. The king doesn't require payment of ten thousand talents but it's still owed. No one paid it. That is not propitiation.

When we sinned against God Almighty, someone had to die for it for our salvation. What do the Muslims teach? You get saved if God says so. That's it. You know, well why would God forgive you? Because He decides to. It's up to Him. Well we don't believe that. We believe that the debt really does have to be paid. In this story there is no debt paid. It is arbitrarily forgiven because the king has pity on Servant A.

3. We have no advocacy. So long as Jesus the High Priest is living at the right hand of God the Father I don't have to worry about falling from grace. Hebrews 7 says that "He ever lives to intercede." I don't have to ever worry about losing my salvation so long as the High Priest lives, because He's going to continually keep His work on the cross before the Father and there will never be a chance of my debt being brought up again, because of faith in Jesus. That's the whole point of intercession. Jesus is at the right hand of God assuring my salvation, keeping the work of Calvary before the Father. Here, there is none of that. There's nothing but a god who is re-angered and reapplies the same debt.

Well then, what are we talking about? Because if it's salvation, if you decide, "No, no, no, Paul and Jesus are just preaching a different salvation, that's just all there is to it. Well, Paul and Jesus and John and Jude… They're all just teaching a different salvation." Well, think about what we have to deal with here. In verse 34 I already introduced to you the fact that you have a man going to jail until he pays. Now think about the problem if you're willing to say that you have to go to hell until your sins are paid for. It's like there's two ways to get saved: either Jesus paid for your sins or you can. Now it will take you ten thousand years, but at least it's just ten thousand years and not an infinity. Well that certainly does seem like a wasted trip for Jesus from heaven. There is a plan B. You can either trust Jesus as your Savior or you can go to hell and pay for your sins and then get out. Well, I don't think that's what the passage is teaching. It's not because my system says it doesn't work; it's because I've already shown you three things that are missing from this passage that are present with New Testament salvation. Propitiation, intercession, and salvation by faith. All of them are not in this passage. So I have to believe that verse 34 is not talking about some sort of go to jail in hell until you pay for your sins.

Also, if the jail that Servant A puts Servant B into is not hell, then the jail the king put Servant A into cannot be hell, because the parable is not parallel then. There's no proof that this is an after death judgment.

So, what is it then? Well, here's what I think: does Matthew use this language any other place in Matthew? And he has, one other time. Matthew 6.

Matthew 6:9-13 showcases the Lord's Prayer. In the middle we read "Give us this day our daily bread. And forgive us our debts, as we forgive our debtors." Now, there's an explanation to follow after He closes the prayer in verse 13 in verse 14.

> *For if you forgive men their trespasses, your heavenly Father will also forgive you: But if ye forgive not men their trespasses, neither will your Father forgive your trespasses.*

Well, we have a couple thoughts once again. Is this passage, just like Matthew 18, teaching that in order for you to have your sins forgiven you have to be a forgiving person? Well, there's a number of reasons why I would say yes and no:

1. First, the "no": It's incredibly difficult for your heavenly Father, which you did not have until you got saved, to punish you like a lost person while He's still your heavenly Father. Only saved people have a heavenly Father. So how can you be punished by your heavenly Father like a lost person if you're unsaved? The other thing is, it's just poor theology. "You're saved if you're forgiving. You're not saved if you're not forgiving." I mean, you could potentially be unsaved and saved fifteen times a day.

2. Second, the "yes": There are two ways in which a person could talk about forgiveness. One is God as your judge and the other is God as your Father. And let me just propose a scenario to you if I could. Let's just say that I was elected to be a district judge. Let's say that my son is involved with

tomfoolery and stupidity and all manner of dumbness downtown. And he decides to monogram vehicles with his initials in his key. There is a solid chance that I'll find out about it, both as his father and as the judge. This is not a perfect illustration but it will illustrate enough what I'm trying to say. He has his day in court. He admits his guilt and the person whose car he defaced drops the charges. I as the judge will not bring judgment upon him because the charges have been dropped. But I'm also his dad. I will take off that gown at the end of the day and I'm no longer his judge. He has nothing to worry about as far as serving the sentence of a convict. But I am going to blister his hind end when we get home because I'm his dad.

There are two ways in which God can judge you, judge me. One was taken care of at Calvary. "Believe on the Lord Jesus Christ and thou shall be saved" (Acts 16:31). You'll never have to worry about being under condemnation again and God will continually work on your heart, time after time after time, to make you a forgiving person; that's true. But if you decide as a Christian, as one of the sons of the Father to ask for forgiveness in this manner and not grant forgiveness in this manner, then you will be worked over by your heavenly Father. It says nothing about being in danger of hellfire. It says forgiveness. Why do we have 1 John 1:9 in the Bible? "To confess our sins and He is found faithful to forgive us our sins." Is it so that we can be saved? No, it is because we are saved that we have the ability to come to God and ask for forgiveness.

I don't want anyone reading this to think that I am decreasing the load of responsibility upon us to be forgiving people. Now, this might seem kind of irrational. Why is it that I am just going to put my brother in prison, but God, if I am unforgiving, will put me to tormentors? Remember it is a parable. It is not doctrinal, it is not a doctrinal teaching passage; it is a parable. It's not like an epistle. It's a story being told to illustrate Biblical truth. So it's not like Jesus is saying, "This is exactly how it'll happen and oh here, by the way, here's the tormentors." But if you have ever met a miserable Christian you will know someone who is being tormented. I want you to know the reason many Christians you know are being tormented in bitterness and anger and despondency, is because they are ridiculously irrational Christians. If you are bitter and angry there's a solid chance that you've got someone in your jail, and you are with the tormentors. And you're going to stay there until you forgive the debt.

It is not a light thing to be irrational. I have always been humored by the lost world who thinks that God is irrational. "If I was God I would take better care of my world and not let hurricanes and tsunamis and tornados. If I was God I would not let my children die of starvation. If I was God..." As if God needs permission to be anything to anybody. How about those of us who have been forgiven amazing amounts of sins against our king? It is so irrational to be American more than Christian. You can sit around and sulk about how you have a right to hold a grudge if you want to, but you're the one that's going to be with the tormentors. "You better let them out of prison or I'll leave you with the tormentors."

We have been forgiven absurd amounts of offense against God and all we can think about is how we've been wronged. "They've taken my rights. They've stepped all over me. They have..." Yes, I know and I'm not trying to reduce the depth of the pain that you're feeling. And I don't think Jesus is either. Nor do I think that He is magnifying your plight. I don't think that He's saying, "Ah, what you went through is nothing." But I do think He's saying, "Have some perspective." In your little, "I need time to recover," you have been holding a grudge for five and seven and thirteen and seventeen years. You need to ask God to forgive you and write a letter of forgiveness to somebody and ask their forgiveness for being such a jerk. So how irrational are we when we keep someone in our jail?

Oh, we need to be careful because while we're keeping people in jail for their offenses against us... I know it hurts, I know you could use that hundred pence, I know they should say sorry. I know they should. I know they should say it like they mean it. I know they should. I know they should stop doing it all the time. I know they should. I know you could use that hundred denarii. I know. But you're the one with the tormentors. And so am I. Let's not spend any time with the tormentors. Let your brother and sister out of jail.

Chapter 19

19:1-2

Now it came to pass, when Jesus had finished these sayings, *that* He departed from Galilee and came to the region of Judea beyond the Jordan. Jesus did not go through Samaria, the middle region, then.
2 And great multitudes followed Him, and He healed them there. Like Matthew 4:32-33, 8:16-17, 9:35, 12:14, 14:14, and 15:29-30. One might surmise that the doctors had nothing else to do. Seems like this is a sneak peek into the kingdom. Again, He shows Himself "qualified" by healing.

19:3

The Pharisees also came to Him, testing Him, and saying to Him, "Is it lawful for a man to divorce his wife for *just* any reason?" They are referencing a very nebulous passage in Deuteronomy 24:1 (as discussed more in verse 7). What is "uncleanness?"

for every cause. One should expect, then, Jesus to answer the question that is asked with this same specificity. This is how Matthew treats it. Let's look at Mark's version:

> *Mark 10:2 And the Pharisees came to him, and asked him, Is it lawful for a man to put away his wife? tempting him. 3 And he answered and said unto them, What did Moses command you?*

The person who cites only Mark as an argument for the "never divorce" better have a reason why they would ignore the Matthew guidance.

> *Matthew 19:9 And I say unto you, Whosoever shall put away his wife, **except it be for fornication**, and shall marry another, committeth adultery: and whoso marrieth her which is put away doth commit adultery.*

> *Mark 10:11 And he saith unto them, Whosoever shall put away his wife, and marry another, committeth adultery against her.*

It could be that Mark doesn't include the exception clause because his audience wouldn't know about the "every cause" question introduced by the antagonizers in Matthew's record. It seems like this speaks of an abuse that had developed out of the Deuteronomy 24:1-4 allowance of divorce for "unclean-ness." There are really two "exception clauses:" One is in the question of the Pharisees while the other is in the answer from Jesus. Neither "for every cause" in their question nor "except for fornication" in Jesus' answer are found in Mark's record. These must, therefore, be related. Probably, Mark's audience would not know about this abuse and that its explanation would have taken more time on the topic than Mark wanted to give. Since Mark didn't include "for any cause" there is no need for Jesus to give "except for fornication." Mark's Gospel did not have the purpose of giving the causes for divorce that were within God's acceptance.

19:4-6

And He answered and said to them, "Have you not read This is funny because this is all they do!

6 So then, they are no longer two but one flesh. Therefore what God has joined together, God created the **together-**ness, and He did it through the sexual union.[73]

19:7

They said to Him, "Why then did Moses So they will pit **Moses** (verses 4-5, the author of Genesis 1-2) against **Moses? command to give a certificate of divorce, and to put her away?"** It seems like Joseph considered this course of action found in Deuteronomy 24:1-4 back in Matthew's first chapter.

19:10

His disciples said to Him, "If such is the case of the man with *his* **wife, it is better not to marry."** Strange thing for **disciples** to say considering there is no better picture of the Gospel (besides baptism and

---

[73]Not just the command to procreate (Genesis 1:27) or the nakedness (2:25), but also the definition of the sexual union as defined by Paul (1 Cor 6:16) make it clear.

the Lord's Supper). Everybody seems to love extremes: Leave the door open to divorce any time, or "don't get married."

19:11-12

But He said to them, "All cannot accept this saying, but only *those* **to whom it has been given: 12 For there are eunuchs** a simple word meaning "bed keeper." **who were born thus from** *their* **mother's womb,** Some were born without the ability to have sexual relations. **and there are eunuchs who were made eunuchs by men,** made unable to perform sexually to perhaps work in a royal office (as the kings of Judah were promised concerning their young men in the prophets). **and there are eunuchs who have made themselves eunuchs for the kingdom of heaven's sake.** This seems to be quite figurative since Heaven and Hell are discussed for the self-maiming person in 18:8-9 and it appears figurative there. **He who is able to accept** *it,* **let him accept** *it.* **"** Since I have already said I believe this to be figurative, let me say that: 1. I think Paul's letters, particularly 1-2 Corinthians, were influenced by the Gospel of Matthew; 2. I think the Gospel of Matthew may have made it to Corinth before Paul did (Acts 18:8-10). So, with that in mind, let's see the parallels[74] between these two tracts of Scripture and what is meant by **eunuchs who have made themselves eunuchs for the kingdom of heaven's sake.** It is honorable to know you have the gift of singleness (see chart citing 1 Corinthians 7), but it is heretical to expect others to do the same (1 Timothy 4:1-2).

19:13-15[75]

Then little children not the Pharisees (19:2) and not the rich young ruler (19:16 and following), but insignificant under-achievers.

---

[74]Other parallels between these two are found in later chapters of this commentary in the same format.

[75]More on my commentary on Mark (10:10-13).

and pray, these are related actions, and the touch from Jesus is related to His prayer.[76]
Jesus will always get what He prays for. Are we sure we want Jesus touching our children and praying for them? **for of such** not the Pharisees and not rulers [despite the fact that Jesus says he lacks but one thing (see verse 13)]; not even the disciples!

Couplets in Matthew		
Event	1st Occurrence	2nd Occurrence
Marriage & Divorce	5:31-32	19:1-10
Desperate Avoidance of Hell	5:27-30	18:7-9
Forgiveness Promised for the Forgiving	6:14-15	18:35
"Sign of Jonah"	12:40	16:1-4
Mass Feedings	14:15-21	15:34-36
Children & Jesus	18:1-14	19:13-15

Little children 18:6 says these "little" ones are saved through believing.

19:16-26

Mostly covered in my commentary on Mark (chapter 10).

24 And again I say to you, it is easier for a camel to go through the eye of a needle than for a rich man to enter the kingdom of God." The "Kingdom of Heaven" (verse 23), then, is the same as this **Kingdom of God.**

19:27

…Therefore what shall we have?" He wouldn't **follow** You for "treasure in Heaven;" what about us?

19:28

So Jesus said to them, "Assuredly "Amen" I say to you, that in the regeneration, when the Son of Man sits on the throne of His glory, you who have followed Me will also sit on twelve thrones, judging

---

[76]More on ordination in my commentary on Acts (chapter 6).

the twelve tribes of Israel. Here is a good hint that Jesus was starting a New Israel. This makes sense: Jesus is the "New Moses" as we have been discussing. He is going to begin again (**regeneration**),[77] and if we have the literal, ethnic tribes of Israel ruling, it won't be the literal sons of Jacob ruling them.

---

[77]Used only in Titus 3:5 and here.

Chapter 20

"For Jesus says "keep reading" with this little word **for.** It seems, then, that this parable serves as an answer to Peter. The man gets "treasure in Heaven" if he "leaves all and follows" Jesus, so Peter is interested in what he gets for "leaving all." This connection is further reinforced when we realize the Gospel is answered with a desire to rule in the kingdom. They simply aren't getting the concept. They are told they will all get a "denarius" and they then want "spots 1 and 2" in the passage to follow.

No, these disciples didn't change at all: Keep the kids away (chapter 19) and keep the blind away (end of this chapter). Not only that, Peter probably thought there was much to gain from the beginning of the story as Jesus is building His cabinet (Matthew 16:18). Peter and the disciples think they're better than the kids and the blind—of course the disciples have their mama talk for them (20:20).

the kingdom of heaven is like There is no chance the listener was thinking this would take 2000 years to transpire.

a landowner who went out early in the morning Mark 13:35 names this as the last watch of the night. This could have been as early as 3 or 4am. **to hire laborers for his vineyard.** He doesn't tell us anything about the nature of this **vineyard** regarding ethnicity because everybody involved in the immediate context is Jewish; nor is he speaking about the evils of capitalism.

20:2-7

3 And he went out about the third about 9am.

5 Again he went out about the sixth about noon **and the ninth hour,** about 3pm. **and did likewise. 6 And about the eleventh hour he went out and found others standing idle, and said to them, 'Why have you been standing here idle all day?'** The manager of the vineyard is not in a hurry. He knew these were here **all day,** and did not hire them. Apparently, it can take all day to get one in the vineyard and it proves

fine for this "lord." **7 They said to him, 'Because no one hired us.'**
Whether the first hour or the 11th hour, the laborer never chose the "lord
of the vineyard." Rather, He **hired** them. If one is in the kingdom then, it
was because they were found and **hired. He said to them, 'You also go
into the vineyard, and whatever is right you will receive.'** Notice how
the system doesn't work so that there is a predictable pay-off.

20:8-12

**12 saying, 'These last *men* have worked *only* one hour, and you
made them equal to us who have borne the burden and the heat of
the day.'** "We worked 12 hours and got the same lousy "denarius." This
is a story of a man who wanted some to do His work and He paid them
all handsomely. The issue here is that the disciples' hearts are not right.
They are angry that they got in right away and that there are others who
get in…eventually…while getting paid the same.

only **one hour** It seems as though Jesus is saying that the "rich young
ruler" will get saved, and that he will get the same "denarius." In the
Kingdom to come, learn the disciples, everybody gets rich. It seems as
though Jesus is forecasting his salvation. See the spreadsheet of the 12
parallels between the Corinthian epistles and the Gospel of Matthew.
Look at this passage

> *1 Corinthians 15:3-8 For I delivered to you first of all that which
> I also received: that Christ died for our sins according to the
> Scriptures, 4 and that He was buried, and that He rose again the
> third day according to the Scriptures, 5 and that He was seen by
> Cephas, then by the twelve. 6 After that He was seen by over five
> hundred brethren at once, of whom the greater part remain to
> the present, but some have fallen asleep. 7 After that He was
> seen by James, then by all the apostles. 8 Then last of all He was
> seen by me also,* **as by one born out of due time.**

This bold portion is one Greek word and is found only once in the New
Testament. Paul sat under a teacher, we find out from the book of Acts,
in Jerusalem. He was often around the peers of Jesus. Here, Peter and the
apostles saw Jesus (and became believers) first, while He describes

himself as one who was "born" later than expected. It seems that Paul, like Peter, lost it all…and found Christ…"late," in the 11th hour.

the heat of the day We're not talking about a minister who started at the beginning of the church age. The disciples are not still working (directly) in the vineyard.

		Matthew	Corinthians
1	Avoidance of judging	7:1-2	11:31
2	Wisdom: Christ's person	11:25	2:6-7
3	Stewards of mystery	13:11-12	4:1-2
4	Faith in the Gospel	17:22-23 & 18:6	15:1-4
5	Offending unbelievers	17:27	10:32
6	Church Discipline	18:15-17	5:12-13
7	After restoration	18:21-35	2 Cor 2:6-9
8	Presence "in spirit"	18:20	5:3; 2 Cor 2:10
9	Marriage Definition	19:4-6	6:15-16
10	Possibility of divorce	19:6	7:26-28
11	One cause for divorce	19:9	7:2, 14-15
12	Kingdom Eunuchs	19:11-12	7:6-8; 7:27-33

20:13-16

15 Is it not lawful for me to do what I wish with my own things? Or is your eye evil because I am good?' This is almost exactly the question posed to Jonah (Jonah 4).

 16 So the last will be first, and the first last. This is the only part of this entire parable found in the Gospel of Mark.

20:17-19

More can be seen on this passage in my commentary on Mark (10:32-34).

20:20

Then came to him the mother of Zebedee's children. We find out from later on in the book, this is Salome. This is Mary, the mother of Jesus' sister. So James and John the sons of Zebedee were Jesus' first cousins.

worshipping him, and desiring a certain thing of him We find her all through Jesus' ministry. We find her in Luke 8; we find her at the cross. So here is one of the parents who steps up from the crowd and says, "Well, here's what I would like. I would like for you to give me something."

20:21

Jesus said unto her, "What wilt thou?" She saith unto him, Grant that these my two sons may sit, They are better than kids, than blind man, and the rich man, and now...each other. **the one on thy right hand, and the other on thy left,** being a part of the kingdom is not nearly good enough. **in thy kingdom.** "Hello! I just told you I'm going to die. Why did she all of a sudden make this association: my son is going to sit on the right hand and left hand? Here's why:

> *19:27 Then answered Peter and said unto him, Behold, we have forsaken all, and followed thee; what shall we have therefore? And Jesus said unto them, Verily I say unto you, That ye which have followed me, in the regeneration when the Son of man shall sit in the throne of his glory, ye also shall sit upon twelve thrones, judging the twelve tribes of Israel.*

"So, okay, this is good. This is good. All right, this is good. All right, we all get a seat. All right, now, I want to sit the closest to the king and then we're going to have my mom ask for it." We find out that's exactly what happened. Now, please notice that Jesus knows who asks. It's one of those things like my son when we have company over, he sends the company to come and ask us if they can watch a movie; if they can play a game; if they can go in the backyard and strip the bark off of trees. You know, that kind of thing. And we all know that the reason that they're coming to ask is because Jake has told them to come and ask.

20:22

You know not what you ask. Are you looking over their mother's shoulder, Jesus addresses them. **able to drink the cup?** He looks past mom to James and John, the two brave men that are going to help them lead the kingdom and says, **Are you able to drink the cup that I drink of and to be baptized with the baptism that I am baptized with?** And they say unto him, "Yup, **we are able."** Now, fast forward a week. Jesus is in the garden of Gethsemane asking that if possible the cup be taken from him and James and John said, "We can drink your cup. I mean, you're just going to be crucified" (four verses earlier). In any regard, the first martyr was James, the son of Zebedee. He had his head taken from Herod in Acts 12:4.

20:23

Ye shall drink indeed of my cup, and James was the first martyr who died in Acts 12, he had his head taken. And John was the last apostle who died. He wasn't martyred, he got away by merely being boiled in oil.

but to sit on my right hand, and on my left, is not mine to give. Can you imagine Jesus saying, "It is not up to me where my cabinet sits in the kingdom?" Let that sink in. You have Jesus saying, "I don't have the authority to give you a particular place in the kingdom." But who has it? **It shall be given to them for whom it is prepared of my Father. And when the ten heard it, they were moved with indignation against the two brethren.** So please don't think that the other ten were really good natured guys. The fact is, James and John beat them to the punch. James and John saw their angle. Can you remember what happened to Peter last which might have made James and John think they had a chance of sitting at the right and left hand of Jesus? In chapter 16 Peter told Jesus that he really wasn't going to die; he really wasn't going to rise again from the dead. There wasn't any need to rise from the dead because he wasn't going to die. They weren't going to let their King die. Remember that?

And Jesus said, "Get behind me, Satan." Not very many people had the prestigious place, of being called "Satan" by Jesus. Very few are in that elite group. In fact, I think just one, alright? So Peter is probably in the eyes of the other apostles, probably slipping down in his placement. Remember, we're dealing here with a real group of people. I mean, think about it: they get the opportunity to rule with a king in his kingdom and they're not sure when the kingdom is going to start; they are suspecting it's going to start very soon because they're approaching Jerusalem and it's Passover when there will be probably, Josephus says, over two million people in the city of Jerusalem.

20:25

Discussed more in my commentary on Luke (22:23-27).

But Jesus called them unto him, and said, Ye know that the princes of the Gentiles exercise dominion over them. Jesus prayed in John 17, "I pray not that you would remove them from the world, but that you should keep them from the evil one." Jesus said, "Don't take them from the world, just keep them protected while they're here." 1 Corinthians 7 says we use the worldly system, but we are not in love with it.

20:27

whosoever will be chief among you, let him be your servant. Practice what you preach. You get to be called "great," or, "chief" in the kingdom of heaven (5:19). This is certainly not in an army leadership manual. You're saying that we have to become like little children and servants or slaves to our fellow man in order to be called "great" or "chief" in the kingdom (18:1-6)? I want to be able to say "I'm a mighty warrior-leader." I want to make things happen.

20:28

Even as the Son of man came not to be ministered unto, but to minister, and to give his life a ransom for many. Just back in verse 19, Jesus is forecasting that he's going to be delivered to the Gentiles, first betrayed, verse 18, then condemned to death, verse 19, "delivered to the Gentiles to mock, and to scourge, and to crucify him: and the third day he shall rise again." So it looks like on the outside Jesus is a victim, but Jesus is very clear in verse 28, "I am not a victim. I am laying my life down because it is the ultimate act of service." Now, if you and I lay our lives down for someone else, perhaps it would be a great act of service but it would not affect my eternity. But when Jesus lays down his life for many, he becomes their ransom! This, too, is a developing theme in the book of Matthew.

> *Matthew 1:21 and will call his name Jesus, for He shall* **save His people from their sin.**

Why? So who is it that we're hostage to that requires a ransom? What is it that we're hostage to? Our sin. Jesus said, "I'm going to come and I'm going to do a snatch-and-grab and I'm going to yank you out of sin's clutches." John 8:31, "If you serve sin, you are a slave of sin." Jesus said, "I am coming to rescue you from your sin." Everyone wants to be rescued from the Romans in their lives. It might be a job you don't like. It might be a "house that's too small." I'm not trying to pick on anyone. I'm just thinking of all the things that cross through this 38 year old, 2016 American. The things that go through my mind that I would love to be delivered from. Everyone wants to be delivered from the Romans, but how many of us are just craving for a Savior to ransom us from our sin? Everyone wants to go to heaven but, "Dear God, I'm not going to give up my sin." Find some application in that.

20:29-34

See this handled under 1:21

21:1[78]

And when they drew nigh unto Jerusalem. And of course the
question is: when did this begin? Well, look at the last chapter, verse 17.

> *And Jesus going up to Jerusalem took the twelve disciples apart
> in the way.*

and were come to Bethphage, unto the Mount of Olives. The last
year of Jesus' life begins with the feeding of the 5,000 in Matthew
chapter 14. So, if you do the
simple math with me, you
realize that very precious
little of Jesus' life is covered
in the Bible. Very little. So
when you see glimpses of it,
like He as a child is visited
by the wise men in Matthew
2, when you see Him as a 12-
year-old in Luke 2, those are
very special, special glimpses
into the young life of Jesus
and they're there for a reason.

Usages of Zechariah in Matthew

1. Matthew 24:31 refers to Zechariah 2:6
2. Matthew 19:26 alludes to Zechariah 8:6
3. Matthew 21:4-5 quotes Zechariah 9:9
4. Matthew 9:36-37 quotes Zechariah 10:2
5. Matthew 27:9-10 quotes Zechariah 11:12
6. Matthew 24:30 refers to Zechariah 12:10
7. Matthew 26:30-31 refers to Zechariah 13:7
8. Matthew 21:1-22 alludes to Zech 4:1-7 & 14:1-5
9. Matthew 24:16-20 refers to Zechariah 14:4-5
10. Matthew 25:31 refers to Zechariah 14:5
11. Matthew 27:45-53 alludes to Zechariah 14:5-6

21:3

**And if any man say ought unto you, ye shall say, The Lord hath
need of them.** Who's them? The donkey and her colt. Ok? "The Lord
needs these animals of yours."

21:4

**All this was done, that it might be fulfilled which was spoken by the
prophet, saying, Tell ye the daughter of Sion, Behold, thy King
cometh unto thee, meek, and sitting upon an ass, and a colt the foal
of an ass.** So Matthew says, "I want you to know that I am writing this
because this is fulfillment of Zechariah 9:9." Now you are seeing Jesus

---

[78]Much more can be found in Mark's version of this episode, discussed in my
commentary on Mark (chapter 11).

come in on a donkey, on a colt, the foal of an ass and you know that he has been called the King of the Jews and if you are a Jew and you know the Old Testament, you are going to think about this Scripture. And we wonder why they went running after palm branches ready to call him the Son of David, the righteous one entering into the gates of Jerusalem crying יָשַׁע (yaw-shah) or hosanna.

21:9

And the multitudes that went before, and that followed, cried, saying, Hosanna to the Son of David: Blessed is he that cometh in the name of the Lord; Hosanna in the highest. This is the King. He is about to enter the gates. He is the righteous one, the Son of David. Matthew 1:1 says he is the Son of David. They know this and they know Psalm 24, Psalm 118, Zechariah 9, and Malachi 3.

21:11-13

Discussed in my commentary on Mark (chapter 11).

21:14

And the blind and the lame came to him in the temple. It is significant that lame people are in Jerusalem at all, let alone they are in the temple, because lame people were despised in Jerusalem. Back 1100 years earlier when Joab took the city of Jerusalem away from the Jebusites, the Jebusites in Jerusalem looked out over the wall and said, "We could set the lame people up against the doors and you are not getting in." And they said from that point on King David hated lame people and would not allow them in Jerusalem. Here we are 1000 years later. The Son of David, the Messiah not only enters Jerusalem, but enters the temple, and now follows him in lame people to be healed. That is significant, friends. That is a big deal, because Jesus is better than David.

21:15

And when the chief priests and scribes saw the wonderful things that he did, and the children crying in the temple, and saying, Hosanna to the Son of David; they were sore displeased. That is the chief priest and the scribes. They wanted only their kind of chaos, the chaos that allowed for money changers and for selling animals for sacrifice, but not the chaos that called for worshipping a Nazarene. Nazarene was kind of like the wrong side of the tracks. Nazareth was not a pretty place. So there is everything to be displeased about here if you are a chief priest or a scribe.

It says that **the children were crying in the temple and saying, Hosanna** Psalm 118:25 The Hebrew: Yasha` 'anna'. The Greek sounds like **Hosanna.** So Psalm 118:25 is being fulfilled in this passage and looks forward to an ultimate fulfillment (says the final verses of Matthew 23).

21:16

And said unto him, Hearest thou what these say? So the scribes and the chief priests are saying, "Jesus, you need to correct them, because they are way out of line here."

And Jesus saith unto them, Yea; have ye never read.... Think about it, now. Who is he talking to? That is all they do is read the Old Testament. The scribe's job is to copy it verbatim, line by line, letter by letter. Haven't you read... have you ever read Psalm 8:2?" Jesus asks these folks this question six times in Matthew.

"Out of the mouth of babes and sucklings thou hast perfected praise?" Why is he quoting out of Psalm 8:2? Jesus is talking to a crowd who mistook biblical literacy for a regenerate lifestyle.

By the way, Jesus authoritatively quoted a translation. It is not the Hebrew.

Moreover, this single line out of a poem was authoritative in the instruction of the character of God. Probably, David wrote this about himself being the youngest of many brothers, but we also find the timeless truth that God's character is reflected in choosing the mouths of children to stifle the enemy. By the way, with the address of Jehovah in Psalm 8:1, this is an overt statement of Jesus declaring His worthiness of receiving worship as Jehovah—or at least, in the place of Jehovah. Away with the ridiculous notion that Jesus did not feel as though He was God.

Also, Jesus quotes from Deuteronomy in chapter 4; Genesis in chapter 19; Psalms here; Hosea in chapter 9; Micah in chapter 10; Malachi in chapter 11; Numbers, 1 Samuel, 1 Kings, and Jonah in chapter 12; Isaiah in chapter 13; Jeremiah in chapter 21; Exodus in chapter 22; 2 Chronicles in chapter 23; Daniel in chapter 24; Joel and Zechariah in chapter 25. The 39 books of the O.T. were in 22 books in the original Old Testament and Jesus quotes from 17 of those 22 books just in Matthew…all of this without proper "authority" or teaching (21:23). He demonstrates here that there was no "canon within a canon" or superior genre. Rather, He quotes the Psalms here as a way of showing that Psalms is just as authoritative as Genesis or any other book. He also had no issues saying they were about Him. We are expected to read the Psalms and believe them on that same level.

In other words, the reason you don't think Jesus deserves your worship is because you don't think He has that much authority. With a culture that has a great cause for why we shouldn't have to obey the authority God places over us. The answer to their question of "authority" (21:23) should have provided their motivation to worship this same Jesus.

thou hast perfected praise? So what kind of **praise** does God **perfect?** Or, to take it from the Hebrew in Psalm 8:2…what does God ordain as the **praise** to Himself:

1. Audible: Jesus said it was right. This is not an issue of personality; it's an issue of obedience. Jesus would have never said "Sssshhhh, we're in church!"
2. Visible: They are waving palm branches. God did not **perfect** the kind of **praise** that keeps the hands in the pockets.
3. Sacrificial: They could have been doing other things. They furthermore sacrificed their self-respect. Were children feeling weird acting this way? Maybe. Revelation 4 has men who cast their crowns before God's throne, and we find these crowns are emblematic of all that was behind the achievement of them and all the accolades from them.
4. Emotional: God **perfected praise** that caused people to act like there was a party going on in the streets of that city.

5. Thoughtful: Somehow, these children knew Psalm 118. Who taught them this? They were saying things they were taught. They were using Scriptural lyrics? How thoughtful!
6. Inconvenient: People took time out to expend energy in this act of **praise.**
7. Unsettling: Mostly everybody around was uncomfortable. "Don't you hear them?! Shut their mouths" (21:15)! Jesus provoked all of this. It's not every day that somebody claiming to be the Son of God comes presenting Himself as King.

17 And he left them, and went out of the city into Bethany; and he lodged there. We are down at the last approach to Jerusalem for Jesus. He goes through Bethany and Bethpage at the beginning of this story. You see that in verse one. Bethany is about two or three miles from the town of Jerusalem. He came down the road from Bethany into the eastern gate, into the temple.

21:18-22

This **in the morning** reference tells us that Matthew probably used Mark's material[79] for Mark gives us more information about the timetable of these proceedings. This same time marker is missing in verse 12 of Matthew's account and seems, then, to show us that they are the same cleansing of the temple and Matthew simply did not transfer that information.

This passage is further discussed as well in my commentary on Mark (chapter 11).

21:23[80]

Now when He came into the temple, the chief priests and the elders of the people confronted Him as He was teaching, and said, "By what authority This is the same word used by the centurion in chapter 8:5 and following and the same word Jesus uses in 10:1 when sending out his disciples to the Jews (10:5-6) and then to the nations (28:18). **By**

---

[79]We have already discussed this earlier in Mark's commentary.

[80]More can be found regarding these following verses in Mark's commentary, chapter 11.

what authority does He have fervor to purify the Father's house? What a strange thing to need proper **authority** to do.

21:24-27

27 So they answered Jesus and said, "We do not know." And He said to them, "Neither will I tell you by what authority I do these things. If "John" had heavenly authority, so did Jesus. If they couldn't be honest about John, then Jesus need not give them more to reject (Matthew 7:6).

21:28-32

31 Which of the two did the will of *his* father?" They said to Him, "The first." Jesus said to them, "Assuredly, I say to you that tax collectors and harlots enter the kingdom of God before you. This is further proof that the fig tree of earlier verses is not "ethnic Israel," but rather the system of religion championed by "ethnic Israel:" **tax collectors and harlots** were Jews/ethnic Israel, and so, they brought fruit and therefore, are not the fig tree—regardless of their ethnicity. By the way, active extortioners and **harlots** do not go to the **kingdom.** It says, they repented (verse 29).

21:33-46

See my commentary on Mark (12:1-12).

Chapter 22

And Jesus answered and spake unto them again by parables, This is the 3rd parable in a row. 21:32's parable had a declaration that the non-Jewish rulers would get the kingdom. Then, 21:38 seems to be saying the same thing (especially when considering 21:45-46). Verse 46 contains a 3rd group: the multitude (in addition to the chief priests and the disciples). This multitude has their new king. He heals; he feeds; he can probably slay an army. Then, he tops it off by raising the dead (John 11). Jesus is their hero.

This parable is aimed at, first: the priests; then, the multitude **and said,**

22:2

The kingdom of heaven is like unto a certain king, which made a marriage [feast] for his son, The bride is not the big deal of this marriage.

22:3

And sent forth his servants to call them that were bidden to the wedding: invitations had gone out, and now it was time to get those who would have been flattered to attend…right? "We don't know when the ceremony will be, but when we know…you'll be expected." **and they would not come.** What audacity! The king calls but they do not come!

22:4

Again, he sent forth other servants, saying, Tell them which are bidden, Behold, I have prepared my dinner: my oxen and *my* fatlings *are* killed, blood was spilled for this feast. Great expense and cost were expended by the King. **and all things *are* ready: come unto the marriage.** Everybody should be saying "how lavish! How generous!" It's not every day you get invited. It's not everybody that gets an invitation. This is a reflection of the character of the Lord. You don't have to like that He didn't invite everybody at first. Those who "were bidden; for whom it was prepared." Certainly you can see that the chief priests and Pharisees were in view here.

22:5
But they made light of *it*, think it weird or futile or secondary in importance; making light of a King's invitation to a feast for His son. One might say, "That's ridiculous! Who would do that?"

Exactly, that's the point. Why would anybody look at the lavish invitation from the King, and think "lightly about it?

and went their ways, one to his farm, another to his merchandise:

22:6

And the remnant Those who did not go to check on the crops or resume their place at the market. **took his servants, and entreated *them* spitefully, and slew *them*.** The bride is of such insignificance in this parable, that she's not mentioned (or in 25:1-11) because the focus is the bridegroom.

22:7

But when the king heard *thereof,* he was wroth: Very angry. His teeth were grinding. **and he sent forth his armies, and destroyed those murderers, and burned up their city.** Take this in for a moment. In A.D. 70, approximately 40 years later, the King burned their city because of this generation of priests—this crowd—not just because they were so flippant as to tend their farms in lieu of a feast, but to also kill heralds of this fantastic news. They weren't coming to collect taxes. So before anybody says "How severe a judgment! This is worth burning a entire city for attacking a few servants?" I would say "How depraved is man to look at the invitation of the King who owes us nothing and say 'I have to tend the animals and my business. I have a system and money is on the line, and I really don't have time…'?"

Some who were not complacent, were caustic. Some were flippant, others flagrant. The bottom line is that they all burned up together in the city. "I'm just passive! I'm not angry, I'm not attacking him! I'll just get to it sometime!" They all burned up together. We know the Lord rewarded this generation according to their works (Matthew

16:27-28), but I want to remind you not to hang out in the same crowd with those who are antagonistic killers. We often see ourselves as "not too bad," and we often think the King as over-reacting and say stupid things like "Why is the King so angry?"

22:8

Then saith he to his servants, The wedding is ready, nothing has changed. *While a military campaign is taking place, dinner is getting cold. To burn a city over a spurned dinner invite seems extreme, but Christ was rejected by an entire nation* (D.A. Carson said this somewhere). **but they which were bidden were not worthy.** If I were in this position, I would find "worthy ones." What does he do?

22:9

Go ye therefore into the highways, and as many as ye shall find, That's not very high criteria: "Just find them." **bid to the marriage.** "What do they need to look like, Lord?"

"They need to look like they can walk to the palace."

It's startling that He deems some "unworthy" and then finds more unworthy people to take their place. Really, I guess that's how Bill Sturm got saved. The Lord blinded Israel as a nation "that the purpose of election might be fulfilled" (Romans 11).

Matthew 21:28 is the man who "repented" and is "publicans and harlots that enter the kingdom." "Who in the world wants extortionists and traitors and women of the street to be a part of their kingdom?" Jesus does. He changes them anyway…into saints. Matthew of all people can testify to that. Nobody goes into the kingdom as a harlot or a publican and stays that way. Once they get to the dinner, they are changed.

22:10

So those servants went out into the highways, and gathered together all as many as they found, both bad and good: and the wedding was furnished with guests. That is when I would back up and say "they lived happily ever after." There is, after all, a full table at the feast. Isn't that just what the King wanted? Many songs have been written on it. Many sermons have been preached on it. Many have gotten lost in the glory of simply arriving at the feast. However, we must be qualified guests. All kingdom participants are qualified guests…

22:11

And when the king came in to see the guests, he saw there a man which had not on a wedding garment: This seems strange. There must be something cultural we don't understand here.

22:12

And he saith unto him, Friend, This also seems strange…particularly since Judas Iscariot is greeted the same way in the Garden of Gethsemane later in the drama. I wonder if Jesus was trying to communicate with him?

It's also used in the parable at the beginning of chapter 20 where those who toiled all day think they got ripped off—working only for a penny in the heat of the day. The owner responded with…"Friend?" How tender is our Lord? Imagine, here, the King looking tenderly and sternly at a man and saying, "Friend, how did you get in here?"

how camest thou in hither not having a wedding garment? My first question was, "Why are we experiencing this sort of two-climax account? Why are we indicting the Pharisees and chief priests, and then we indict the guests? We thought one of the points of the parable was that the chief priests were not worthy and their city was burned. It must be, then, that Jesus is talking to the multitude since they were just sure He was a prophet. They have been with Jesus, eating the loaves and fish, watching the miracles, and they are now pictured as sitting pretty at a wedding feast…naked. Isaiah 28:20 speaks of those in judgment as those with a bed too short and a sheet too narrow. They may as well be nude. You will not be comfortable and you will not be covered.

> *Hebrews 4:13 Neither is there any creature that is not manifest before the eyes of Him with Whom we have to do.*

All of the sudden, we don't have a man that feels like a guest anymore. We have a man that feels like an imposter. Those people that were in the crowd for weeks or months may have been thinking, "Well at least we're not being condemned with the priests and Pharisees" and here Jesus then includes them on the parable with a stern warning to them: "Make sure you have the proper garment." Honestly you wouldn't even know where this came from if you didn't have Isaiah's reference (Isaiah 61:9-10).

I cannot find in Matthew where the Lord requires a garment; we're dealing with a garment. Isaiah is the only place where we find a garment and where we find a wedding context. With Matthew's mind so often on Isaiah's prophecy, it is not surprise that Isaiah gives us light on this.

So whose fault is it that the man has no garment? It is not the Lord's! In this custom there was a time when the man putting on the feast would supply the garment. The King's surprise at the lack of garment is proof we're not dealing with some sort of "particular atonement" application. No, the idea is that this man was provided the necessity and chose to leave it unemployed. How audacious is it to say "I have another place to be?" Very. But how audacious is it to leave a garment at home which a man provided for you to attend his garment.

Romans 11 speaks about the "goodness and severity" of God, and in this parable we find both. "How did you get in here thinking you were 'good to go'?"

And he was speechless. This is after Matthew 7:21-23, apparently, since there was an answer on the lips of those under examination in 7:22-23 where they appear to be saying "we have been sitting at your table for years!" There He doesn't argue with them, but they were not righteous as "workers of iniquity." Apparently, in this story, he has run out of arguments or defenses. "You provided me a garment and I chose not to wear it."

Matthew 13:38 introduces the tares among the wheat that exist undetected, in the kingdom. You don't belong in the kingdom if you are one "who does iniquity" and it can, therefore, be summarized as "having the proper garment." It is, as Isaiah says, a "robe of righteousness," after all.

22:13

Then said the king to the servants, Bind him hand and foot, and take him away, and cast *him* into outer darkness; there shall be weeping and gnashing of teeth. If I was a king with all of this power, where he can just say, I am not sure I would go through the trouble of "binding hand and feet." This seems so extreme and "over the type." If I'm not careful here, I find fault. "It's so excessive." It's a little like the conversation that says "Why an eternal Hell for sins done in time? How severe indeed!" I will come back and say "How depraved are you to not wear the garment of which you have been provided!" The fault lies not with the King who punishes, but the man who despised the provision of the King!

If He seems extreme, then "kiss the Son, lest ye perish from the way when His wrath is kindled but a little" (Psalm 2:12). Be on the right team. Choose Christ. Jesus preached election, and then laid the blame at the foot of the man who did not wear His garment.

22:14

For many are called, but few *are* chosen. The man who was kicked out of the marriage feast wasn't kicked out because the food wasn't prepared for Him; because the animals weren't slain for his pleasure. The death that took place for that supper to be furnished was for him too. The man couldn't say "What a trick! This dinner wasn't for me!" No, the prohibition for his attendance at the feast has more to do with what the man was wearing. The meal, the garment, the invitation were provided.

Some of those who were not **chosen** were a part of the **many.** Think that through. Same week in Jesus' life:

> *Matthew 20:28 The Son of Man came to give His life a ransom for **many.***

Some say "Ah! He didn't die for all; he died for many."

Two can play that game. In that cute, wonderful system, you have fewer than the many getting into the kingdom (Matthew 22:14). Who did He die for? "Many." Not all the "many" stayed at the wedding. You will never be able to say, "God, I wasn't called! I wasn't paid for!" Again, if the King didn't provide the garment to the man, why was He so surprised the man didn't wear it? This is why Peter said "Make your calling and election sure." Church folks, looking like they belong in the kingdom, are a fantastic mission field some times.

This man was thrilled about the Son being married. Who wouldn't be? He is tickled about the wedding. He is thrilled about being able to be at the feast. You couldn't get this many any more excited about the Son. He loved being "churchy" around the "church folk." Somehow, he didn't wear the salvation garment Jesus provided. If you don't, the King will be shocked and so will you.

The man was unlike those who couldn't find time to consider the marriage. There are a plethora of bible studies today, it seems. Here is a man who never told himself He couldn't take time to be around the Son. He probably walked miles. He gave much thought to the marriage. Imagine the distance he walked to get there. Every step was a step of contemplation concerning what the feast would be like. He was tickled it was at the castle, and when he got there…he didn't belong there. He was **worthy** in that he came (22:8). How many people couldn't even find the time to come!? He is like a lot of people today who "made a commitment and came to Jesus."

Based on 22:10, **this man may have been a <u>good</u> guy**. We find no where that he was a **bad** guy. We don't have any evidence that this guy was beating his family, driving recklessly, or laundering money, do we? This could have been a good man. He was probably starting to fit in, and then…the King showed up. Now, he realizes He doesn't belong with God's people.

Regarding this garment, we consider 2 Corinthians 5:21. Regarding the warning of verse 14, we remember 2 Corinthians 13:5. When He "comes in His kingdom" (Luke 23), you do not want to be found without His salvation garment.

22:15[81]

…Master, we know that You are true, and teach the way of God in truth, and You don't care for any man: for You regard not the person of men. And so, not only did they embrace the occupiers but

---

[81]More on this in my commentary on Mark (12:13-17).

they were absolutely wonderful flatterers. As a matter of fact, Nicodemus tried this. "We know You're a teacher come from God. No man can do these miracles except God be with Him" (John 3:1-2). Jesus said, "Except a man be born again he cannot see the Kingdom of God." Jesus just… "Don't need your praise. Don't need your appraisal. I already heard from the sky that I'm the Son in whom He is well pleased. I don't need you telling Me anything good about Me."

Tell us therefore, What do You think? Is it lawful to give tribute unto Caesar, or not? And by the way, this is not the same tax spoken of earlier (17:24).

And Jesus perceived their wickedness. Jesus has a knack for reading peoples' minds. Consistently. Like we just read it, where Peter comes marching into the house in Capernaum and Jesus says, "So what do you think, Peter? Who should they charge tax?" You remember when the Queen of Sheba went to Jerusalem to visit with Solomon and said he told her all her questions. "I know what you're thinking. You want to know this, this, this, and this." Here's Jesus doing that very same thing. Jesus perceived their wickedness. He wasn't one of these guys that said, "You know, I'm going to give you time to think about how you feel about Me. You might not be fully on My team here but I'm going to give you time to develop."

22:21

Then saith He unto them, Render therefore unto Caesar the things which are Caesar's. Jesus is all too wise. He's the great Solomon.

and unto God the things that are God's. He is arguing for God's ownership of the Herodians who bare the image of God.

> *Matthew 6:24 No man can serve two masters: for either he will hate the one, and love the other; or else he will hold to the one, and despise the other. **You can't serve God and money.***

The Herodians are facing what Jesus said you'd be facing: a struggle between two gods: money or God, and you can't serve them both. And here Jesus is exemplifying that truth when He demands of these Herodians that they make a choice between Herod and Caesar, and God.

You see, there's a lot of people playing both sides. A lot of people are playing both sides.

And the Lord is stressing to the Herodians, "You go ahead and give God what's His. Right now you're not doing a good job of that." It's not that they weren't good taxpayers, it's that they were horrible at giving God what was His. In all three cases (verses 21, 23, and 34) the Lord is answering with two answers the one question of the Herodians. "Do we pay tribute?" And the Lord says, "Yes, in a way," and then He goes a step further and says, "Give yourselves to God." To the Herodians, to the Pharisees, to the Sadducees, they ask one question; they get their answer and then they get the answer they need from the Lord.

In the parable before these three passages, everyone wanted to know, "How do I get to the feast? How do I get to the feast? How do I get to the feast?" Jesus answers that question and then says, "Not only do you need to be at the feast, you need to be wearing the right clothes."

So, in four consecutive passages the Lord says, "Not only to the feast, you need to be in the right clothes." He says, "Not only do you need to pay tribute to Caesar, you need to pay tribute to God. Not only do you need to know that the marriage problem is taken care of at the resurrection, but there actually is a resurrection and you should see the need to be ready. Not only do you need to know that your first commandment is with God and you can feel good about that, but that will bleed over into the second area of your life, your life with your neighbor." And that is what Jesus does. He answers the questions that we have and then answers the questions we need to be answered.

This is the third time that I can find that Genesis is referenced in the book of Matthew.[82] Here we are talking about Genesis 1:26 and 27, and the reader should see my commentary on Mark where I deal with what it means to be "made in His image" (appendix on Genesis).

22:23-28[83]

---

[82] Matthew 18:22 probably recalls Genesis 4:23-24 while Matthew 19:4-5, Genesis 1:27 & Genesis 2:24.

[83] See this covered more in my commentary on Mark (12:18-27).

This is, by the way, at least the 4th time the book of Deuteronomy is quoted in Matthew.

22:29-33

31 But concerning the resurrection of the dead, have you not read what was spoken to you so it was written as a record of what God told Moses, and yet Exodus 3 was **spoken to** Jesus' audience. Galatians 4:24 says Mt Sinai is in Arabia. By extension, then, it is God's Word to us. These strange "Sadducees", by the way, did not believe the "Scriptures" in a real sense. They did not hold to any portion besides Moses' works. Yes, Job 19:25, Isaiah 26, Ezekiel 37, Daniel 12:3 speak of this, but then Jesus quotes a portion from what they do, in fact, believe.

33 And when the multitudes heard *this,* they were astonished at His teaching. Just as in 7:28 and 13:54.

22:34-36[84]

But when the Pharisees heard that He had silenced the Sadducees, they gathered together. 35 Then one of them, one breaks from a gaggle. He just left his group and now...**a lawyer,** an expert of Moses' law...and the Talmud...and the Midrash...and the Mishnah of those days.

22:37-40

Matthew 5:17 assures us that Jesus obeyed every part of the law and thus assures us of salvation having died for us. There does appear to be another sense here, and that is that the Son of God perfectly loved the Father and perfectly loved His neighbor as Himself. That Sermon on the Mount is a sermon that only Jesus has ever obeyed—being perfect as the Father (Matthew 5:48).

40 [z]On these two commandments hang all the Law after the Pharisees and Herodians want to know about the "lawfulness" of paying taxes; and

---

[84]See more in my commentary on Mark (12:28-34).
[z]Matt. 7:12; Rom. 13:10; Galatians 5:14; James 2:8

after the Sadducees want to know what "Moses said", this man wants to ask about the "great commandment of the law." **and the Prophets."** Here, again, Jesus gave more than what was requested. He didn't just sum the **law,** but He also summarized the **Law and the Prophets.**

Matthew records nothing about the man's response. Matthew wants us to see this is not the main issue. God has an economy that doesn't allow much room for man's approval.

22:41-42[85]
So continues a conversation that takes place on Tuesday of passion week, and includes the last part of chapter 21 and continues all through chapter 25. This day has the most Scripture written than any other day in Jesus' life. **41 While the Pharisees were gathered together, Jesus asked them,** This is a sneak peek at the last day (22:1-10, "how did you get in here"; he was speechless"). See verse 46 and see their obvious ending: "speechless". **42 saying, "What do you think about the Christ? Whose Son is He?"** He asks the question we all must answer. Eternity hinges upon our answer.

They said to Him, *"The [b]Son* of David." Jeremiah 23:5 is a beautiful reason to expect this answer.

22:43-46

44 *'The LORD said to my Lord,*[86] This command from the Father to the Son which follows has much to do with 21:9 (which is a quotation of Psalm 118) and the listeners would see these as implications of their murder of Him and His exaltation (anyway).

"Sit at My right hand, mentioned again to the high priest in Matthew 26:64.

---

[85]More in my commentary on Mark (12:35-37).
[b]Matt. 1:1; 21:9
[86]See appendix on "finding the Father in the O.T" in my commentary on Ephesians.

Chapter 23

23:1-12

Then Jesus spoke to the multitudes about those who had questioned him in all of chapter 22. **and to His disciples, 2 saying: "The scribes and the Pharisees sit in Moses' seat.** A special **seat** from which the teacher of the day would expound the Scripture text just read from the podium. One can see both the reading and the sitting demonstrated in Luke 4 by Jesus.

5 But all their works they do to [d]be seen by men. They make their phylacteries broad from the Old Testament requirement to put the Scriptures between one's eyes. Perhaps the literal exaggeration of a hyperbole. Little scrolls would have a portion of Scripture in this little box strapped on the arms and foreheads.

6 They love the best places at feasts, the best seats in the synagogues, Too bad they didn't listen to Solomon (Proverbs 25:6).

7 greetings in the marketplaces, and to be called by men, 'Rabbi, Rabbi.' A Hebrew word meaning "great one." **8 But you, do not be called 'Rabbi'; for One is your Teacher, [4]the Christ, and you are all brethren.** Apparently there are no higher titles than "brother." **9 Do not call anyone on earth your father; for One is your Father, He who is in heaven.** Jeremiah 31:35-40 will speak to us again when we deal with 23:39, but here we see Jeremiah 31:9 speaks of God's **Father**hood to Israel. By the way, Jeremiah 31:15 was already quoted by Matthew in his 2nd chapter. It seems, then, that Jeremiah 31:9 is certainly on Matthew's mind here with this recording of Jesus' words.

This isn't an blanket prohibition of children calling their male parent **Father** since Jesus Himself uses this title for the "dad" in this very book. This is for those who are aching to have this title but do not reflect the character of the **Father** (it seems that we cannot improve on the story in the last half of Luke 15).

---

[d]Matt. 6:1–6, 16–18
[4]NU omits *the Christ*

Not only that, but we find out from this passage that the hearts of these "scribes and Pharisees" (23:2) was about being noticed as a life-giver. In other words, these were your early sacradotalists.[87] They really felt as though they gave life through their actions as religious leaders. So when these people wanted to be called **Father** that wanted to be known as those who give life. In other words, they are going to usurp the true **Father** of His notoriety. Since this was so abused by those in that setting, the injunction was in using this "life-giving" title to refer to these "scribes and Pharisees."

If this were not so, Jesus' first indictment includes a charge that they will not have any life themselves (23:13).

10 And do not be called teachers; for One is your Teacher, the Christ. He says it twice in three verses.

23:13-14

"But woe to you, He is done talking about them and is now turned to them and speaks to them. **scribes and Pharisees, hypocrites! For you shut up the kingdom of heaven against men; for you neither go in yourselves, nor do you allow those who are entering to go in.** This first distress pronounced on these people is for their confusing of the way to Heaven for others.

14 [7]Woe awful distress. This should be seen with the backdrop of the opening verses of Matthew 22 and should be instructive to the awful fate awaiting that group of people: the burning up of their city and the destruction of a nation, but then came all the questions from those who were really not seeking illumination or inspiration or information; they were seeking to trap a man to kill Him—and they do so some 72 hours later. They were wanting God to approve of their current condition—both they and their temple and its system. **to you,** There are 8 **woe** statements in this passage.

---

[87]Those who believe you gain life by partaking the sacraments by particularly sanctioned peoples.
[7] NU omits v. 14.

23:16

"Woe to you, blind guides, who say, ^m'Whoever swears by the temple, it is nothing; but whoever swears by the gold of the temple, he is obliged *to perform it.*' You can promise, but don't mention the temple treasury.

23:17-22

19 Fools and blind! He calls them this three times in four verses.

23:29-30

30 and say, 'If we had lived in the days of our fathers, we would not have been partakers with them in the blood of the prophets.' The parable in chapter 22 was about them and they assure their listeners that they would never have killed **the prophets.** "Give me the chances my dad had and I would have done better."

23:31-33

32 Fill up, then, the measure of your fathers' *guilt.* This very week they will do what they could not at the tower of Babel (Genesis 11); they will reach into Heaven and strike down God. **33 Serpents, brood of vipers! How can you escape the condemnation of hell?** This seems a little more Christ-like than the often coined "If you died today are you 100% sure you would go to Heaven?" He was so disturbed over what they had brought on themselves that He assumed **damnation** for them.

23:34-36

Therefore, indeed, I send you prophets, Did you get that? Jesus is claiming to be Jehovah. He is claiming to be the one that sent these to them. **wise men, and scribes: *some* of them you will kill and crucify, and *some* of them you will scourge in your synagogues and persecute from city to city, 35 that on you** same as "this generation" (verse 36). That is to say, the entirety of the nation's stored wrath will be dumped

---

^mMatt. 5:33, 34

on the generation that was living in Jesus' day **all these things shall come upon this generation.** This curse from killing God's messengers will **come upon this generation.** So, that **generation** is the recipient and "Jerusalem" is their location (23:37).

23:37-39

"O Jerusalem, Jerusalem, This bemoaning is nothing more than spawning from sheer terror. "For years I have tried to keep you from this moment, but you didn't want me." He still speaks as Jehovah for there is no chance Jesus is speaking of three years of ministry. No, rather you have God speaking out of a dreadful fear of His Own wrath and His Own character demanding said justice. When you read the book of Ruth with continued reference to "dwelling under"; when you read that Boaz is the Christ figure and stands in the place of Jehovah in that context for Ruth, you see here that Christ is claiming to act on behalf of Jehovah.

38 See! Your house the temple in which they are standing. He did indeed leave the house as was seen in the absence of God's glory behind the veil (27:51).

39 for I say to you, you shall see Me no more till you say, [j]**_Blessed is He who comes in the name of the_ LORD!' "** Isaiah 1:1-7, Jeremiah 25:2-9, Ezekiel 5:5-8, Micah 1:1-4, and Zepheniah 4:1-4 show God speaking as Himself in the human armies coming against Jerusalem. However, they also use language of the Lord coming out of His place. These in Jesus' day should have acknowledged God's working in the days of their fathers. For He would do it again (Matthew 22:7).

Jesus is claiming that He will live after He dies. How do I know that? Because Jesus has already told His disciples three times, Matthew 16, Matthew 18, Matthew 20, that the Gentiles were going to seize Him, kill Him, and that He would rise again the third day. Jesus saw a day soon coming when He would return to these people and they would say, "Blessed is He that comes in the name of the Lord." And these are a people, this Jerusalem city, are a people that have not yet welcomed Him thusly. The day is still coming when Jerusalem will receive their king.

---

[j]Ps. 118:26; Matt. 21:9

They didn't do it in chapter 21, and for two chapters—all of this Tuesday of Passion Week—Jesus has been declaring that they have serious trouble coming, and He has promised in verse 39 there will come a day when they will welcome Him as He is worthy. He's not only promising of the resurrection, He's promising, basically, His second coming.

Now you have to decide whether you think Malachi 3 still needs to be fulfilled. If it has (in the "Palm Sunday" episode), you need to ask Jesus why He brought up another coming to the city of Jerusalem, because that is what takes place in the last verse of chapter 23. Now then, let's consider, does Israel have a future in God's economy?

We're going to talk about "yes" because Jesus said so right here. Consider the difference in circumstances between what occurred in 21:1-8, and what is promised in 23:39. Apparently, these things will be different when He returns:

1. Unlike chapter 21 of Matthew, those accompanying Him into the city of Jerusalem in the future will not be children. They'll not be peasants. They'll not even be other Jews. They will be saints.

Jude 14: And Enoch also, the seventh from Adam, prophesied of these, saying, The Lord cometh with ten thousands of His saints, to execute judgment upon all that are ungodly, and to judge all that are ungodly among them of all their ungodly deeds which they have ungodly committed.

We have Enoch prophesying of a day when the Lord would return with all of His saints.

I promise you, when the Lord returns He will have Revelation 19, the armies of heaven, with Him. He is the Lord of hosts. The reason Malachi chapter 3 calls Him that twice in that passage is because when "He comes suddenly to His temple," in the future, He will have His hosts with Him. Oh, it'll be a fantastic difference. He came quiet and meek, and the best they could do was get some people together to wave some palm branches. It was an impressive sight, I have no doubt. But you wait until the heavens crack open and the Lord God descends and Jesus Christ comes back with all the hosts of heaven. That is probably one major reason why the Jews will then say, "Blessed is He that comes in the name of the Lord."

2. The response of Israel's leadership will not be one disdaining worship, but will be rather leading the procession. They'll be the ones welcoming Him. You might remember in 21:10 it was the city that was moved, not the Jewish leaders. When Jesus returns it will in fact be the Jewish leaders who will be saying, "Please come in."

Psalm 24 speaks of this. You should put this right next to 21:10. You should put Jude 14 right next to 21:9 (and you should put Zechariah 14 and 1 Thessalonians 3:13 and Revelation 19). "when He returns with all of His armies," right next to verse 9. You say, "I can't fit it all next to there." Try anyway.

Did you know that over the Eastern Gate of Jerusalem, right now, is nothing but stone? It's sealed up and Ezekiel 44:1-3 says that it's supposed to be sealed up until "the Prince" passes through it. We needed some Mohammedans to take over the Middle East to seal the Eastern Gate. We needed them to seal the gates because there's an entrance fit only for the King. Psalm 24: "Lift up your heads, O you gates; and be lifted up, you everlasting doors; and the King of glory shall come in. Who is this King of glory? The LORD strong and mighty, the LORD mighty in battle. The Lord of hosts is His name."

3. Business as usual will be remarkably different. What is Jesus doing when He comes into the temple of God (21:12)? They will not be selling sacrifices and taking advantage of people in the temple court. They will not be selling the right to worship God in the temple court. The Levites will need to be purified and they will be purified. They will offer themselves and they will be purified, Malachi 3:3, as with fuller's soap. They will be purified as silver. It will be remarkably different when the Lord returns. They will say, "Blessed is

He who comes in the name of the Lord." It will be as Jesus said: a house of prayer for all nations.

4. Every mouth will worship the Lord Jesus. It won't be just the children. Jeremiah 31 says, Say no more, Know the LORD: for they all will know the Lord, from the very least to the greatest.

5. His disciples will not soon be disappointed. You know, when the disciples were walking Jesus in to the temple, or into Jerusalem, they really think, "Boy, this is really about to take off for us. We're about to have no more issues. All the bills are about to be paid." Think this through now. They're about to be a part of the cabinet of the new kingdom, aren't they? And now Jesus is being not received by Jerusalem. It wasn't just a few days later when they all forsook Him and fled. When you and I meet with the Lord in Jerusalem, we will not be disappointed. No follower of Christ, who understands the plan of God, has ever been disappointed. God has never owed anybody anything.

6. Instead of a foal he'll be riding a horse. Revelation 19 says He's on the back of a white horse. That's the way conquerors come to their new thrones. They come to a white horse. They come on a white horse. I will tell you there is one thing that is the same. Referencing Matthew 21:14 the blind and the lame come into the temple and He heals them. Be encouraged. This won't be completely different than the next time He returns. There still won't be any blind and lame people in the temple.

Now then, having given you six things that are different, let me give you a very short list of things that you should do (knowing this short list). In other words, so what?

1. You should be very grateful that God keeps His promises. See this is how I kind of work with the resurrection: The resurrection is as historical as Washington crossing the Delaware. I have no problem believing in the resurrection because I have no problem believing that a bunch of dudes I never met signed a piece of paper I never could read (when I saw it); they declared us free

from England. I accept all of that as historical fact and so I have no issues accepting the resurrection just as historically. It doesn't become non-historical just because it's in a religious book. When God makes promises, I can believe those.

2. When I know that this is going to happen it makes me want to be sure that their Father is my Father. If you've never put your faith in the Messiah, you're in the same place that Jerusalem is within this text). If you've never put your faith in what Christ did for you on the cross, how He died for you, every sin you ever would commit, every sin that you could commit, and rose from the dead, God is not your Father and you have plenty to fear in the day of His wrath.

3. Pray for it to be sooner rather than later. Psalm 125 says we're supposed to pray for the peace of Jerusalem. Why would we want to pray for it to happen sooner than later? Well, it's kind of like this. If it happens sooner, humanly speaking, less people die and go to hell. If it happens sooner, rather than later, then we can get started with this kingdom thing and get on with heaven on Earth. We are commanded in the last chapter of the book to pray, "Even so, Lord Jesus, come quickly." "What do we have to do? Let's wrap this thing up." We're not supposed to think like eight-year-olds anymore. "Well, Lord, I'd like You to come back but can You wait until next Tuesday? I want to go to Bible camp first. I want to get married first. I want to have my first kid first." We want to experience that amazing stuff on this Earth, but I just have a feeling that that will pale in comparison to the kingdom to come.

4. Save your money. You'll get your free trip to the Holy Land.

5. Remember who you are in view of Romans 11:25-29. If God can blind an entire ethnicity for two millennia, then it is the grace of God that you and I know King Jesus tonight. They will believe on Him, in mass, as a nation, and be born again. Their scales will be peeled off and they will be born again and saved and usher in their King just as soon as the "fullness of the Gentiles" arrives.

24:1-2[88]

Then Jesus went out after just pronouncing utter distress and "woe" upon those living in His day. **and departed from the temple,** This makes a lot of sense when we see 23:38 and the mentioning of "the house" (or, "you can have it!") **and His disciples came up to show Him the buildings** that which John 2 tells us took 46 years to build. **of the temple.** So they are moving towards the "Mount of Olives" (23:3) after having pronounced an empty house (23:38).

24:3

Now as He sat on the Mount of Olives, the disciples came to Him privately, saying, "Tell us, when will these things be? The woes pronounced on these people in 23:35-36 and the promise of 24:2 that the temple and its buildings would be destroyed. **And what *will be* the sign of Your coming, and of the end of the age?"** If Jesus doesn't fix their understanding, they are going to think these three things occur (at least in part) at the same time. The fact that we have talk concerning the end of the world (24:35) inhibits our adoption of what we might call the "full Preterist" view (the view that all things are to be fulfilled in only the first century around A.D.). Furthermore, 24:26-27 require such a public coming that shoving this into a private rapture—let alone a private coming in A.D. 70—borders on the weirdness of 2 Timothy 2:17. We have already talked about the reality "dual interpretation" and we see 24:15 was already fulfilled before Christ and yet Jesus says it will occur again. In other words, in Jesus' time, Daniel 11:30 was history and prophecy.

24:4

And Jesus "started telling them about things—after an entire chapter of pronouncing distress and judgment on a people living in His time period (not on an ethnicity)—that they nor their children or grandchildren or great grandchildren or great great...etc., would not see"—or so the modern dispensational perspective on this chapter would lead us to

---

[88]See more in my commentary on Mark (13:1-4).

believe. You mean Jesus has been spending two chapters promising judgment on those people in that time, and then He continues with information that will not affect them for 100 generations!?!? Come now. All of the "you" references in the verses to follow should alert us to the fact that Jesus has not changed His perspective. Bishop Ussher in his book "Annals of World History" says that 1.3 million Jews died around 70A.D. It seems like a person would call that "Great Tribulation" (24:21). Then, to top it off, Jesus said that all these things mentioned in these verses would indeed take place to those people living at that time giving us our second of two fantastic bookends (23:36; 24:34).

In a sermon that Luther preached on Matthew 24:15–28, first printed in 1525, the Reformer taught that the "abomination of desolation" (Matt. 24:15) had occurred when "Emperor Cajus, as history tells, had put his image in the temple at Jerusalem as an idol, for the people to worship."[89]

24:5-8[90]

6 And you will hear of wars and rumors of wars. The **wars** are not necessarily seen. The real chore is to get us to love historical setting of which we can find much writing so that we know we can love our Bibles that we already believe. In other words, we almost feel like we have to have permission to believe Jesus' words in 24:34. Matthew 10:23 and 16:27 keep telling us to believe that it will really occur in that generation.

rumors of wars This is the first of five discernible parallels between Matthew 24 and the book of Daniel (this is found in Daniel 11:25-27).[91]

24:21-22

---

[89]Martin Luther, Twenty-fifth Sunday After Trinity sermon. In Sermons of Martin Luther, Vol. 5 (Grand Rapids, MI: Baker, 1995), 36378 at 3667.

[90]See more in my commentary on Mark (13:5-23).

[91]The others are Matthew 24:15 with Daniel 11:31; Matthew 24:21 with Daniel 12:1; Matthew 24:6-14's reference to "the end" with Daniel 12:4-6; and Matthew 24:30 with Daniel 7:13.

22 And except those days the **days** of "great tribulation" mentioned in verse 21. **should be shortened, there should no flesh be saved: but for the elect's sake** don't you think it's strange that Matthew hasn't used this word (other than the aforementioned parables) other than here—when he is speaking of "great tribulation?" Is it to assure the reader that they are there by God's gracious and Sovereign design?

those days shall be shortened. I think that like we have a calendar that pulls out and you have all kinds of slots on it and you can see that the days rotate and so that even though there might 31 or 32 or even 40 slots—depending on who published the calendar—they might be designed for a certain amount of days, but not every month has 31 days. I would suggest, to keep everyone guessing, there is still this element of surprise when it comes to the coming of the Lord. Remember, there is no coming of Christ until verse 30. This could be how there are no people that know when He shall come (24:36).

Let me get this straight…God, you may speed the movement of the cosmic bodies for your **elect?** Then, what else would you do for your **elect?** If He hasn't changed in His character then His view of His **elect** hasn't changed either. He still reaches down into "great tribulation" and shortens days for His **elect.** He did it in A.D. 69-70; He'll do it at the ultimate end; He does it today for us…and the world benefits (much like Laban did with Jacob and Potiphar did with Joseph). There is, after all, much prayer occurring (verse 20). Those who have received a penny and a garment—they are chosen by God, **elect** by God to be in "Great Tribulation," and to save the world ("no flesh shall be saved"). These days of "great tribulation" are so awful that they deceive or destroy everyone but the **elect** and so awful that only the prayers (verse 20) of **the elect** will shorten them (verse 22).

He, therefore, still stops those days just shy of it being too much for you…or it would wipe you out. Just before this eats you alive, the "days will be shortened." What makes God acts is that He hired us, clothed us, and because we are His **elect.**

for the elect's sake I would not have said it this way. I am too soteriologically "Reformed:" I would have said "for the sake of God's glory" or "for the sake of God's notoriety." I would have been more exact and extravagant (I speak in jest). He rather says "I will do this for you. I'll stop the world for you."

24:24

For there shall arise false christs, and false prophets, and shall shew great signs and wonders; insomuch that, if it were possible, they shall deceive the very elect. When it says there are many false christs, know that the antichrist is probably the most influential one, but definitely not the only one. 24:4, 24:11, and 24:23 show us that there would be times when believers would be **deceive**d **if it were possible.**

the very elect. The 2nd time in 3 verses this word is used (see also verse 31 for the 3rd time; that verse should be proof enough that **elect** is not just "ethnic Jews." Jesus is not coming to gather Jews simply because of their "ethnicity." Isaiah over and over again calls Jews the **elect.** Colossians, moreover, calls believers the **elect** in his 2nd chapter.

Matthew 22:14, however, uses this same word (translated "chosen")—as does Matthew 20:16, and so we should see that the **elect,** according to Matthew are those who have been hired at the 11th hour (20:16) and those with proper garments at the feast (22:14). Otherwise, we would have to see only ethnic Jews getting the denarius and getting the garment. Imagine saying, as some do, that there are saved people in Jerusalem at this time, but they are not **elect.** So we have those who are saved but are not a part of the **elect?** Not only that, but why are these unsaved ethnic Jews—which are supposedly the **elect** in the theology of some—almost deceived? Do we suppose they were about to pursue "false christs" and be drawn away from the real Christ when they are Christless **elect?** It's dizzying to make these **elect** ethnic Jews.

While the **elect** are not immune to "sorrow" (verse 8-12), they do have a special promise here: they will endure (10:22; 24:13) and not be **deceive**d.

24:26

Wherefore if they shall say unto you, Behold, he is in the desert; go not forth: they are going to "hear of wars and rumors of war—becoming unsettled." Then verse 15…"you're going to see something…then flee" (verse 16). Disobedience to this instruction from the Lord will lead to separation (24:40)…perhaps through an enemy awaiting you. If you leave early, you will find it is not the safe place and you will be judged. In other words, doing the right thing at the wrong time is doing the wrong thing.

behold, he is in the secret chambers; believe it not. "These false christs are going to be saying there is a secret showing of Christ over here. Come on over to our building, come over to our cave, come over to his field and you will see Christ. He is coming again." Now does Christ come again? 24:30, right? And before he comes again publicly you have people lying about secret comings of Christ. It is interesting that the chiefest sin that brings on mass death and birds of prey are those who seek to unseat the Christ—or even misrepresent Him.

24:29-30

Immediately after the tribulation of those days Compare it with verse 21, and you find out the **tribulation** is the Great tribulation.

shall the sun be darkened, and the moon shall not give her light, and the stars shall fall from heaven, and the powers of the heavens shall be shaken. Should we assume that Jesus used this same kind of language, but in a literal way, for future states of planet earth?[92] Perhaps (after considering the words of the apostles), but not primarily so [see table above, crafted originally by my friend and boss previously, Pastor Sean Harris of the Berean Baptist Church (Fayetteville, NC)].

A Comparative Analysis of the Christ's Olivet Discourse to Paul's Letters to the Church at Thessalonica			
Biblical Text	Matthew & Mark	1 Thessalonians	2 Thessalonians
1. Warning about Deception	24.4/13.5		2.3
2. Labor Pains/Pregnancy	24.8 (birth pains)13.17	5.3	
3. Tribulations/Persecutions	24.9/13		1.4
4. Abomination of Desolation	24.15/13.14		2.2-3
5. Coming (Parousia G3952)	24.3,27,37,39	2.19; 3.13; 4.15; 5.23	2.1; 2.8-9
6. Visible Descent from Heaven	24.30	4.16	1.7
7. Clouds	24.30/13.26	4.17	
8. Great Power/Day of the Lord	24.30/13.26	5.2	1.9-10; 2.2; 2.8-9
9. Archangel/ Angels	24.31/13.27	4.16	1.7
10. Sound/Shout	24.31	4.16	
11. Gathering/Caught Up	24.31	4.17	2.1
12. Souls from Heaven Coming	24.31/13.27	3.13; 4.14	1.10
13. People from Earth Gathered	13.27	4.17	2.1
14. Thief	24.43	5.2	
15. Watch	24.42/ 13.35-37	5.6	
16. Drunkards	24.49	5.7	
17. Destruction/Judgment	24.51	5.3	1.5-9

---

[92]See my commentary on Mark (13:27) for more on this.

30 And then shall appear the sign of the Son of man in heaven: same generation (24:34) that would be given no sign except the **sign** "of Jonah" (Matthew 12:38-40; Matthew 16:1-4): One who is apparently dead, rising from the dead, and appearing to a godless people.

24:31[93]

And He will send His angels with a great sound of a trumpet, and they will gather together His elect from the four winds, It seems as though this is the Gospel declaration taking great effect through the work of **angels.** First, consider the connection between Matthew's Gospel and Hebrews:

1. Both speak about "swearing" (Matthew 5:33-34; Hebrews 6:19-20).
2. Both (and only these both) quote the 8th Psalm in the New Testament (Matt 21:16-17; Hebrews 2:6-7).
3. Both quote Psalm 110 (Matthew 22:44; Hebrews 1:13).

It seems reasonable, then, to consider that Hebrews 1:14 speaks to the role of **angels** for those who "'shall be' heirs of salvation."

from one end of heaven to the other. Whoever **the elect** are before (as seen in Matthew 20 and Matthew 22 parables), they must be here. To say he meant something different separated by four chapters (chapter 20) and/or occurring on the same day (Tuesday of Passion Week, Matthew 22) is ridiculous. There is nothing secret here where the **elect** are being removed. Jesus is talking to His disciples (24:3) and using the 2nd person plural as if to say that they are going to see much of what He has described here. Now, the disciples are the recipient of church discipline (Matthew 18:15-20), and it is hard to fathom that these disciples are merely "Israel." Why would "Israel" be given church discipline and managing church membership? What about chapter 26 where the disciples are getting the Lord's Supper? This is only 12 hours before His death and 48 hours after this passage in chapter 24. Are we going to say that "Israel" was given the Lord's Supper? If so, why does the church practice it? If the disciples are the church in chapter 26 on Thursday, why would they be "Israel" 48 hours earlier on Tuesday? The **elect**

---

[93]Here is another reminder to reference my commentary on Mark (13:27).

cannot change identities in the same week. What about chapter 28? Did "Israel" get the Great Commission—including baptism? How does it make you feel to hear that "God didn't give His Great Commission to the church?" or "The church doesn't have authority to baptize from Jesus?" If that's hard to believe, then imagine saying that the disciples are "the church" in chapters 18, 26, 28, but in chapter 24 they are "Israel."

This coming of Christ is sooner than expected (24:36; 24:43 24:50, 25:6-11; 25:14), but it is not without signs. The building of an "ark" is hardly invisible or private or secret. Animals in groups of as many as seven and the wrath of God coming in a flood was not signless (24:37). So there must be a way for this coming to be "after the tribulation" (24:29) and still unexpected. 24:21 tells us how we can find this coming both "after the tribulation" and yet, unexpected. Perhaps this means that though the "tribulation" is on the calendar for seven years, it can be shortened.

The purpose of this coming is to divide the wicked from the godly [Noah from those outside; those in the field; those at the mill; the five from the five (25:1-11); the "Good and Faithful Servant" from the slothful servant (25:14-30); the sheep from the goats (25:31-46)]. This should tell us that Christ wasn't trying to teach all kinds of little elements of end-times doctrine: He was simply preaching the suddenness of His coming, and the separation that occurs. Oddly enough, 26:1 identifies one named Judas who would be separated from the disciples.

24:32-35

34 Assuredly, I say to you, this generation will by no means pass away till all these things take place. Again, we know that we can search the histories of Josephus and Ussher to see that these things did indeed **take place** in that **generation.**[94] Because of our respect to Jesus' statements here and in 23:36, we believe the Scripture—with or without

---

[94]See my commentary on Luke 21:32 where I discuss another consideration on this passage—albeit not the safest in our perspective of Jesus' veracity (in my estimation).

our external proofs. Having said that, it seems like we should remind the reader that the apostles related their understanding of "end times" doctrine to these words of Jesus and applied them to geography quite different than Jerusalem. We see, then, the following context is not intended on being a comfort, but a warning (echoing Matthew 10:23 and 16:27). There is nothing comfortable about a coming flood (24:37), a thief coming to my house (24:43), a returning boss-man (24:47), an unexpected arrival of an extremely important party (25:11), or the return of a business owner (25:14)[95]—even if I know they are coming. Knowing a thief is coming rather sets us on edge.

Doors are found all throughout this passage. For example, the end of verse 33: "It is near, even at the doors." And then, you know what kept people out of the ark, right? A door. We see it reappear in 25:11 with the parable of the ten virgins. This passage is full of notions of you being left outside the door and that is why the two parables at the end of chapter 24, the account of Noah, this parable of the ten virgins, and even this next parable. What is happening to this man? He is being cast out into darkness (25:30).

24:41-44

Two *women will be* grinding at the mill: one will be taken and the other left. The "unready" are swept away from their fellows in judgment like those outside the "ark" (24:38)

43 But know this, that if the master of the house had known what [8]hour the thief would come, he would have watched and not allowed his house to be broken into. He is not stealing away anybody (as whimsically supposed by many today), but rather breaking into somebody's house. 1 Thessalonians says that believers are not overtaken (5:4), thus necessitating their presence for it to be a salient point. **44 Therefore you also be ready, for the Son of Man is coming at an hour you do not expect.** At least Paul (1 Thessalonians 5:1-3) and Peter (2 Peter 3:9) isolate Jesus from a calamitous "day of the Lord" when

---

[95] All of these cases point to separation—just as 25:31-46 culminates in separation.

[8] Lit. *watch of the night;* See Mark 13:35.

using this language, but in this address, Jesus wants the listener to fear His coming—not anticipate it with delight. We must, therefore, be dealing with a coming of Christ in judgment rather than in deliverance of His people. The warning of Noah (24:36-38) sets the tone for the entirety of these five stories.

25:9-15

But the wise answered, saying, '*No,* lest there should not be enough for us and you; but go rather to those who sell, and buy for yourselves.' No endorsement of communism or socialism here: "get your own." 25:28 seems to teach the same. He takes from the "have nots" and gives it to the "haves."

15 And to one he gave five talents, to another two, and to another one, to each according to his own ability; ability determined responsibility.

25:23

His lord said to him, 'Well *done,* good and faithful servant; you have been faithful over a few things, I will make you ruler over many things. Enter into ʳthe joy of your lord.' They get the same affirmation: "five talents" and "two talents." Well, can we hear about the guy who didn't hear this affirmation but still gets to enter the kingdom? No…this person doesn't exist (25:30). Just as there are no middle grounds affirmed in the next passage (25:31-46)—recognizing some who might be "sheep" but did not do works "unto Jesus".

25:30

And cast the unprofitable servant ᵘinto the outer darkness. There will be weeping and gnashing of teeth.' Just like 24:51.

25:31-40

ʳPs. 16:11
ᵘMatt. 8:12; 22:13

When the Son of Man shall come in His glory, and all the holy angels with Him, then shall He sit upon the throne of His glory: And before Him shall be gathered all nations: and He shall separate them one from another, as a shepherd divides his sheep It seems like we can either guess who the **sheep** are or we can ask Matthew.

"Matthew, who are the **sheep**?"

First, let's identify some players here. We have three groups of people in this drama: **Sheep; Goats;** Brethren (25:40). We have this group of people known as Christ's brethren in the passage.

> *Matthew 12:47: Then one said unto Him, Behold, Thy mother and Thy brethren stand without, desiring to speak with Thee. But He answered and said unto him that told Him, Who is My mother? And who are <u>"My brethren?"</u> He stretched forth His hand toward His disciples, and said, Behold My mother and <u>"My brethren!"</u> For whosoever shall do the will of My Father which is in heaven, the same is My brother, and sister, and mother.*

Jesus said His brethren are those who do the will of His Father.

> *Matthew 28:9 As they went to tell His disciples, Jesus met [the ladies], saying, All hail. And they came and held Him by the feet, and worshipped Him. Then said Jesus unto them, Be not afraid: go tell <u>My brethren</u> that they go into Galilee.*

So, in chapter 12 the brethren are His disciples, the ones who do the will of the Father; chapter 28, the brethren are His disciples. Right in the middle we have the term brethren being used again. We would be very foolish to decide that Matthew means something totally different.

So whoever the sheep are they are the ones who treated the believers well. We could guess, but I'd rather not. Let's go with what Matthew already told us. That's called being a Bible student, right?

Now, let's talk about **the sheep**. We could guess who **the sheep** are, but let's not do that.

> *Matthew 10:5: These twelve Jesus sent forth, and commanded them, saying, Go not into the way of the Gentiles, and into any*

city of the Samaritans enter ye not: But go rather to the lost
sheep *of the house of Israel.*

Matthew 15 Behold, a woman of Canaan, not a Jew, came out of
the same coasts, and cried unto Him, saying, Have mercy on me,
O Lord, Thou Son of David; my daughter is grievously vexed
with a devil. But He answered her not a word. And His disciples
came and besought Him, saying, Send her away; for she cries
after us. But He answered and said, to who? To the woman who
is crying after Him, I am not sent but unto the lost **sheep** *of the*
house of Israel.

All through this passage, all through this book, Jesus has already
identified **sheep.** They are Israel and the ones He is going after are the
lost **sheep** of the house of Israel.

You have **sheep** who treat Christians well and are received into a
kingdom. Now, what happens around the AD 70 context is you have
Christians who have been told to wait for something before they leave
Jerusalem (24:15). And who are these Christians going to be surrounded
by in Jerusalem? Jews. So there's some AD 70 context there. I just want
you to see Jesus is careful to tell us who these folks are.

25:41-45

Then shall He say also unto them on the left hand, Depart from Me,
you cursed, into everlasting fire, prepared for the devil and his
angels: Now, nothing is gained by downplaying the fire in 25:41.

I suppose the references to hell as a place of "eternal fire" (Matt.
25:41) or "burning sulfur" (Rev. 20:10) are symbolic, if for no
other reason than that the demons are disembodied spirits and
thus cannot be punished by fire in the literal sense. But what of
that? **The purpose of imagery is to point beyond what literal**
language can convey. If a literal burning by fire is bad, the
reality of hell's suffering must be immeasurably and
inexpressibly worse. Even if the suffering is only mental,

internal, or psychological, it is something that produces an eternal "weeping and gnashing of teeth" (Matt. 25:30).[96]

If fire is a symbol of what hell is, and not really fire, than how bad is it if the word they use to symbolize it is fire? So you gain nothing by saying it's a symbol if the symbol you use to symbolize it is fire. So you gain nothing by saying it's a symbol. It's still awful.

"Oh, I think hell is not really fire. I mean what kind of sense would that make? I mean, people who die right now go to hell. How can you have a fire?"

The point is, even if you want to say "it's not a real fire," you gain nothing: if fire is a symbolic word, how bad is it to use the word fire?

Jesus is talking about Himself in verse 31 when the Son of Man shall come, and He calls Himself the King. That is pretty audacious. Let's not forget this is Tuesday night (with the Good Friday scenario) of Passion Week here. He's about to wear a crown of thorns in 72 hours. Less than 72 hours. In two and a half days Jesus, the King of glory, is going to wear a crown of thorns and be beaten with a mock reed. And He's going to have a sign above His cross that says, "This is the King of the Jews." Think about how Jesus looked through that in this passage, to the day when He would come again in glory.

45 Inasmuch as you did it not to one of the least of these, you did it not to Me. And these shall go away into everlasting punishment: but the righteous into life eternal. The word "hell" is not used. We're going to call it hell because it's fire and it's for the wicked, so I'm going to use the normal word hell for our discussion. In verse 41 and here in verse 46 we find the idea of what we normally call "Hell."

Please also notice that Hell is not prepared for the goats. Verse 34 says "the kingdom" was "prepared" for the "sheep", but verse 41 says that "everlasting fire" was "prepared for the devil and his angels." God did not intend on anyone going to the flame from the foundation of the world. No one begins their journey on earth having been destined for the fire.

---

[96] James Montgomery Boice, *The Gospel of Matthew* (Grand Rapids, MI: Baker Books, 2001), 544.

Then there's this idea of this **punishment.** I'm not happy about hell and I think that that's my problem. Yeah, I do. Because if God does something, it's holy.

> *25:41 Depart, ye cursed, into <u>everlasting fire.</u>*

> *25:46 And these shall go away into* **everlasting punishment***: but the righteous into life eternal.*

If you have a King James Version, one word is eternal and, one word is everlasting (both in verse 46). It's the same in the Greek; same word. So know this, if you're going to say, somehow, that the punishment is not everlasting then you also have to say that the life in the kingdom is not everlasting. We've got to be consistent.

Look, I think if we stay in this verse we're going to see that if in verse 46 the punishment is not forever than you also have to say that the life is not forever. I wish that I could say to someone, "If you are unfortunate enough that you go to the fire that the fire will go out and one day you will cease to exist" (a doctrine known as annihilationism). The problem is, I am not comfortable saying that if I go to heaven that that doesn't last forever (**life eternal**). It's the same term used for both.

Someone would say, "Well, it's not the flame that lasts forever. You're not conscious of it. It is the punishment, in its effect, that lasts forever; but you're burned up right away. So it is not "eternal conscious punishment." Well how does that work for heaven? Are you comfortable saying that? "You go to heaven but you don't really know you're there. You cease to exist." We've got to be fair with the passage, folks.

Now look, I might be wrong, but we better have a good reason why I'm wrong. I can talk to you about the prayers of saints are incense before the Lord (Revelation 8), and the torment of the wicked is incense before the Lord (Revelation 14). That is to say, it is just as pleasing for people to be in the lake of fire as it is for people to pray before the holy God of heaven. It is holy and righteous and I don't understand it, but I accept is as God's perfect will, and I don't like it. And so what do I do? Do I sit around and act embarrassed about what my Lord says? No, I give the gospel out so that less people have to go to the flame.

Chapter 26

26:1-2[97]

…and the Son of Man will be delivered up to be crucified." Said first in chapters 16, 17, and 20.

26:3-5

Then the chief priests, the scribes, and the elders of the people assembled at the palace of the high priest, we should be suspicious of any religion whose head has a **palace.**

26:6-9

8 But when His disciples so strange how Matthew includes himself on this. It would have been easier to say "the disciples, but mostly Judas." It is us…not that guy Judas."

26:10-13

11 For you have the poor with you always, but Me you do not have always. Deuteronomy 15:11 is here cited.

26:14-16

16 So from that time he sought opportunity to betray Him. Whether it's Eden or Bethany, we see altogether quickly how treasoning our hearts are against the High King of Heaven. Judas did not have to do this. He was offered, Matthew 19:28, an opportunity to reign.

26:17[98]

Now the first day of the feast Just like that, it's two days later. When you are about to endure what Jesus knows He will endure, what do you do for a day? What of this missing day? Remember from the opening of

---

[97]More can be seen in my commentary on Mark (14:1-11).
[98]More can be seen in my commentary on Mark (14:12-16).

the chapter, we spoke of this feast, as prescribed by Exodus 12, lasting a total of 8 days following the Passover meal.

26:18

And he said, Go into the city to such a man, This sounds an awful lot like 21:1-2, but that is a different town. Probably, this is John-Mark's father and Jesus had previously known him. He identifies him as carrying something in another Gospel's account so this is not as arbitrary as Matthew's account makes it sound. Why John-Mark? In the book of Acts there is another meeting in the upper room (Acts 1) while it is probably later identified as Mark's home (Acts 12:12). **and say unto him, The Master saith, My time is at hand;** What a very sobering reality: "any time now, it will be my time." It really makes a person wonder, "Why now?" What has happened to make this the "right time?" One would wonder if verse 24 sheds a little more light on this. In other words, what do a "time at hand" (26:18) and a prophesied death of the "Son of Man" (26:24) have in common in light of Old Testament backdrop? We do know, after all, that if anything was "written" it is a reference to the Old Testament. So the question is "which Old Testament prophet" discusses the death of the Son of Man and places an element of time with it? Consider the identification of Daniel's prophetic focus in Daniel 7:13-14 as the Son of Man, and then consider the time element Daniel sees placed alongside this Son of Man in Daniel 9:21-27 as it relates to the Son of Man's death.

Some questions are now evident: Is this what Jesus was talking about? If so, did the Jews understand the connection; is it reasonable for Jesus, a Jew, to make the connection between the "Son of Man" of Daniel 7 and "Messiah the Prince" of Daniel 9? You be the judge (see Matthew 26:63-64).

It seems like another question should follow: Is it realistic that Jesus would be thinking about Daniel? Is it realistic that Matthew would be thinking of Daniel? You be the judge:

	Daniel	Matthew

Son of Man Coming with Clouds	**7:13**	**24:30**
Rumors of War	**11:25-27**	**24:6**
Abomination Desolation	**11:31**	**24:15**
Great Tribulation	**12:1**	**24:21**
"the end"	**12:4-6**	**24:6-14**
Death for the Son of Man	**7:13-15; 9:21-26**	**26:18-24**

Well, then maybe the next question is did Jesus really do the math? Was Jesus really expecting to die because of a prophecy in the Old Testament? Certainly His Father and the Holy Spirit were already communicating to Him. They did, after all, tell Him about a fish with a coin in it, right? They did, empower Him to do miracles and He did do so within the scope of His Father's will, correct? So we don't assume that Jesus was dependent on just the book of Daniel for these statements in Matthew 26, but what if it did inform Him?

What if He really did do the math and found out that 69 weeks of 7 years brought us to 483 years and what if He really did multiply that by a Jewish year of 360 days and found Himself dying on the very week where those 173,880 days would expire? What if He did know when those 62 weeks of Daniel 9:26 began and when those 156,240 days would end?

This becomes even more grave and gravely more sober when we consider that it was quite possibly known at one time by those same Jews that they could do the same math and see that this Son of Man, marked by miracle after miracle, was living among them; that this same Son of Man, riding on the foal of a donkey was the One song of prophetic trumpet blasts from 500 years before.

So, then, why no math, when they saw Jesus heal a man of palsy "that ye may know that the Son of man hath power on earth to forgive sins…Arise, take up thy bed, and go unto thine house" (Matthew 9:6)? Why no math when just before healing a man with a withered hand,

Jesus said "the Son of man is Lord even of the sabbath day" (Matthew 12:8)? Why no simple math when just after Jesus healed and deaf and dumb man Jesus said "whosoever speaketh a word against the Son of man, it shall be forgiven him: but whosoever speaketh against the Holy Ghost, it shall not be forgiven him, neither in this world, neither in the world to come" (Matthew 12:32)?

All of these questions, in my opinion, find their quintessential absurdity in a man named Judas who heard Jesus say three times: "The Son of man shall be betrayed into the hands of men" (Matthew 17:22), "the Son of man shall be betrayed unto the chief priests and unto the scribes, and they shall condemn him to death" (20:18), and "the Son of man is betrayed to be crucified" (26:22)?

This is what makes the actions of Judas in this passage deplorable and ignorant. You almost wonder if Judas is in His right mind. I get the idea that he isn't even sure if he's the guy doing the betraying at this point (see verse 25). It's almost like he might be trying to accomplish something as described previously in this chapter that would drive Jesus to do something enormous. He knows the power of Jesus.

We see what appears to be almost a shock in his confession in the next chapter when he says "I have betrayed innocent blood" (27:4). It is as if he did not think Jesus would actually die through his actions. Perhaps this is why he settled for such a stupid price of 4-months pay. Perhaps he wasn't after the money.

I wonder, when did he start to doubt that he was doing the right thing? When did he finally realize that Jesus wasn't going to kill all the Romans? When did He doubt that Jesus, though all powerful as the "God of Angel Armies" described in Matthew 24:31, would not actually use them at the disposal of the Romans in this chapter? Who can blame Him for thinking that Jesus, the Son of Man, would be the conqueror of the Romans? Daniel 7 does make it look like the 4th beast would see the dawn of the Son of Man's kingdom? So, when did Judas start to doubt?

It seems reasonable that he began to doubt when, later in this same chapter, Jesus tells another of His disciples in Judas' own presence that He was not going to use His angels, His holy ones, as described in

Daniel 7. He had to first die. This, however, should not have been a surprise to Judas. Jesus told Judas and all the others that He was to be a "ransom for sinners" (in Matthew 20:28) long before He would be a conquering King returning from Heaven.

So what is the take-away. Be careful how you hear! This is the whole point of the soils of Matthew 13. Some listen wonderfully and bring forth fruit. Some only hear a little and the wicked one snatches the seed away. Others hear with joy and desire just a little truth before the cares of this world choke out what little faith they had. One wonders whether Judas had considered that He needed to listen a little more closely.

I will keep the passover at thy house with my disciples. Again, one perusal of Exodus 12 and the reader will soon see that the Father presides over the house on this most somber night. Jesus, the head of the Father's Household (Hebrews 3's argument) leads His family (Matthew 12:48 and following) during this Feast.

26:20[99]

Now when the even was come, he sat down with the twelve. The sense of the originals doesn't exactly get represented in most translations. It is more of a "as evening was coming, he was sitting down with the 12." You get a stage being set by Matthew; a sort of drawing the reader to the sobriety of the moment: "as the sun was setting, the Son was setting." A moment dawned on which we would talk about death.

26:24

The Son of man goeth as it is written of him: See comments on verse 18. If we are correct in drawing the connection between Christ and the Son of Man knowing His "time," then we find a very human distinctive here about Jesus: He is learning about Himself from the Scripture too.

26:25

Then Judas, which betrayed him, answered and said, Master, is it I? Maybe he's trying to shroud his involvement; or, maybe there's

---

[99]More to be found in my commentary on Mark (14:17-21).

something else. See comments under 26:18. **He said unto him, Thou hast said.** This is a colloquialism from that day of "you said it" or "you couldn't be more right."[100] This phrase comes up again later in the chapter with Caiaphas.

26:27-28[101]

And he took the cup, and gave thanks, and gave it to them, saying, Drink ye all of it; For this is my blood of the new testament, which is shed for many for the remission of sins. Once again, in view of Matthew 20:16 and Matthew 22:14 where it says "many are called and few are chosen", we see that the provision is for myriads more than will take part. We do not minimize that the primary objective of the "ransom" was for the elect hostages, but we do, as we did in Matthew 24 remind ourselves that the blood of Jesus Christ—while not efficacious for the un-elect many—is legitimately offered and potentially effective for those same number who will never experience life. There was one, therefore, at this supper, that appears to have been a part of the "many" and is not, however, a part of the kingdom. Think about it. Judas was a potential recipient for the remission of sins by the blood of Jesus. Before one takes issue with that, you need to be reminded that Judas was promised, upon His continued devotion to Christ, one of the 12 thrones in the New World (Matthew 19:28).

Still yet another observation: If remission of sins didn't occur until the next day, then we know the cup had no saving merit and the blood, the next day, brought **remission of sins,** and the New Covenant is brought by this same shedding of the blood. Moreover, this same New Testament is brought by Christ through His death as the Ultimate Moses. This, again, is not new to the reader:

Event/Fact	Moses	Jesus
Mass death preceding arrival	Exodus 1	Matt 2

---

[100] Jim Bishop, *The Day Christ Died* (New York: Harper & Brothers, 1957), 87.

[101] More details in my commentary on Luke (22:19-38).

A trip to Egypt	Exodus 3	Matt 2
An Exodus from Egypt	Exodus 12-14	Matt 2
Preceded by a prophet	Exodus 3	Matt 3
Major Opposing Figure	Exodus 4	Matt 2
A baptism	1 Cor. 10:1-2	Matt 3
Both hear from Heaven	Exodus 19:19	Matt 3; 17
40 days/nights	Ex 24:18; 34:28	Matt 4
Miracle Worker	Exodus 3	Matt 4
A mountain for a law	Exodus 19	Matt 5-7
Mediator of a Testament	Exodus 24	Matt 26:28

26:29

But I say unto you, I will not drink henceforth of this fruit of the vine, until that day when I drink it new with you in my Father's kingdom. It's probably impossible to exhaust the full, rich meaning of what the Lord's Supper is and does for the soul of the believer, but one thing it does for the spirit and mind is that it reminds us of the supper in the kingdom—forecasted by Matthew 8:11 and Matthew 22:1ff; or, rather, the "supper that is the kingdom." The Lord's Supper, then, celebrates the horror of the death of God's Son and the Honor of the Coming of Christ for all God's Sons. Calvary is the height of God's love and the extent of God's wrath.

This statement also, albeit on the way, tells us what Jesus did not drink post resurrection (Matthew 28).

26:30

And when they had sung an hymn, they went out into the mount of Olives. Wonder of wonders. What does one do who is in God the Father's will in the darkest of nights? What do those do who understand little and feel much for their Master? They sing. Ridiculous…if there is nothing of which to sing.

It seems, as they are leaving the upper room, that this would be a good time to talk about all that the streets of Jerusalem have seen. It would be a great opportunity to wax eloquent concerning "what the streets would say if they could talk." However, that would not be helpful to understanding Matthew's intent with the text. Seriously, we could go right over to John's gospel and we could talk about how they passed where the blind man was healed (John 9) or where the woman taken in adultery (John 8) or…you get the idea. We will refrain here so we can be true to the text. There is much here of which we can and should glean.

26:31[102]

Then saith Jesus unto them, All ye shall be offended because of me this night: for it is written, I will smite the shepherd, and the sheep of the flock shall be scattered abroad. This is a quotation from Zechariah and we are not surprised at this:

1. Matthew 9:36-37 quotes Zechariah 10:2
2. Matthew 19:26 alludes to Zechariah 8:6
3. Matthew 21:4-5 quotes Zechariah 9:9
4. Matthew 21:1-22 alludes to Zech 4:1-7 & 14:1-5
5. Matthew 24:16-20 refers to Zechariah 14:4-5
6. Matthew 24:30 refers to Zechariah 12:10
7. Matthew 24:31 refers to Zechariah 2:6
8. Matthew 25:31 refers to Zechariah 14:5
9. Matthew 26:30-31 refers to Zechariah 13:7

The shocker here is not that he quotes Zechariah, but that He knew that the Father was doing the smiting. This seems so counter-intuitive because it was Jesus Who was "moved with compassion because He found sheep who had no shepherd" (Matthew 9:36). It must be that these are sheep in a different sense as these 11 remaining disciples are not "lost sheep of the house of Israel" (Matthew 10:5). It seems illogical, therefore, to change the usage of "sheep" in relation to the "shepherd"

---

[102]More to be seen in my commentary on Mark (14:26-31).

unless we have contextual reason to do so…such as a quotation from the Old Testament.

See Zechariah 13:1-8: This is a glance of a day (or a time) when there is forgiveness (verse 1), purgation (verses 2-3), repentance (verse 4-5), and refinement (verses 8-9). What we haven't talked about is verses 6-7. It is so hard to understand what is going on here. The repenting false prophet of verses 3-5 is somehow saying that He has been wounded in his friend's home. Furthermore, we don't know if this is the cause of his repentance, or the result of the repentance, or unrelated to his repentance.

Then…God speaks in verse 7 and continues through verse 9. We don't know if, once again, He speaks in reaction to the repentance and forgiveness taking place in this day or if his actions of verses 7-9 are related to this "great day" at all—particularly since "the day" is not mentioned after verse 4.

Thirdly, there is a long-standing habit of seeing Jesus speaking in verse 6 as a forecast of being crucified because of the actions of the friend, but then what do we do about His denying to be a prophet (verse 5) or his involvement in the corrupt ministry of the prophet (verse 4)?

What if, however, in the big picture, Christ is identified with the repentant prophet—becoming one with a sinful nation of Israel— epitomizing the sinful nation of Israel as one if its leaders, a prophet?[103] What if, this identifying with a sinful nation who loves its false prophets is what allows for this forgiveness of sins found in verse 1? Then, we have a probable prophecy of His betrayal and forsaking of friends surrounding the time when His hands were wounded in crucifixion authorizing such a fountain to be opened in Jerusalem; and, we have probable cause for judging those who are not a part of the redeemed in verses 8-9 (Acts 17:31).

There is no question that this is involved and there is much I am missing in the writer's intent of this passage—particularly since we have not exegeted the book of the prophecy of Zechariah. One thing is sure:

---

[103] It's not foreign. You may remember that in Matthew 3, Jesus is involved with a "baptism for repentance"—having no sin of which to repent. One of the possibilities is that He is identifying with a sinful nation.

forgiveness of sins is a gushing reality where there was once a wounding of hands, and this reality is the scheming of the One Who said He would wound His shepherd. One thing is equally as sure, the Shepherds wounding is related to the forgiveness of verse 1. Sadly, and surely though, sheep do not understand the confusing methods of their shepherd by the hand—the Roman hand, the Jewish hand, the Herodian hand, the Imperial hand, the Satanic hand, the Iscarian hand—of the Jehovah Who speaks in this passage.

The truth is, when we read Psalm 23 and we find sheep who are comforted with their shepherd's rod, we find the Shepherd as Jesus and we as the sheep and we find comfort in that he protects us with the rod—from our wandering selves by breaking our legs; from our wounding foes by breaking their necks. Yet, somehow, we find that the Shepherd was the first recipient of the Rod, and therefore, His bearing the rod in Zechariah is from the wrath-distributing hand of the Thrice-Holy Judge. We, meanwhile (after Calvary), behold the tender, protective rod of a Father-facing brother Who ever lives to intercede for us.

Without the Father smiting the Son, there is no fountain opened in Jerusalem for forgiveness.

26:32-33

33 Peter answered and said unto him, Though all *men* shall be offended because of thee, *yet* will I never be offended. It's hard to imagine not being willing, once again, to accept news of the Gospel—which is not really a Gospel to Peter. The smiting of the shepherd? That is not such good news. What about the resurrection, though? It's not even noticed—not any more than chapter 16 where Peter, again, insists that Jesus' resurrection—whatever it means—is a moot point because He will not be allowed to die.

26:34-35

35 Peter said unto him, though I should die with thee, yet will I not deny thee. Likewise also said all the disciples. So here on this walk from the upper room to the garden of Gethsemane we have two very difficult topics: God's involvement in killing His Messiah, and Peter's overwhelming confidence in Himself. I suppose this is why so many of us are careful to tell what "we would do" in a situation if we were the ones under pressure.

Really, though, can you imagine arguing with Jesus? Why wouldn't Peter have learned from this? The last time He argued with Jesus, Jesus called him "Satan." Doesn't make Peter sit back and think…"maybe I should ask, 'Lord can I avoid this?' Isn't there a way to posture myself so that I don't run away from the Lord? Isn't there a way I can keep from being a coward, Lord?" But we see nothing but an ill-mannered, unfriendly, misguided disagreement that majors on will power and speaks almost nothing of God's power. Since Peter doesn't understand about his failure in the big moments with the big things, I guess it's time for him to learn from his failures in the small things…

26:36-39[104]

37 And he took with him Peter and the two sons of Zebedee, and began to be sorrowful and very heavy. This may mean that Matthew got the report from one of these four people in the garden. In view of the record of Jesus' prayer during the napping of the disciples, the likely source is Jesus Himself.[105] **39 And he went a little further, and fell on his face, and prayed, saying, O my Father, if it be possible,** A very sober reality that not all possible things would please God. **let this cup pass from me: nevertheless not as I will, but as thou *wilt.*** This is doubtless what Jesus was talking about with the mother of James and John in Matthew 20. One would wonder how those two mere men could simply drink the same cup. How is that even possible? Particularly since James was beheaded early and John died of old age.

26:42

O my Father, if this cup may not pass away from me, except I drink it, thy will be done. Some of the commentators are helpful to point out that this request is different than the last. The previous request was "if it be possible" (26:39) and this one is **if this cup may not pass away**. It is

---

[104]More can be found in chapter 14 of my commentary on Mark (14:32-42).

[105]If Mark was written first, then it may be that the young man running from the scene of the arrest (in Mark's Gospel) is the source. Even if Mark wasn't written first, it could be that the testimony of Mark was written down by Matthew first (then Mark, perhaps).

as if Jesus now knows that this cup is not going to pass away, and this prayer, instead of one of more relief is one of more resignation to the will of the Father. The phrase that "Jesus prayed a second time" puts me in mind that "Elijah prayed again" (James 5:18), but...the heavens don't drop down rain at all as they did for Elijah. This Jesus, better than Elijah, drank the bitterness of a closed up and silent Heaven. Instead, this holy resignation, perfect submission, finds refreshment for us; salvaging for us; ransom for us (Matthew 20:28). I like what Carson says here:

> *"Not your will but mine" changed Paradise to desert and brought man from Eden to Gethsemane. Now "not my will but yours" brings anguish to the man who prays it but transforms the desert into the kingdom and brings man from Gethsemane to the gates of glory.*[106]

Or, perhaps, the great commentator—the Apostle Peter (who by the way, was there)—said it this way:

> *1Peter 2:21 For to this you have been called, because Christ also suffered for you, leaving you an example, so that you might follow in his steps. 22 He committed no sin, neither was deceit found in his mouth. 23 When he was reviled, he did not revile in return; when he suffered, he did not threaten, but* **continued entrusting himself to him who judges justly.**

Indeed, this was an act of faith by Jesus.

The cup What is this? I have heard many fanciful sermons and have enjoyed most of them. I have been acquainted with a good many Old Testament references through commentaries and study Bibles that this **cup** is "the wrath of God." The only issue I see with this is that when I feel like I need to choose between an Old Testament backdrop against which a writer may have been writing or a more finely-tuned contextual understanding within that writer's own objectives, I must pick the more localized understanding. So the question: Does Matthew use this terminology already? Yes, Matthew 20 and only in Matthew 20 do we find the **cup** being used in this manner.

---

[106]Frank E. Gaebelein, ed., *The Expositor's Bible Commentary, Matthew, Mark, Luke (Vol 8)* (Grand Rapids: Zondervan, 1984), 545.

*Matthew 20:22-23 But Jesus answered and said, Ye know not what ye ask. **Are ye able to drink of the cup that I shall drink of,** and to be baptized with the baptism that I am baptized with? They say unto him, We are able. 23 And he saith unto them, **Ye shall drink indeed of my cup,** and be baptized with the baptism that I am baptized with: but to sit on my right hand, and on my left, is not mine to give, but it shall be given to them for whom it is prepared of my Father.*

I think we can agree that James and John (in this context) did not drink of the wrath of God. It must be, then, that Christ's **cup** referenced in both places was a cup of suffering. Now having said all of this, one could say that part of Christ's cup was the wrath of God,[107] and that "drinking of the cup" (Matthew 20:22) means that they did not have to drink all of the cup. How could they? How could they drink the full cup as Jesus did? So it seems permissible to say that this **cup** of which Jesus was to drink involved that which no other could suffer. Now, James, he drank of the cup and was beheaded (Acts 12) while John was exiled on an island and drank of his cup. We can move forward to a dreadful time on the cross that next day:

Matthew 27:45 Now from the sixth hour there was darkness over all the land unto the ninth hour. 46 And about the ninth hour Jesus cried with a loud voice, saying, Eli, Eli, lama sabachthani? that is to say, My God, my God, why hast thou forsaken me?

We already had a two-part conversation when we discussed Matthew 1:1. The question of "did God actually turn His back on Jesus?" was discussed then and Isaiah 53:10 should be mentioned in passing here. However, the main issue that all should be able to settle on is that Jesus at least believed He was alone.

The reader should not find it difficult to believe that Matthew was thinking about Isaiah. There is such a pattern. Was it the act of Isaiah 53:6—God "laying the iniquity of us all on Him"—that which made Jesus feel completely alone? What is it about feeling the awful

---

[107] One really should read Psalm 75, and notice with fresh eyes, verse 8 where Christ is then drinking the very bottom of the cup for the "Wicked of the earth" who have caused such disorder to the very world in which they live (75:3-4).

weight of sin upon your shoulders that made you feel like "God had forsaken" you? Probably, the weight of sin brought with it the absence of God.

At this point, conversations take place about "how an omnipresent God (Jeremiah 23:23-24; Psalm 139) can be absent from anywhere?" Good question. So maybe, we could say as Scripture says that there is a sense in which God is absent from places where there is massive amounts of sin. Can you think of a place full of so much sin as the place where all the sins of mankind were dumped on the Son?

Then, imagine the death that Adam experienced when he died "in that day" (Genesis 2:17) of his sin (Genesis 2:17; 3:7-9). If "death" is a sense in which people experience a separation from God, how much of a death it must have been to die that day? For the first time in Creation, man was not walking with his God. Adam, as the federal head of his home, felt the weight of the sin of himself and Eve as they walked alone in the garden and hid themselves among the shrubbery of the Garden. Then, find this Jesus in a garden; find him bearing the sin of Adam and all Adam's children. 7 billion people in this day. 100 years ago, there were about 1.6 billion,[108] all of which—for the most part—are dead today. 8.6 billion sons of Adam, and that speaks only for the last 200 years. Then, .9 billion people were alive 200 years ago, probably all dead 100 years ago. 9.5 billion sons of Adam; all their sins with all the guilt—judicially-speaking and emotionally-speaking—were "laid on Him." .6 billion 300 years ago.[109] That means that if there were no people born and dying between these benchmarks (which we know there were many), over 10 billion people lived in the last 300 years alone! 10 billion sons of Adam—with their lawbreakings against a holy and righteous God—were laid on Him!

Is there any wonder that the very Son of God requested another way if there were another way. But is there also any confusion as to how God can be so angry with those who reject Jesus? After this unspeakable cost (mentioned in Matthew 20:28), is there really any wonder that God

---

[108] https://ourworldindata.org/world-population-growth/ [accessed May 9, 2016]

[109] https://www.census.gov/population/international/data/worldpop/table_history.php [accessed May 9, 2016]

is so infuriated with those who balk at this cost and endeavor to play by the rules of their own economy?

26:43

And he came and found them asleep again: for their eyes were heavy. I don't think there's anything deep to say here. We find this word **sleep** used multiple times in the book of Matthew and it isn't always negative, but the thing that these disciples should have considered was that when you're sleepy, you stand up.

26:44

And he left them, and went away again, and prayed the third time, saying the same words. Well, that doesn't seem very deep now, does it? I guess that means those are not the "vain repetitions" we thought about in Matthew 6:

> *6:6 But thou, when thou prayest, enter into thy closet, and when thou hast shut thy door, pray to thy Father which is in secret; and thy Father which seeth in secret shall reward thee openly. 7 But when ye pray, use not **vain repetitions**, as the heathen do: for they think that they shall be heard for their much speaking.*

So know this, whatever "vain repetitions" means, it doesn't mean to ask for the same thing three times. Apparently the dissuasion to use repetition is to avoid mindless incantations that have no heart behind them. On the other hand, we can see that there is plenty of heart behind Jesus' prayer. Moreover, this is a two way communication. Jesus went from a request in verse 39 to a request in verse 42 with a certain increased level of awareness as to the will of God. This is anything but "vain."

26:45

Then cometh he to his disciples, and saith unto them, Sleep on now, and take *your* rest: I'll mention here that we have before us a good piece of training: when you have two translations that disagree,[110] you don't have to do either of the extremes: 1. Throw your hands up and say

---

[110]Your translation may read "Are you still sleeping?"

"what's the use? I don't know Greek!"; nor do you have to 2. Shrug your shoulders and say "what does it matter? It doesn't change the meaning of the overall text."[111] I will only say here that neither the Nestle-Aland's 27th edition[112] nor the *Textus Receptus* contain this in question form if all we are doing is considering punctuation in the Greek New Testaments. We do understand, however, that Greek punctuation was added after the era when the New Testament was written. We actually find out, as a matter of fact, that "The form of a Greek question is not necessarily different from a statement; the punctuation and context are your main clues."[113]

So, if we suspect that the punctuation is not concrete or "set in stone," we consider the context. If Judas is walking up as Jesus is speaking and verse 46 occurs just beyond verse 45 (which appears to be the natural reading of the passage), then there is no time for the three disciples to "sleep on and rest," for Jesus says, "the betrayer is here, get up."[114]

behold, the hour is at hand, and the Son of man is betrayed into the hands of sinners. We are faced with the reality of Daniel 9 and its great accuracy. We are also faced with the reality that our prayers do not always affect the timing of something (although they may) as much as they may affect the experience of that very same thing.

26:46

Rise, let us be going: behold, he is at hand that doth betray me. These are the words of somebody who indeed knows that it is the doing of His Father and the time is right. Think about all the ways somebody could have reacted to this—knowing the discomfort that followed both during and after the arrest. Eventually, one must simply set their face like a rock (Isaiah 50:7) and proceed to the Father's will.

---

[111] This may be the most harmful to the understanding of a "verbal, plenary inspiration of the Bible." If a phrase is made up of words, and a paragraph of phrases, it doesn't take too many words to change the meaning of a paragraph.

[112] Eberhard Nestle et al., *The Greek New Testament*, 27th ed. (Stuttgart: Deutsche Bibelgesellschaft, 1993), Mt 26:45.

[113] William D. Mounce, *Basics of Biblical Greek: Grammar*, ed. Verlyn D. Verbrugge, Third Edition. (Grand Rapids, MI: Zondervan, 2009).

[114] This reading actually agrees with Mark's account.

Be that as it may, imagine Jesus' prayer life informing Him that what His Scripture-reading life had informed Him was right and that His Father was equipped and able to carry Him through—carry Him through to death, that is. Remember, friends, Jesus had never been dead before. What if part of His "cup" was the human uncertainty of what that would be like? I want a Scripture life that informs me of the future, yes. But I want a prayer life that informs my emotions as well. "Let's get up and go meet the will of my Father." Totally unpleasant. Completely unenjoyable. The will of the Heavenly Father found in the confused face of a friend. The will of God the Father found in the eyes of perhaps indifferent soldiers and indignant priests. They are there to conquer, and so is Jesus—through surrender to the Father.

26:47[115]

And while he yet spake, lo, Judas, one of the twelve, "Matthew, we haven't forgotten." What is he doing here with this phrase **one of the twelve**? It seems like he is writing this out of shock. **came, and with him a great multitude with swords and staves,** Even Jesus acts like this is irrational. Look at verse 55 where Jesus brings up the point that they had apparent opportunity earlier with the same apparent fire power. What is He getting at? The end of verse 54 tells us Jesus was in effect telling them as they heard him rebuke the sword-swinging disciple: "The only reason we are even talking is because Scripture said this would happen. If My Father's will, as revealed in Scripture, were not playing out here, I would fry all of you, and you knew it then as well as you do now."

We could let the **chief priests and elders of the people** off the hook for seeking to bind Jesus if they were nowhere around during his miracles and if they only heard his teaching and if they felt like he had hundreds hiding out with Him in the garden. We would even let them off the hook if they arrested Him already. Oh, no, We find right away that Jesus speaks to the whole lot of them—calling them to bear witness that there are reasons why they did not do it before, and now they are doing it under the darkness.

26:48-49

---

[115]More in my commentary on Mark (14:43-52).

49 And forthwith he came to Jesus, and said, Hail, master; and kissed him. Such a strange greeting from somebody who seeks to harm you? This is a word that prior to this time is used three times by Matthew (2:10; 5:12; 18:13), and each time is translated as "rejoice." So this is meant to be a cheerful, honorific greeting. When the word is used in chapter 27, it is a mock greeting to Jesus as "king." When it is used after Jesus' resurrection in chapter 28 it is a cheerful, consoling greeting to the women who found the empty tomb. This is another clue to me that Judas was either the most heinous, hateful, cocky, gloater of a former friend that could ever be conceived…or that he was intending on this being a happy occasion after all. Satan-possessed, Satan-obsesses, Satan-impressed…whatever you wish to say, he was fooled and bewitched, but something tells me that the greeting of Judas and the response and actions of Jesus after Peter's cavalier act of defense of Jesus signal a forthcoming, shocking awareness: Judas had indeed delivered the Messiah, the Son of Man, to death. Remember his sorrowful realization in the next chapter.

26:50

And Jesus said unto him, Friend, wherefore art thou come? Here, as in Matthew 26:45, we have a difference of opinion as to whether it should be a question or a statement. The ironic thing is that while the some versions pose a question in verse 45, here they post a statement instead of a question.

Because of our myriad of parallels between Adam in Eden and Jesus around His death, I side with the question form of this translation. Remember, we have already seen the disparity between Jesus and Adam in the prayer of Jesus. In our second brush with Eden in this passage, we find God asking a particular friend that was walking with Him a soul-searching question. "Why are you here?" seems simple enough. Of course, so did "Adam, where are you?" You see, once again—as pointed out in 1:1—Jesus is the ultimate and perfect Adam and the flesh-crazy, manipulative arm of "making things happen" and nationalism has never produced anything God-glorifying: not in Eden and not in Gethsemane; and certainly not in America.

26:51

And, behold, one of them which were with Jesus stretched out *his* hand, and drew his sword, and struck a servant of the high priest's, and smote off his ear. It is s strange action this man, identified by John as Peter, takes. What is he doing? First of all, Matthew must know it's Peter. He knows from verse 37 that there were only three men who entered the garden with Jesus. Why did he not know which of these men it was if he knew of the event taking place? Since we must assume that he knew who it was, why did he not mention Peter? Was it because he had already singled Peter out so many times and was seeking to show a little more deference? Was it because he was about to showcase Peter as the denier? Was it because Judas was to be the biggest villain? Who knows?

26:52-53

53 Thinkest thou that I cannot now pray to my Father, and he shall presently give me more than twelve legions of angels? Does anybody else think it's marvelous that Jesus, after having to bend his will to the Father's, feels the power still to ask this same Father for immediate deliverance from this hour? What a mystery is taking place here! I tell you that this is so far outside of my understanding. It seems as though Jesus is aware He could come out of this place and yet…at the same time…he cannot! Surely, Matthew is not seeking to mislead us! Surely, Jesus did not forget what He just prayed! The only thing I can say is that "this really did happen and I have no idea how to grasp or help others to grasp this phenomenal relationship between the God the Father and His Only Begotten Son!" All I can say is that since He did not ask His Father to deliver Him that this is yet another display of His submission. In other words, by Jesus' actions, He was saying "Although I have the access; and although I have the enablement…I do not have the authority to ask for such a thing!"

Or, even more powerfully, the pain that Jesus has felt, is feeling, and will feel is not at all between the forsaking disciples, the betraying deceiver, the jealous priestly class, or the disoriented Roman pontiff. This is the coordination of God satisfying His Own justice. This is the provision of the Father, using human instrumentality, to ransom those same wicked human instruments through the spotless Son of Man (Matthew 20:28). Or, more concisely said, "This is a conversation between God the Father and His Son Jesus. This is a drama between the Godhead; not silly, fickle, sons of Adam."

So it is today. As we submit, as ransomed souls, to the Father of all spirits made perfect (Hebrews 12), we—although we may be entangled by the snares of men—are a part of a conversation with the Father, about plans from the Father, to bring glory to the Father by His Son Jesus in like manner as we have seen Him display even here.

This is what we do when we hear of unpleasant days ahead for the church. When we hear of our young ladies being the subject of a bill that just passed a house subcommittee requiring them to be a part of the draft we are tempted to fret. When we know of a possibility of losing our tax exempt status; when we consider that our religious liberty will probably be sacrificed before the cries of a sexually depraved, morally decadent and ever-increasingly secular society, we ask the Father to remove our cup. We do so today…and if it becomes clear that we are to carry a cross…we look at one another and say **arise, let us be going.**

When God calls us to different fields and we find ourselves quaking in our shoes; when He bids us follow Him to difficult tasks and hard burdens and vulnerable times, we ask for relief from heavy hearts and mental dilemmas; then we embolden our hearts by the Spirit of God and say **arise, let us be going.**

Thinkest thou that I cannot now pray to my Father, and he shall presently give me more than twelve legions of angels? This has the idea of "calling the Father to His side with 12 legions of angels." One understands that Jesus uses the number 12 as before in this book (Matthew 19:28) to refer to this "New Israel", and is a sort of rebuke to Peter and the others that He [Jesus] is not limited to the aid of 12 disciples, but has the help—should He call headquarters—of angels…not just angels, but thousands of angels; not just angels, but "twelve thousands of angels."[116]

26:54-55

---

[116] John Peter Lange and Philip Schaff, *A Commentary on the Holy Scriptures: Matthew* (Bellingham, WA: Logos Bible Software, 2008), 487; it seems to go without saying that this source (as well as others) hold to a legion being 6000 soldiers.

55 In that same hour said Jesus to the multitudes, Are ye come out as against a thief with swords and staves this can also be a club or stick.

26:56

…Then all the disciples forsook him, and fled. I wish I knew more about Matthew. We find his conversion in chapter 9 and his calling to apostleship in chapter 10. In this short chapter, 3 times (26:8; 26:35 before this), Matthew courageously confesses to his complicit cowardice. "I left the Lord too."[117]

From a strictly pragmatic side, what is it about people that tell their story of rejection of God's will like Matthew? Why do those who find liberty in Christ also relish mentioning their old lives? It seems the reason is simple: we want people to see how deep the pit of our rejection of Christ, our fear of the unknown, and our capitulation to the fads and styles and voices of the day—just how deep that pit was. The reason we discuss how we were among those who "fled" is so that they too will rejoice with us when they see what deliverance and cleanliness and mercy look like.

Today, we have a clear-cut Gospel to believe: Christ died for our sins to deliver us from them (Matthew 1:21 and 20:28) and rose again. Matthew was not such a believer as seen in Matthew 20 & Matthew 26. He denied the entire drama by his own admission. He was not, in any

---

[117] Let's get the conversation out of the way. Did Judas have to betray? Did Matthew have to leave? The honest truth is that in some cases (such as here looking back at the prophecy of Zechariah in Matthew 26:31), the prophecy appears to be speaking from an omniscient perspective as if to be saying "here is what will happen with or without anybody's permission because…it just will."

Other times, such as was discussed in 26:18 and 26:24, and in this episode (verse 54), the prophecies are a script that must be followed…so let's do what we're supposed to do. What was the motive? Was Jesus moved to fulfill them out of obedience to the Father or out of the realization that "the Father would make it happen anyway so let's get this over with?" The answer will tell you if you are a theological liberal who believes that these folks were just self-fulfilling the prophecies or if you are an inerrantist who believes these were truly divines who both felt compelled to obey and resigned that God's will must—absolutely must—be done (with realities that the fear of the Lord keeps us from interfering with His very obvious work).

way, a New Testament believer prior to this chapter so all the questions about "whether or not the disciples lost their salvation" is moot. What is not so cloudy is that God's character is on display here. If anybody felt like they were beyond the reach of Heaven on this night—it was Matthew. If anybody felt like it was brainless to hope in a resurrection or a new life afterward or an afterlife with this same Jesus and God the Father, Matthew was among them. What about you? Have you been following from miles behind? Have you found yourself deep in sin—surely nobody will find you and nobody's looking for you?

Do you think that the character of the Lord Jesus has changed? Do you not remember that the very same Lord Whom you forsook in this chapter of your life was the One for Whom you forsook all to follow in chapter 9? Do you not remember that you would have never gone from "forsaking all" to "all forsaking" had the Lord not passed by your life to begin with? Do you think that you are feeling the weight of your own failures leaving your very mind as you read this because the Lord has forsaken the One who has forsaken Him? I say unto you, that the One Who drank the cup for you drank even your sin of forsaking Him? Will you believe that this is so, and return to Him and find healing and forgiveness? Will You? You have not out-sinned God's grace. You can do no worse act than you have already done. Your sins have crucified the Savior. What worse can you do?

26:57

And they that had laid hold on Jesus led him away to Caiaphas the high priest, where the scribes and the elders were assembled. So they already knew they were about to see the one that is being arrested. You have a group of people going to the garden of Gethsemane to get Jesus. You have another group of people assembling the council. They are elders, the 70 elders that make up the Sanhedrin. The Sanhedrin began back during the time of Moses. You might remember the father-in-law of Moses in Exodus 18.

They were being assembled. Now this is very unlawful. It was against Jewish law to have a trial in the middle of the night. Why? Well, for a number of reasons, one of which is it is difficult to get witnesses since they are all in the bed and you probably don't know where they all live. You might know where they work. You don't know where they all live probably.

And so there are a lot of things wrong with this. If you want a good book on everything that was wrong legally with this night I recommend reading *The Murder of Jesus* by John MacArthur. It is probably 230 pages. It is the opinion of some that this meeting took place on the Southwest corner of the temple mount.[118]

26:58

But Peter followed him afar off unto the high priest's palace, and went in, and sat with the servants, This word for "servants" here is only used one other time in the book of Matthew (5:25) and it is there understood to be a person in charge of executing judgment or guarding a prison or something to that effect. These are the ones, it seems who are in charge of making sure people like Peter are not allowed into the courtyard.[119] **to see the end.** So the first time reader sees the end of verse 56 and then says, "well, Peter has followed after, at least."[120] Then, sadly, we read the end of the chapter and find Peter bolting out the gate into the night.

How does Matthew know this? I thought all the disciples left the Lord back in verse 56? Just like Peter followed the party, it seems Matthew could have done the same thing, right?

I've heard a good many messages about Peter "following afar off" and "warming himself by the enemy's fire," but it seems like Matthew wants us to know that Peter was wanting to **see the end.** Was Peter still hopeful that Jesus would rise up and call those angels he told Peter about? "Was Jesus a sort of Valkyre plot that was just attempting to get into the temple to bring the whole thing down?" Or, was Peter hoping for a last minute acquittal? Maybe he was just trying to buy time

---

[118] Jim Bishop *The Day Christ Died* (New York: Harper Brothers, 1957), 247.

[119] I discovered this after noticing that the HCSB translates this as "temple police" instead of "servants."

[120] John's Gospel has this possible because John got Peter in the door.

to get Jesus released. Maybe his very denials are his buying time to get closer to Jesus?

One thing is certain: Peter was seeking to circumvent the death of Jesus on the way to the revolution. This really is the issue. If Jesus dies, he must die. That is the point of Jesus "come after me with your cross" on the heels of his first preaching the Gospel in Matthew 16:20ff.

26:59

Now the chief priests, and elders, and all the council, sought false witness against Jesus, to put him to death; Isn't that ironic? The religious people are willing to lie. The religious people of the day are so concerned with having their position secured in the temple that they are willing to actually look for false witnesses. What kind of people are we dealing with here? People that are willing to find someone that will disprove that Jesus is the Messiah.

26:60-61

But found none: yea, though many false witnesses came. Now look at this. What kind of group are we dealing with here? "We need liars down at the high priest's house. Oh, thank you for coming." Think about that. They filled the place with false witnesses. They are desperate to kill their Messiah, unbelievable.

yet found they none. One understands from Mark's account that these are not contradictory statements. While some of the more modern versions have this second phrase missing in them it is because their underlying Greek texts or manuscripts do not have them.[121] It is my philosophical choice to believe the church had the correct text for all if not most of its history than to assume that the more modern discoveries reflect the original reading.

So…when Matthew says this second time that "they found none," he is speaking of a particular type of false witness: the kind made

---

[121] A text would be the conglomeration of two or more Greek manuscripts and are typically published by a person or a committee or an organization.

up of two or more which actually agree, making a single, valid witness. In Mark it speaks of two where in Matthew it summarizes them as one valid voice.[122]

It seems that, at this point, Matthew is seeking to establish Jesus' innocence. He does go to some lengths to include some in this band who hold to Jesus' innocence: Consider Judas.

*Matthew 27:3 Then Judas, which had betrayed him, when he saw that he was condemned, repented himself, and brought again the thirty pieces of silver to the chief priests and elders, 4 Saying, I have sinned in that I have betrayed **the innocent blood**. And they said, What is that to us? see thou to that.*

Here, the one responsible for this entire fiasco, humanly speaking, is declaring that Jesus is indeed "innocent" following the obviousness of Jesus' condemnation.

*Matthew 27:18 For he knew that for envy they had delivered him. 19 When he was set down on the judgment seat, his wife sent unto him, saying, Have thou nothing to do with **that just man**: for I have suffered many things this day in a dream because of him.*

Pilate's wife even thinks Jesus is a "just man." Then, there's Pilate himself:

---

[122] By the way, this is precisely what occurs when Matthew speaks of a singular cockcrowing following Peter's betrayal while Mark speaks of two cockcrowings. A particular cockcrowing of which Christ spoke in Matthew is comprised of two cockcrowings in Mark. That is to say, the cockcrowing of which Jesus spoke in Matthew was not that of which He spoke without the second crowing of that rooster. This works also in the story of Jairus. Matthew 9 seems clear enough that the girl is dead prior to the interruption of the woman with the issue of blood. This is established when Jesus tells those who think she's dead that she is just sleeping without any further explanation. Matthew's reader would assume the child is dead and that Jesus knew it prior to the interruption. Mark, on the other hand, has a second visitor from the master's house (Mark 5:34) telling Jesus of the death of the child following the interruption. Well, what of it? Matthew, as with these "false witnesses" being a summary of two agreeing false witnesses—and with the "cockcrowing" being a summary of two cockcrowings—is in Jairus' story summarizing two messengers from the house into one.

*Matthew 27:22 Pilate saith unto them, What shall I do then with Jesus which is called Christ? They all say unto him, Let him be crucified. 23 And the governor said, Why, **what evil hath he done**? But they cried out the more, saying, Let him be crucified. 24 When Pilate saw that he could prevail nothing, but that rather a tumult was made, he took water, and washed his hands before the multitude, saying, I am innocent of the blood of **this just person**: see ye to it.*

Now, what about you? Have you found fault with this Christ? To find fault with God the Father is to find fault with His Son. Often, many of us have incomplete theologies. We believe God is Omnipotent. We think to ourselves: "God can bless anybody like in Job 42. If He can, then why doesn't He do so divorced from the 'Hell on earth' He serves up to Job in the meantime?" If God can shape Joseph with means that are not so abrasive or aggressive, then why not do it? Why allow so much pain? These are good thoughts and they are thoughts of those like me and you that are convinced God is all-powerful and all-knowing, but we are not so sure He is "all-nice." Until we realize that all things are God-wrought for His glory, yes…but also for our good, will probably continue to find fault with our Lord.

Remember, we are talking about the Son Who said in the 9th chapter of this book that "the Son of man has power on earth to forgive sins." That is to say, He can do on earth what was only to be done in Heaven to this point. He is the only Heavenly agent heretofore given Who can say "the will of Heaven is being done on earth" in answer to the prayer He prayed. To see that Jesus is on trial in Matthew's Gospel as the agent of the Father is not only to establish the perfection of the sin offering Who died to ransom us from our sins (Matthew 20:28), but also to re-establish that the Kingdom of Heaven is righteous and is representative of a righteous Lord (Matthew 22:1-12) who sets up His Son as King.

That is to say, if we find fault with Jesus here, at the hands of His enemies, we have fault with the God of Heaven. We are, as you might expect, intrigued at the very notion that we are considering God's fitness to be adored. Yet, as tender, delicate people who feel the weight of health and hearing and wealth and welfare and bills and blights, we are sometimes interested in asking "Does God do all things well?"

Of course, the Ultimate application to me is the reality that there is no overly aggressiveness I have experienced when I consider how infinitely aggressive the Father was with His Own Son in directing Him to drink the cup of my extraordinary sins. How "extreme" can we blame God of being? Can we find fault with God after all of this? When we step back after living through this drama from the bleachers, we find blood- curdling awareness that God is faultless, Christ is faultless, and we—we are the ones seeking to find fault.

61 And said This fellow said, I am able to destroy the temple of God, and to build it in three days. If that were possible, Jesus would be a wizard. So right here they are trying to get Jesus to confess to being a worker of magic and a wizard and they have him. They can stone him right then and there legally.

> *Leviticus 20:27 A man also or woman that hath a familiar spirit, or **that is a wizard, shall surely be put to death: they shall stone them with stones:** their blood shall be upon them.*

There are some other issues that wouldn't allow the Jews to kill Jesus on this day because of the Passover. Isn't it amazing? God planned the crucifixion of Christ on a day when the Jews were not allowed to kill Jesus. Therefore, they had to find something he was worthy of death on a day that they could not kill him because the ordinary way that they killed people was by stoning. And Jesus had to be cursed by God and the only way to be cursed by God according to Deuteronomy 21:22 and Galatians 3:13 is for him to be nailed to a tree.

This shows up again in 27:40 where those on the ground begin taunting Him as He hangs on the cross. The truth is, Matthew is not telling everything he knows here. Of course, he may not have known anything about what the Holy Spirit was communicating here.[123] Do you remember Jesus saying "I will build my church and the gates of Hell will not prevail against it" (Matthew 16:18)? It's the same word here. Jesus does not deny that He said this, so Matthew is at least leaving the door open for the reader to think that Jesus may have said it. So, when did He

---

[123]The reader is tempted to jump to John 2 and the explanation found there but we have no indication that this was in the purview of Matthew's audience.

possibly say this? One idea is Matthew 16:18. Jesus tears down this temple in which He stands, but how? And then, how can we say that He has **built it in three days**?

Seven facts are presented:

1. The tearing down of the temple happened **three days** before it was built (from this passage).
2. God used to meet with His people in the tabernacle, then the temple (Exodus 40; 2 Chronicles 6-8).
3. The veil was ripped, thus effectively destroying the temple—making it of no effect.

*Matthew 27:51 And, behold, **the veil of the temple was rent in twain from the top to the bottom; and the earth did quake,** and the rocks rent;*

More than this, it showed to the world that there was no God in that temple—effectively destroying it.

4. Three days later, Christ did ascend out of *hades*, the land of the dead (see Psalm 16:8-10 with Acts 2:24ff).
5. Jesus connects the church being built to the gates of this place called *hades* (Matthew 16:18).
6. Jesus promises to meet in the midst of His church (Matthew 18:15-20).
7. The church, must be, the built up temple that was established at Christ's resurrection when the gates of hades could not hold Him, and He meets with us today.

26:62

And the high priest arose, and said unto him, Answerest thou nothing? Now, if Jesus were able to pull of this wizardry then I could see the demand for justice, but I am confused as to why it would be such an outrage if Jesus had simply claimed to be able to do this. **what is it which these witness against thee?** I am afraid I would have said, "What is there to answer, numbskull? You haven't had two witnesses agree. What do you want me to answer?" So this is the problem. They can't render Jesus guilty without two agreeing witnesses. So the high priest knows the only way that they are going to be able to get him and condemn him is if he will in the ears of 70 witnesses—confess. And Jesus, "as a lamb before his shearers is dumb opened not his mouth" (Isaiah 53:7).

1. Matthew 1:23 quotes Isaiah 7:14
2. Matthew 2:23 refers to Isaiah 11:1
3. Matthew 3:3 quotes Isaiah 40:3
4. Matthew 4:14-16 quotes Isaiah 9:1-2
5. Matthew 8:17 quotes Isaiah 53:4
6. Matthew 11:4-5 refers to Is 8:13-14, 35:4-8, 42:3 & 61:1-2
7. Matthew 11:23 refers to Isaiah 14:12-14
8. Matthew 12:17-21 quotes Isaiah 42:1-3
9. Matthew 13:14-15 quotes Isaiah 6:9-10
10. Matthew 13:40-43 refers to Isaiah 13:6-8
11. Matthew 15:8-9 quotes Isaiah 29:13
12. Matthew 15:21-28 refers to Isaiah 22:22-23:18
13. Matthew 22:11 echoes back Isaiah 28:20
14. Matthew 26:62 reminds us of Isaiah 53:7

26:63

But Jesus held his peace. And the high priest answered and said unto him, I adjure thee by the living God, some newer versions[124] say this simply means that the High Priest is placing Jesus under oath. Again, knowing Jewish jurisprudence it is astounding to me that the high priest is so concerned with "holy matters" like "oaths before God" when he has been so complicit with discarding this same law in matters pertaining to how Jesus is being tried. **that thou tell us whether thou be the Christ, the Son of God.** Having no witnesses and no guilt, the High Priest—as desperate as ever—seeks an admission of guilt through confession from the man Himself.

On another note, one might notice the difference between the question from the high priest and the question from Pilate. One was concerned about his confession to claims of being the Christ, therefore

---

[124] Such as the NRSV.

substantiating the need to kill Him for blasphemy. One, if you'll notice 27:11, was concerned about the civil ramifications of one within the Roman Empire claiming to be King. The reason Pilate asks Jesus of His claims to be a King is because, although there is no mention by Matthew, the question was spurred by the mob who told Pilate Jesus claimed to be a King. One might notice that in both cases, Jesus answers in the same Hebrew hyperbole: "you said it."

26:64

Jesus saith unto him, Thou hast said: nevertheless I say unto you, The word is 2nd person plural. Today we would say "I say unto you all…" **Hereafter shall ye see the Son of man sitting on the right hand of power, and coming in the clouds of heaven.** See comments under 16:27-28 and 24:31. Suffice to say this was Jesus rebuking the head agent for the old temple—promising the destruction of that temple. Contextually, this makes sense in view of verse 61. When would the temple be destroyed? Within the purview of those there standing.

26:65

Then the high priest rent his clothes, saying, He hath spoken blasphemy; what further need have we of witnesses? behold, now ye have heard his blasphemy. See commentary under 3:13-17. After remembering that the high priest had here disqualified himself we remember also that this "blasphemy" was a capital crime:

> *Leviticus 24:16 And he **that blasphemeth the name of the LORD, he shall surely be put to death**, and all the congregation shall certainly stone him: as well the stranger, as he that is born in the land, when he blasphemeth the name of the LORD, shall be put to death.*

26:66

What think ye? They answered and said, He is guilty of death. It was against Jewish law for you to both hear a case and render a verdict on the same day. It doesn't matter how guilty he was. You were not allowed to do that on the same day. Lots of injustices took place. And yet "as a lamb before her shearers is dumb, so he opened not his mouth" (Isaiah 53:7).

26:67-68

68 Saying, Prophesy unto us, thou Christ, Who is he that smote thee? Jesus just claimed to be the fulfillment of Daniel's chapter 7 prophecy. Surely, if He were—they would reason—He could prophesy. Peter, without question, is wondering "will this be when Jesus has had enough? Will He finally beckon His angels?"

26:69-75

See commentary on 10:2.

Chapter 27

When the morning was come, all the chief priests and elders of the people took counsel against Jesus to put him to death: One should take a look at the many times this is used through Matthew. No less than three times these folks are huddling and being bothered by this Jesus Who is a threat to their security, and get this…this are seeking a way to kill Him…

> After Jesus healed on the Sabbath:
>
> *Matthew 12:14 Then the Pharisees went out and **plotted** against Him, how they might destroy Him.*

> After Jesus announced some of them would not be allowed to stay at the wedding feast:
>
> *Matthew 22:15 Then the Pharisees went and **plotted** how they might entangle Him in His talk.*

This couple of words, **took counsel** (or "plotted"), are used again in verse 7 and are found when they are seeking to determine what to do with the money Judas had returned.

27:3

Then Judas, which had betrayed him, when he saw that he was condemned, repented himself, and brought again the thirty pieces of silver to the chief priests and elders, Here is another good proof that those who repent or regret poor choices are not necessarily going to Heaven. Acts 1 seems to indicate that Judas will not be in Heaven and Jesus, calling Judas a "devil," seems sold on the reality that Judas is not a child of God—having later calling Him the "son of perdition" (John 6:70; 17:12). There seems to be little proof that Judas, albeit misdirected into having his new lease on life as a cabinet member for the new anti-Rome government, ever really trusted Christ as Messiah who would die for the sins of the world (John 1:29 versus 2:11). Contextually, Matthew

---

[125]Concerning 27:1-2 and 27:11-23, please see my commentary on Mark (15:1-14).

26:24 are going as far as to say that Judas has some punishment that greatly exceeds the potential good that could have resulted from his life.

The reality is that we don't know why he decided to be so anti-Judas all of the sudden. Rather, he doesn't appear to regret his wrongness more than he appears to regret the shame of his actions. Hating how sin makes me feel is not exactly the same as hating sin. "Lord, help us to remember that feeling guilty is not the same as agreeing with you about the lostness of my sinful heart."

Again, God hasn't changed and neither have men or women. A so-called repentance may be nothing more than a self-hate for failing at something (for those who are always achieving). It may be a loathing of feeling tainted or dirty more than a loathing for failing the Lord's standard. These things may drive us to desperate reliance on the Gospel—the only thing that can make us "worthy" or "clean"—but they are not a replacement for the Gospel. The person who is moralizing himself or herself may simply be realizing that "things need to change," but may not actually see the real danger that all sin is condemnation and wrath from which we must be acquitted or relieved or saved. Look at verse 5 for a proof that Judas sought reformation.

Let me go a bit further here and say you can have a repugnance or an aversion to particular sins; that is to say, you can agree with God on the sinfulness of certain things and the absolute corruptible character of certain sins above certain sins as God does when He calls them "abomination," and still not be forgiven. Judas was. We find that even his "blood money was repulsive."[126] If anybody had a fruit of "hating the old life," it was this guy.

---

[126] Stuart K. Weber, *Matthew*, vol. 1, Holman New Testament Commentary (Nashville, TN: Broadman & Holman Publishers, 2000), 458.

If a preacher would have said "so called free love is adultery." Judas would have nodded. If the drunk would have been denied the title "alcoholic," Judas would have folded his arms in agreement. If you were to have a rally against lustful sins like homosexuality and for traditional, biblical marriage, Judas would have attended and bought the t-shirt. If there were legislation passed that murderers would no longer be excused for so-called "temporary insanity," Judas would, at this point in his life, said "amen" and "that's right." If we preached that pastors who do not practice integrity in their dealings and appropriateness in their relationships should be not only excused from their positions, but kept from future pastorates, Judas would have agreed with an index finger in the air. Yet, somehow, he was not saved.

		Matthew	Corinthians
13	One getting saved "late"	20:12-14	15:8
14	Proper Garment Before King	22:8	2 Cor 5:21
15	Be sure you're in	22:14	2 Cor 13:5
16	Expectation of Resurrection	22:30-32	15:35-44
17	Deliverance of His Elect	24:24	10:13
18	Inheriting the Kingdom	25:31-38	15:50
19	Two kinds of sorrow	26:75; 27:4-5	2 Cor 7:10

27:4

Saying, I have sinned in that I have betrayed the innocent blood. Another lesson is how one can be convinced of Christ's flawless character. We mentioned this last chapter, but there are many people who think Christ is sinless, but that doesn't change how they mistreat Him or assume upon His forgiveness or believe He can be manipulated. "God, help me to not assume you will overlook my sin simply because I think your sacrifice was perfect." Judas is in some company here: with Pilate's wife, with the council, with Pilate. Many, many people who are probably not in Heaven today are convinced of the finest Christologies ever written.

One of my favorite songs is "Come, Behold the Wondrous Mystery" by Matt Papa.[127]

Come, Behold the wondrous mystery, He the perfect Son of Man;
In His living, in His suffering Never trace nor stain of sin.

If you can imagine, Judas would have said the same concerning Jesus. He would have sung a great many of our songs, and yet, He was not on the right side of this conflict.

And they said, What *is that* to us? see thou *to that.* Here again, one may find themselves without worldly friends, dejected by anti-Christian movements, only to realize that it is not a given that if one is denied by the world, they are automatically accepted by God. No, here we see that there is no connection in Judas' life between rejection from the hordes of the wicked one and a long home in Heaven. Again, the world will eat you up and spit you out. Just think about how nervous the "left" got when Hillary Clinton unwittingly called an unborn child…a "person."[128] After this world uses you and gets what they want from you, they will spit you out and send you packing. Even the pornography industry—after you have aged and have done unspeakable things that, after years and years have finally desensitized the audience to need more and more indecency on the screen—will kick you to the curb for a younger, more risqué disgust.[129]

27:5

And he cast down the pieces of silver in the temple, and departed, and went and hanged himself. Here, now, we relook at the comparison between Matthew and the epistles of Paul to the Corinthians.[130] The comparisons continue as we discuss the response of Judas with that of Peter.

---

[127]Philip Webb, ed., *Hymns of Grace* (Los Angeles: Master's Seminary, 2015), 184.
[128]http://observer.com/2016/04/hillary-clinton-exposes-the-lefts-own-abortion-extremism/ [Accessed May 30, 2016].
[129]http://sdgln.com/news/2016/01/04/recent-epidemic-gay-porn-stars-dying-young-more-lgbt-support-needed [accessed May 30, 2016].
[130]We have discussed 12 already.

What do we learn from this comparison? Life or death results from one's repentance. Either one repents and finds life or one repents and finds death. Again, here is a quite repentant man—wanting nothing to do with his sin or its fruit—yet he does not belong to Jesus. What an awful way to end your life. Listening to the Puritans pray drives us to wish for a better prospect where we can confidently say:

> *Death dismays me but my great high priest*
> *Stands in its waters,*
> *And will open me a passage,*
> *And beyond is a better country.*
> *While I live let my life be exemplary,*
> *When I die may my end be peace.*[131]

No, rather Judas presents for us what may have been Matthew's juxtaposition of those cursed on trees: Jesus with the Father; and Judas all alone:

> In Judas's case, however, there is no scriptural warrant for the sentimental notion that he was actually saved. For the Jews, a hanging would have confirmed God's curse (Deut 21:23).[132]

Some might say this was the ultimate act of Satanic depression or the ultimate act of Hellward rebellion. How can he get so far as to kill himself? Did he really feel like he would find mercy any other way than to go and find refuge within the community of God's Christ?

> If Judas had gone to Christ, or to some of the disciples, perhaps he might have had relief, bad as the case was; but, missing of it with the chief priests, he abandoned himself to despair: and the same devil that with the help of the priests drew him to the sin, with their help drove him to despair…And some have said, that

---

[131]Arthur Bennett, ed., *The Valley of Vision* (Carlisle, PA: Banner of Truth Trust, 2014), 155.

[132] Craig Blomberg, *Matthew*, vol. 22, The New American Commentary (Nashville: Broadman & Holman Publishers, 1992), 408.

Judas sinned more in despairing of the mercy of God, than in betraying his Master's blood.[133]

27:6

And the chief priests took the silver pieces, and said, It is not lawful for to put them into the treasury, because it is the price of blood. Once again, the irony here is that these chief priests are so concerned with anything legal after these successive kangaroo courts.

27:7-10

8 Wherefore that field was called, The field of blood, unto this day. 9 Then was fulfilled that which was spoken by Jeremy the prophet, saying, And they took the thirty pieces of silver, the price of him that was valued, "the price of him that was valued" may be a figure of speech referring to an economical fact that people were worth something in regards to slavery. The reader would have gotten this right away. In other words, Christ was sold for what may have been the price of a healthy man slave. **whom they of the children of Israel did value; 10 And gave them for the potter's field, as the Lord appointed me.** Much of what we read here can be found before prophesied (Jeremiah 19:1-10 & Zechariah 11:12-13).

How do we explain this apparent discrepancy (that it is really a morphing of the two rather than **Jeremy**? Well, the first thing that came into my mind was what I was taught in a small Bible college in Virginia Beach by a mighty man of God who simply said that "Jeremiah" or "Jeremy" was the first book of a group of books within the Hebrew canon that contained—also—Zechariah. In other words, Zechariah and Jeremiah were books within a book within the Old Testament and Jeremiah was the first book or the longest book and so the entirety of that particular section was known as "Jeremiah"—even though it was really in Zechariah.[134]

---

[133] Matthew Henry, *Matthew Henry's Commentary on the Whole Bible: Complete and Unabridged in One Volume* (Peabody: Hendrickson, 1994), 1763.

[134] Robert Jamieson, A. R. Fausset, and David Brown, *Commentary Critical and Explanatory on the Whole Bible*, vol. 2 (Oak Harbor, WA: Logos Research Systems, Inc., 1997), 61.

This reason seems like a reality for four reasons: 1. We have such a small amount of evidence that Matthew's original work said anything other than what we read here; 2. We have to believe that Matthew at least thought he was correct; 3. The likelihood that Matthew was wrong about something about which he could have easily found himself corrected is quite low; 4. Matthew was an expert in Judaism.

27:11

And Jesus stood before the governor: and the governor asked him, saying, Art thou the King of the Jews? Although Pilate is probably simply asking Jesus questions using His Own words, this is a real building upon a theme which begun with the genealogies and the wise men and carrying through the kingdom language of Matthew. Yes, this is the charge of the priests and elders, but it has a bigger picture, and that is the aim of Matthew.

27:14

And he answered him to never a word; The ESV says "not even to a single charge." **insomuch that the governor marvelled greatly.** Or as the NASB says, he was "quite amazed." Eight times, Matthew tells us about people being amazed: Three times to the disciples; three times to the multitudes, once to Jesus. This is the only time in Matthew that someone **marvels greatly.** It could be that Pilate is looking for a way to calm this thing down by declaring Jesus acquitted or maybe, to have his hearing put on the calendar after the Passover? But Jesus gave him nothing!

27:19

When he was set down on the judgment seat, his wife sent unto him, saying, Even a pagan woman could see it.

27:32-35[135]

33And when they had come to a place called Golgotha, (third "G" word in this drama after Gethsemane and Gabbatha).

---

[135]More in my commentary on Mark (chapter 15).

34 they gave Him sour wine mingled with gall to drink. But when He had tasted *it*, He would not drink. Some have said it was an act of cruelty in giving him nothing to satisfy His thirst while others have said it was an act of mercy as a sort of analgesic. **35 Then they crucified Him, and divided His garments,** presumably this was valuable because it belonged to a notorious criminal. **casting lots, that it might be fulfilled which was spoken by the prophet:…**in Psalm 22.

27:36

Sitting down, they kept watch over Him there. This is true to the originals. It isn't merely looking at Him, but "watching over Him" to be sure nobody will interfere with His death.

But Isn't this us? People who, we're told, sinned when Adam sinned (Romans 5:12), did we become quite a bit better in 4000 years until this day of Christ's death? Death reached us when Adam died. When Adam sinned, we sinned. Would we have done more than these soldiers this day in sinning by seeking their solace in a tree? Usually we think we would not have done what Adam and Eve did, even though Scripture says so.

Only here they are not seeking to find fruit to satisfy their taste, they are seeking blood to satisfy themselves? Both those in Eden and here at Golgotha seek fulfillment to cover our curiosity. As if being unfittingly clothed wasn't bad enough—revealing our own shame in the garden; we then find Our Lord unclothed in this paramount rebellion we have held against Our Jesus. We took His clothes. We brought the thorns in Genesis 3 and we made Him wear them in Matthew 27.

Then, as one journeys into Genesis, they find themselves—once again—on the side of those who build a tower to Heaven for the sake of their own notoriety. Is there a greater tower of babel that takes place than here at Calvary's Hill where we tell God that "we will not have His Son to reign over us?" Many feel like they're the exception. Yet, if we were given the opportunity, we would crucify Him again.

Isn't this us? Sitting down and watching Him die? Were we not the ones mobbing around the Lord Jesus, stripping Him, mocking Him, inflicting pain on Him? Were we those who gave Him no reprieve for His pain; found amusement in His anguish? We were indeed. Since we were; since this is us…What do we see?

We see One wearing our sins in the form of dripping blood and spittle. The main plot is a God-ward reality. Matthew 20:28 says this is the Son of man "giving His life as a ransom for many." As we sit here and gaze on the merciful Christ, we find One Who suffered for our hatred, our malice, our disgust. One Who today is reminded, since He knows no time, of the cost of our pettiness, our forgetfulness of His grace, and our idolatry. Sit here with me and see the cost of our little pet sins, our selfishness, and our anxiety wrapped up in so-called rights. We see a witness to just how dark our hearts really are.

We see the Creator Who is being nailed to wood He created; being spat upon by people He created; receiving vinegar from the hands He formed in the wombs of their mothers; desiring water comprised of molecules He concocted.

We see One Who shows Himself to the nations like Romans and Africans—Africans who will carry the very implement of his own salvation.

We see One Who wears a crown with joy. This is not the end of the story. The day is coming when He will wear the crown He deserves. Here, He wears the one we deserve.

We see One to Whom the world will bow, and they won't do so mockingly.

27:37-40

37And they put up over His head the accusation written against Him: THIS IS JESUS THE KING OF THE JEWS Remember, this is a major theme of Matthew—particularly because it opens with the lineage of the King and an introduction by the wisemen looking for him.

40 and saying, "You who destroy the temple and build it in three days, save Yourself! If You are the Son of God, come down from the

cross." This is much the same language of Matthew 4 and the temptation of Satan. He often works through difficult people.

27:41-43

43 He trusted in God; Can anybody think of a finer compliment than "He trusts God?" How wonderful! Of course, since so much of this comes from Psalm 22, it seems natural to see Psalm 22:9's reference to Jesus' trust in God beginning at infancy.[136] They did not think Jesus was correct. They did not think Jesus was on the right side. They did not think Jesus was protected by God. Isaiah 53:3-5 says they believed just the opposite. What was undeniable to these godless people was at least this: **He trusted in God.** We spoke of this briefly in our discussion of Matthew 2 where Jesus is being carried by the Father out of the grasp of Satan, but I wanted to reintroduce to you the reality that Jesus is not only known as the Jehovah in Whom we should trust, but that He is the One Who trusted Jehovah!

And who can blame Him for trusting the caring Heavenly Father? When the Father has been trustworthy to give Jesus safety through Egypt, in raging seas, under the attack of first, Satan and then the demons, and numerous attacks on his life…Jesus finds it to be a natural part of His existence to trust the Father…but what about when the story isn't going to turn out just right?

Jesus found the following to be true about what might happen when they "trust in God."
1. One can be trusting in God and have His Words misused (verse 37).
2. One can be trusting in God and surrounded by lawbreakers (verse 38).
3. One can be trusting in God and feel worthless (verse 39, 43).
4. One can be trusting in God and be attacked by Satan (verse 40).

---

[136]Some measure was taken to show the fulfillment of Psalm 22 in the life of Jesus here: http://www.sermonaudio.com/sermoninfo.asp?SID=1212121937452 [accessed 1/23/17].

5. One can be trusting in God and not exerting their rights (verses 40-43).
6. One can be trusting in God and feel alone (verses 45-46).
7. One can be trusting in God and be misunderstood (verse 47-49).
8. One can be trusting in God and die (verse 50).

But when we trust the Father…
1. We die in the perfect will of God in His perfect timing (verse 50). I provide for you an anecdote:

[After a clear direction from the Lord to missions endeavors in Burma, and] In compliance with a hint from Miss Hasseltine, Mr. Judson wrote to her father asking his consent to the proposed union. The following extract shows the candor and frankness of Mr. Judson; his devotion of purpose, and sense of the sacrifice a parent must make in giving up a daughter under such peculiar circumstances:

"I have now to ask, whether you can consent to part with your daughter early next spring to see her no more in this world; whether you can consent to her departure for a heathen land, and her subjection to the hardships and sufferings of a missionary life? whether you can consent to her exposure to the dangers of the ocean; to the fatal influence of the southern climate of India; to every kind of want and distress; to degradation, insult, persecution, and perhaps a violent death? Can you consent to all this, for the sake of Him who left his heavenly home, and died for her and for you — for the sake of perishing immortal souls — for the sake of Zion, and the glory of God? Can you consent to all this, in hope of soon meeting your daughter in the world of glory with a crown of righteousness, brightened by the acclamations of praise which shall redound to her Saviour from heathens saved, through her means, from eternal woe and despair?"

The parent thus honorably addressed, obeyed the voice of duty at the sacrifice of feeling, and gave his daughter to the cause of missions, for the sake of the first great Missionary, who had freely given his life a ransom for many….love for

Christ can loosen the coils of selfishness, and that faith can relinquish the brightest jewels of the heart.[137]

2. People find their way to God (verse 51).
3. Life finds its way where there ought to be none (verse 52-53).
4. Truth finds new outlets (verse 54).
5. Endurance is fostered in the hearts of Christ's followers (verse 55-56).
6. Courage is birthed in the life of the timid (verse 57-58).
7. The body of Christ is honored (verse 59). I refer, in our application of course, to the church (Matthew 16:18).
8. Deliverance does, in fact, come (28:1).

27:45-49[138]

27:50

And Jesus [t]cried out again with a loud voice, and [u]yielded up His spirit. Even in His dying, He maintains control of His life.

27:51-53

Then, behold, [v]the veil of the temple was torn in two This did a number of things: 1. It showed that the real presence of God resided elsewhere rather than behind the veil (Matthew 16:18; 18:19); numbers 2-3 are found in my commentary on Mark (15:37-39).

from top to bottom; and the earth quaked, Notice the order. Perhaps this was Matthew's way of showing us that the earthquake did not necessarily cause the tearing of the veil. **and the rocks were split, 52 and the graves were opened; and many bodies of the saints who had fallen asleep were raised;** So three miracles take place at the death of Christ (torn veil; earth quake; resurrected saints). **53 and coming out**

---

[137] J. Clement, *Memoir of Adoniram Judson: Being a Sketch of His Life and Missionary Labors* (Roger Williams Heritage Archives, 1853), 24–25.
[138] See my commentary on Mark (13:33-36).
[t] Luke 23:46; John 19:30
[u] John 10:18
[v] Ex. 26:31; 2 Chr. 3:14; Heb. 9:3

of the graves after His resurrection, they went into the holy city and appeared to many. With the absence of the punctuation in the originals, along with the absence of **and** in the originals before **coming out** the reader is left with some liberty to assume the saints were raised after the resurrection. This seems likely both theologically (1 Corinthians 15:23) and literarily as it says they didn't leave their **graves** until **after [Jesus'] resurrection.**

27:54-56[139]

Perhaps the greatest miracle; the fourth perhaps and greater than the three mentioned under verse 52 is the conversion of a godless man.

27:57-61[140]

60 and laid it in his new tomb which he had hewn out of the rock; Jesus, in keeping with 8:20, has no place to lay His head—not even in death.[141]

27:62-66

63 saying, "Sir, we remember, while He was still alive, how that deceiver said, 'After three days I will rise.' Why did the critics believe the intent of Jesus' words more than His disciples? Why did they assume the disciples would cover up their grief by leading others to believe their Lord had indeed risen? Such mysteries baffle me.

64 Therefore command that the tomb be made secure until the third day, lest His disciples come by night and steal Him away, The "stolen body" (28:13) would better have been "stolen" before the guards arrived.[142] **and say to the people, 'He has risen from the dead.' So the last deception will be worse than the first."** What was the "first

---

[139]More in my commentary on Mark (15:40-41).

[140]More in my commentary on Mark (15:42-47).

[141]This is furthermore seen in his staying with people in their homes—as in the case of 8:14-15 and 9:1-8.

[c]Matt. 16:21; 17:23; 20:19; 26:61; Luke 13:33

[142] Craig Blomberg, _Matthew_, vol. 22, The New American Commentary (Nashville: Broadman & Holman Publishers, 1992), 424.

deception?" **65 Pilate said to them, "You have a guard;** apparently the priests had their own assigned soldiers and this would make sense in light of 28:11 where they report first to them. **go your way, make it as secure as you know how." 66 So they went and made the tomb secure, sealing the stone and setting the guard.** Not a single writer of any ethnicity or era has proven evidence of the body of Jesus yet buried.

Before the 2nd Saying at the cross	After death of Christ at the cross	After death of Christ at the cross	At the burial & Sunday at the tomb	At the burial	Sunday Morning at the tomb	Sunday Morning at the tomb	Sunday Morning at the tomb
Mary, Jesus' Mother							
Mary, Cleophas' wife	Mary, mother of James and Joses	Mary, the mother of James the Less and Joses.	"Other Mary"	Mary, the mother of Joses	Mary, the mother of James	Mary the mother of James	
His mother's sister	The mother of Zebedee's children	Salome			Salome		
Mary Magdalene	Mary Magdalene	Mary Magdalene	Mary Magdalene	Mary Magdalene	Mary Magdalene	Mary Magdalene	Mary Magdalene
						Joanna	
John 19:25	Matthew 27:56	Mark 15:40	Matthew 27:61 & 28:1	Mark 15:47	Mark 16:1	Luke 24:10	John 20:1

Chapter 28

28:1-4[143]

Now after the Sabbath,[144] **as the first day of the week** Matthew identifies days of the week by number no other time;

2 And behold, there was a great earthquake; The second grand earthquake in three days occurs (see 27:51), and it seems to have been caused by **an angel** It was angels that orchestrated the safe passage of Jesus in the times of Herod the Great (chapters 1-2). It was angels that ministered to him following the temptation in the wilderness (chapter 4). It's angels that Jesus has been promising would be involved in the judgment of the great day (chapters, 13, 16, 24, 25), and it is angels that Jesus said were at His disposal. To think that it is but one that came down to roll the stone away from the door…

An angel of the Lord another grand prooftext that there has always been more than one **angel of the Lord.**

3ᵈHis countenance was like lightning, and his clothing as white as snow. Other Scripture tells us that this was done so that the empty tomb could be seen. **4 And the guards shook for fear of him, and became like ᵉdead men.** Frozen from fear? They certainly had a story to tell. At

---

[143]More can be found in my commentaries on Mark (chapter 16) and Luke (24:1-7).

[144]In my desire to remain purely Matthean, I include this here and, with my integrity, I cannot remember the true source (but it is not me): *Mary Magdalene and the other 3 women approached the tomb while it was still dark (John 20:1). They immediately run (full of fear and supposing the body was stolen) to tell Peter and John who return to a grave as "dawn began" (Matthew 28:1) and inspect the grave clothing. As they leave without saying a word, Mary and the other women notice two angels inside the tomb (Luke; John) and one on the stone (Matthew) who preach the Gospel (resurrection of the dead Savior) to them and send them to the disciples. Mary Magdalene still believes the body has been stolen (Matthew 28:8). Jesus makes Himself known to the ladies after their thinking He was the gardener (compare Matthew 28:9-10 and John 20:11-18). They proceed to tell the disciples of their seeing Christ (Mark 16:10-11; Luke 24:10-12; John 20: 18). Peter returns to the tomb again for another look (Luke 24:12) and afterwards sees Jesus Himself (Luke 24:34; 1 Corinthians 15:5).*

ᵈDan. 7:9; Mark 9:3; Acts 1:10
ᵉRev. 1:17

any rate, we come away with an understanding that angels are not "cute." Matthew may be playing on a dead stone rolling at the quaking of the earth with these men becoming "shaken" into an inanimate state themselves…like stones.

28:5-10

But the angel answered and said to the women, "Do not be afraid, this amazing Gospel opens with hopes that Joseph…the other "just man" would also not be afraid of the angel (1:20).

7 Go a closing theme (reaching back to Matthew 10:5 and drawing a contrast with "go not" and "go") repeated in 28:10 and 28:19.

10 Then Jesus said to them, "Do not be afraid. Taken with verse 8, Jesus says "keep the joy" (verse 9) and drop the fear. **Go and tell My brethren** Isn't this something? He calls His disciples **brethren.** This is not unique to Matthew, and He, like, the other Gospel writers (and the Hebrews writer) seem to get Psalm 22:22 where "Christ is not ashamed to call them brethren" (Hebrews 2:11) as they record Jesus' singing a hymn with His disciples after the Lord's Supper. **Brethren** also helps the interpreter with Matthew 25:31-46 and identification of that third party.

28:11-15

11 some Which means **some** did not come **into the city**. This may have been the **some** they blamed for "sleeping" and were mysteriously in exile. This explains how Pilate may demanded the entire outfit's death: he couldn't account for the **some** who were blamed for sleeping and didn't come **into the city.**

Chief priests notice how they were accountable to them, rather than to Pilate, primarily (27:65). Apparently there were soldiers entrusted to the Jewish leadership from Pilate (as was seen in the garden arrest three nights previous (John 18:3).

12 When they had assembled with the elders and consulted together, they gave a large sum of money to the soldiers, Of course, this—in addition to Jesus' paying taxes (Matthew 17:24-27), Judas' selling Jesus for 30 pieces of silver (Matthew 26:15), and Judas' trying to return the money (Matthew 27:3-10)—is mentioned only in Matthew, and shows the personality of this author.

13 saying, "Tell them, 'His disciples came at night and stole Him away while we slept.' Now, we know there were two groups of people who were enemies of Jesus that admit there was, in fact, an empty tomb. When you realize that the tale was told among the Jews until the time of the authorship of this passage (verse 15), we have a third group (in addition to the soldiers and the chief priests). Doubtless, the man who condemned Jesus (the Governor; verse 14) did indeed hear of this empty tomb—making, perhaps, the 4th witness. The reality is that if the Governor or the "Jews" doubted it, they could go and see that the body was not in the tomb. What does this prove? Only that they knew the tomb was empty.

> *Not only did the Jewish leaders not disprove the witness concerning the empty tomb, but their polemic [offensive tactic] even admitted it. One well-known principle of historical research generally recognizes what one's enemies admit.*[145]

14 And if this comes to the governor's ears, we will appease him and make you secure."

> *The evidence is finely balanced between the two views, since the guard ultimately answers to Pilate (28:14) but first reports to the chief priests (v. 11). If the guards are Roman, it is understandable that they would tell the Jews to whom they had been delegated what happened. It seems less likely that Jewish police would be in any danger from Rome for failing to carry out their assignment.*[146]

28:16-20

---

[145] Gary Habermas *Five View of Apologetics* (Grand Rapids: Zondervan, 2000), 110.
[146] Craig Blomberg, <u>Matthew</u>, vol. 22, The New American Commentary (Nashville: Broadman & Holman Publishers, 1992), 425.

17 When they saw Him, they worshiped Him; but some doubted.
The reader is left to wonder what or why they **doubted.** And, in all
fairness to the disciples, we don't know if the **some** are in contrast
(because of **but**) with the **eleven/they. 18 And Jesus came and spoke
to them, saying, "All authority has been given to Me in heaven and
on earth.** "The whole world is mine" is not only in contrast to the claims
of Satan in chapter 4's account of the temptation, but is also a signal that
the one claiming possession can take possession at the right time (Psalm
24:1; Revelation 5:5, cross referenced with Jeremiah 32:6 and
following).

19 Go therefore It seems this is the end of "the generation book"
introduced in Matthew 1:1. It answers Isaiah 53's troubling plea as to
whom will "declare his generation." Who will carry on His name if He
dies before He has children? A clear vision now sees that His death
brought children who would then carry on His name.

With the seeming preoccupation with Psalm 22, we see that He
shall have a "seed counted to him for a generation" (as seen in Psalm
22's finale).

and make disciples of all the nations, nations is not the same as
"tribes" (as in Matthew 24:29-30). There is therefore no reason for them
to see this as a mandate to stay in the land of Israel. Rather, this is a
sharp contrast between the "go not" commission of 10:5 and its
particularity to the Jews. **baptizing them in the name of the Father
and of the Son and of the Holy Spirit, 20°teaching them to observe
all things that I have commanded you; and lo, I am with you always,
even to the end of the age."** This is the work of church planting (Acts
2:42-47), and we are guaranteed that we cannot fail—He superintends
His work until the age is over[147] and builds His church all the while
(Matthew 16:18).

°Acts 2:42

[147]See my commentary on Ephesians (the footnote on 1:21) for more on this.

Made in the USA
Columbia, SC
23 December 2018